Rubin



21.11.91

(work copy)

# Text Generation and Systemic-Functional Linguistics

COMMUNICATION IN ARTIFICIAL INTELLIGENCE SERIES

Artificial Intelligence (AI) is a central aspect of Fifth Generation computing, and it is now increasingly recognized that a particularly important element of AI is communication. This series addresses current issues, emphasizing generation as well as comprehension in AI communication. It covers communication of three types: at the human–computer interface; in computer–computer communication that simulates human interaction; and in the use of computers for machine translation to assist human–human communication. The series also gives a place to research that extends beyond language to consider other systems of communication that humans employ such as pointing, and even in due course, facial expression, body posture, etc.

*Communication in Artificial Intelligence Series Editors:*
Robin P. Fawcett, Computational Linguistics Unit, University of Wales Institute of Science and Technology
Erich H. Steiner, IAI EUROTRA-D and University of the Saarland

*From Syntax to Semantics: Insights from Machine Translation*, eds: Erich Steiner, Paul Schmidt and Cornelia Zelinsky-Wibbelt

*Advances in Natural Language Generation: An Interdisciplinary Perspective*, 2 volumes, eds: Michael Zock and Gérard Sabah

*Text Generation and Systemic-Functional Linguistics: Experiences from English and Japanese*, Christian M.I.M. Matthiessen and John A. Bateman

Further titles are in preparation

# Text Generation and Systemic-Functional Linguistics

## Experiences from English and Japanese

Christian M.I.M. Matthiessen
*and*
John A. Bateman

Pinter Publishers, London

First published in Great Britain in 1991 by
Pinter Publishers Limited
25 Floral Street, London WC2E 9DS



**British Library Cataloguing in Publication Data**

A CIP catalogue record for this book is available from the British Library
ISBN 0 86187 711 X

Typeset by Mayhew Typesetting, Rhayader, Powys
Printed and bound in Great Britain by SRP Ltd., Exeter

# Contents

# List of figures

# Foreword

It gives me a very special pleasure to write this Foreword, because I have no less than three reasons for being delighted that this important and impressive work has now appeared.

This book gives the first full account of the development of the NIGEL grammar and the Penman framework for generation — first for English and then for Japanese. The NIGEL grammar has been described as 'the largest systemic grammar and possibly the largest machine grammar of any kind' (McDonald, Vaughan and Pustejovsky (1987:179)). It therefore goes far beyond the 'mini-grammars' (and even the 'midi-grammars') that are more typically used to exemplify the theoretical discussions in computational linguistics (CL). Indeed, it illustrates the way in which a new range of challenges arise when a rather fuller range of linguistic coverage is attempted. For its size and its richness alone, then, it must command respect. But it is far more than merely an account of a large grammar; the NIGEL framework includes, as well as the grammar itself, components that control the grammar, including an 'inquiry semantics'.

***

At this point it is right to pay a special tribute to the crucial role in the development of the NIGEL framework played by William Mann. Mann was by background a computer scientist with no special training in linguistics, but it was he who had the double insight to see, back in the late 1970s, the potential value for the project in text generation that he was planning of (1) giving the theoretical initiative, as it were, to the linguistics rather than to the computing, and (2) within linguistics, selecting a theory little in favour with computer scientists at the time (with the notable exception of the pioneering work by Winograd (1972) and Davey (1978)): Halliday's systemic functional grammar (SFG).[1]

In due course, Mann was joined at the Information Sciences Institute (ISI) of the University of Southern California by Matthiessen, and, working within the overall framework initiated by Mann, Matthiessen gradually took on more and more responsibility for the detailed development of the NIGEL grammar and the semantic components above it. Other systemic linguists (including myself for a brief period) have contributed fragments, but above all Halliday himself has been a regular visiting consultant throughout the development of NIGEL.[2] Later Bateman, working at the University of Kyoto, adapted the original NIGEL framework for Japanese (Bateman, 1986), and later still he replaced Matthiessen at ISI when Matthiessen moved to the University of Sydney. In all of these complex variations of personnel — and many others not mentioned here — Mann played a crucial unifying and integrating role.

But as well as steering the Penman project successfully throughout the 1980s, Mann has made a significant theoretical contribution, with Sandy Thompson, by developing rhetorical structure theory. This is a model for monologue discourse which is having a considerable influence in CL circles, with which NIGEL interacts (as described in this book). Thus Mann's contribution to the work reported here — whether in terms of the original conception of the project, its overall structure, the work with Matthiessen on NIGEL in the early years, the year-in year-out direction of the project throughout the 1980s, or his particular theoretical contribution at the level of discourse structure — has been of fundamental importance. Without William Mann there would have been no NIGEL.

***

The first of the three roles in which I welcome this book is my role as the co-editor of two books already published by Pinter, in the *Open Linguistics* series. These are *New Developments in Systemic Linguistics, Volume 1: Theory and Description* (co-edited with M.A.K. Halliday, and published in 1987) and *Volume 2: Theory and Application* (co-edited with David J. Young, and published in 1988). Together, the two books are intended to give an overview of recent work in systemic linguistics.

The particular purpose of the second volume is to illustrate the fruitful interplay between theory and application in the many areas in which systemic linguistics has been applied. But one reviewer of that volume, while generally welcoming it, chastised the editors for not including a chapter representing the important field of computational linguistics. In fact, as was explained in the Foreword, we had originally intended to have just such a contribution — indeed, to have two: one by each of Matthiessen and Bateman. Now the full truth about that double omission can be told. The fact is that when Matthiessen's contribution finally came in — which was just as the shape of the book as a whole was being finalized — it turned out to be about *thirty thousand* words in length — itself approaching half the length of a substantial book! I was immediately struck by both the quality of the account given there of the NIGEL framework and the impossibility of including it in the intended volume (unless we cut out several of the existing valuable contributions). Thus was born the idea of the present book. I asked Christian Matthiessen and John Bateman to consider joining forces to provide the definitive account of NIGEL, set as it is within the overall framework of the Penman Project. As I said in the Foreword to Fawcett and Young, 1988 (p. x), the present work 'should be thought of as an integral part of *New Developments in Systemic Linguistics*' because 'no picture of the theory and its applications would be complete without a chapter reporting work on the NIGEL grammar.'

Thus the present volume, while belonging squarely in the series *Communication in Artificial Intelligence*, also belongs in principle in the *Open Linguistics* series, as a book-length example of the fruitful interplay between theory and application in the field of computational linguistics. But note that, despite the length of treatment allowed, this book is still not a full account of current work in this field, as we shall see below; this is essentially the account of one major project in this field that was developed and complemented at two sites: the NIGEL framework.

***

Second, I welcome this significant book as a fellow researcher in this field. In my role as Director of the COMMUNAL Project, which is also at heart a text generation project and which also uses systemic functional grammar, I pay tribute to the courage, imagination, intelligence and sheer hard work with which the researchers on NIGEL and Penman attempted — and succeeded at — their enormous task. By so doing they made it easier for others to attempt to build more or less related models. These include Bateman's Japanese model, Patten's SLANG (Patten, 1988), the GENESYS component in the COMMUNAL Project at Cardiff (Fawcett, 1988; Fawcett and Tucker, 1990; Fawcett, 1990; and Tucker, to appear), and two recently begun projects: the KOMET Project at Darmstadt of Steiner, Bateman and colleagues (Steiner *et al.*, 1990; Wanner and Bateman, 1990), and even more recently started work by Matthiessen and colleagues at Sydney.

Let me make explicit one particular aspect of the debt owed to the pioneering work of Mann and Matthiessen by the rest of us. We have been like cross-country skiers following the tracks of a trail blazer, with the way (partially!) smoothed before us. The key point is that the task of implementing SFG computationally was very different from — and much greater than — that of implementing the current post-Chomskyan models, e.g. in parsers. The reason is that relatively little work had been done on turning SFG, which had been developed primarily for the hand analysis of texts, into a fully explicit, generative model. The effect is that a great debt is owed to the NIGEL team by those of us who have come after — whether we have been building explicitly on the base of the NIGEL framework for work on another language (as at Kyoto and Darmstadt) or exploring alternative ways of controlling the grammar (as with Patten at Edinburgh) or developing both a new framework and an alternative SFG (as at Cardiff). The great advantage shared by us all has been that we have known that, in principle, *the task is doable.*[3] It is this single fact, in my view, that has been the biggest contribution to giving us later workers in this new field of research the confidence to keep going on those occasions when, if we had not known that others had solved similar problems in a similar framework, we might have been overfaced (to use a good North Country word) by various problems of implementation. For us at Cardiff it was not that we borrowed solutions to the problems from NIGEL (because we did not, believing in the value of seeking our own solutions and so enriching the available experience) — but that we knew that it could be done.

***

I wrote in the Foreword to the *New Developments in Systemic Linguistics: Theory and Description* (Halliday and Fawcett, 1987):

> The very notion of developing a theory and then applying it is — or should be — a nonsense. The fact is that theories develop most creatively when descriptions of language that 'realize' them are tested in applications of various sorts — and, very often, the theories are stretched by the exercise and in due course reworked. It might therefore have been . . . appropriate . . . if we had given the second volume some such title as 'the theory-description-use-theory cycle'.

The position taken by Matthiessen and Bateman is precisely the same. As they say (Chapter 1, Section 1.1): 'Application is in fact an opportunity to work on theory'. Thus, this work is not 'merely' the application of a complex theory of language to an equally complex and challenging task (as if any application were 'mere'); it is equally a contribution to linguistic theory.

In particular, it is a major contribution to the further development of systemic linguistics. But newcomers to this theory should not be daunted; the book is written in such a way that you will be led gently into an understanding of the theory — and in due course an understanding of some of the issues that arise when building computational models of SFG: issues both for the implementation and for the theory.

Thirdly, then, I welcome this book in my role as a student of language and a fellow explorer of the systemic functional route to a better understanding of this all-pervasive and ever-fascinating phenomenon. This work should interest all linguists, irrespective of whether they happen to believe that theory should be tested and developed in the research paradigm of the computer, as it is in this case.[4]

There seems to be a view among linguists working in non-systemic frameworks that there is essentially just one systemic linguistics, i.e. that of Halliday (e.g. 1985). This is fairly far from the current reality. The fact is that Halliday does not lay down a currently 'correct' version to which all true believers should adhere. Indeed, he himself often offers alternative positions (e.g. on 'transitivity' in Halliday, 1985). He has long recognized the 'ineffability of language' (Halliday, 1984), and tolerates and encourages the exploration of alternative approaches within the general systemic framework. Thus the NIGEL grammar as developed by Matthiessen (and, as stated above, by many others who have visited ISI and worked on it) is in some respects different from the grammar found in Halliday, 1985, and the GENESYS lexicogrammar and generator in the COMMUNAL Project at Cardiff is different in many significant ways from both. Similarly, new ideas potentially significant for SFG theory are also appearing in the KOMET Project at Darmstadt (e.g. Wanner and Bateman, 1990).

Others working in the systemic framework (but not necessarily in the computational paradigm) have developed yet other ideas, some published (e.g. many of the contributions in Halliday and Fawcett, 1987; Fawcett and Young, 1988, and Davies and Ravelli, to appear). But many interesting ideas are simply presented at the annual International Systemic Congresses or discussed in local groups, without being formally published. Sometimes accounts of these ideas find their way into *Network*, the newsletter for those who want to keep up with news of the systemic linguistics community, but more often, regrettably, they do not.[5]

There is almost as much difference between some of these systemic approaches (e.g. those of Halliday, Fawcett, Gregory and Martin) as there is between members of the broad family of 'post-transformationalist' theories, such as generalized phrase structure grammar (GPSG), lexical functional grammar (LFG) and government and binding (GB). The importance of the present book in this respect is that it sets out the case for doing things in the way that they have been done in the NIGEL framework more clearly than is usually done in SFG, and that it discusses — though inevitably briefly — at least some of the alternatives. So yet another service that this excellent book performs is to provide a beginning — in a way that Halliday's key text *Introduction to Functional Grammar* does not (and, given its purpose, could not) — to the serious discussion that is now needed of the many questions that arise within systemic linguistics. Typically, these do not get discussed in depth in a forum more public than, for example, the research seminars held to thrash out current problems in the

COMMUNAL Project — and in similar semi-formal groupings, wherever systemic linguistics are at work.

The 'Introduction' to Halliday and Fawcett (1987) sets out eight 'new developments' (or, in another terminology, 'issues') within systemic *linguistic theory*. In building the GENESYS sentence generator in the COMMUNAL Project we have deliberately set out to broaden the collective SFG *computational* experience in two ways. First, we have chosen to explore alternative routes to solutions to many of the same problems that arose in developing NIGEL (e.g. by using the declarative language of Prolog rather than the procedural language of Lisp); by using a different but equally well-tested SFG description of English in which the networks are explicitly at the level of semantics (based on Fawcett, 1980); by giving central status to the selection expressions as a semantic representation; and by attempting to design the realization rules so that they are intrinsically reversible (see O'Donoghue, 1991). Second, we have additionally built, or begun to build, components that would in principle have been built for NIGEL if there had been time, and which will no doubt be developed in due course (e.g. the realization of meaning in intonation (Fawcett, 1990); the integration of meanings realized lexically in the same network as that for meanings realized grammatically and intonationally (Fawcett and Tucker, 1990; Tucker, to appear); the use of probabilities and preferences in system networks (Fawcett, to appear a and b); discourse modelled as social interaction (Fawcett, van der Mije and van Wissen, 1988). All of these innovations, like those in NIGEL, raise questions of principle and should contribute, in the spirit of the present book, to future discussions of systemic theory.

Here, in conclusion, is a selective checklist of questions that are raised in the context of work in the computational paradigm, and on which a SFG linguist or computational linguist should have (or be working towards having) a position. Virtually all are as relevant to those who want a good description of language for, let us say, describing a text of literary or social interest as they are to building better models for text generation or understanding. The hope of all those working in the demanding and exciting field of CL is that the various pressures on us to deliver working systems — pressures that our confidence in systemic theory enables us to feel well able to meet, given time and adequate resources — will not prevent us from somehow finding more time than we have had in the past to give to considered discussion, comparison and experimentation in relation to these matters.

1. Can the system networks in the lexicogrammar be semanticized further than they are in NIGEL, without overstraining the realization rules (or 'statements')?

2. Given that 'realization' rules/statements are inherently 'actualization' rules/statements, are they also genuinely 'realization' (i.e. inter-stratal) rules/statements?
3. Is it necessary to postulate a higher stratum of even more 'semantic' choices, still within the semiotic system of language, as opposed to their being part of the 'belief system' or 'upper model' (assuming the rough equivalence of these terms)?
4. What is the role of probabilities in (a) generation and (b) understanding?
5. At what level of planning is it most appropriate to handle register and other types of variation that are open to users of a language?
6. Should there be, in a SFG approach, a role for anything remotely like the standard notion of a 'lexicon' that is separate from the 'grammar' (e.g. in parsing)?
7. What is the relationship of the traditional linguistic concept of a 'description' of a language to the computational concept of language as a processing device for turning (very roughly) 'meanings' into 'sounds' and back? Are there 'neutral' descriptive models?
8. Should models of producing text be derived from models of understanding text, or *vice versa*, or from 'neutral' descriptive models?
9. What is the role of 'gates' (roughly, one-feature systems)? Are all gates essentially of the same type, or are some part of the system network and some part of the realization apparatus?
10. What is the full range of possible ways of handling the inter-stratal relationship of realization (which has been much less fully discussed so far than networks), and what is the optimal apparatus and notation?
11. What should the criteria be for deciding between alternative approaches within SFG to phenomena such as the 'clause complex' (e.g. 'hypotaxis' vs. 'embedding')?
12. The final question to be raised here is the one that is perhaps the largest of all for linguistics. If a SFG generator, with its system networks and realization rules, is the 'sentence planning' stage of text planning (i.e. if it is the last of possibly three broad stages of planning a text), then how far is linguistics an autonomous discipline? Just as most systemicists (and many others) would now reject the Chomskyan notion of 'autonomous syntax', claiming that 'meaning potential' (or 'semantics') has to be given its due place in the picture, so too it may be misleading to try too hard to produce 'autonomous linguistics' models — in the sense of models that generate, from a base that specifies the meaning potential (as in SFG), all and only the grammatical strings of words for a language. Any adequate model must find ways of handling the various constraints that are needed *at the*

*appropriate level*. But are all of these 'levels' within the semiotic system of language itself? In other words, is the concept of 'generation', in its formal language theory sense rather than its natural processing sense, still exerting an undue influence on the field?

Matthiessen and Bateman touch on almost all of these issues — and indeed on many others — and on some they have a clearly stated position. When they take a position it must be treated very seriously, because it has been tested in the fire (and sheer hard slogging work) of a computational implementation. It is for their contribution to the developing discussion of these and other crucial questions of linguistic theory that I personally welcome this book most of all. And for other readers, such as those who are simply seeking a clear exposition of how a SFG can be used in text generation, the book will be equally valuable.

*Robin P. Fawcett*
*Radyr, June 1991*

## Notes

1. Most researchers in parsing have preferred to work with broadly Chomskyan models of language that are explicitly influenced by the concepts and procedures of formal language theory; this is despite Winograd's seminal work on natural language understanding, which used systemic grammar (Winograd, 1972) and Winograd's continuing use of it, e.g. as the basis for the linguistic descriptions used in his widely used textbook *Language as Cognitive Process* (1983).
2. Indeed, the name 'Nigel' is itself an indication that Halliday is the 'father' of the grammar, in that 'Nigel' is the name used for Halliday's son in Halliday's celebrated account of Nigel's language development in *Learning How to Mean* (Halliday, 1975).
3. Winograd, 1972 and Davey, 1978 were earlier breakthroughs, but it was the sheer size and range of coverage of NIGEL that gave the additional confidence.
4. Nonetheless, it is significant that the testing and development *have* been done in this way; computational implementation has in the last decade — and for good reasons, I believe — become one of the leading ways of testing the validity of a linguistic theory. This should be alongside, as always (1) the time-honoured but ultimately unverifiable test of whether or not descriptions of actual texts based on a detailed description of a language give the analyser a sense of insightfulness, and (2) the potentially valuable but in practice still unreliable craft of psycholinguistic testing.
5. Those of us working in higher education these days are almost all too busy with teaching and administration to give as much time as we should to writing — and, indeed, all too often, to reading. Those with research posts may similarly have pressures on them to produce working models that cut down drastically the time that is left for interaction with co-researchers (whether orally, or through the writing and reading of papers) and too on the time for simply letting ideas develop. Research students: make the most of your few golden years; they may never come again (or only with a great struggle)!

## Bibliography


Bateman, J.A. *Text Planning for a Systemic Functional Grammar of Japanese*. Technical Report. Kyoto, Japan: Department of Electrical Engineering, University of Kyoto, 1986.

Berry, M.M., Butler, C.S. and Fawcett, R.P. (editors) *Meaning and Choice in Language: Studies for Michael Halliday. Volume 2 Grammatical Structure: a Functional Interpretation*. Newark, N.J.: Ablex, to appear.

Davey, A. *Discourse Production: a Computer Model of Some Aspects of a Speaker*. Edinburgh: Edinburgh University Press, 1978.

Davies, M. and Ravelli, L. (editors) *Advances in Systemic Linguistics: Recent Theory and Practice*. London: Pinter, to appear.

Fawcett, R.P. 'Language generation as choice in social interaction'. In Zock and Sabah (editors) 1988b, 27–49, 1988.

——— 'The computer generation of speech with semantically and discoursally motivated intonation'. In *Procs of 5th International Workshop on Natural Language Generation*, Pittsburgh, 1990.

——— 'A systemic functional approach to selectional restrictions, roles and semantic preferences', to appear a. Accepted for *Machine Translation*.

——— 'A systemic functional approach to complementation', to appear b. In Berry, Butler and Fawcett, to appear.

Fawcett, R.P. and Tucker, G.H. 'Demonstration of GENESYS: a very large, semantically based systemic functional grammar'. In *Procs of 13th International Conference on Computational Linguistics*, Helsinki, Volume 1 pp. 47–9, 1990.

Fawcett, R.P. and Young, D.J. (editors) *New Developments in Systemic Linguistics, Volume 2: Theory and Application*. London: Pinter, 1988.

Halliday, M.A.K. *Learning How to Mean*. London: Arnold, 1975.

——— 'On the ineffability of grammatical categories', in Manning, Martin and Mc Calla 1984. pp. 3–18, 1984.

——— *An Introduction to Functional Grammar*. London: Arnold, 1985.

Halliday, M.A.K. and Fawcett, R.P. (editors) *New Developments in Systemic Linguistics, Volume 1: Theory and Description*. London: Frances Pinter, 1987.

Kempen, G. (editor) *Natural Language Generation*. Dordrecht: Martinus Nijhoff, 1987.

McDonald, D.D., Vaughan, M.M. and Pustejovsky, J.D. 'Factors contributing to efficiency in natural language generation'. In Kempen 1987, pp. 159–81, 1987.

Manning, A., Martin, P. and Mc Calla, K. *The Tenth LACUS Forum 1983*. Columbia: Hornbeam Press, 1984.

O'Donoghue, T.F. 'A semantic interpreter for systemic grammars', In *Procs ACL Workshop on Reversible Grammars*. Berkeley, California, 1991.

Patten, T. *Systemic Text Generation as Problem Solving*. Cambridge: Cambridge University Press, 1988.

Steiner, E.H., Bateman, J.A., Maier, E., Teich, E. and Wanner, L. *KOMET: Department Plan*. Technical report. Darmstadt, Germany: GMD/Institut fur Integrierte Informations- und Publikationssysteme, 1990.

Tucker, G.H. 'Cultural classification and system networks: a systemic functional approach to lexical semantics', to appear. In Berry, Butler and Fawcett, to appear.

Wanner, L. and Bateman, J. 'Lexical cooccurence relations in text generation'. In *Procs of 5th International Workshop on Natural Language Generation*, Pittsburgh, pp. 31–8, 1990.

Winograd, T. *Understanding Natural Language*. Edinburgh: Edinburgh University Press, 1972.

——— *Language as Cognitive Process. Volume 1: Syntax*. Reading, Mass: Addison-Wesley, 1983.

Zock, M. and Sabah, G. (editors) *Advances in Natural Language Generation Vol. 2*. London: Pinter, 1988.

# Acknowledgements

The research discussed in this book has been carried out throughout the 1980s in several places: we are greatly indebted to the many people who have contributed in various ways over the years. Without the insight of Bill Mann the Penman system would not have come into existence: he conceived of the system, involved us, and directed the Penman project for most of the 1980s. We have benefited from our many discussions with him — just as with the other project members and co-workers at ISI: Robert Albano, Susanna Cumming, Ed Hovy, Bob Kasper, Johanna Moore, Cécile Paris, Lynn Poulton, Norman Sondheimer, Yu-Wen Tung, Richard Whitney and others. To Yu-Wen we also owe a special debt for his research on parallel generation, which forms the basis of our Chapter 10, and the work presented in Section 12.5 is joint work with Cécile Paris. Furthermore, several visitors and consultants have been crucial: Robin Fawcett, Peter Fries, Michael Halliday, Ruqaiya Hasan, Jim Martin, Sandy Thompson and others. Kary Lau at ISI receives a special mention and thanks for her work in preparing the final versions of most of the figures for the book.

The research contexts at Kyoto University and GMD/IPSI in Darmstadt have been very significant in expanding and supplementing the work at ISI. Thanks are due here to Professors Makoto Nagao and Jun-ichi Tsujii for being very supportive of the development of our prototype treatments of Japanese at Kyoto, and to the eager and thorough participation of the students, particularly Gen-ichiro Kikui, Atsushi Tabuchi and Li Hang; John Bateman offers further special thanks to Wendy (Jones) Nakanishi for prompting his foray into Japanese linguistics.

As will be abundantly clear from the book, our fundamental theoretical debt is to Michael Halliday. He has also provided constant support and encouragement in many exchanges around the globe. Bill Mann, Paul Schachter, Sandy Thompson and Mayumi Masuko commented on earlier materials on which we have drawn in preparing this book, and Cécile Paris and Erich Steiner have both made many helpful and detailed comments on the book drafts themselves. Robin Fawcett suggested that we should transform a book chapter into a book and so he is responsible for the existence of the present work! Through his own closely related research, he has been a constant source of inspiration, always willing to help and challenge.

As the above begins to suggest, it would almost be easier to list the places, countries, and continents where parts of this book have *not* been written, either by one of us individually or by both of us together, than those where they have been. This has naturally presented various technical and organizational problems and so, finally, we would like to thank Pinter Publishers, particularly Vanessa Couchman, Heather Bliss and Nicola Viinikka, for continued patience in the face of ever postponed delivery dates!

# 1 Introduction: text generation as an application of linguistic theory

The nineteenth century saw the culmination of the Industrial Revolution in the Western World. The revolution was a material one in many respects and the sciences that came of age at the time were the sciences of matter — inanimate and animate. Physics has accordingly emerged as the paradigm for doing science and this further foregrounds the material interpretation of our world. However, there are signs in modern physics that we need another kind of interpretation, a semiotic one where information plays a major role. This is not a new way of looking at the world, of course. The question of how to manage and represent information was as important in the sixteenth and seventeenth centuries when the modern scientific period started in the West and was in its predominantly taxonomic phase as it is now. But this complementary semiotic interpretation of our world has only recently come into prominence.

One central reason for this is that we now have tools for studying and manipulating information that are likely to be as important as the telescope, the microscope, and the steam engine were for the development of the scientific material world view — tools such as the tape recorder and the computer. These tools allow us to record and disseminate information in ways that were not made possible by the two previous milestones in the manipulation of information, the inventions of writing and printing.

The most elaborate and sophisticated information system we know is natural language and that is good reason to focus on disciplines that provide insight into language. There are several, of course, reflecting the various levels at which language exists (social, psychological, neurological, aesthetic, and so on). Indeed, this multiplicity is likely to prove one of the focal points in the breakdown in the traditional disciplinary boundaries and to be important in the foundation of a more thematic approach to the exploration of our world. It already figures prominently in two major interdisciplinary developments — cognitive science and semiotics.

## 1.1 Text generation

This book lies at the intersection of two paradigms for working on and with language: it is concerned with the exchange between linguistics and artificial intelligence (AI) in the context of TEXT GENERATION. Text generation can be characterized as one mode of information processing: information that is stored at a higher order of abstraction than wordings (grammatical structures and lexical terms) is organized and re-expressed over a number of steps so that it can be presented as a worded text. Together with text-understanding, parsing and machine translation, text generation is often known as natural language processing (NLP) and is pursued within computational linguistics.[1] This book deals with the application of linguistic theory and description to the task of text generation, drawing on AI techniques and methods.

Text generation research is motivated by the need to present information stored in or produced by the computer in a data base, an expert system or the like — information that would not otherwise be accessible to a person who is not a computer expert. Research on text generation thus usually involves getting the computer to function as a writer for some fairly restricted writing task (or occasionally as a speaker; cf. Sigurd, 1984; Davis and Hirschberg, 1988; Davis and Schmandt, 1989): given a need for text, the computer will produce text automatically in response to this need. We can see text generation and text understanding as complementary processes for communicating with the computer, i.e., exchanging information with it, in our own terms — those of natural language. Looked at in this way they represent a natural extension of the history of programming languages, which started out as machine languages, but have developed more and more to accommodate human principles for organizing information.

One kind of reason, then, why one might want to build a text generator would be to automate the production of weather forecasts by building a weather forecast generator. The generation process would involve finding the relevant information about yesterday's, today's and tomorrow's weather, organizing this information according to the format of weather forecasts, and then wording this information by means of grammatical structures and lexical items (cf. Isabelle, 1984; Kittredge, 1987). We will see many other applications of text generation of this kind below.

Another kind of reason for constructing generators comes from within linguistics. It is increasingly being realized among those working on text generation in a purely computational context, i.e., at departments of computer science or electrical engineering, research institutes concerned with computational research, and within the computer industry, that it is important to be aware of text generation as an application of linguistic theories and principles (we motivate this position more in Chapter 3). However, this has not yet been so well accepted among the linguistic community. As an application of linguistic theory, text generation stands in the same relationship to theory and description as do, for example parsing, pedagogic grammar, contrastive analysis, typological studies, the quest for linguistic universals, and literary studies. Linguistic theory is responsible to all applications such as these and they all involve theory revision and extension. Application is in fact an opportunity to work on theory. Thus, it is necessary to appreciate the value of *text synthesis* as a complementary approach to text analysis in the study of text and the other semiotic systems instantiated in text.

This has already motivated a number of linguistic researchers to work on issues related to the creation of text — with or without computers: Bengt Sigurd's (e.g. 1984) COMMENTATOR system developed at Lund University is a good example of the former, and Fawcett (1973, 1980), Halliday (1973, 1977), Chafe (1977, 1979), and Dik (1987) are good examples of the latter;[2] also, current work at Sydney University exemplifies both kinds of work. This tendency is certain to increase with the ready availability of ever more powerful, and yet cheaper, computers: linguistics departments will no longer be unable to afford machines capable of running the sophisticated software necessary for meaningful linguistic research. Text synthesis could then become just as valuable to discourse study as speech synthesis has become to phonetics. But the initiative for this needs to come from within linguistics, which is why it is important for linguistics also to conceive of text generation as a linguistic research task.

## 1.2 Systemic-functional linguistics

The particular approach to language around which we will centre our account of the application of linguistic theory to text generation is SYSTEMIC LINGUISTICS, which originated in Britain but is now used and developed internationally. Systemic linguistics started with M.A.K. Halliday's work in the early 1960s and has been developed by him and others into a holistic theory of *language in context*. Halliday's immediate linguistic environment was that created by Firth in the 1930s through 1950s.[3] One important theme was text in context, a way into language emphasized by the anthropologist Malinowski, who influenced Firth and also later systemic linguists. Halliday has also been influenced by, e.g., Prague School linguists, Hjelmslev, and Whorf.

In the systemic interpretation, language is seen as a resource for making meaning. This resource is organized functionally according to a small number of simultaneous highly generalized functions (metafunctions), concerned with the representation of experience (ideational), symbolic interaction between speaker and listener (interpersonal), and the presentation of information as text in context (textual). This resource is also stratified into subsystems forming three levels of abstraction ((discourse) semantics, lexicogrammar and phonology/graphology). Lexicogrammar is the unified resource of grammar (syntax and morphology)[4] and lexis (vocabulary). Grammar and lexis are simply different aspects of the same system; both are simultaneously ideational, interpersonal, and textual. For instance, ideational lexis is the (taxonomic) organization of vocabulary as denotation, interpersonal lexis is the connotative organization, and textual lexis is concerned with the use of lexical resources in the creation of cohesive text.

In systemic linguistics, each level of the linguistic system is organized as a network of interrelated choice points (a system network), making explicit what resources are available. Selections from this network are realized (expressed, coded) by structures, items, etc. Choice is thus the primary principle of organization, not structure. The linguistic system as a whole is furthermore 'embedded' in context, which can be interpreted as higher-level semiotic systems (e.g., systems of social relationships and ideological systems).

The reasons for our choice of systemic linguistics as the theoretical linguistic foundation in text generation will emerge below (particularly in Chapter 5), but it is important to note in the present context that systemic linguistics differs sharply from Chomskyan linguistics, with Government and Binding theory as the current principal manifestation (Chomsky, 1981), and the various frameworks that have been presented as alternative ways of answering the questions about language that Chomsky is concerned with (Lexical Functional Grammar — LFG: Bresnan and Kaplan, 1982; Generalized Phrase Structure Grammar — GPSG: Gazdar, Klein, Pullum and Sag, 1985; and so on). First of all, systemic linguistics interprets and represents language not as a rule-system for generating structures but as a *resource* for expressing and making meanings. The interpretation of language as a resource makes a fundamental difference when we build a text generation system since the purpose of such a system is precisely to express and make meanings. Second, systemic linguistics has expanded the boundaries of linguistics and made them more permeable from outside. It can thus help facilitate the interdisciplinary exchange we are concerned with.

These and other related differences should be emphasized in the present context since the image of linguistics in computational areas is often the Chomskyan one. This is probably one significant factor in the occasional wholesale rejections of linguistics that may be observed within Natural Language Processing, which is unfortunate since there are other ways of doing linguistics, other ways of conceiving of, and theorizing about, language. Even when the Chomskyan contributions, particularly in the area of syntax, are accepted, the systemic alternative (as well as others, of course) is worth considering. Many areas which are crucial to computational linguistics (functional grammar, discourse, context, register, and so on) simply fall outside Chomskyan theorizing but are part of the systemic domain. We will illustrate many of these areas explicitly in the chapters below: thus, our choice of systemic linguistics as the theoretical foundation for our work on text generation is motivated both because it addresses issues that are crucial to natural language generation and because it facilitates the interdisciplinary exchange we believe is now necessary.

## 1.3 Organization of the book

We have divided our discussion into four parts to show the progression from the opening up of the exchange between work on text generation and systemic linguistics through particular research applications and conclusions that can be drawn from them so far to future directions building on these conclusions. The specific context of our discussion is provided by two particular text generation systems with which we have been involved: the Penman system for the generation of English text and the Kyoto system for the generation of Japanese text.

Part I, Text generation and systemic linguistics: opening the exchange (Chapters 2–4), introduces text generation and systemic linguistics. Chapter 2 deals with the model of text generation in natural language processing and Chapter 3 gives a brief interpretative survey of past work on text generation within a computational setting. Chapter 4 takes up the issue of the exchange between linguistics and text generation, indicating what the division of labour has been up to now.

Part II, Systemic linguistics and text generation: the basic theoretical framework and two computational instantiations (Chapters 5–7), lays the linguistic foundation for the rest of the discussion and introduces two research applications. Chapter 5 is a very brief synopsis of those aspects of systemic theory that are particularly relevant to text generation. Chapter 6 presents this framework as it is embodied in the two research applications, focusing on the level of grammar. Chapter 7 draws on the grammars of Japanese and English to illustrate the use of the framework.

Part III, Up to and beyond the limits of the basic framework (Chapters 8 and 9), explores the question of how far the current computational modelling of systemic theory has taken us and where we have to return to the theory for insights into how to revise the model. We divide this discussion along two dimensions of organization drawn from systemic theory: Chapter 8 discusses extensions within grammar in terms of the METAFUNCTIONAL decomposition of grammatical resources, and Chapter 9 discusses extensions that go beyond the grammar to higher STRATA of the linguistic system.

Part IV, Future directions for computational systemic-functional linguistics (Chapters 10–12), takes up a number of issues that are only beginning to be explored and that are thus one step beyond those discussed in Parts II and III in the evolving exchange between theory and application. Chapter 10 addresses the possibility of parallelism in text generation based on multi-functional systemic theory and Chapter 11 turns to the task of developing dynamic interpretations and representations of the linguistic system. Chapter 12 explores the relationship between the general and the specific in text generation — the tension between the generalized notion of text generation and the specific generators created for generating reports, encyclopaedic entries, etc. — in terms of the systemic concepts of context and register variation.

Finally, to conclude the book, Chapter 13 briefly discusses other related systemic-functional work that is currently under way and which we feel will be important for the future of computational linguistics, systemic linguistics, and their interaction. We organize this in terms of the dimensions of components of the theoretical framework as developed throughout the book — this should be of use to readers who wish to follow up on particular aspects of the theory and practice of systemic-functional linguistics in general and its application to computational natural language processing in particular. Further collections of references are provided in supplemental tables following Chapters 2, 3 and 5 and a general glossary of terms precedes the bibliography.

## Notes

1. Natural language processing has not previously been taken to include work on various kinds of data processing where the computer is used as a research tool to examine and discover statistical patternings. However, more recent results in the analysis of large-scale corpora are finding their way into natural language processing proper.
2. There are also examples within psycho-linguistics; but they tend to be further away from the problems we are concerned with here.
3. It has to be emphasized that the Firthian environment was fundamentally different from the American linguistic environment in which Chomsky grew up

and reacted against. Many of the issues and insights that have only appeared on the agenda in the late 1970s and 1980s as a reaction against the version of generative linguistics developed in the 1960s were already on Firth's agenda (see e.g., Henderson, 1987).

4. Note that the term grammar is thus used in its traditional sense and not in its more recent Chomskyan sense of '(model of) the linguistic system', where it can come to include not only syntax and morphology but also semantics and phonology.

# Part I Text generation and systemic linguistics: opening the exchange

## 2 The model of text generation in natural language processing

As we will see in our historical overview of text-generation systems in Chapter 3, such systems vary quite significantly in basic design. In this chapter, we discuss briefly what a text generation system of the early 1990s looks like when conceived in computational linguistic terms and identify a number of key components, presenting them in terms of one design.

### 2.1 The design of a representative generation system

In the design of a text generator, one general tendency is to distinguish between *resources* such as knowledge resources, a user model, rhetorical resources, grammatical resources, and lexical resources; and *processes* or procedures that employ these resources. Examples of processes include knowledge selection, text planning (organization), lexicogrammatical expression, and editing. The general process of generating text is often seen as *goal pursuit* — a powerful metaphor developed within AI which defines processes that may be performed in order to achieve as yet unrealized but desirable states. In the particular case of text generation, therefore, *communicative goals* are specified and the generator produces a text in order to attain these goals.[1]

A simple design is diagrammed in Figure 2.1. For concreteness, we will centre our opening description on Mann's (1982) design plan for the Penman generator, which, as one of the broadest scoped generators that has been developed, offers an orienting framework for most of the features we

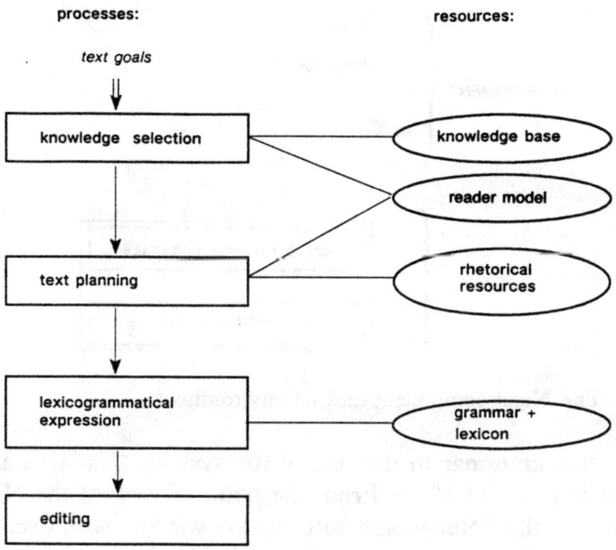


**Figure 2.1** Simple sequential generator design

need to introduce. It has also provided the starting point for a number of current developments in text generation (e.g., Matthiessen, 1989; Steiner *et al.*, 1990a), text analysis (Kasper, 1989b), and machine translation (Bateman, 1989b; Hovy, 1989a) and so continues to be relevant for current research efforts.

The generator starts by invoking a subprocess, KNOWLEDGE SELECTION (also called SEARCH), which extracts the relevant knowledge from the knowledge resources of the generator. The selection process can be guided by a model of the intended user, the user model (also sometimes called the reader or hearer model), so as to avoid including information already known to him or her and to include background information not known to him or her.[2]

Text PLANNING then arranges the extracted knowledge into a RHETORICAL STRUCTURE using the strategies offered by the rhetorical resources, again consulting the user model if available. In Penman, for example, the overall organization of the text is planned in terms of *Rhetorical Structure Theory*. The result is a hierarchy of rhetorical units, each terminal unit typically corresponding to a non-embedded clause.

The process of LEXICOGRAMMATICAL EXPRESSION then takes over and executes the text plan by turning it into wordings, relying on the lexicogrammatical resources. In Penman, for example, the process of lexicogrammatical expression uses the *Nigel* component of the system, which is organized into two levels (strata): a systemic-functional grammar and a semantic interface

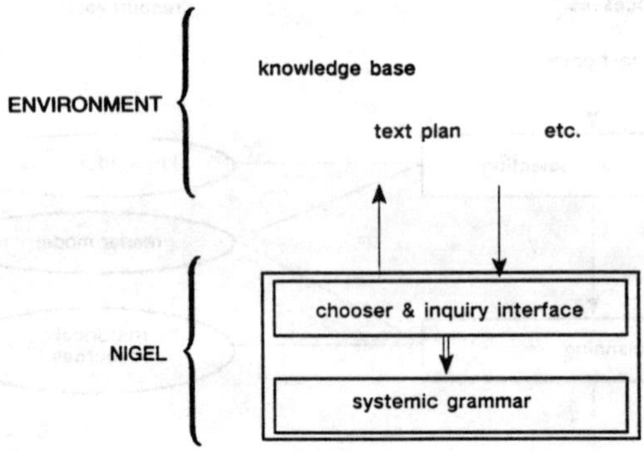


**Figure 2.2** The Nigel component and its environment

that relates this grammar to the rest of the system; this latter is called the chooser and inquiry interface. From the point of view of the Nigel component, the rest of the Penman generator — knowledge base, user model, and rhetorical resources, etc. — constitutes the *environment* in which Nigel operates; we will discuss this environment and what it contains in Part III in some depth. The chooser and inquiry interface interacts with the environment to obtain information needed to make motivated grammatical choices, as depicted in Figure 2.2. We will return to the theoretical foundations and practical details of this component in considerable depth in Part II.

Finally, the generator may also include a simple monitor or EDITOR that tries to improve the final output. In future, more sophisticated systems, editors will have to be given the capability of parsing and understanding the text produced by the generator but such integration of generation and understanding has not been achieved in systems developed in the 1980s.

## 2.2 An example of a generated text

In order to ground our discussion of text generation somewhat, and to give a more concrete idea of the role and interaction of the components of our idealized text generation system as we have presented them, consider the following text. This is a text actually generated by the Penman system when driven by a rather sophisticated text planning component drawn from work on Explainable Expert Systems (Swartout and Smoliar, 1987). The particular instantiation of the Explainable Expert System at issue here is Johanna Moore's 'Program Enhancement Advisor' (PEA), a program which engages in a dialogue to suggest to users improvements in the style of their Lisp programs (Moore and Paris, 1989).

You should replace (**setq x 1**) with (**setf x 1**). **Setf** can be used to assign a value to any generalized-variable. **Setq** can only be used to assign a value to a simple-variable. A generalized-variable is a storage location that can be named by any accessor function.

This text is generated in the following stages (referring also to Figure 2.1). First, there is a rather sophisticated degree of dialogue planning (this text is only one turn from a more extended dialogue between user and system) which sets up a context of communicative goals that are being achieved. The top level goal responsible for this text is to recommend to the user that s/he replaces the first Lisp form given for the latter. In order to achieve this goal, the system knows from its library of plans that a good strategy would be to explain the differences between the Lisp forms. This allows the user also to understand why it is that one form may be preferable to another. This, therefore, can trigger an operation of knowledge selection, where the system has to retrieve knowledge from its knowledge base of differences between the types of Lisp forms that are being considered. These differences should not be differences that the user already knows about; nor should they be differences that are irrelevant to the current goals of the user. In both cases, therefore, the retrieval must consider the model of the user that the system has in order to be aware of the user's goals and knowledge.

The system also knows from its rhetorical resources that there are various ways of relating the two pieces of information that one Lisp form should replace another and that there are differences between the two forms. In this case, there is a rhetorical relation of motivation which can have particular consequences for the linguistic forms that are appropriate.

When all these pieces of information have been found, and the rhetorical relations that hold between them have been selected, they can then be passed on to a lexicogrammatical component in order to construct appropriate grammatical and lexical expressions for them. The result of these operations is the text above.

## 2.3 Deep and surface generation: stratal height

Researchers often draw a distinction between *deep generation* and *surface generation*: knowledge selection and text planning constitute deep generation and lexicogrammatical expression is surface generation. Broadly speaking, surface generation has received most attention and has been the first area of research to be addressed. Although the distinction between deep and surface can be useful for certain purposes, it has also been harmful as it has invited the interpretation that all the important choices are deep ones. This distinction is now being questioned: many 'surface' phenomena such as the selection among synonyms and the sequencing of the elements of the clause turn out to have very deep significance and have to be modelled in deep generation. This is to be expected from a functional linguistic point of view (cf. for example, Halliday, 1967/8 and work on Functional Sentence Perspective from the Prague School). The general point here is that all the stages in text generation (as shown in Figure 2.1) are meaningful, but they represent meaningful options at different orders of abstraction. We will not rely on the depth metaphor and the theory it embodies; instead, we will draw on another spatial metaphor, where the subsystems of the overall system are organized into levels (strata) arranged according to symbolic height and abstraction from higher levels to lower levels.[3] Levels are related by realization and there is no implication that lower levels are less meaningful than higher ones.

## 2.4 More sophisticated designs and design issues

The simplicity of the generator design in Figure 2.1 lies partly in the strictly sequential arrangement of the processes indicated in the diagram in contrast to a model where they are interleaved.[4] Knowledge selection and text planning should in a general model probably be interleaved rather than staged. On the one hand, the need to express certain knowledge has implications for text planning. For instance, the need to express a procedure can often call on text planning resources for sequential organization. On the other hand, text planning will also raise the need to select knowledge. For instance, if text planning determines that the user needs to be given background information, evidence, motivation, and so on, the relevant knowledge to support this rhetorical strategy has to be selected.

Furthermore, we will eventually have to design generators that can plan and execute texts stage by stage rather than in one go. This will be particularly important when we move towards designs of more interactive generators for (casual) conversation.

To reflect the interaction between text planning and knowledge selection, we can redraw the diagram from Figure 2.1 as shown in Figure 2.3. Here, editing has been left out of the diagram; resources are diagrammed inside process boxes; and the products produced by the processes are italicized.

According to this design, incoming text, or communicative, goals, which are stated in terms of the prospective user, are analysed and handed off to text planning. Text planning interacts with knowledge selection in building a text plan — knowledge organized into some kind of rhetorical structure. Both processes consult the user model. A sentence generator such as Nigel then realizes this text plan as a text worded in English.[5] In addition, current work is considering the production of spoken texts, where a further

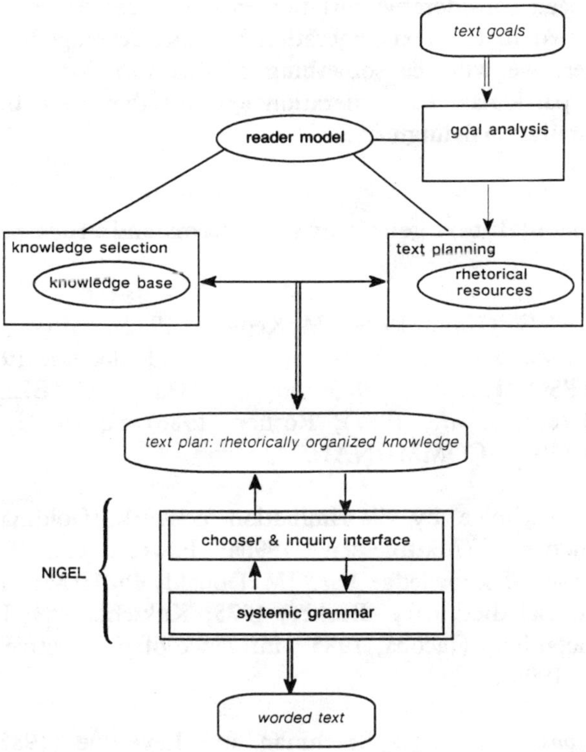


**Figure 2.3** Generator design with interaction

component is added to realize the results of lexicogrammatical generation as spoken output with appropriate intonation.

The two design sketches in Figures 2.1 and 2.3 indicate some of the fundamental variables in the design of a text generation system:

- What are the processes and the resources?
- What is the *stratal* arrangement of the resources — how many strata are there; which resources are stratally higher; which resources are stratally simultaneous? The two designs differ in the arrangement of knowledge base and rhetorical resources. They are stratally differentiated in the first design, whereas they are not in the second model.
- What is the *staging* of the generation processes? The stratal arrangement of the resources will determine the overall staging of the generation processes, but there are still different stagings. Are the processes sequential or interleaved? To what level of detail does planning have to articulate the text being generated before realization in linguistic form can commence?

There has been considerable variation in how these design questions have been addressed in the text generation systems developed to date. In the next chapter, we will see something of this variation as we describe a number of particular text generation systems that have been developed within computational linguistics.

## 2.5 Supplemental: text generator subsystems and processes

*Subsystems*

*Grammar:* FUG (Kay, 1979; McKeown, 1982); SFG (Davey, 1978; Patten, 1988a; Part II); ATN (Simmons and Slocum, 1972; Goldman, 1974); APSG (Heidorn, 1975; Sowa, 1983a); MUMBLE (McDonald, 1980; Meteer, *et al.*, 1987); Rösner (1986) SEMSYN; Fawcett and Tucker's (1990) COMMUNAL.

*Lexis:* lexical choice by discrimination network (Goldman, 1974); by system network (Matthiessen, 1990a; Fawcett and Tucker, 1990); lexicalization of knowledge base (McDonald, 1981; Matthiessen, 1981); use of phrasal dictionary (Becker, 1975; Kukich, 1983; Hovy, 1988b); idioms/metaphors (Jacobs, 1985); influence of perspective (Wanner and Bateman, 1990).

*Knowledge base:* see e.g., Brachman and Levesque (1985) for general references; further: perspective (McCoy, 1986), views (Jacobs, 1985), knowledge selection (McKeown, 1982; McDonald and Conklin, 1983; Moore and Paris, 1989). Also Part III. cf. also user modelling.

*Rhetorical resources:* rhetorical schemas (McKeown, 1982; Kukich, 1983; McCoy, 1986; Paris, 1987, 1990); rhetorical structure theory (Mann and Thompson, 1987; Hovy, 1988a; Moore and Paris, 1988); use of focus (Grosz, 1978; Sidner, 1981; McKeown, 1982; Grosz and Sidner, 1986). Also Part III.

*Semantics for guiding lexicogrammatical expression:* chooser and inquiry semantics (Part II); situation-specific semantics (Patten, 1988a).

*User modelling:* as lists of facts acting as filter (Mann and Moore, 1980), user's domain goals (McKeown *et al.*, 1985), user misconceptions (McCoy, 1986), degree of user expertise (Paris, 1987; Bateman and Paris, 1989, 1990), user interest, affect, group membership (Hovy, 1987a, 1989b).

*Conception of generation and global organization of processes*

Generation as problem solving (Patten, 1988a); as hierarchic planning (Appelt, 1985); as mixture of global and local, interleaved planning (Hovy, 1988b).

## Notes

1. The distinction between processes and resources corresponds to the differentiation in Fawcett's (1980) systemic model between the problem solver, the central processor of the system, and the resources it works with such as affective states, 'knowledge' of the universe, 'knowledge' of the addressee's informational state, and semantics.
2. Although the need for a user model has been recognized for some time, there has been rather less work on this resource than the others; it is, however, now coming to receive considerable attention, e.g., Kobsa and Wahlster (1988).
3. Perhaps the depth metaphor should be abandoned altogether (as a number of linguists have done). The alternative metaphor of symbolic height is used within theories where stratification and realization are fundamental organizing principles.
4. cf. de Beaugrande (1984: 102ff.) on the contrast between what he calls a sequential-stage relay model and a parallel-stage interaction model. This is also under consideration in current work on text generation generally (Hovy *et al.*, 1988; Emele *et al.*, 1990b).
5. In fact, further 'interleaving' will almost certainly be required. In particular, once the process of lexicogrammatical expression has started, it will need support by 'local' text planning such as the planning of referring expressions. In addition, it is also good design to permit hearer feedback to be able to interact with planning so as to avoid inappropriate and potentially costly planning directions.

# 3 The development of text generation in relation to systemic linguistics

We now offer a brief survey of the development of text generation, noting its relevance and interactions with systemic linguistics. Systemic notions will be introduced here only as the need arises; Part II provides a more systematic introduction. We will start with interaction between systemic linguistics and natural language processing (NLP) before systemic work was used in the service of text generation, since it serves as a background to later work on generation. We then move on to the core systemic concept of 'register', since this provides us with a powerful interpretive framework for work on text generation generally. Finally, we move to the interpretative survey itself.

## 3.1 Systemics and NLP before text generation

The interaction between computation and systemic linguistics did not start with text generation; machine translation and parsing preceded. Machine translation (MT) is automatic translation from one language to another by means of a computational system. Parsing is automatic grammatical analysis. This ordering reflects the general development of computational linguistics in which text generation is a more recent development than machine translation and parsing (and text understanding).

The interaction can be said to have started with Michael Halliday's participation in an early machine translation project in Cambridge in the mid-1950s led by Margaret Masterman. Other participants included Martin Kay and Arthur Parker-Rhodes. One outcome of this work was Halliday's (1956) paper on the potential for a mechanical thesaurus as a strategy for coping with the lack of translation equivalence; the thesaurus has remained central to the systemic theory of lexis, as we shall see below. Another outcome was Parker-Rhodes's (1978) proposal of a graph notation for the representation of meaning — this differs from most semantic nets (e.g., Simmons and Slocum, 1972; Findler, 1979; Sowa, 1983b) in that he takes account of textual (e.g., Halliday's information focus) and interpersonal meaning, that range of meaning concerned with the social interaction involved in language, in addition to ideational meaning, the expression of propositional content and views of reality. All three areas are held by systemic linguistics to be crucially involved in all instances of language use; we will introduce them in detail below.

Martin Kay went on to develop the highly influential FUNCTIONAL UNIFICATION GRAMMAR (FUG) as a grammar for computational uses (first described in Kay, 1979). This has turned out to be more like systemic functional grammar in terms of the representational resources that it provides than any other linguistic grammar (Kay, 1986; and for a comparison of the two, see Kasper, 1987a, 1988). For instance, as in systemic functional grammar, the specification of a grammar in FUG makes it possible to write grammars using 'functions' and 'features' (see Chapter 6 below) and to specify different fragments of grammatical descriptions that can be unified or accumulated as a description is built up in parsing or generation. Unification is essentially like set union; but they are not identical: see Kay (1979). FUG has been employed as the basis for a number of grammars used in text generation[1] (for example by McKeown, 1982 — see below) and its control mechanism, unification, is at the heart of many current grammar formalisms (e.g.: Categorical Unification Grammar, Uszkoreit, 1986; Head-driven Phrase Structure Grammar, Pollard, 1985, Pollard and Sag, 1987; etc.; see Shieber, 1986, for a general overview).

A further significant interaction occurred around 1967 when Terry Winograd studied with Halliday in London; the influence of systemic theory on him can be seen both in the milestone artificial intelligence system SHRDLU (see, e.g., Winograd, 1972) and in the general introduction to NLP that he presents in Winograd (1983). SHRDLU was a system capable of answering questions about the arrangement of blocks of various shapes and colours on a table top and complying with commands to manipulate those blocks. SHRDLU was significant in a number of ways. Perhaps the most obvious importance from a systemic point of view is Winograd's use of a systemic grammar for the analysis of natural language input to the system at a time when most attention on linguistic grammars was directed towards transformational work and there were few grammatical alternatives available in computational linguistics.[2] But SHRDLU is also of interest in other respects. In particular, it demonstrated what can be achieved in artificial intelligence by creating a well-bounded, so-called *micro-world* — in this case, the blocks world of the SHRDLU system. In the next section, we relate this micro-world approach to the important systemic concept of register, or functional variety of language (variety according to use); this will permit us below to suggest a means by which one of the most prominent criticisms of the micro-world approach, lack of generalizability, may be countered (Chapter 12).

Winograd and his work have influenced the development of text generation in at least two ways. One of the first text generation systems to be built, Davey's (1978) PROTEUS, was subsequently also based on a systemic grammar. In addition, Winograd's student David McDonald developed a systemic-like grammar (the early MUMBLE grammar of McDonald, 1980), which later developed into one of the primary generation grammars and has been used for a variety of generation tasks (e.g., McDonald and Conklin, 1983; Rubinoff, 1986; Meteer, 1989). Winograd's work also showed some of the merits of a procedural approach to semantics; Fawcett (1980) discusses this and other aspects of Winograd's system in relation to systemic theory.[3]

Even prior to detailed work on text generation, therefore, there had been significant, if sometimes indirect, interaction between systemic linguistics and natural language processing. Although the flow of information in this interaction was mostly from systemic linguistics, and its perspectives on language and language use, into computation, there were attempts to exchange information in the other direction, i.e., from computation into systemic linguistics — for example, one of the first attempts to provide formalizations of aspects of systemic theory in computational terms was Henrici's (1965) computational analysis of the *system network*.

The system network had been developed by Halliday in the early 1960s (cf. Halliday, 1963, 1964, 1966) as a theoretical tool for representing the organization of linguistic systems as choice, i.e., for representing paradigmatic organization (examples are given in Part II). Henrici developed a program for making automatic selections of the linguistic alternatives defined by a system network (forming 'selection expressions' of grammatical features), thereby demonstrating that the notation formerly developed within linguistics could find application as a computational formalism and could, as a consequence, potentially support automatic generation.

One result of Henrici's analysis, however, was the identification of a number of problems (e.g., the analysis of 'recursive logical systems' that we will return to in Chapters 8 and 11), where the notation did not lend itself to immediate implementation. This revealed areas where the informal understanding of the notation used linguistically was not sufficient for constructing the more detailed specifications necessary for computational formalization. This is important since it shows where the linguistic notation and its properties are not as well understood as they ought to be. Although some of the problems raised by Henrici have now been addressed, the majority of aspects in systemic theory have not yet received adequate computational elucidation.

This illustrates the general delay between initial theoretical formulation and a principled, non-*ad hoc* computational model of the theoretical construct. This kind of delay is not a drawback; rather, it points to the importance of working with a framework which operates with a wide range from informal theorizing to fully explicit formalization. This we motivate further in the following chapter.

Although computational work that serves to improve and develop the formalization of systemic theory now forms a growing body of research,[4] most previous work on text generation has not yet explicitly contributed to the exchange of information between systemic linguistics and computation in either direction. This is to a certain extent comprehensible in terms of an initial explosion of development and systems where specialized techniques could make rapid progress; we will see something of this manner of development below. The text generation research community has also been rather small, although it now seems to be growing steadily,[5] and it was perhaps necessary for text generation to establish itself — its goals, methods, and areas of concern — prior to taking stock of the more global environment of concern about text. The research questions asked in text generation are often different from the ones we find in work on parsing, for example. Whereas work on parsing is often concerned with the formal behaviour of different kinds of parsing algorithms and problems posed by syntactic constructions given special attention in formal syntax, it seems reasonable to say that generation is treated primarily as a functional problem.

As capabilities become more sophisticated, however, there is an increasing need for comprehensive theories of the task being undertaken. The cost of redesign whenever a new functionality or domain of application is required simply becomes too high. It is essential to achieve generality and extensibility in text generation systems and a solid body of theory development that goes beyond the immediate needs of the day is essential for this.

To show this rather more clearly, we will relate a number of prominent 'text generation' systems — construed rather widely — to one body of theory, i.e., systemic-functional linguistics. As already remarked in connection with the overview of a text generation system in Section 2.1, text generators vary considerably in design. They can be (and have been — cf. McDonald, Meteer, and Pustejovsky, 1987; Kempen, 1986) compared and contrasted in terms of the techniques they use, the resources they rely on, etc. While different designs clearly reflect different concerns and preferences on the part of researchers, there is another significant reason for the variation. Here we present a particular interpretation of their differences and similarities by motivating system design in terms of the concept of *register* from systemic theory (Halliday, 1978; Halliday and Hasan, 1985, and Chapters 5 and 12). This, we suggest, provides a rather more global view of the contributions of particular systems to the general task of generating text than that possible in contrastive accounts of system designs.

## 3.2 Text generation and register

It is well known that languages vary according to the language user's geographical and social background — this is called dialectal variation. But there is another kind of linguistic variation as well, one that is more immediately important to computational linguistics. This is variation as a function of use. It is called *functional variation* (or register variation) and a particular functional variety is called a *register* just as a regional variety is called a dialect.[6] For instance, sports commentaries are linguistically quite different from weather forecasts, fairy tales quite different from detective stories, air traffic control interactions quite different from unhurried telephone calls between close friends, etc.

Use is determined by three components in the context of use: field, tenor, and mode. Field is the social activity accompanying the language processing and also the 'subject matter'. Tenor is the social relationship being enacted by the interlocutors (e.g., in terms of power and expertise); it is their enactment of social distance. Mode is the role being played by language itself, e.g., in terms of medium (spoken/written) and rhetorical purpose (instruction, persuasion, etc.). Different conventional settings of field, tenor and mode values correspond to different registers. Thus recipes can be characterized very broadly as field: culinary activity; tenor: expert to non-expert; and mode: written instruction. As we will see in our discussion below, it is also possible and illuminating to recognize the relation that holds between field and the construct 'knowledge base' and between tenor and the construct 'user model' in computational systems.

The designs of text generation systems reflect the purposes for which texts are to be generated. That is, *different registers tend to lead to different kinds of designs of text generators*. While this may be of interest theoretically of itself, the relationship drawn to register has considerably more significant consequences. Registers not only relate context to types of language, they also focus on the relationships *across* types of contexts. That is: the theory of register imposes an organizational classification on situations and contexts which allows us to relate the rather diverse-appearing properties of language use in differing contexts and of text generation systems supporting those language uses.

Thus, for example, it is now possible to make the connection between Winograd's SHRDLU, mentioned above, and systemic register theory quite explicit: what Winograd's system can do corresponds to a fairly closed register. This is not a drawback; rather, it is an indication of how work of this kind might be guided by register theory. Once a particular 'language processing task' has been located in a register space, we will have a fair idea of what it will take to construct a system that can deal with the task. This is of considerable importance in natural language processing. The micro-world approach of AI has come under attack because, it is argued, it does not deal with the general issues of 'intelligence' (cf. Dreyfus, 1981). However, one thing register theory is intended to do is to relate specific to general and closed registers to more open ones. That is, we can think of a micro-world as a very restricted field of discourse which, by means of the theory of register, should be relatable with other micro-worlds and to more general characterizations. We will discuss this in more depth in Chapter 12.

In general, therefore, we can by means of the systemic-functional interpretation of language as a resource that is always used in particular contexts relate and motivate differences in text generator design — even quite radically different-seeming designs as those producing fully planned utterances and those relying on 'canned text'. The latter are simply the limiting cases of extremely restricted registers — what Firth termed restricted languages. Slightly less restricted are generators which are able to rely more heavily on lexis than on grammar by using a so-called phrasal lexicon, as in Kukich's (1983) stock market report generator, which uses lexical items such as *display a hesitant mood early in the day* and *display a hesitant mood late in the day*. Since lexicogrammar realizes semantics, registerial differentiations are also projected through lexicogrammar; in fact, the registerial differences speakers are probably most aware of are lexical ones such as these.

Register also strongly affects grammatical and textual organization, however. For example, other text generation systems have generated extended text but have relied on the organization of the domain or field to organize the text rather than on an independent set of rhetorical strategies. Thus we find systems that will just trace through procedures such as computer programs and 'translate' them into English — a method sometimes called direct translation or direct replacement (see Swartout, 1983; Kukich, 1983; and McDonald, 1986, for some discussion).

Furthermore, text generators have often been one-register generators — game transcript generators, story generators, stock market report generators, and so on — and this has made certain design simplifications possible. For example, some systems have been designed for registers where it is possible to achieve results without generating text extending beyond a sentence (cf. Appelt, 1983; Jacobs, 1985). The significant differences in registers addressed also motivates how some areas of text generation, e.g., story generation and expert system explanation, have constituted fairly distinct lines of research in text generation. We will suggest below how such barriers can be lowered in a theoretically motivated and beneficial fashion.

In the next section, we focus on four significant text generation systems. We will motivate the design of each in terms of the register or registers for which it is intended to create text. We will also draw attention to other text generation systems during the discussion as an indication of the breadth of application of the interpretation we offer.

## 3.3 Text generators: a brief interpretative survey

We will approach our survey of text generation systems as follows. First, we will describe briefly the capabilities of the systems mentioned; this will also lead to a characterization of the contexts in which the systems were to function. Then we will show how the capabilities and the design decisions taken to achieve those capabilities follow from those contexts. We also make reference to the general components of a text generation system as set out in Chapter 2, for placing the components of the systems we describe here, and run an additional loose chronological organization throughout.

We have noted that work on text generation started later in computational linguistics than work on machine translation and text understanding; indeed, the earliest work in 'language generation' was not text generation at all: rather, it was random sentence generation for the purpose of testing grammars (cf. Yngve, 1962; Friedman, 1969). Accordingly, the grammar components of text generation systems have had the longest history of development. As the focus moved to text generation proper, the need to use a grammar to express particular information rather than to generate random structures was increasingly foregrounded. From this point on, questions concerning the effect of context — i.e., in the simplest case, what semantic information to express[7] — become relevant and we can raise register-related issues. Although a number of researchers have worked with the use of a grammar in isolation for presenting pregiven semantic information (e.g., Simmons and Slocum, 1972), perhaps the earliest — and still one of the most impressive — attempts to build a complete *text* generation system was Davey's (1978) Proteus system, built in the early 1970s. It is with this system, therefore, that we begin.

### *3.3.1 Davey's PROTEUS*

PROTEUS was a genuine text generation system in that it planned and produced texts rather than focusing only on the lexicogrammatical expression of individual sentences. It generated short transcripts describing games of noughts and crosses (tic-tac-toe) played on the system. The quality of the output was due partly to the sophistication of Proteus' grammatical component, a systemic grammar.[8] The following game transcript was produced by Proteus:

The game started with my taking a corner, and you took an adjacent one. I threatened you by taking the middle of the edge opposite that and adjacent to the one which I had just taken but you blocked it and threatened me. I blocked your diagonal and forked you. If you had blocked mine, you would have forked me, but you took the middle of the edge opposite the corner which I took first and the one which you had just taken and so I won by completing my diagonal.

The text illustrates some of the strengths of Proteus:

- It can group coherent moves into combinations of clauses, or 'clause complexes'.
- It can discover and signal contrasts (*but*).
- It can handle fairly complex referring tasks.

An attempt at a diagram of generation in Proteus is given in Figure 3.1. Davey (1978: 110) offers the following summary of how Proteus generates text:

The input of the program is a list of moves in a game of noughts and crosses. The moves are taken to have occurred in the order given and must be legal in that order.

The list of moves serves the role of the knowledge selected from the knowledge base that we saw in Chapter 2. Proteus then *selects* the information to be expressed from this list:

Given this list of moves, the program decides what moves are to be described in the first sentence and then describes them, making each move on a board in its memory as it describes it.

It then returns to the list of moves, to design and construct the next sentence, repeating the cycle until it has described the last move.

Moves are grouped into a sentence (clause complex) to reflect 'tactical coherence' in a game — coherence according to the organization of the field of games of noughts and crosses. Proteus was able to generate extended text

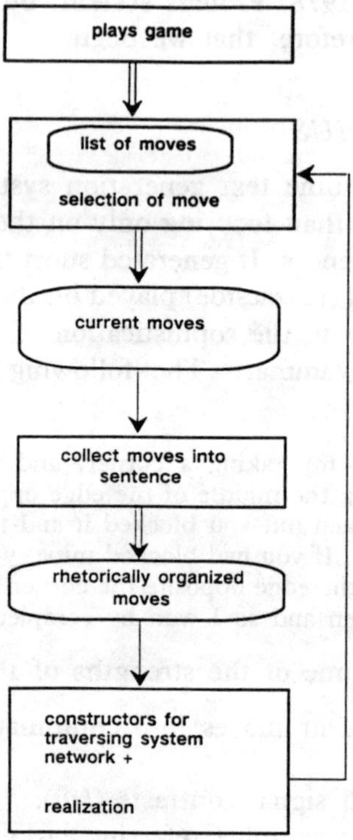


**Figure 3.1** Generation in PROTEUS

but did not use a general theory of text organization: the organization of the *game* guides the organization of the text; rhetorically, it is dependent on and specific to the field of playing noughts and crosses.

In this approach, then, text organization is ensured only by the organization of the ordered set of semantic propositions to be expressed. A number of other systems, while appearing rather different in terms of the texts they produce, also rely on this 'field-oriented' mode of text generation. For example, the first story generator, Meehan's (1977) TALE-SPIN, constructed in the mid-1970s, focused on generating an appropriate story *plot*. These plots, as an organized collection of propositions to be expressed, again provided the principal mode of text organization development.

The need to create a plot is of particular importance in story generation, and this has probably contributed to work on story generation remaining fairly distinct from work on other kinds of text.[9] Stories constitute a family of registers that is fairly different from those normally attempted in text generation, all of which are non-fictional. However, this difference in register should not serve to isolate this kind of text generation from others. Here is an example of a TALE-SPIN story:

Once upon a time George ant lived near a patch of ground. There was a nest in an ash tree. Wilma bird lived in the nest. There was some water in a river. Wilma knew that the water was in the river. George knew that the water was in the river. One day Wilma was very thirsty. Wilma wanted to get near some water. Wilma flew from her nest across a meadow through a valley to the river. Wilma drank the water. Wilma wasn't thirsty any more.

It is, of course, easy to see how this text could be improved by giving TALE-SPIN better resources for creating clause complexes, ellipsis, reference, and so on, but this would involve more sophisticated grammatical and textual resources. The ability to relate the general notion of text to particular kinds of texts such as stories, reports, transcripts, and definitions that the theory of register offers would provide for the usability of such resources from other text generation systems where they have been more at the focus of development.

A further example of where the availability of general resources for text generation would have been useful is Clippinger's (1978) ERMA, from the mid-1970s, which attempted to simulate a patient in a psychoanalytic situation, drawing on the analysis of natural transcripts. Although Clippinger was influenced by Winograd's work and originally intending to make direct use of Halliday's systemic-functional grammar, the lack of a readily controllable systemic-functional grammar at that time effectively prevented this. However, as we shall describe below, the computational development of semantic interfaces for systemic-functional grammars has developed considerably in recent years, making this kind of application very much a possibility. With the addition of an explicit orientation to register variation (see Chapter 12), this will become an increasingly attractive option.

We have seen in this section a text generation system which places a strong emphasis on the grammatical component and some which have suffered from lacking one; there have also been systems which have concentrated on the lexical resources of the linguistic system, for example, Goldman's (1974, 1975) BABEL system to which we now turn.

### *3.3.2 Goldman's BABEL*

The innovation in BABEL was the use of hierarchical discrimination networks for lexical selection. For example, processes of ingesting food, air, smoke, etc. are discriminated step by step in a taxonomy: first 'take' is distinguished as ingesting for the purpose of becoming healthier, next the ingesting of fluids or objects is distinguished from the ingesting of gas; 'smoke' is distinguished from 'inhale' and 'breathe', and so on; the

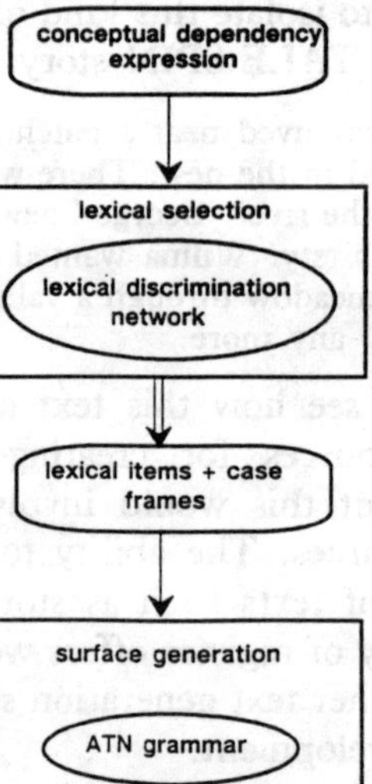


**Figure 3.2** Generation in BABEL

discriminations continue until individual senses such as 'inhale' and 'take' have been reached.

The input to the generation process is a conceptual dependency expression (e.g., Schank, Goldman, Rieger and Riesbeck, 1973). The first step is to select appropriate lexical items by means of the lexical discrimination networks. Next, these are linearized and specified morphologically in the traversal of a transition network grammar as shown in Figure 3.2.

We can see from the generation process in BABEL as shown in the figure that an explicit ordering of lexical selections with respect to grammatical selections has been imposed. The relative orderings of these two subprocesses was deliberately left unspecified in our sketch of a representative text generation system in Chapter 2. According to systemic-functional theory, lexis and grammar are not differentiated 'stratally' — i.e., in terms of the levels of the linguistic system — and so it is to be expected that there will be strong interactions between lexical and grammatical selections.[10] In order to handle the constraints that lexical selection appears to have on grammatical structure, Goldman adopts the approach of doing lexical selection before the grammar is traversed.[11] In this respect, Goldman's model is more like Dik's (1978, 1987) Functional Grammar and current 'lexicalized' grammars (Abeille *et al.*, 1989; Bresnan, 1982; Pollard and Sag, 1987) than like systemic lexicogrammar. Such approaches start with the selection of predicate frames from the lexicon and these then pass through the syntactic and pragmatic components of the model.

There are other possible organizations, however; for example, lexis and grammar can be integrated in one unified specification, as has been suggested for systemic lexicogrammar (Halliday, 1961; Hasan, 1987; Matthiessen, 1990a), or, procedurally, grammar might be explored before lexical selections are made (as is the case in the original Penman architecture that we describe in Chapter 6). Again, we can relate the choice of system design to the types of language for which systems are intended — i.e., to their target registers. The more constrained the lexical selections are for a given register (cf. the fixed idioms of the stock market reports we referred to earlier or use of a Phrasal lexicon such as in Jacob's (1985) PHRED system), the more lexical selection will need to be able to drive the grammar.

This does not argue, however, that lexis needs to be seen as a distinct component of a text generation system. On the contrary, Goldman's work serves as an illustration of an approach to lexis in generation that has some of the properties of systemic lexis: both are based on the thesaurus model of lexis rather than the dictionary model. Further, it is very easy to re-represent the distinctions made in Goldman's lexical discrimination nets by means of a system network, since discrimination networks are a special case of system networks (cf. Matthiessen, 1990a).

A more appropriate view, then, of the *resources* of lexis is one in which they present finer classifications of broad grammatical categories. Naturally the use of these resources is sensitive to the particular contexts of that use but, as we shall see in Part IV, this applies equally to grammatical alternations and does not constitute a distinguishing feature of lexis. Placing lexis before grammar procedurally is not a solution to constraining the grammar that generalizes well *across* registers: in the worst case it can result in the reduplication of major discrimination processes both within the grammar and within the lexical selection component.

### *3.3.3 McKeown's TEXT*

All of the systems we have mentioned so far, and PROTEUS and BABEL in particular, generate without explicit treatments of text structure. To the extent that any multisentential text appears, this is a direct reflection of the underlying 'knowledge' or 'semantic content' to be expressed. Most registers, however, require more sophisticated organization; indeed, the selection of domain knowledge is not even sufficient uniquely to determine a particular register and so, in order to generalize, text generation systems need further possibilities for organizing the texts they produce.

One important move towards this was made in the early 1980s by McKeown (1982, 1985), at a time when several of the current lines of research into text generation were started, including work on the Penman system. McKeown gave her system, which was called TEXT, a rhetorical component, which had the resources to support text organization that was not a direct translation of the organization of the information in the knowledge source.

Here is an example of a definition generated by TEXT (ONR = Office of Naval Research; DB = data base):

[1] A guided projectile is a projectile that is self-propelled. [2] There are 2 types of guided projectiles in the ONR database: torpedoes and missiles. [3] The missile has a target location in the air or on the earth's surface. [4] The torpedo has an underwater target location. [5] The missile's target location is indicated by the DB attribute DESCRIPTION and the missile's flight capabilities are provided by the DB attribute ALTITUDE. [6] The torpedo's underwater capabilities are provided by the DB attributes under DEPTH (for example, MAXIMUM OPERATING DEPTH). [7] The guided projectile has DB attributes TIME TO TARGET & UNITS, HORZ RANGE & UNITS and NAME.

Importantly, the knowledge source of the system was a navy data base which had not been built to support text generation. The method of translating directly from the knowledge source would not have produced very good text and certainly not the text above. Considerably *more* information needs to be appealed to in order to create texts such as this. In particular, RHETORICAL STRATEGIES that serve to organize information appropriately for its expression are crucial.

McKeown approached this problem by examining a range of texts where a clear discourse purpose was evident in order to discover the kinds of text organizations that were employed. Three data base query types were built into the system as available discourse purposes: requests to define a concept, requests to compare two objects, and requests to describe available information. McKeown found that certain recurrent text patterns were sufficient to describe the achievement of these purposes. These patterns she formalized as the following set of rhetorical strategies: *constituency*, *identification*, *attributive*, and *compare and contrast*. Each of these strategies was defined in terms of a transition network including statements of the kinds of knowledge which were necessary in order to fill in the components of a selected schema. This makes it possible to choose between a variety of strategies for a single discourse purpose; for example, the constituency schema could be used for both the *define* and *describe* discourse purposes but particular states of knowledge of the system might support selection of one rather than the other.

The schema responsible for the example text above is the *constituency*

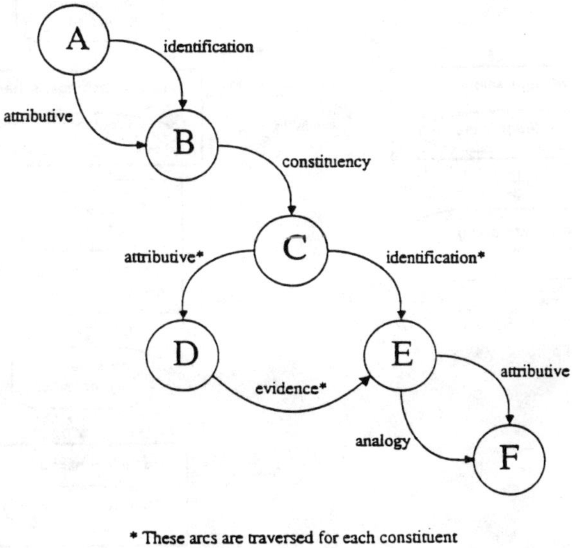


**Figure 3.3** TEXT's constituency schema

schema. It is shown in transition network form in Figure 3.3. The schema may be considered in terms of four basic steps:

(i) identify the item to be described or defined as a member of some generic class or present attributive information about it;
(ii) present the constituents of the item;
(iii) present characteristic information about each constituent;
(iv) present attributive or analogy information about the item.

In slightly more detail, and following Figure 3.3, the numbered sentences of the example text can be placed in correspondence with the components of the schema thus:

1. identification of guided projectile
2. constituency of guided projectile
3. identification of first component of projectile: missile
4. identification of second component of projectile: torpedo
5. attribute concerning missile
6. attribute concerning torpedo
7. attributive information concerning guided projectile

Figure 3.4 diagrams the overall organization of TEXT. It is based on McKeown (1982: 16) and has been adapted to maintain comparability with

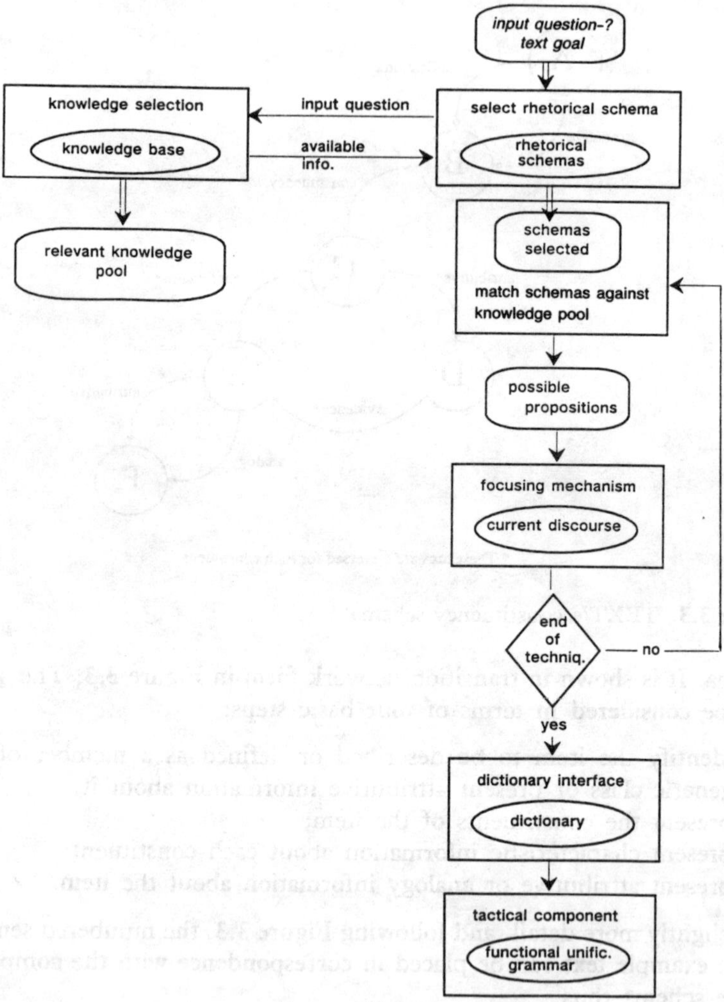


**Figure 3.4** Generation in TEXT

the design sketch in Figure 2.3. McKeown (1982: 14–15) summarizes her procedure for generating text as follows. Assume that we have asked the system a question such as 'What is guided?' In response to the input question, semantic processes in the system produce a relevant *knowledge pool*. For example, if the task is to define an object, such as a guided projectile, this search for knowledge identifies 'the area around the questioned object containing the information immediately associated with the entity (e.g., its superordinates, subtypes, and attributes)'. Next, *rhetorical selection* takes place:

A characterization of the information in this [knowledge, JB & CM] pool is then used to select a single partially ordered set of rhetorical techniques from the various possibilities.

A formal representation of the answer (called a 'message') is constructed from the relevant knowledge pool which matches the rhetorical techniques in the given set.

To guide the selection of what to say next, the system uses a focusing mechanism. This is really a mechanism for selecting the next *discourse topic* (rather than focus) by consulting a model of the current discourse:

The focusing mechanism monitors the matching process; where there are choices for what to say next . . ., the focusing mechanism selects that proposition which ties in most closely with the previous discourse.

This mechanism, which is based on Sidner (1978, 1981), is also used to influence decisions within the grammatical component.

The ordered messages that come out of the generation process as described so far (knowledge selection, rhetorical schema selection, and topic selection — what McKeown calls the strategic component of the generator) are lexicalized in the dictionary interface before they reach the grammatical component:

The dictionary stands as interface between the strategic and tactical components. Input to the dictionary is in message formalism; the dictionary takes a single proposition as input which consists of a predicate and its instantiated arguments . . . Dictionary output is the deep structural representation for the English sentence to be generated, specified in Kay's (1979) functional notation. (op.cit., p. 192)

McKeown calls the output of the dictionary interface a deep structural representation. Alternatively, we can interpret it in terms of systemic theory as ideational lexis (i.e., denotative lexis as opposed to interpersonal and textual lexis), including transitivity configurations ('case frames'). The tactical component contains other aspects of lexicogrammar and these are unified with the output of the dictionary interface:

Once the message has been constructed, the system passes the message to a tactical component[12] which uses a functional grammar (Kay, 1979) to translate the message into English. (p.15) A sentence is produced in Kay's formalism by unifying the input, which is specified in the same formalism as the grammar, with the grammar. The input to the unifier is a deep structure representation of what is to be generated. The output is a surface syntactic representation of the sentence which is linearized using the patterns it contains. (op.cit., p. 219)

McKeown's sentence generator is also of interest as its grammar is of the kind developed by Martin Kay (1979), a Functional Unification Grammar (FUG), whose representational resources, as already mentioned, resemble systemic-functional grammar in many respects (cf. Winograd, 1983: Ch. 6). McKeown selected the framework because of its functional nature: 'It was selected because of the ability to directly encode in the grammar tests on focus and theme for determining which construction to use, information which the strategic component supplies for this purpose' (McKeown, 1982: 210). In this respect, grammars expressed in the FUG-formalism can closely resemble systemic-functional grammars. The grammar of TEXT is also a *general* grammatical component; we will return to the significance of this in Section 3.3.5 below.

Finally, note that, as in the BABEL generator, lexical selection takes place before the 'tactical component' is entered. In contrast with BABEL, both the dictionary interface and the syntax operate with the same formalism — functional unification grammar — which is an important simplification.

McKeown's work on rhetorical organization is highly relevant to the present discussion for two reasons. First, it contrasts in interesting ways with Rhetorical Structure Theory, a theory of text organization developed within the Penman project that we will describe below. Second, it is similar in some important respects to Hasan's (1978) Generic Structure Potential in systemic theory: see Matthiessen (1988c ms).

We have seen how TEXT can support a number of different text types, depending upon the particular purpose for which a text is being generated; i.e., to define, to compare, and to describe. Further rhetorical strategies for further text types have also been studied, for example in Kukich's (1985) stock market report generator ANA. Discourse purposes constitute another of the dimensions along which registers vary. Thus, in these cases we see the beginnings of text generation sensitive to register even within a single text generation architecture — at least at the level of text organization.

Further development centring around the TEXT architecture has also led to a consideration of another dimension of register variation. In work on the TAILOR system (Paris, 1984, 1987, 1988), it was noted that in addition to discourse purpose influencing text structure, rhetorical organization also varied according to the level of a system user's *expertise* in the domain of discourse. The texts generated by McKeown's TEXT system are concerned with object-oriented fields — the properties, parts and types of vessels and other objects in the navy world. Paris discovered that for domain novices, *process-oriented* texts were more appropriate. She thus permitted sensitivity to levels of user expertise to select between combinations of McKeown's *constituency* schema and a new *process* rhetorical schema that sought to express more of the causal relations that could be found in the underlying knowledge base. In addition, McCoy's (1986) ROMPER system similarly defined new rhetorical schemata for a rather different kind of responsiveness to a user — correcting a user's misconceptions concerning objects and their descriptions.[13]

The need to generate text sensitive to a user, hearer, or reader is not, of course, restricted to issues of text organization. Referring expressions (e.g., Appelt, 1985; Dale, 1989), lexical selections, and grammatical constructions all need to be constructed relative to states of user knowledge and interpersonal relationships. The first, and most significant, text generation system to permit these 'interpersonal' aspects of language use to permeate and influence the generation process fully across all these levels of the linguistic system was Hovy's (1987a, 1987b, 1988) PAULINE.

### *3.3.4 Hovy's PAULINE*

Hovy's text generator PAULINE was the first to include explicit representation of a speaker's stylistic, rhetorical, and affective goals and to allow for significant variation in the texts produced in response to variations in these goals. A representative of the variation that PAULINE is capable of producing is the following pair of texts, which both describe a hypothetical American primary election between Carter and Kennedy (Hovy, 1989b: 41–2):

> Carter and Kennedy were the candidates in a primary in Michigan on 20 February. Carter lost to Kennedy by 1335 votes. At present, Kennedy has a better chance of getting the nomination than before. Carter is also closer to getting the nomination than before. Both Carter and Kennedy want to get the nomination.

> Kennedy diminished Carter's lead by getting all of 21850 votes in the primary in Michigan. In a similar case, Carter decreased Udall's lead in a primary in 1976, and he easily trounced Udall to be nominated by 2600 delegates. I am real glad that Kennedy is now closer to getting the nomination than before.

The research question that motivated Hovy's construction of PAULINE was: 'why and how is it that we say the same thing differently to different people, or even to the same person, in different circumstances?' Both the example texts here were generated with respect to the same knowledge base; yet they are very different in grammatical form, lexical selections, and textual organization.

Whereas the differences in McKeown's TEXT system were restricted to textual organizations governed by the generated text's discourse purpose, the differences in PAULINE's texts are motivated by a set of 12 RHETORICAL GOALS which are appealed to at various stages during the generation process. Importantly, they can apply just as well to lexical selection (e.g., in the selection of *trounce* rather than *beat*) and grammatical organization as to textual organization and topic selection (e.g., in the second text an additional fact is mentioned to support the statement that Kennedy is significantly closer to gaining the nomination). Furthermore, the rhetorical goals are predominantly concerned with the interactive situation and interpersonal relationships presumed to hold between speaker and hearer. Thus, for example, there are rhetorical goals of FORMALITY, TIMIDITY, PARTIALITY, FLORIDITY, RESPECT, HASTE, etc. The first text above was generated with rhetorical goals and values formality: colloquial, partiality: impartial, detail: details, haste: somewhat planned; the latter with values formality: colloquial, partiality: implicit, details: all (details and interpretations), haste: planned.

The recognition of rhetorical goals of these kinds serves to introduce into the model a new rhetorical *level* which supports new possibilities for stratal kinds of reasoning that are quite important in the context of text generation. PAULINE's rhetorical goals influence the text generation process in two ways, which Hovy has described in terms of *prescriptive* and *restrictive* planning. The former corresponds with top–down planning, i.e., the kind of planning within AI that works by successive decomposition of a complex goal into ever more simple goals until these can be achieved by means known to the system (cf. Sacerdoti, 1977), and concerns goals that once achieved can be forgotten. Tasks which are prescriptive 'act over and give shape to long ranges of text'. The latter type of planning offers a means of selecting between alternatives that were left open by the prescriptive planning. Restrictive planning is intended to handle goals that are difficult to conceive of as being achieved once and for all; for example, the goal of being polite needs to be continually oriented to during generation of a text — there does not come a point, before the end of the text, where the goal can be said to have been achieved and be flushed. We can make a theoretical generalization about these kinds of goals: they are concerned with the tenor component of context (cf. Section 3.2 above) — maintaining interpersonal relationships; and the linguistic resources tend to express them prosodically rather than segmentally.

PAULINE fleshes out considerably the control of linguistic variation according to speaker–hearer relationships. As the first generator to be specially designed for producing differing texts for the same underlying knowledge base content, it goes a long way towards multi-register generation. Clearly, with all the rhetorical goals and the possible values with which they may be assigned, PAULINE can generate an immense number of differing texts. Rather more problematic with the approach, however, is the lack of organization among the rhetorical goals and the theoretically unconstrained interaction between them and the grammar and lexicon.

PAULINE makes use of a phrasal grammar/lexicon consisting of a collection of generation experts that know which rhetorical goals to query in order to select between possible alternatives. It is difficult to see how generalizations can be drawn and the control of its grammar transported to other generation systems.

Nevertheless, PAULINE remains an impressive demonstration in the computational context of the need to allow speaker–hearer relationships to affect text generation in a way that is considerably broader than attention to expertise.

### *3.3.5 General grammar components*

A criticism that we have just made of PAULINE is that its grammar, although extensive in capabilities, is not an easily isolatable component of the system. Indeed, a number of text generation systems have previously constructed grammar components almost from scratch. It would clearly be beneficial if there existed a general grammatical resource which met the needs of many generation tasks. We can now define this task, the task of achieving a reusable grammar component, in register terms — and in doing so answer the question as to why, in the past, so many experimental systems have felt the need to attempt to write their own grammars.

A reusable grammar component needs to be just the opposite of most earlier text generation systems — it needs to be register *non-specific*. As soon as register-specific details are built into the design of a grammar component, it becomes unsuitable for those text generation contexts that seek to generate text for a different register.

Fortunately, the task of creating a register non-specific grammar is exactly the task that a linguist attempting to construct a grammar for a language usually takes on. Grammar descriptions are *general* accounts of grammatical resources; they need to describe the abstract linguistic potential of the grammatical stratum of a language prior to its differential use in context. It is therefore natural to expect that linguistic grammar description and the task of creating a reusable grammar component for text generation systems should be closely related and mutually supporting. Somewhat less fortunately, until recently this has been very much the exception rather than the rule.

Perhaps the first attempt to create a truly general, reusable and broad coverage grammar component was McDonald's (1980) MUMBLE. As already suggested, McDonald was influenced by his teacher, Terry Winograd, and the early MUMBLE grammar could be said to belong to what we might call the systemic-functional 'family' of grammars. However, after a number of applications of the MUMBLE grammar, a new version was created (MUMBLE-86: see Meteer *et al.*, 1987) which is based on Tree Adjoining Grammar (e.g., Joshi, 1987) and which, in the terms we will introduce in Part II, includes only realization rules. Thus, the present system presupposes that all aspects of choice are handled outside of the grammatical component — i.e., it does not include the systemic part of a systemic-functional grammar. Furthermore, the linguistic content of MUMBLE in any of its instantiations remains eclectic and does not make contact with an established body of linguistic research.

While this has permitted certain questions concerning grammar formalisms and their use to be addressed most profitably, for generation the problem of *choice* between the alternatives that a language provides always remains. Theories and mechanisms which make the choice problem approachable are crucial.

The Nigel grammar of the Penman system was another attempt launched at the beginning of the 1980s to construct a reusable grammar component for text generation. In this case, however, there was an early commitment to working with an established linguistic theory and tradition in which there already existed a sizeable body of descriptive work. This continues to contribute not only to the development of the grammar itself, but also to the development of the theory of how the grammar is to be controlled — i.e., how it is to be made responsive to its situated use in context for the generation of language in any register which may be required. We feel that these design criteria should be foregrounded in any approach that seeks to construct a grammar component for text generation. A number of current text generation systems, including SPOKESMAN (Meteer, 1989) which uses MUMBLE-86, are approaching this problem in terms of higher levels of semantic abstraction. It is particularly important, therefore, to have theoretical guidance when we move so far from readily observable surface details. Aspects of the particular guidance that systemic-functional linguistics can provide form much of the content of the rest of this book.

## 3.4 Survey of the survey

Our 'historical' interpretative overview of the development of text generation has been selective and we have left out a number of systems that should be included in a general survey.[14] Our main purpose has been to show the kinds of information that a text generation system must exercise control of if it is to be able to create a technically sophisticated and theoretically interesting range of texts. We have approached this in terms of the systemic-functional conception of register — the idea that language is deployed differentially according to its context of use. Contexts can further be decomposed into a number of types of information and, as will be explained in more detail in Part II, we have focused here on three principal types:

- the propositional content to be expressed;
- the discourse purpose of expressing that information;
- the interpersonal relationships between speakers and hearers, between speakers and their knowledge, and the properties of the interactive language situation itself.

From this basis, we have been able to show what certain text generation systems have when compared with others, and what kinds of language use fall within their capabilities. Clearly, when information sources of any of these three kinds are missing, or when a system lacks the grammatical sophistication to make use of that information, then the functionality of the system is compromised. For the particular generation of texts in particular registers this can be justified. For general text generation capabilities, however, it cannot.

Just as there are generation systems that we have not mentioned, or described in the depth they deserve, here, there are also dimensions of register variation that support those systems that we have not described. For example, one of the rhetorical goals defined by Hovy in PAULINE was 'haste', and this naturally points to a rather important potential property of the language situation: i.e., it may occur in real-time. This brings its own set of constraints and necessities to bear; some of the work on MUMBLE has focused on this issue, and the generation system of de Smedt and Kempen (1987) pays considerable attention to it.

Another variability is in the mode of the linguistic interaction, e.g., whether it is written or spoken. The systems we have discussed have been predominantly concerned with written texts, although there is work on speech generation also (e.g., Sigurd, 1984; Fawcett, 1990). Another kind of mode variability is the very choice of language that is made; again most of the systems described here have been based on English text generation, although there is substantial text generation work in other languages, most notably perhaps, German (e.g., Rösner, 1988; Emele, 1986). All of these dimensions of variation should be included in a complete account of the language and its contexts of use.

Another important line of research has been that of Patten (1986, 1988a). Patten was the first in generation to attempt to implement the process of being sensitive to register itself. Patten (1988a) makes an important contribution in showing how another aspect of systemic theory, socio-semantic systems, can play a fundamental role in text generation. Essentially, this means identifying semantic systems that are adapted to specific contexts of use and using these to 'drive' the selections in the grammar (cf. Halliday, 1973). We will return to this topic in some more detail in Chapter 12.

We have now seen that systemic functional grammar has been used successfully in text generation — as in Davey's Proteus and the two projects discussed in this book. We have also seen examples of independent developments within computational linguistics that parallel systemic ideas outside of grammar in interesting ways — Goldman's approach to lexis and McKeown's rhetorical schemas in particular. Finally, we can note that in addition to the work that we have mentioned so far or with which we will be centrally concerned below, computationally oriented explorations of systemic-functional grammar are now again closing the circle of development that we mentioned at the outset of this chapter. Although work on machine translation and analysis preceded work on text generation, with the increased understanding of the linguistic resources that that work on text generation has enabled, research in these areas is being taken up again — for example, by Steiner *et al.* (1988), Steiner and Reuther (1989), Bateman (1989b, 1990b), Bateman, Kasper, Schütz, and Steiner (1989), and Hovy (1989a) in machine translation, and Kasper (1988, 1989b) in analysis. Interestingly, both of these areas of application need to be developed across a wide variety of registers and so call for, where appropriate, register non-specific specifications of linguistic resources — e.g., for grammar. Thus, once again, the need for future natural language research, text generation included, to move beyond the register limits that we have seen at work in the majority of earlier systems is highlighted.

## 3.5 Supplemental: text generators

### The 1970s

| System | Text type | Main features: grammar | discourse | user | other |
|---|---|---|---|---|---|
| Simmons and Slocum (1972) | | ATN 'grammar' for parsing semantic nets and building syntactic structures | — | — | |
| Goldman's (1974) BABEL | | ATN grammar | — | — | lexical choice by means of discrimination networks |
| Chester (1976) | logical proofs | | | | |
| Meehan's (1977) TALESPIN | stories | | according to plot generator | — | (no textual control) |
| Davey's (1978) PROTEUS | game transcripts | SFG | field-based; contrast | — | — |
| Clippinger's (1978) ERMA | | | | | 'psychological modelling' |
| Mann and Moore's (1980) KDS | fire alarm instructions | (very simple) | 'fragment and compose' | list of facts known by user as filter | |

**The 1980s**

| System | Text type | Main features: grammar | discourse | user | other |
|---|---|---|---|---|---|
| McDonald's (1980) MUMBLE sentence generator; through 80s (Meteer *et al.*, 1987) | logical proofs, scene descriptions (as part of GENARO), etc. | SFG-like grammar, later TAG | — | — | various knowledge representations |
| PENMAN (throughout 80s) | reports (navy, electronic mail and calendar), advice, terminology definitions | SFG (Nigel) | RST | user modelling planned | chooser and inquiry semantics; metafunctional breadth; upper model |
| McKeown's (1982) TEXT | navy data base reports | FUG | rhetorical schemas | — | selection among schemas guided by focus mechanism |
| Kukich's (1983) ANA | stock market reports | — | rhetorical schemas | — | phrasal dictionary |
| McKeown *et al.*'s (1985) ADVISOR | advice | FUG | rhetorical schemas | user's domain goals used to tailor advice | |
| Appelt's (1985) KAMP | utterances giving advice in equipment assembly | FUG | — | user beliefs taken into account | based on hierarchic planning |

| | | | | | |
|---|---|---|---|---|---|
| Jacobs's (1985) PHRED | utterances as help to UNIX users | pattern-concept pairs | — | — | treatment of some metaphors |
| Emele's (1986) FREGE | task-independent | FUG | — | — | object-oriented implementation |
| Rösner's (1986) SEMSYN | task-independent | FUG | — | — | German generator |
| Kehl's (1986) GOETEX | geometric constructs | SEMSYN | — | — | object-oriented implementation |
| McCoy's (1986) ROMPER | responses to user misconceptions | FUG | schemas for discourse strategies in responses (no optionality or repetitions) | classification of misconceptions | perspective separated from object represented in knowledge base |
| Paris's (1987) TAILOR | 'encyclopedia entries' | FUG | rhetorical schemas | selection of information according to user's expertise | |
| Rösner's (1987) SEMTEX | news stories | SEMSYN | — | — | — |
| de Smedt and Kempen (1987) | | incremental | — | — | psychological model |
| Danlos (1987) | | | | | |
| Hovy's (1987c) PAULINE | 'reports' (news) | phrasal grammar | | different user settings | other contextual factors; rhetorical level |

| System | Text type | Main features grammar | discourse | user | other |
|---|---|---|---|---|---|
| Patten's (1988a) SLANG | regulatory utterances | SFG | — | — | situation specific semantics systems; problem-solving approach |
| Iordanskaja, Kittredge and Polguère's (1988) GOSSIP | weather reports | Meaning-text-model | — | — | — |
| Dale's (1989) EPICURE | recipes | | | | |
| Fawcett and Tucker's (1990) COMMUNAL | | SFG | systemic interaction model | user modelling planned | cognitive model |

## Notes

1. Although it needs to be noted that, in many respects, it is better to conceive of Functional Unification Grammar purely as a *formalism* rather than as a particular brand of grammar as such. FUG provides a formalism, mechanisms, and notations for representing grammars but does not itself intend to commit to a particular brand of linguistic theorizing. That is, FUG does not provide an ontology of 'scales and categories'; for instance no distinction is made between features and functions as they are used within systemic linguistics (see Chapter 6). There is only the very general distinction between attribute and value.
2. Within computational linguistics itself, Woods was developing transition network grammars (Woods, 1970).
3. In the 1970s, there was an opposition between a procedural approach to the representation of meaning and information in general and a declarativist one. The current preference is to separate procedures from declarations, as was done in the overview in Figure 2.1 by distinguishing processes (procedures) from declarative information (resources). One reason is that this makes it possible to rely on the same resource in generation procedures as well as in parsing procedures. In this connection, it is important to remember that the *system networks* that constitute a systemic grammar (Chapter 5), can be read both as declarations (classifications) and as procedures, although *logical recursive systems* (Chapters 8 and 11) constitute a special 'dynamic' type.
4. See, for example: Brew (1990), Cummings (1987), Fawcett and Tucker (1990), Kasper (1987a, 1989b), McCord (1975, 1977), Mellish (1988), Patten and Ritchie (1987), Steiner (1990), and Teich (1989, 1990).
5. As can be seen from the growth of the American and European international workshops on text generation: Appelt (1984), Kempen (1987), Paris, Swartout and Mann (1990), Zock and Sabah (1988), Dale, Mellish and Zock (1990) and the 1988 AAAI workshop on text realization and planning (Hovy *et al.*, 1988).
6. Related concepts include the traditional notion of genre, the Prague School 'functional dialect', and sublanguage in computational linguistics.
7. To some readers, our inclusion of the information to express as part of 'context' may still appear unfamiliar. It rests upon the systemic notion of *metafunctional diversification* that we introduce in Part II. As the discussion in this chapter develops, we will introduce implicitly each of the three metafunctionally motivated components of context posited within systemic theory and use them in our characterizations of generation systems. The reader is therefore encouraged to review this chapter when more familiar with Part II, although we have attempted to make the present chapter as self-contained as possible.
8. The particular version of systemic grammar that Davey drew most heavily on was the one Hudson had developed by the early 1970s (see Hudson, 1971).
9. Although the association of story generation with a distinct school in artificial intelligence/natural language processing — Schank's Yale School — should probably also not be ruled out as a contributing factor to this separation.
10. This is corroborated by current computational work; for example, Danlos (1984) goes to the extreme of suggesting that the interactions are so complex as to be unpredictable and virtually arbitrary.
11. I.e., in metafunctional terms, ideational lexis, including transitivity seen from lexis, is distinct from and precedes grammar.

12. Unwritten-up work by Stephen Bossie.
13. Rather earlier, in the late 1970s, Mann and Moore (1980) built at the Information Sciences Institute a text generator known as KDS, which stands for knowledge delivery system. One of the strengths of the KDS system was that it included a reader/user model (cf. Figure 2.1) that enabled the system to filter out information that could be assumed to be previously known to the reader. However, this served more as a filter on the process of expressing knowledge than as a positive contribution to text organization itself.
14. For rather more general surveys of work on text generation and explanation, see Mann *et al.* (1981), Kempen (1986), McKeown and Swartout (1987), Paris (1991), Bateman and Hovy (1991).

# 4 The exchange between linguistics and text generation

In the previous chapter we saw that text generation has drawn on AI and computational linguistics rather more than it has on linguistics. However, we think linguistics has more to offer than has been made use of to date. At the same time linguistics can benefit from work on text generation. A process of genuine *exchange* between the two disciplines, with important benefits for both, is now, we believe, an important direction to follow. To expand this exchange between linguistics and text generation, we need to identify more clearly what linguistics has already contributed and what are further possible exchanges. The nature and potential of the exchange guide the remainder of the discussion in this book.

## 4.1 Where have products come from?

We can think of a design such as the one diagrammed in Figure 2.1 as a shopping list for the researcher in text generation. The distinction between resources and processes is significant since it has tended to determine what is taken from linguistics and what is taken from artificial intelligence and computer science: linguistics has provided text generation with models of resources rather than accounts of processes; process models have been taken primarily from computational linguistics and artificial intelligence. There is also a tendency to rely more on linguistics in the area of the grammatical 'core' of the linguistic system.

Examples include the following:

Davey's (1978) Proteus generator, Patten's (1988a) SLANG, the Kyoto generator and the Penman generator include grammars taken from systemic linguistics, but the generation algorithms were not taken from systemic linguistics. The grammars are implemented in different ways; Patten's

grammar is represented as a production system but the others are not.
There is a family of grammatical frameworks developed largely in linguistics — feature and function grammars (cf. Winograd, 1983: Ch. 6), including systemic-functional grammar, generalized phrase structure grammar (GPSG: Gazdar *et al.*, 1985), and lexical functional grammar (LFG: Bresnan, 1982); but the processes for using them in parsing and generation come from computational linguistics — including the basic computational notion of unification (cf. Shieber, 1986).
In her development of rhetorical schemas, McKeown (1982) used Grimes's (1975) work on rhetorical predicates, but in her implementation of a process for using them she used transition nets from computational linguistics.
The representation of resources in Rhetorical Structure Theory (e.g., Mann and Thompson, 1987) is related to various proposals in linguistics; but the processes of using them in generation come from the AI planning paradigm (Hovy, 1988b).
The representation of knowledge in generation systems (e.g., NIKL: Moser, 1983; LOOM: MacGregor and Bates, 1987; MacGregor and Brill, 1989; frames: Minsky, 1975; Hayes, 1977; semantic networks: Woods, 1975; Findler, 1979), although drawn largely from artificial intelligence and computational linguistics, received significant early input from work on semantic representation in linguistics (Samlowski, 1976) — particularly work concerned with developing notions of 'deep case' such as Fillmore's case grammar (Fillmore, 1968).

Figure 4.1 illustrates the distribution of sources of input to three levels of concern in the study of language: grammar, discourse, and meaning. There are, of course, examples of joint developments, such as Lexical Functional Grammar and Rhetorical Structure Theory, and it will probably make less and less sense to try to locate the origin of ideas in linguistics or computational linguistics as joint development becomes more prevalent.

## 4.2 How can linguistics benefit?

What can we learn from the application of linguistic work in text generation? From the picture we have sketched it is clear that there is a gap in linguistic theory building: there are few PROCESS ACCOUNTS in linguistics. Martin (1985) identifies this gap and suggests that it is necessary to operate with dynamic models as well as synoptic (static) ones:

Having argued for the importance of both a synoptic and a dynamic perspective on two very different semiotic systems, genre and bridge, the question naturally arises

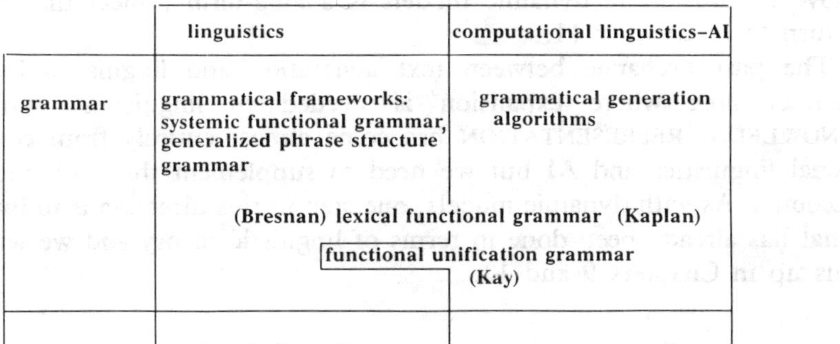


**Figure 4.1** Contributions from linguistics to areas relevant to text generation

as to whether these two perspectives are relevant to language as well. The answer that most linguists have implicitly given since Saussure is *no*; a synoptic perspective has almost exclusively dominated linguists' work on phonemes and clauses. Now that linguists have begun to turn their attention to texts, however, the answer is no longer so simple (p. 260) . . . much of the difficulty linguists have experienced in text generation probably stems from the importance of dynamic systems in this enterprise. Linguists come to discourse equipped with synoptic generative models, not dynamic ones. (p. 272)

There is, then, a clear need to explore dynamic models in linguistics. One step in this direction is to interpret the relevant work in computational linguistics and AI in terms of linguistic theory. For instance, how do the grammatical generation algorithms used in text generation systems relate to the categories of grammatical theories? what kind of theory of text organization does hierarchic planning in AI presuppose? and so on. This move towards more dynamic models is a long-term project that we will return to in Chapter 11.

The past exchange between text generation and linguistics indicates another area where expansion is needed in linguistics. Work on KNOWLEDGE REPRESENTATION has come almost entirely from computational linguistics and AI but we need to supplement this with linguistic accounts. As with dynamic models, one step in this direction is to interpret what has already been done in terms of linguistic theory and we will take this up in Chapters 9 and 12.

## 4.3 Domain of theorizing and alternative metaphors

It might be argued, of course, that 'knowledge' lies outside language and is a matter for cognitive psychology rather than linguistics. But linguistics can make a contribution by providing an alternative metaphor for knowledge, i.e., an alternative way of looking at knowledge: knowledge is meaning; or rather, the information looked at as knowledge can also be looked at as meaning. Therefore, language can give us insights into how it is organized. In effect, this often happens in any case but the linguistic organization is stated in cognitive terms; for instance, lexical semantics is discussed in terms of conceptual organization.[1]

Related to the separation of knowledge from language is another knowledge-language kind of duality — the separation of thinking from semantic processing. For example, Levy (1979) contrasts what he calls a text-based approach to communication[2] with the mind-based approach he explores. He focuses on speaking as mental activity (pp. 184–5):

> Cohesion, I will argue, is most certainly REALIZED THROUGH the speaker's language resources, but its ultimate reference point must be found in the structure of the linguistic content and in the flow of the speaker's thought processes . . . The central thesis of this chapter is that the study of discourse must come to terms with the mental activity of the speaker, that it must make reference to the processes in which he is engaged while speaking. I will attempt to show that the speaker encodes important components of his thought processes in his utterance (the very thought processes that lead to the production of that utterance) . . . I will argue that much of the cohesive properties of discourse [footnote omitted] are best captured by reference to the speaker's mental states and that the current research on text grammars is not only mistaken (as Halliday and Hasan imply) by imputing structure where there is none but also that it is working at the wrong level of description to capture the salient generalizations.

As Levy points out, his 'mind-based' perspective comes from AI, but we also find it in linguistics. For instance, we find it in the nineteenth-century and early twentieth-century grammarians in notions such as psychological subject and psychological predicate and it has recently become more popular again in linguistics, now as 'cognitive linguistics'. But the mind-based approach to communication is much more widespread than any particular approach within a particular discipline: Whorf (1940/56) pointed out many years ago that it is the common-sense model of language and thought, what he called natural logic (p. 207) —

Natural logic says that talking is merely an incidental process concerned strictly with communication, not with formulation of ideas. Talking, or the use of language, is supposed only to 'express' what is essentially already formulated non-linguistically. Formulation is an independent process, called thought or thinking, and is supposed to be largely indifferent to the nature of particular languages.

The mind-based approach of AI is arguably an embodiment of the common-sense view of natural logic. Whorf pointed to two fallacies in natural logic, both of which arise because language is usually backgrounded to the task at hand in communication and so outside 'critical consciousness' (p. 211):

First, [natural logic] does not see that the phenomena of language are to its own speakers largely of a background character and so are outside the critical consciousness and control of the speaker who is expounding natural logic. Hence, when anyone, as a natural logician, is talking about reason, logic, and the laws of correct thinking, he is apt to be simply marching in step with purely grammatical facts that have somewhat of a background character in his own language or family of languages but are by no means universal in all languages and in no sense a common substratum of reason. Second, natural logic confuses agreement about subject matter, attained through use of language, with knowledge of the linguistic process by which agreement is attained.

Whorf suggests that agreement between two people can only be attained through the 'amazingly complex system of linguistic patterns and classifications' which they share. They reach agreement by linguistic processes or else they fail to agree.

As an alternative to the position of natural logic, Whorf emphasized the importance of linguistic processes:

the background linguistic system (in other words, the grammar) of each language is not merely a reproducing instrument for voicing ideas but rather is itself the shaper of ideas, the program and guide for the individual's mental activity, for his analysis of impressions, for his synthesis of his mental stock in trade. Formulation of ideas is not an independent process, strictly rational in the old sense, but is part of a particular grammar, and differs from slightly to greatly between different grammars.

The contrast between the two positions Whorf identified is important in the development of text generation systems since the different positions lead us to look for guidance from different sources in designing those systems. If we pay attention to the alternative Whorf suggests, it follows that linguistics has a central role to play in creating models of 'knowledge' as well as of the processes of creating text. That is, it can and should do more than supply the components for expressing the flow of thought.

Since Whorf made these observations, other aspects of the 'background' system have come into focus in linguistics, notably semantics and rhetoric and their interaction with context, and it is functional linguistics that has served to expand the territory.[3]

## 4.4 What contributions can linguistics make?

We have just suggested that it is functional linguistics that has expanded the territory of linguistic theorizing and description, but it is fair to say that computational linguistics has paid considerably more attention to formal linguistics than to functional linguistics. The area where linguistics has made the largest contribution is grammar (i.e., syntax + morphology), which is also one of the main areas of formal linguistics. Areas that lie beyond the horizon of formal linguistics have received much less attention. Consequently, we think many of these areas contain ideas that are important to the development of text generation and which functional linguists interested in making contributions might focus on; for example (cf. Chapters 5 and 12 for the interpretation of context, etc. in systemic theory):

- Context. Text is produced in *context* and linguistically motivated theories of context can complement current work. For instance, more sophisticated generation systems will have to make purposeful choices reflecting the social relationship between writer and reader or speaker and listener.
- Register. Future text generation systems will have to move from being generators of particular kinds of text such as stock market report generators or game transcript generators to being more flexible systems, systems with broader register repertoires. To accomplish this, we will need a register theory that relates the general task of text generation to specific tasks of generating specific types of text within particular registers and that enables the generation system to move between registers and within registers.
- Semantics. Semantics in text generation has almost always meant a fairly formal kind of semantics. Functional semantics can contribute towards the problem of relating communication tasks identified by a text generator and lexicogrammatical resources.

- Semantic styles. Different subcultures may operate with different semantic styles and the control of this range will become increasingly important as text generation systems are used more widely.
- Multifunctionality. There has undoubtedly been a bias towards the ideational function of language — a bias towards 'getting the content' right. Functional linguistics can make contributions from the textual and interpersonal functions.
- Grammatical metaphor. Metaphors that involve grammatical resources play an important role in expanding the resources for making new kinds of meaning. They are reflected not only in grammar (e.g., as nominalizations) but also in semantics and in the construction of particular fields of knowledge. For instance, to handle scientific discourse and knowledge in a principled way, generation systems will have to be able to operate with grammatical metaphor.
- Instantial systems. Language is a dynamic open system; it is always changing in exchange with its environment. For the purposes of text generation, the changes that are embodied in the instantial systems of a given discourse are particularly important. As a text develops, an instantial version of the general system evolves. If the text is a dialogue, the instantial system is constantly being negotiated. When research on text generation turns to longer texts, generation systems will have to be able to record the history of the text in the changing instantial system. (This is already quite obvious for reference, of course; but reference is only one of the clearest cases.)

These are very general observations and it is possible to add others — for example, a functional organization of lexis as a resource and the probabilistic nature of the linguistic system. But it is also important to add more detail and identify detailed contributions and this will be the need that we will be addressing throughout Parts III and IV.

In view of the tendency to draw on linguistics for resources but not for process models, it is natural that our discussion should focus on resources rather than on generation processes. But, at the same time, the interpretation of the processes in terms of linguistic theory is an important task to which we will pay attention. Since the resources in a text generator are all used by automatic processes, they have to be explicit, detailed, and nonambiguous to a degree that is not normally required in linguistics. This raises interesting representational issues that we will also explore in Parts III and IV.

## 4.5 Complementarity

Although some might argue that the picture presented above in Section 4.1 represents the appropriate complementarity between linguistics and computational linguistics/artificial intelligence in the area of text generation, we have suggested that it does not. On the one hand, linguistics already has more to offer than has been consumed up to now. On the other hand, there are gaps in linguistic theory and description that need to be addressed.

We do not think that the complementarity between linguistics and computational linguistics/AI lies in complementary partial coverages of the whole of text generation. Rather, we think the complementarity should lie in abstraction. We have to build complete linguistic models of text generation but these will be more abstract than their computational counterparts.

It is of crucial importance to operate at various levels of abstraction. Abstract linguistic models of text generation are essential both for interpreting our experiences in computational linguistics/AI in terms that are meaningful and useful linguistically — e.g., interpreting experience in computational linguistics/AI with knowledge representation, processes, and so on for linguistics — and for providing computational work with access to insights and accounts in linguistics — relating work in linguistics that has not yet had an impact on text generation to work in computational linguistics/AI. The construction of abstract linguistic models in text generation therefore maintains an essential broad exchange.

But we have suggested that there are important reasons internal to linguistics for exploring linguistic models of text generation; and these reasons evolve around another kind of complementarity — the complementarity of synthesis and analysis. If generation models can in fact complement the analytic mode of study used in discourse analysis and other areas, then text synthesis can indeed come to have the same value in linguistics in general as speech synthesis has had in phonetics.

## Notes

1. Note that this is what is happening in some current attempts to work at a detailed level of semantics; for example: Langacker (1987), Talmy (1987), Jackendoff (1983, 1987, 1990).
2. He attributes the approach to Halliday and Hasan, citing from their work on cohesion (Halliday and Hasan, 1976), but this is a misunderstanding (cf. Fries, 1986), since they have always emphasized text in context, a perspective which goes right back to Malinowski (e.g. 1923). It is also important to emphasize that text is the actualization of the system behind it (see e.g. Halliday, 1977) and that

systemic linguistics has never focused on one to the exclusion of the other. Further, it should be emphasized that text is a high-level semantic process.

3. We can also note here the contact this makes with the broader sweep of much later twentieth-century philosophy of language, including the later Wittgenstein and Heidegger. Both have been considered in more or less explicit relation to AI — for example, by Searle (1980), Winograd (1980), Winograd and Flores (1986), Dreyfus (1972, 1977), Agre (1988).

# Part II Systemic linguistics and text generation: the basic theoretical framework and two computational instantiations

## 5 Dimensions and categories of systemic theory

We will now identify the dimensions and categories of systemic theory that are particularly relevant in thinking about the design of a text generation system. By way of introduction, we will say a few words about the background to systemic theory and the reasons for choosing systemic theory in research on text generation. Since we are describing part of what is, in fact, a general theory of the linguistic system, this chapter is of necessity somewhat long and in places involved. Some readers might, therefore, prefer to read the chapter either following, or in close conjunction with, the more concrete examples of applications of the theory that follow in Chapters 6 and 7 and in Part III.

### 5.1 Background

If we trace the history of Western thinking about language from its beginnings in ancient Greece, it is possible to identify two strands embodying two broadly different orientations (see Halliday, 1977). One tradition is oriented towards philosophy and logic; the other towards ethnography and rhetoric. During any given period, these two traditions may be more or less separate; and they may be balanced or one or the other may dominate. Current formal grammars are manifestations of the philosophico-logical tradition and the so-called Chomskyan revolution has meant that this tradition has come to dominate much of the discussion within and around linguistics. The questions that are asked about language are philosophical ones, putting the opposition between rationalism and empiricism on the agenda again: what is the nature of (linguistic) knowledge; how can this knowledge come to be acquired; what aspects of this knowledge are innate; etc.? The methods of inquiry are also philosophical. And the fundamental conception of syntactic structure was originally derived from traditional grammar and logic, for instance in the translation of Subject + Predicate as NP + VP.

In contrast, systemic linguistics falls within the ethnographic-rhetorical tradition (Halliday and Matthiessen, 1990). The questions that are asked about language are, broadly speaking, ethnographic ones: how does grammar create meaning in context? what is the relationship between grammar and text in context? how does grammar realize higher-order cultural meanings? etc. The methods of inquiry are also ethnographic: naturally occurring texts in context form the 'data base' for empirical work on grammar. The basic linguistic unit is not the sentence (as it tends to be in the philosophico-logical tradition) but text and the fundamental conception of syntactic structure is rhetorical, relating it to its textual environment in monologue and dialogue (e.g., in the Theme + Rheme and Mood + Residue structures, to be illustrated later).

More specifically, systemic linguistics has evolved in the Malinowski–Firth tradition. B. Malinowski (1884–1942) worked in anthropology in Britain in the first half of this century and developed a functional–contextual framework for interpreting culture where language plays a central role. In the course of this, he came to reinterpret language in a number of important respects. J.R. Firth (1890–1960), a younger linguist colleague of his for a while and later the first professor of linguistics in Britain, built Malinowski's ideas about context into a linguistic theory of language. One central theme was context, both the contexts of language and text (Malinowski's context of culture and context of situation), and contexts within the levels of the linguistic system. Another was the centrality of meaning in the study of language and consequently of text in context. A third theme was the equal importance of system and structure. Further, prosody was introduced as a mode of organization in phonology. This intellectual environment was very different from the one in the United States at the time of the 1940s and 1950s and there was no need to rebel to make progress: Firth had opened up the domain of linguistics; he rejected behaviourism and placed meaning at the centre of the stage. Linguists were not then constrained to follow discovery procedures.

Although it has often not been seen, Firth anticipated important aspects of the development of linguistics in the late 1970s and 1980s, for instance in stressing prosodic organization in phonology (cf. Autosegmental phonology) and the importance of context (for some discussion, see

Henderson, 1987). One of Firth's students, M.A.K. Halliday, developed and supplemented Firth's ideas and systemic linguistics evolved out of Firthian linguistics, including other important influences such as Whorf, Hjelmslev, and the Prague School along the way. Firth had concentrated on the 'outer' levels of the linguistic system, semantics and the relationship between language and context on the one hand and phonology on the other, and one of Halliday's first contributions was to propose a theory of the purely internal level, grammar (Halliday, 1961), systematizing a number of earlier theoretical abstractions. This came to be known as scale-and-category theory and can be thought of as protosystemic theory. Two important factors were involved in the transition into systemic functional theory. One was the foregrounding of language as a system of choices (Halliday, 1966) and the other was the discovery of the functional organization of language and Halliday's theory of metafunctions (Halliday, 1970, 1967/8).

We will not explore the development of systemic linguistics here (for overviews, see e.g. Monaghan, 1979; Steiner, 1983; Butler, 1985; Halliday and Matthiessen, 1990) but will pick up part of the current picture in the remainder of this chapter. First, however, we will say something about the reasons for choosing systemic linguistics to provide the linguistic foundation for text generation in particular.

## 5.2 Choosing systemic linguistics

In Chapters 2 and 3, we gave a rough characterization of the text generation task first in terms of an abstract sketch of the processes and components of an early 1990s text generator and then by identifying the major research tasks that have been explored so far. Now we can turn to the choice of a linguistic theory that can contribute towards work on text generation. It is perfectly possible that the idea of choosing *one* theory is a bad one to start with: we may be much better served if we pick and choose from a variety of sources as we assemble a text generator. However, we think there are good reasons to use one theory, at least as a reference point:

(i) there is a greater likelihood of compatibility among the parts if they come from the same theory; and
(ii) we are likely to learn more about the value of one theory if we apply it uniformly.

Although these are, we think, good and valid reasons, text generation systems do not, as a rule and as we have seen in Chapter 3, apply one linguistic theory throughout.[1] In contrast, in our discussions here of aspects of text generation ranging from morphology to social situations and context, we will use systemic theory as a reference point throughout.

We do not think that it is possible to argue conclusively for the choice of one theory over another for the task of text generation; nor do we think that it is desirable. We must emphasize that there is absolutely no reason whatsoever to think that there is only one possible approach to any application of linguistic theory. Moreover, experience with different approaches is extremely valuable. So, we will point to some reasons for choosing systemic theory as *a* theory, one with respect to which we are considering text generation in this book, not as *the* theory with respect to which text generation must be pursued. We will consider (i) the historical perspective, (ii) theoretical comprehensiveness, (iii) descriptive comprehensiveness, (iv) paradigmatic orientation, (v) functional orientation, (vi) theoretical research questions, and (vii) the exchange between theory and research applications.

(i) *Historical perspective.* There is a long history of systemics and computation in the area of lexicogrammar (grammar and vocabulary; Halliday, 1956 and 1962 are early examples) and it has thus been possible to draw on previous work, such as Henrici (1965), Winograd (1972), Davey (1978), Steiner, Eckert, Weck, and Winter (1988) and Patten (1988a). Further, some central ideas on lexical choice (as in Goldman's BABEL) and discourse organization (as in McKeown's TEXT) that have developed independently in text generation relate to systemic theory in interesting ways (cf. the discussion in Chapter 3). The present range of ongoing computational work building on systemic theory — including Fawcett and Tucker (1990), Steiner *et al.*, (1990a) and Matthiessen (1989) in addition to the Penman and Kyoto systems used extensively as illustrations throughout this book — is of course extending this history of interaction up through the present day.

(ii) *Theoretical comprehensiveness.* If we want to choose one linguistic theory, there are, in fact, few linguistic theories that are comprehensive enough. That is, most current linguistic theories are not theories of language but theories of syntax, syntax and morphology, or syntax, morphology, and phonology; but they do not cover semantics in a general way, discourse or discourse organization, cohesion, context, and register (functional variation), all of which will be central to work on text generation. For instance, it is crucial in text generation to know what is the interaction between a textual grammatical function such as Theme, discourse semantics, and the mode variable within context (cf. Fries, 1981; Halliday, 1978). Tagmemic theory (Pike, 1959), systemic theory, and stratificational theory (Lamb, 1966) are probably the only three comprehensive theories with a long tradition of research.

(iii) *Descriptive comprehensiveness.* The current task is to generate English text, so descriptive coverage of English is an important consideration. Of the three theoretically comprehensive approaches just mentioned, systemics is clearly the most comprehensive in descriptive coverage of English. Tagmemics has tended to focus on other languages and stratificational linguistics has not produced comprehensive accounts of English. Among formal theories of syntax, more value has been put on in-depth studies of particular areas of formal theoretical interest than on comprehensiveness (cf. Gross, 1979).

(iv) *Paradigmatic orientation.* In text generation, one of the central tasks is to exercise purposeful *control* over choices (cf. McDonald, 1980; see also Halliday, 1978, on developing text as ongoing choice), which calls for theories which emphasize the important organizing principle of *choice*, i.e., with a strong paradigmatic orientation, reflecting the conception of language as resource. As we have already noted and will see in detail below, systemic theory has a paradigmatic base — the system network — and structural realization is separated from this paradigmatic base.

(v) *Functional orientation.* If we take text generation to be purposeful behaviour and model it as goal pursuit, we need a theory with a *functional* orientation. More specifically, we need a theory that allows us to model language as a resource organized according to the functions it has evolved to serve. There are numerous examples of this in both the computational and non-computational literature but we will see some particular illustrations of the benefits that this orientation brings in our more detailed descriptions below.

(vi) *Theoretical research questions.* There is obviously more theoretical pay-off in applying a theory if the application is likely to throw light on questions within the theory. This is the case with systemic theory, where current questions of research interest include dynamic modelling (cf. Chapter 11 and, e.g., Bateman, 1989a; Martin, 1985; O'Donnell, 1989a; Tsui, 1989; Ventola, 1984, 1987), a task central in text generation, and the representation of context (see e.g. Martin, 1990; Halliday and Matthiessen, in preperation), which is related to issues of knowledge representation in text generation.

(vii) *The exchange between theory and application.* Systemic theory has always been developed in the context of application; application has not been activity unrelated to the development of theory. Halliday (1985c; 1, 6) addressed the exchange between systemic theory and application in this contribution to the Ninth Systemic Workshop:

The theme of the workshop is 'Applications of Systemic Theory', and this suggests to me that it is in the context of what can be done with the theory that we shall be seeking to exchange ideas. The theory has evolved in use; it has no existence apart from the practice of those who use it. Systemic theory is a way of doing things. If the English language permitted such extravagances I would name it not with a noun but with an adverb; I would call it 'Systemically' . . . These very sketchy references will perhaps serve to bring out what I think is a salient feature in the evolution of systemic theory: its permeability from outside. By 'outside' I mean not only outside itself, from other theories of language such as tagmemics and stratification theory, but also from outside linguistics, from disciplines for which language is not the object of study but rather an instrument for some other purpose . . . The value of a theory lies in the use that can be made of it, and I have always considered a theory of language to be essentially consumer-oriented.

There is an important analogy between linguistic theory — metalanguage — and language here: both develop to serve the uses to which they are put. A functional theory of language is designed to bring out the ways in which language is organized according to functional principles; it is also a 'meta-functional' theory in the sense of being organized to serve the uses to which it is put.

## 5.3 Systemic theory

Having motivated the choice of systemic linguistics as a linguistic foundation of research into text generation, we will now sketch the most important aspects of systemic theory in the context of text generation.

The systemic model is different from a componential or modular organization in that it is more highly differentiated: components (modules) may be related stratally (Section 5.5), by rank (as syntax and morphology are; Section 5.8), by axis (paradigmatic axis vs. syntagmatic axis; Section 5.7), or by metafunctions (Section 5.6); the distinctions tend to be lost if they are all treated in the same componential fashion. For instance, if syntax, morphology, and phonology are all set up as components, the difference between the rank relation between syntax and morphology and the stratal relationship between these two and phonology is obscured.

Systemic theory is thus multidimensional and it is always difficult to discuss a multidimensional abstraction step by step since its value lies in its multidimensionality. The following presentation has to be read as an abstract, brief overview; many details will only emerge later. We will proceed by discussing the following dimensions:

- *Resource* (Section 5.4);
- *Stratal organization* (orders of abstraction; Section 5.5);

- *Functional diversification* (diversification according to function: functional spectrum; Section 5.6);
- *Axis* (paradigmatic and syntagmatic organization; Section 5.7);
- *Rank* (hierarchy of units according to potential for occurring as constituents in other units; Section 5.8);
- *Synoptic* and *dynamic* (descriptions of static resources and descriptions of activations of these resources; Section 5.9);
- *Functional variation* (varieties according to use; Section 5.10).

These dimensions determine the modularity of the overall model; the 'modules' are defined in terms of stratal organization, metafunctional organization, rank, and so on.

To conclude the chapter we will then comment on what this extensive range of dimensions of theoretical variation does for us in the context of text generation and model building.

## 5.4 Organization as resource: functional interpretation

Language is interpreted in systemic theory as a RESOURCE for the speaker–listener. It leads to a view of language as essentially meaning potential available to its users — a resource for meaning, both reflectively and actively. The concept of resource is fundamental; it is the basis of a multifaceted kind of functionalism. It is closely related to:

- a functional interpretation of language as a stratal system of systems (see Section 5.5 below), first in the life of the child, before he or she moves into the mother tongue, as a two stratal system, and then under multifunctional pressures, as the tristratal system of adult language (e.g., Halliday, 1975; Painter, 1984);
- an interpretation of language as functioning in context (see Section 5.5 below);
- a multifunctional view of language (see Section 5.6 below);
- the notion of functional variation (see Section 5.10); and
- the paradigmatic orientation, since a paradigm can be seen as a way of identifying the resources available to the language user (see Section 5.7).

As a way of construing language, 'resource' contrasts with notions such as rule system: it represents a functional rather than a formal interpretation, that relates to rhetoric rather than to logic. We can see this clearly in conceptions of grammar. Lowth (1762: x) states the task of grammar as follows:

The principal design of a Grammar of any Language is to teach us to express ourselves with propriety in that Language, and to be able to judge every phrase and form of construction, whether it be right or not. The plain way of doing this, is to lay down rules, and to illustrate them by examples. But besides shewing what is right, the matter may be further explained by pointing out what is wrong.

There are two demands on grammar here — (i) *expressing* and (ii) *judging*. These two demands run through the conceptions of grammar — grammar as resource and grammar as rule system; different theories will give more emphasis to one or the other, partly depending on what tasks they have been designed to deal with. The nature of the grammar will depend on which task is given prominence; as Lowth points out, judging is achieved by laying down rules; e.g.:

When the Verb is Passive, the Agent and Object change places in the Sentence; and the thing acted upon is in the Nominative Case, and the Agent is accompanied by a Preposition. (op.cit., p. 104)

This perspective leads to a conception of language as a rule system. Modern linguistics no longer operates with the contrast between right or wrong. The distinction is seen as a thing of past prescriptivist aspirations but it has reappeared in a descriptivist guise as the distinction between grammatical and ungrammatical.

In text generation, it is clearly more the first demand on grammar that needs to be the driving principle: the task of the grammar is to serve as an expressive resource. The second demand, distinguishing right and wrong or rather grammatical and ungrammatical, is primarily a 'safety' check. While acknowledging the part it may play as a safety check, we should however keep in mind Kay's (1986: 125) observations:

Language is a system for encoding and transmitting ideas. A theory that seeks to explain linguistic phenomena in terms of this fact is a *functional* theory. One that does not misses the point. In particular, a theory that shows how the sentences of a language are all generable by rules of a particular formal system, however restricted that system may be, does not explain anything. It may be suggestive, to be sure, because it may point to the existence of an encoding device whose structure that formal system reflects. But, if it points to no such device, it simply constitutes a gratuitous and wholly unwelcome addition to the set of phenomena to be explained.

For the grammar grammaticality is thus a very secondary concern. Besides, there are other systems at higher levels in a text generator that will affect whether an expression is acceptable or not and to attempt a specification of acceptability that does not consider these complicates the task rather unnecessarily.[2]

## 5.5 Stratal organization

The linguistic resources for making and expressing meanings are inherently symbolic and are thus organized into a number of levels of symbolization. These LEVELS (in Firthian terms) or STRATA (in terms of Lamb's stratification theory) represent different orders of abstraction; they are ordered in relation to one another and higher strata are REALIZED by lower ones (Halliday, 1961; Matthiessen and Halliday, 1989; and many other places): for instance, grammar is realized by phonology.[3] The organization within a stratum, intrastratal organization, will be discussed in some detail below; the central organizing principle within each stratum is choice and the overall organization is a network of interrelated choice points. Selections from this network are expressed by means of structures and items (e.g., lexical items).

### *5.5.1 The strata of the linguistic system*

There have been various proposals within systemic linguistics concerning the number of strata. We will follow Halliday in interpreting (adult) language as tristratal; the three strata are, in order of abstraction, semantics (resource for meaning), lexicogrammar (resource for wording), and phonology (resource for sounding). Minimally, a symbolic system has to have two strata, a semantic stratum and an expression stratum and early child language before the child begins to learn a mother tongue is in fact such a bistratal system (Halliday, 1975; Painter, 1984). It has a semantic stratum and a phonological one but there is no grammatical interface between the two: meanings are coded directly into sounds. Such a system is limited in functionality and the child has to abandon it and begin to learn the mother tongue spoken around him/her both in order to be able to mean more than one thing at the same time and in order to deal with the task of adapting to a wide and growing variety of different communicative contexts while generalizing across these. These two demands on the system, contextual adaptation and generalization, can be met by stratifying the bistratal system in the transition into the mother tongue: the adaptation to different contexts of use takes place at the semantic stratum while the generalization across these different contexts of use is achieved through the development of a grammatical stratum that is 'slotted in' between semantics and phonology.

We can characterize the three strata involved as follows:

- SEMANTICS: resource for meaning. Since it is a resource, meaning is a functional/rhetorical/communicative notion rather than a formal/logico-

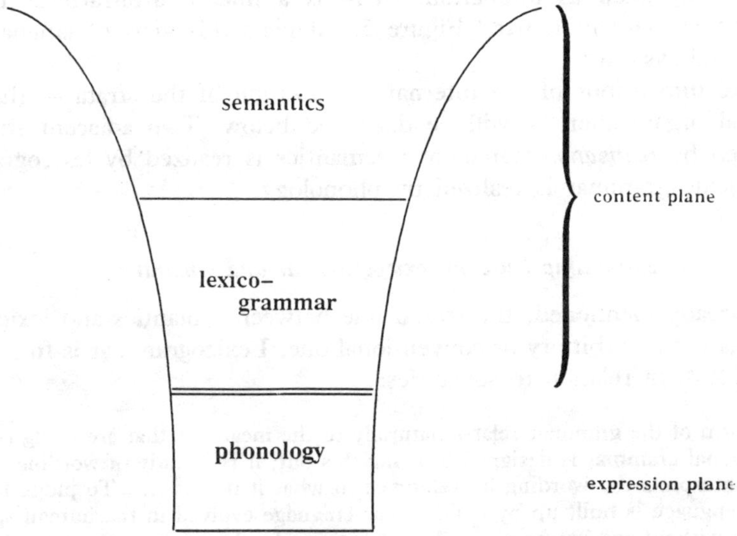


**Figure 5.1** Language as a tristratal system

philosophical one and this is reflected in two ways in the conception of semantics: (i) it is multifunctional (see further below) and (ii) it is a semantics of text (discourse). The latter follows from the observation that text (rather than words or sentences) is the unit of communication.

- LEXICOGRAMMAR: resource for wording meanings, i.e., for expressing them by means of structures and 'words' (more accurately, grammatical and lexical items). Lexicogrammar includes lexis (vocabulary) as well as grammar in one unified system; lexis is interpreted as the most specific part of grammar. Grammar includes morphology as well as syntax; the two are not stratally distinct.
- PHONOLOGY: resource for sounding.[4] It includes intonational resources, which serve to realize grammatical choices directly, as well as resources of rhythm and of syllabic and phonemic articulation, which are not in a direct realization relation to grammar.

Lexicogrammar and one manifestation of semantics (choosers and inquiries) will be introduced in more detail in Chapter 6; a further approach to semantics will be discussed in Chapter 12.

Lexicogrammar is semantically natural and thus functionally motivated; its categories are grammaticalizations of semantic categories. In contrast, the categories of phonology are not 'phonologizations' of grammatical categories; although there are certain grammatically natural areas of phonology such as intonation, there is a line of arbitrariness between phonology and grammar.[5] Figure 5.1 depicts this view of language as a tristratal system.[6]

The dimensions of the internal organization of the strata — the intrastratal organization — will be discussed below. Two adjacent strata are related by *realization* statements: semantics is realized by lexicogrammar; and lexicogrammar is realized by phonology.

### *5.5.2 The relationship between lexicogrammar and semantics*

As already mentioned, the stratal line between semantics and lexicogrammar is not an arbitrary or conventional one. Lexicogrammar is functionally NATURAL in relation to semantics:

> the form of the grammar relates naturally to the meanings that are being coded. A functional grammar is designed to bring this out; it is a study of wording, but one that interprets the wording by reference to what it means . . . To judge from the way language is built up by children, as language evolved in the human species it began without any grammar at all; it was a two-level system, with meanings coded directly into expressions (sounds and gestures). This at least is how children's 'protolanguage' is organized, the symbolic system they construct for themselves before starting on the mother tongue. This is then replaced, in the second year of life, by a three-level system in which meanings are first coded into wordings and these wordings are then recoded into expressions. There were various reasons why this step had to be taken if the system was to expand; it opened up both the potential for dialogue, the dynamic exchange of meanings with other people, and the potential for combining different kinds of meaning in one utterance — using language both to think with and to act with at the same time. (Halliday, 1985a: xvii–xviii)

The semantic naturalness of lexicogrammar helps explain why there has been a fair amount of variation in the assignment of responsibility to semantics and lexicogrammar. Halliday has developed a functional, 'semanticky' type of grammar. This has sometimes been taken to mean that his grammar has taken over semantics but this is not the case. Rather, his semantics is free to expand upwards, as we will see in Section 5.6.2. Others, influenced by Hudson's (1971, 1974, 1976) work, operate with a leaner, more formal grammar and as a result their semantices do some of the work handled within Halliday's grammar.

In general, there are a number of considerations deciding on the division of labour between grammar and semantics; these include the following:

(i) Semantics has to address the task of providing the interface between grammar, which is a purely internal linguistic stratum, and higher-level contextual systems (cf. Halliday, 1973).

(ii) As a result, one approach is to treat the stratum above grammar not as one semantic system but as a repertoire of different semantic systems, adapted to different contexts of use (as is clearly the case in protolanguage) — i.e., as a repertoire of socially specialized communicative strategies (cf. Halliday, 1973; see further Chapter 12). In contrast, grammar is treated as one highly generalized system, serving the range of different semantic systems in different contexts of use.

(iii) Since their responsibilities are different, semantics and grammar operate with different fundamental units — texts in context and clauses, respectively.

(iv) There are a number of recurrent semantic features realized in the grammar such as apposition and causation (see Halliday, 1985a). These realizations are distributed across different grammatical contexts (clause complexes, clauses, groups, and so on) but they can be related at the semantic stratum. One consequence of this is the phenomenon of grammatical metaphor (see Section 5.5.3 immediately below). To describe it, we need to be able to say that certain selections at the semantic stratum can be realized either congruently (e.g., as a clause: *the Roman Empire fell*) or metaphorically (e.g., as a nominal group: *the fall of the Roman Empire*) at the grammatical stratum.

(v) Grammar may leave a number of specifications fairly implicit, for example, by means of the resources of ellipsis. These implicit specifications can be 'filled in' explicitly at the semantic stratum. (The differentiation between grammar and semantics in terms of explicitness has been particularly important in logic-based approaches to semantics involving, for instance, the recovery of quantifier scope.)

In addition, there is a very general but powerful observation: whenever two adjacent strata are set up, the symbolic potential is increased since the possibility of many-to-many mappings is introduced. We can see this quite clearly in the area of speech functions (semantics) and mood (grammar); cf. Halliday (1984). For instance, the differentiation of the semantic option of command and the grammatical option of imperative means that the possibility has been created whereby commands are realized not only by imperative clauses (*Sit down!*) but also by indicative ones (e.g., modulated yes–no interrogative ones: *Would you sit down?*), thus allowing for further more delicate semantic distinctions having to do with, for example, politeness.

### *5.5.3 Grammatical metaphor*

The relation between semantics and grammar is affected by the strategy for creating new modes of meaning known as GRAMMATICAL METAPHOR (e.g.,

Halliday, 1985a: Ch. 10): meanings represented grammatically in one way are re-represented as if they were of another kind; processes are represented as if they were things, modalities as if they were thoughts, commands as if they were questions, and so on. There may be a congruent coding as well as metaphorical ones:

> Language has evolved in such a way that our interpretation of experience (thinking with language) and our interpersonal exchanges (acting with language) are coded into semantic structures that are plausible; and with these has evolved a lexicogrammatical system that extends the plausibility one step further, so that even at one remove we can see (or feel; the process is an unconscious one, until linguistics begins to meddle with it) the sense that lies behind the forms. A congruent expression is one in which this direct line of form to meaning to experience is maintained intact, as it is in young children's language like *man clean car*. A metaphorical expression is one in which the line is indirect . . . There is no very sharp line between the congruent and the metaphorical — there rarely are any sharp lines in language, since it is an evolved system and not a designed one; but the distinction is an important one for text analysis and generation. (Halliday, 1985a: xix)

There are many different types of metaphor; one type involves the representation of a temporal location as a perceiver in a process of perception, as in *1987 saw the large producers and distributors playing it safer than ever before*. Here the reason for selecting the metaphorical strategy is textual; the structure presents *1987* as unmarked Theme (the point of departure or local context of the clause) and groups *the large producers and distributors playing it safer than ever before* as one point of (new) information. The congruent version would organize the information quite differently; e.g.: *the large producers and distributors played it safer than ever before in 1987*.

### *5.5.4 Context: higher-level systems of meaning*

Semantics is the interface between the linguistic system and the higher-level systems of the context in which language is embedded. The number and nature of the contextual systems depend on the purposes for which the model is set up. We will discuss context in text generation from the point of view of grammar in Chapter 9. There is also variation according to different proposals in systemic linguistics. Minimally, it is important to recognize the level of context above the linguistic system as is depicted in Figure 5.2.

As with lexicogrammar and semantics, there is fluidity between semantics and context in the assignment of descriptive responsibility. In the work of, for example, Halliday and Hasan (1976, 1985), semantics is text semantics: the base unit of semantics is text, not a unit defined by grammar. Another, more traditional proposal, is to stratify this level into discourse and semantics (cf. Butler, 1985).

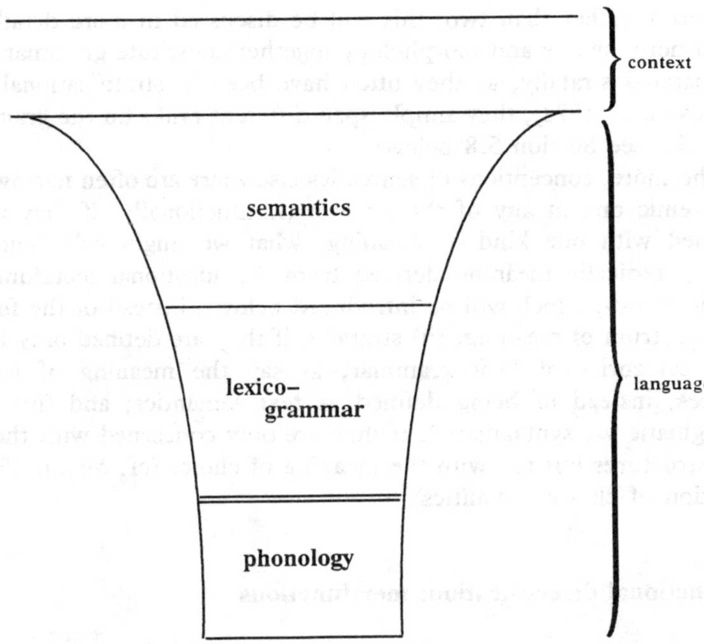


**Figure 5.2** Context and language

Work on the 'stratal' organization of context is one of the current research areas in systemic linguistics, as can be seen in the recent collections of systemic research (e.g., Berry, 1984; Benson and Greaves, 1985; Halliday and Fawcett, 1987).[7]

### 5.5.5 *Relationship to other approaches*

There is a clear rough correspondence between the overall organization of a text generation system such as the one outlined in Chapter 2 (cf. Figures 2.1 and 2.3) and the stratal organization of the model in systemic linguistics. Stratal organization has not in general been explicitly recognized in discussions of the organization of text generation systems, but many of the organizational concerns are similar to the stratal considerations that have long been modelling issues in systemic and stratificational linguistics. Stratal considerations are beginning to play an increasing role in computational systems however. For example, as we saw in Chapter 3 above, the properties of rhetorical goals of the type pursued in Hovy's PAULINE constitute a separate stratum requiring its own consideration.

According to the stratal arrangement above, grammar and lexis constitute one stratum rather than two; this will be discussed in more detail below. Furthermore, syntax and morphology together constitute grammar and are not separated stratally, as they often have been in stratificational models (cf. Lockwood, 1972); they simply span different ranks on the grammatical rank scale (see Section 5.8 below).

Furthermore, conceptions of semantics elsewhere are often narrower than the systemic one in any of three ways: (i) functionally, if they are only concerned with one kind of meaning, what we might call denotational meaning (basically meaning derived from the ideational metafunction of systemic theory, which will be introduced below), instead of the full functional spectrum of meaning; (ii) stratally, if they are defined only in terms of the categories of lexicogrammar, as say the meaning of words or sentences, instead of being defined as text semantics; and (iii) by axis (paradigmatic vs. syntagmatic), if they are only concerned with the meaning of structures but not with the meaning of choice (cf. Mann, 1983a, on the notion of choice semantics).

## 5.6 Functional diversification: metafunctions

The stratal organization is based on abstraction. Within the content plane of language (i.e., lexicogrammar and semantics), there is another type of organization that 'cuts across' the stratal organization: metafunctional diversification. This diversification is reflected in the organization of the content plane as layering — there are simultaneous functional layers.

### *5.6.1 The three metafunctions*

There are three highly generalized metafunctions — ideational, interpersonal, and textual. They do not differ in abstraction from one another as the strata do; rather, they are simultaneous, functionally differentiated perspectives on the linguistic system.

The IDEATIONAL metafunction is, as the name suggests, concerned with ideation: it provides the speaker with the resources for interpreting and representing 'reality'. This metafunction is further divided into two subtypes: the *experiential* and the *logical*. The experiential one represents particular classes of phenomena, such as configurations of processes, participants, and circumstances; it represents wholes in terms of their constituent parts. The logical one represents combinations of phenomena through highly generalized relations, such as addition, alternation, exemplification, sequence and causation.

The INTERPERSONAL metafunction provides the speaker with the

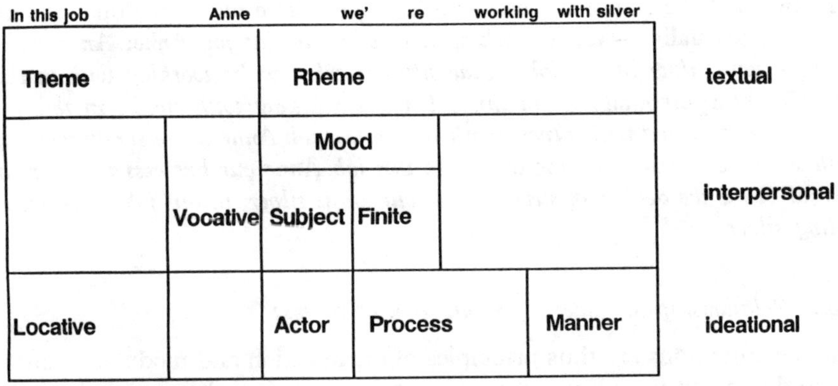


**Figure 5.3** Metafunctional layering in grammar

resources for creating and maintaining social relations with the listener, e.g. by assigning speech roles such as questioner and (intended) answerer and by intruding into the speech situation by giving or demanding comments on what is being said.

The TEXTUAL metafunction enables the speaker in presenting ideational and interpersonal information as text in context; it provides him or her with the resources for contextualizing the information.

We will meet many examples of the three metafunctions in the subsequent discussion, but let us give one initial illustration here in terms of grammatical structure. Consider the grammatical organization of the clause *in this job Anne we're working with silver* (taken from Halliday, 1985a: Appendix I, where a fuller account is given) shown in Figure 5.3.

From a TEXTUAL point of view, the speaker provides a local context or point of departure for the clause — the Theme: *in this job* (domain of interest) and *Anne* (person supposed to attend to what follows). In fact, both of these persist through the remainder of the discourse (a typical feature of the textual metafunction); they set the overall topic and addressee and are not cancelled. The remainder of the clause is the Rheme, which is interpreted in the context of the Theme.

From an INTERPERSONAL point of view, the speaker has selected the declarative mood, expressed as the sequence Subject followed by Finite, and has explicitly identified the addressee (*Anne*). These two choices are both aspects of the speech function of the clause. Furthermore, the speaker identifies 'we' as the protagonist of the statement.

Finally, from an IDEATIONAL point of view, the clause represents a configuration of a Process ('be working') and a participant, the Actor, and two attendant circumstances, Locative and Manner.

Notice that the clause can be varied along all three metafunctional dimensions: (i) textually — *we're working with silver in this job Anne*; *Anne we're working with silver in this job*; *Anne silver is what we're working with in this job*; (ii) interpersonally — *in this job we're working with silver*; *in this job Anne we're working with silver aren't we*; *in this job Anne we're surely working with silver*; and (iii) ideationally — *in this job Anne our business is silver*; *in this job Anne we deal with silver*; *Anne our job is silver*; *in this job Anne we're selling silver*.

### 5.6.2 *Relationship to context: organization of context*

The metafunctions are thus principles of organization and modularity internal to the semantic and grammatical systems. But they also explain how the semantic system relates upwards, to context. To see the nature of this relationship, we first have to look at the three different aspects of context that have been identified in systemic theory (e.g., Halliday *et al.*, 1964; Halliday, 1978; Halliday and Hasan, 1985): the FIELD (of discourse), the TENOR (of the relationship between speaker and listener), and the MODE (of the discourse). These three aspects are categories of context as a higher-level semiotic organization — 'they are a conceptual framework for representing the social context as the semiotic environment in which people exchange meanings' (Halliday, 1978: 110); they can be characterized briefly as follows (from Halliday, 1978: 142–3):

FIELD: the field of discourse — 'that which is "going on", and has recognizable meaning in the social system; typically a complex of acts in some ordered configuration, and in which the text is playing some part, and including "subject-matter" as one special aspect' — 'a field of significant social action'. If a text is self-sufficient rather than an accompaniment that runs alongside some other social activity, the field of discourse is the subject matter of the text but it also includes the activities that make the subject matter relevant — activities such as exploration, learning, and imagining; if the text is 'embedded' in some other social activity, this activity is also included in the field. The notion of field is related to the common notion of domain in computational linguistics.

TENOR: the tenor of the relationship between speaker and listener — 'the cluster of socially meaningful participant relationships, both permanent attributes of the participants and role relationships that are specific to the situation, including the speech roles, those that come into being through the exchange of verbal meanings' — 'a tenor of role relationships'. Tenor thus includes roles that are brought into existence because of language — speech roles — as well as other social role relations. The notion of tenor overlaps significantly with user modelling in computational linguistics.

MODE: the role played by language itself in a given context of situation — 'the particular status that is assigned to the text within the situation; its function in relation to the social action and the role structure, including the channel or medium, and the rhetorical mode' — 'a mode of symbolic organization'. Mode includes most of what in computational linguistics is covered by rhetorical and communicative goals.

Put very simply, field concerns natural reality, tenor intersubjective reality, and mode semiotic reality. As an illustration of how these categories come into play, consider the following example of the characterization of a situation of play involving father and son, taken from Halliday (1978: 115):

field: Child at play: manipulating movable objects (wheeled vehicles) with related fixtures, assisted by adult; concurrently associating (i) similar past events, (ii) similar absent objects; also evaluating objects in terms of each other and of processes.
tenor: Small child and parent interacting: child determining course of action, (i) announcing own intentions, (ii) controlling actions of parents; concurrently sharing and seeking corroboration of own experience with parent.
mode: Spoken, alternately monologue and dialogue, task-oriented; pragmatic, (i) referring to processes and objects of situation, (ii) relating to and furthering child's own actions, (iii) demanding other objects; interposed with narrative and exploratory elements.

The following text develops in this situation:

Nigel [small wooden train in hand, approaching track laid along a plank sloping from chair to floor]: `Here the railway line . . . but it not for the train to go on that.`
Father: `Isn't it?`
Nigel: `Yes tis . . . I wonder the train will carry the lorry` [puts train on lorry (*sic*)].
Father: `I wonder.`
Nigel: `Oh yes it will . . . I don't want to send the train on this floor . . . you want to send the train on the railway line` [runs it up plank onto chair] `. . . but it doesn't go very well on the chair. . . .` [makes train go round in circles] `The train all round and round . . . it going all round and round . . .` [tries to reach other train] `have that train . . . have the blue train ('give it to me')` [Father does so] `. . . send the blued train down the railway line . . .`[plank falls off chair] `let me put the railway line on the chair ('you put the railway line on the chair!')` [Father does so] `. . .` [looking at blue train] `Daddy put sellotape on it ('previously') . . . there are very fierce lion in the train . . . Daddy go and see if the lion is still there. . . . Have your engine ('give me my engine').`
Father: `Which engine? The little black one?`
Nigel: `Yes . . . Daddy go and find it for you . . . Daddy go and find the black engine for you.`

| | contextual categories | metafunctionally differentiated resources of the linguistic system | |
|---|---|---|---|
| field: socially significant action | manipulation of objects<br>movability of objects & their relation to fixtures<br>assistance of adult | transitivity<br>process type and participant structure<br>type of movement & location<br>benefactive | ideational |
| tenor: relationship between interactants | interaction with parent<br>determination of course of action<br>enunciation of intention<br>control of action<br>sharing of experience<br>seeking corroboration of experience | person<br>mood and polarity<br>demand, 'I want to'<br>demand, 'I want you to'<br>statement/question, monologue<br>statement/question, dialogue | interpersonal |
| mode: the role played by the text itself | dialogue<br>reference to situation<br>textual cohesion: objects<br>processes | ellipsis (question–answer)<br>exophoric reference<br>anaphoric reference<br>conjunction | textual |

**Figure 5.4** Relationships between categories of context and metafunction in grammar

According to Halliday (e.g., 1978), each of the three metafunctions tends to serve to project one of the three different aspects of context; he sets the following correspondencies as a working hypothesis:

field — ideational
tenor — interpersonal
mode — textual

That is to say, the field tends to determine ideational meanings, the tenor interpersonal ones, and the mode textual ones. For instance, the significant social action is reflected in the ideational resources of transitivity, whereas the tenor of the relations between speaker and listener is reflected in selections of mood and modality.

Figure 5.4, based on one given in Halliday (1978: 117), illustrates the relationships between the categories of context and the metafunctional resources of the linguistic system.

To sum up, there is functional differentiation both in context and in the linguistic system; the functional differentiation of context and language is added to the stratal diagram in Figure 5.5.

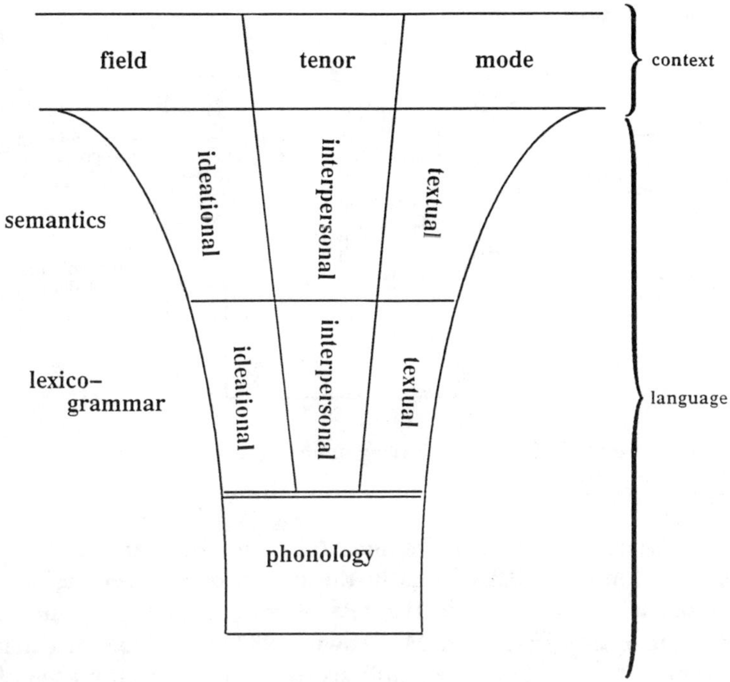


**Figure** 5.5 Functional layering

*5.6.3 Relationship to other theories*

The metafunctions are, as already noted, simultaneous within one stratum. However, outside of systemic linguistics they have sometimes been modelled in a way that is closer to stratal organization; that is, some kind of extrinsic ordering is imposed on the decisions and their consequences. For example, the functional components of Functional Grammar are ordered in a stratal sort of way (cf., e.g., Dik, 1978). This is often tied to a lexical conception of the ideational metafunction. As an alternative to systemic-functional lexicogrammar, we can set up a model with an ideational lexicon or dictionary that precedes syntax, which includes textual and interpersonal syntax — what is often thought of as more 'surfacy' syntax — as shown in Figure 5.6.

The 'common alternative' is not a specific model, but it reflects design features that are quite common. Thus, the lexicon of a Functional Grammar (e.g., Dik, 1978, 1987) contains the basic predicate frames of the model. The same is true of the predicate argument structures of lexical

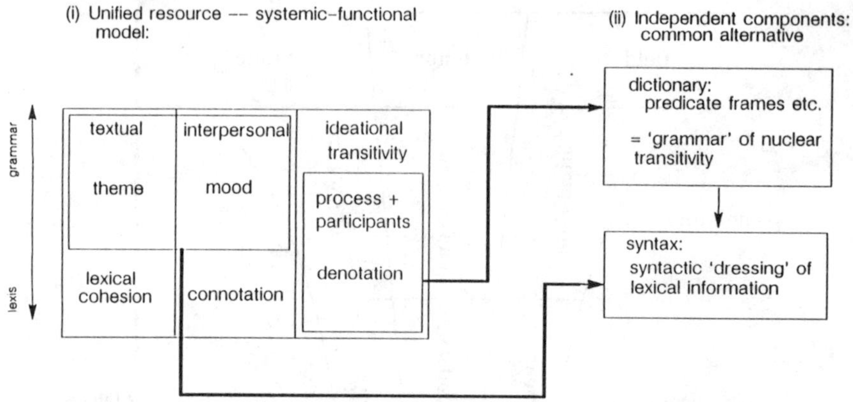


**Figure 5.6** Systemic-functional lexicogrammar and alternative

items in Lexical Functional Grammar (cf., e.g., Bresnan, 1980, 1982). We have also seen examples of this in the design of text generation systems: ideational lexis may precede the rest of lexicogrammar (as in Goldman, 1974, McDonald, 1980, and McKeown, 1982, introduced in Chapter 3).

Within text generation, the emphasis has typically been on the ideational function of language and the field component of context. The latter corresponds roughly to the knowledge base of generation systems. One of our concerns here will be to widen this perspective in a systematic and theory-driven manner.

The beginnings of this movement have already been mentioned in our interpretative survey in Chapter 3, where we noted the value of considering text generation systems in terms of the registers of the texts they generate. This demonstrated a move beyond simple considerations of field (corresponding to computational knowledge bases and domain models) to include notions of tenor (corresponding to user models, although with an *intersubjective* emphasis — cf. Bateman, 1985b) and situation types (corresponding, e.g., to notions such as the scripts of the Yale school — cf. Schank and Abelson, 1977).

Although systemic theory is the only approach that recognizes the particular set of metafunctions described above, functional components or uses are widely recognized — as in the work of Bühler (1934), various Prague School linguists such as Firbas (1966) and Daneš (1974), Dik (1978), Givòn (1983), Foley and Van Valin (1984). One unique feature of Halliday's systemic theory of metafunctions, however, is the differentiation between the experiential and logical subtypes of the ideational metafunction. We

| | characterization | related typologies | major resources |
|---|---|---|---|
| ideational | ideation -- interpretation and representation of the world in and around us | semantic<br>representational<br>denotative<br>**propositional content**<br>cognitive | transitivity (process + participants + circumstances)<br>Loc \| Actor \| Proc \| Goal<br>Tom. we'll fix it won't we? |
| interpersonal | interaction between speaker and listener; **assignment of speech** roles and modal-attitudinal comments | conative-expressive (pragmatic) | **mood & modality;** key<br>Mood (Su \| Fi) ...we'll<br>Moodtag (TSu \| TFi) ...won't we |
| textual | presentation of ideational & interpersonal information as text in context; control of **textual statuses and** conjunctive development of text | pragmatic<br>**discoursal**<br>functional sentence perspective | theme; information; conjunction<br>Theme \| Rheme<br>Tomorrow we'll |

**Figure 5.7** The metafunctions and related schemes

will see later that it is crucial to an understanding of various issues in text generation.

Furthermore, current functional theories are often essentially bifunctional rather than trifunctional. Either the interpersonal metafunction is left out of the theory of grammar (opposed as an extrinsic theory of speech acts) or it is treated together with the textual one as some kind of 'pragmatic' function — a largely undifferentiated area of 'style', 'social affect', etc. We will see later that it is essential to differentiate the two in text generation, both from a grammatical point of view and from a semantic/conceptual perspective. Also, in contrast to the views proposed by, for example, Leech (1983) and Butler (1987, 1988) that the interpersonal and textual metafunctions should be seen as extrinsic to the lexicogrammar, as is found according to a more traditional tripartite division into grammar, semantics, and pragmatics, we have found the metafunctional hypothesis to produce a coverage of phenomena that is unusually broad for an explicit computational account. It certainly, therefore, deserves to be taken further and we will organize much of our discussion below in the terms it provides.

The three metafunctions are tabulated in Figure 5.7 together with related

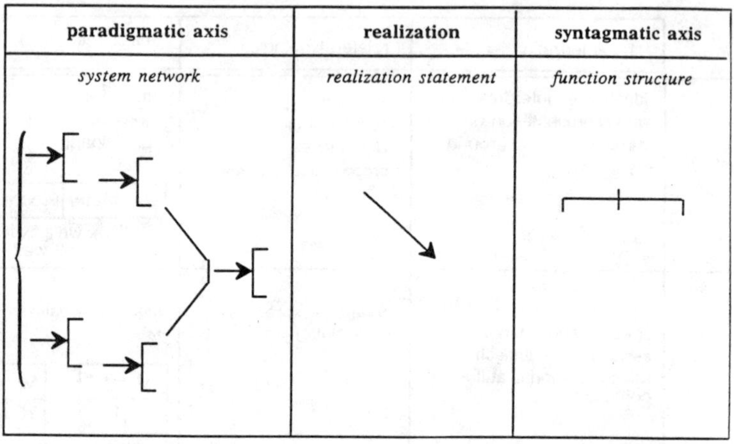


**Figure 5.8** Axis and inter-axis realization

terms from other theories and examples of grammatical resources from the grammar.

## 5.7 Axis: paradigmatic and syntagmatic

We now turn to the basic principle of the internal organization of each stratum or level within the overall system.

### *5.7.1 The differentiation of the two axes*

Recall the emphasis on the interpretation of language as a resource rather than a rule system for specifying structures. All strata in the linguistic system are construed as paradigmatically organized resources — resources of meaning, wording, and 'sounding'. Syntagmatic specifications are derived by means of realization statements associated with paradigmatic selections; i.e., syntagmatic realizations are always given in particular paradigmatic contexts — see Figure 5.8.

As the figure indicates schematically, paradigmatic organization and syntagmatic organization are represented by means of different modes of representation. (This follows from the priority given to the paradigmatic organization, but it is unusual among linguistic theories. Even in stratificational linguistics, the same mode of representation is used for both paradigmatic organization and syntagmatic organization.)

### 5.7.2 *Modes of representation*

Paradigmatic organization is represented by means of SYSTEM NETWORKS, which are networks of interrelated choice alternatives — the systems of systemic theory. The choice alternatives of a system are represented by features. The systems of the system network are ordered in DELICACY, from least delicate (most general) to most delicate (most specific). System networks apply to all strata and to all metafunctions. We will discuss system networks in more detail in Section 6.1 of the next chapter.

Syntagmatic organization is represented by means of FUNCTION STRUCTURES, configurations of constituent functions. An example of a function structure was shown in Figure 5.3. The concept of function structure is less general across strata and metafunctions than the system network, but it has been applied to all strata and metafunctions.

As already mentioned, REALIZATION statements are used to 're-express' the features of the system networks as syntagmatic specifications. While delicacy is the principle of paradigmatic organization, constituency is the principle of syntagmatic organization. We will return to syntagmatic organization in more detail in Section 6.3 of the next chapter.

### 5.7.3 *Relationship to other approaches*

Like European structuralism[8] in general and the Firthian tradition in particular, systemic theory emphasizes the paradigmatic axis as well as the syntagmatic one. It differs from most other traditions — including Firthian theory and stratificational linguistics — in giving each level a paradigmatic base.

Unlike European structuralism, American structuralist linguistics focused more on syntagmatic organization than on paradigmatic organization (and the models were, accordingly, item and arrangement or item and process models rather than item and paradigm models). This emphasis was taken over by transformational linguists (where paradigmatic relations were modelled as syntagmatic ones, e.g., as *structure* changing transformations, as is clear when we compare them with the more recent metarules of early GPSG: Gazdar *et al.*, 1985).[9] In fact, most current theories not only of syntax but also of semantics, 'discourse', and other subsystems still emphasize syntagmatic organization and do not have a paradigmatic base: structures are generated by means of structural rules instead of being generated as realizations of paradigmatic selections.

The paradigmatic organization represented by the system network of systemic theory is often implicit in the rules intended to specify syntagmatic properties.[10] That is, while syntagmatic rules may be optional and include alternatives, these instances of choice are all local and incidental to the syntagmatic specification (cf. Sampson, 1980); they are not explicitly related as a network of interrelated choices, which is what constitutes an independent statement of paradigmatic organization.

The primacy of paradigmatic organization in systemic theory corresponds to the basic need in text generation for control over the generation process. The need for explicit accounts of control is now being felt in approaches to text generation based on current theories of syntax other than systemic-functional grammar: what is typically achieved is a statement of the constructions that are possible that lacks methods for constraining those possibilities appropriately with respect to particular communicative needs.[11]

The need to refer to a 'map' of possible choices and the logic of their interrelatedness has emerged quite independently in AI in general. Patten (1988a) demonstrates and builds on the convergence between the systemic paradigmatic interpretation of language and research on problem solving in AI, particularly in organizing solution spaces and in developing methods for searching these according to the interconnectedness of the choice alternatives. We also find graphs in AI for representing choice — discrimination networks and decision trees. They resemble the system network, but are less flexible since they are more constrained.[12] In our survey of generation systems, we noted Goldman's (1974) account of lexical choice based on discrimination networks.

## 5.8 Rank

The overall organization of language in context is based on orders of abstraction: the levels of Section 5.5. The organization of structure within the levels of lexicogrammar and phonology is, further, RANK-based.

### *5.8.1 Rank-based organization*

The units of lexicogrammar and phonology are ordered discretely on a scale according to their 'constituency potential' — from 'largest' to 'smallest'. Each value on this hierarchic scale is called a RANK; and the scale itself is the RANK SCALE. Units of a given rank (say clause in the grammar or syllable in the phonology) consist of units of the rank next below in the ordering (say groups and phonemes, respectively). This ranking type of organization is familiar from systems in general — cf. subatomic particle–atom–molecule; cell–organ–organism; city–county–state–nation; etc. Through RANKSHIFT, a unit of a higher rank may serve as if it were of a

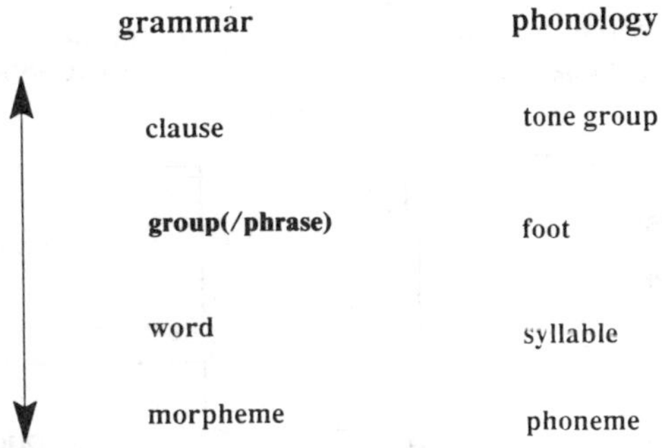


**Figure 5.9** Rank in English grammar and phonology

lower rank (e.g., a clause may serve as if it were a group); rankshift always means *down*ranking.

The theory does not fix the number of ranks present at any level. English grammar and English phonology both have four ranks,[13] as shown in Figure 5.9. Rank is also applicable at the semantic stratum. If the approach of situation-specific semantices is taken, we will, however, find more than one semantic rank scale. We will touch on this issue in Part IV.

### *5.8.2 Relationship to other frameworks*

The grammatical rank scale in English spans clause and group (/phrase) as well as word and morpheme. Outside systemic linguistics, it has often been broken down into two different components or strata as syntax and morphology, as shown in Figure 5.10. However, in a systemic-functional grammar there is no reason for this separation. Both syntax and morphology show the same kinds of paradigmatic and syntagmatic organization — they manifest the same kind of 'item and paradigm' grammar (cf. Hudson, 1973). Word grammar stands in the same relation to group grammar as group grammar does to clause grammar — groups consist of words and clauses consist of groups. Further, syntax and morphology, i.e., clauses, groups, words, and morphemes, both stand in the same kind of realizational relation to phonology.

The rank-based constituency of systemic-functional grammar (and phonology) differs from the immediate constituency of formal grammar (and phonology). The former is associated with minimal functional bracketing, while the latter works with maximal bracketing in terms of grammatical classes (Hudson, 1971; Halliday, 1985a: Ch. 1). The nature of constituents has been important in developing a framework for associating them with semantic correlates; see below.

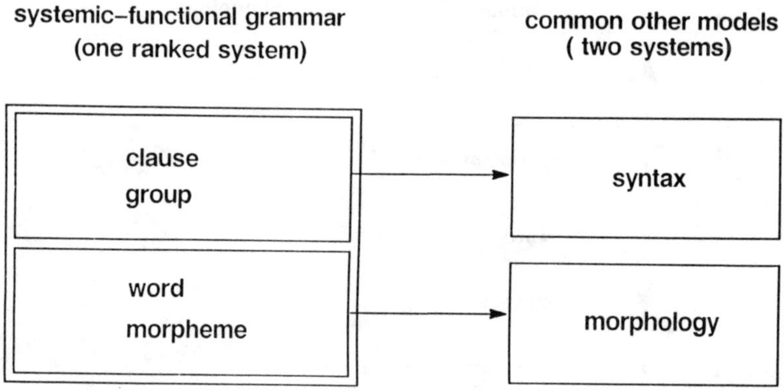


**Figure 5.10** Systemic-functional grammar and alternative

The resources of grammar and semantics are diversified according to the metafunctions presented above in Section 5.6. Within each metafunction they are distributed across the different classes of unit of each rank. It is thus possible to specify a 'map' of the resources, locating each one according to its metafunctional and rank 'address'. Thus, we have as an example the following organization for English:

| | ideational | interpersonal | textual |
|---|---|---|---|
| clause | TRANSITIVITY | MOOD | THEME |
| group, verb | TENSE | MODALITY | VOICE |
| group, nom. | MODIFICATION | PERSON | DETERMINATION |

Each of the identified resources, TRANSITIVITY, TENSE, MOOD, etc. is a functional region of the lexicogrammar of English that can be described in relative isolation from the others. This scheme has been used extensively in modularizing the Nigel grammar of English that we will see in detail in Chapter 6. It remains, however, a simplified illustration; for more detailed accounts of English, see Halliday (1985a) and Matthiessen (1990b).

It is also worth noting that rank-like organization is reflected in knowledge representation in AI in the framework of scripts, and especially now in the more modular 'memory organization packets' (e.g., Schank and Abelson, 1977; Schank, 1982; Schank and Kass, 1988).

## 5.9 Synoptic and dynamic

The dimensions and categories of the theory outlined above serve in a characterization of the linguistic system at rest — a static or SYNOPTIC

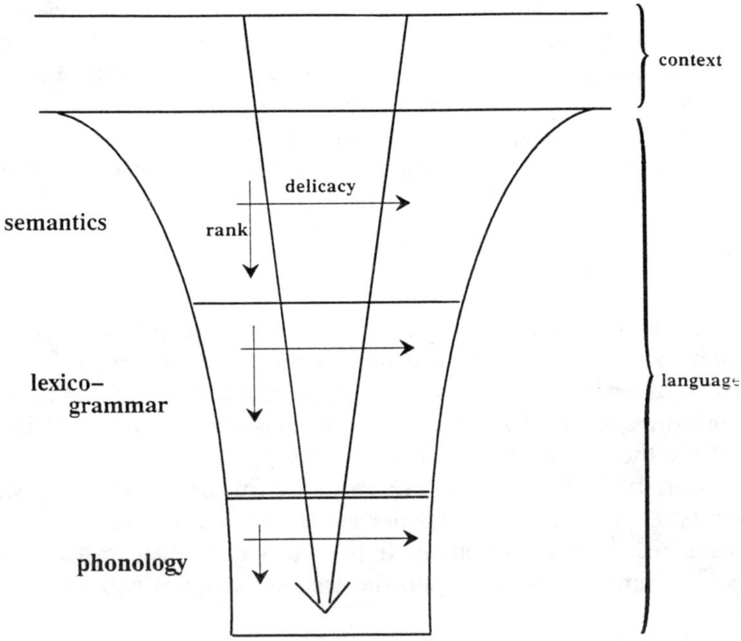


**Figure 5.11** Activation

view of the potential of the system, of the resource that the system offers. But the theory also has to take account of the actualization of the potential. In the context of text generation, this means that the theory has to specify the constructs from which generation algorithms can be built. In general, it is assumed that if it is sequential, actualization of the system potential means

(i) moving down the stratal organization; and
(ii) within a given stratum, moving towards increasing delicacy and decreasing rank.

Furthermore, it is assumed that the metafunctions are, in principle, activated in parallel. A graphic representation of activation is given in Figure 5.11.

The overall directions of the activation 'movements' are the predominant ones; they do not exclude operations such as shunting between strata and moving backwards in delicacy from a preselected feature in a system network to determine what features it presupposes, both of which, as we shall see in Chapter 6, are frequently required.

The activation of the system potential is an area where a good deal of work is needed and issues associated with a DYNAMIC view of the linguistic system and the context in which it is embedded have come into focus in current systemic research (cf., e.g., Bateman, 1989a; Martin, 1985; O'Donnell, 1989a; Tsui, 1989; Ventola, 1984, 1987). We will introduce generation algorithms in Chapter 6 and then develop more the relationship between computational algorithms and linguistic theory in Chapter 11.

## 5.10 Functional variation

We have met two fundamental principles of the organization of language in context as they are conceived of in systemic theory, stratification and functional diversification. We now need to take account of *variation* within the linguistic system. Two basic types of language variation are identified in systemic theory (see e.g. Halliday *et al.*, 1964; Gregory, 1967; Gregory and Carroll, 1978; Halliday, 1978): DIALECT (including sociolect) variation and REGISTER variation. The former is variation according to user and has long been recognized, of course. It is of less immediate concern in work on text generation at present than the second, which is variation according to use.

This second type is a generalization of the traditional notion of *genre*; it is an outgrowth of Firth's conception of RESTRICTED LANGUAGES (cf. also the Prague School notion of functional dialect; e.g. Havránek, 1932). Halliday (1978: 35) characterizes a register as 'what you are speaking (at the time), determined by what you are doing (nature of social activity being engaged in), and expressing diversity of social processes (social division of labour)'. A register is determined by the contextual variables field, tenor, and mode. The theory of functional variation of this kind is register theory.

As we described in Chapter 3, register variation is of fundamental importance in text generation and coming to grips with register variation is one of the major challenges we are faced with: full text generation systems (as opposed to sentence generator components) are always very restricted in register; they are story generators, stock market generators, weather forecast generators, game commentary generators, and so on.

Different registers constitute different principles of using the linguistic system; they have different text structures (generic structures – described below) and different semantic systems. The different uses occur in different contexts of situation and the different semantices interface these different uses with one unified lexicogrammar; these relationships are depicted in Figure 5.12.

The approach of setting up situation-specific semantic systems as a way of interfacing between specific uses and the generalized grammar is one of

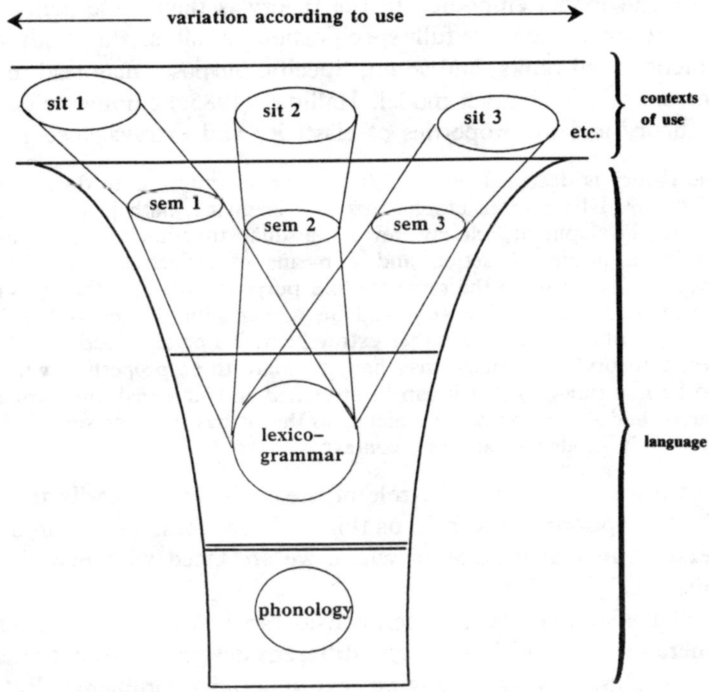


**Figure 5.12** Functional variation

the approaches to semantics in systemic linguistics. It has been used in text generation and we will return to it in Part IV.

## 5.11 Flexibility

The dimensions and categories of systemic theory that we have now introduced do not lead to a unique, restrictive model. That is not their purpose; rather they are intended to provide the linguist with a 'flex-model' so that he or she can play off strata, ranks, axes, and so on against one another. In the practice of analysing language use and understanding, we require a framework that can reveal to us as much of the organization that motivates that language as is possible. Systemic-functional linguistics takes the standpoint that language is only revealed in its systematicity and patterning along many simultaneous dimensions. Focusing on overly narrow descriptions then runs the risk of destroying the very phenomenon we wish to understand.[14]

The overall model embodied in the theory is then quite deliberately an extravagant one: there is full specification at all strata, both axes, all metafunctions, all ranks, and so on. Specific purposes may lead to reduced versions of the full abstract model. Halliday (1985c) comments on the role of the theory and its properties of elasticity and extravagance:

> Systemic theory is designed not so much to prove things as to do things. It is a form of praxis. I have often emphasized that language, both in nature and in its ontogenetic development, clearly reveals a dual function; it is at once, and inseparably, a means of action and a means of reflection. Linguistics, as a metalanguage, has to serve the same twofold purpose. Systemic theory is explicitly constructed both for thinking with and for acting with. Hence — like language, again — it is rather elastic and rather extravagant. To be an effective tool for these purposes, a theory of language may have to share these properties with language itself: to be non-rigid, so that it can be stretched and squeezed into various shapes as required, and to be non-parsimonious, so that it has more power at its disposal than is actually needed in any one context.

To this we would add that the role of theory is not primarily to constrain possible descriptions but to help us think of new ones. This is an important consideration in text generation where we are faced with new descriptive problems.

As we have seen, there has been considerable variation in the designs of text generators. In certain respects, different designs represent alternative, mutually exclusive ways of solving text generation problems. But, at the same time, the differences are often due to the partialness of the models: to put it in terms of the full systemic model, they may be designed for one register, they may give priority to one of the metafunctions (always the ideational one), they may give priority to ideational lexis over grammar, and so on.

## 5.12 Summary

In this chapter we have introduced in some detail the principal dimensions and categories of systemic linguistics, explaining how these interrelate to provide a rich multidimensional view of language that can cast considerable light on the many problems of text generation in particular, and of language in general.[15] In the remainder of our discussion, we will explore various aspects of the theory we have just sketched in the context of text generation. In the remainder of this part of the book, we will stay at the lexicogrammatical stratum and its interface to higher strata of organization. In Part III, we will take a closer look at the metafunctions and then move to the question of how to organize context. Part IV then problematizes and explores dynamic grammar and the influence of context on grammar.

## 5.13 Supplemental: systemics and computational linguistics: some points of contact

| Systemics | Computational linguistics/AI | |
|---|---|---|
| | Implementation of systemic notion | Independent, similar abstraction |
| Language as resource: network of interrelated options | | Organization of situations in problem solving (Patten, 1988a) |
| System network | Henrici (1965) | discrimination net, decision tree, lexical discrimination nets (Goldman, 1975); feature structures (Kasper, 1987a; Emele and Zajac, 1990); classification in knowledge representation (MacGregor and Bates, 1987) |
| Stratal organization | | arguments about levels of organization: Hovy *et al.* (1988) |
| Systemic lexicogrammar | Winograd (1972) Davey (1978) McCord (1977) Patten (1988) Nigel (Part II) Kyoto system (Part II) Fawcett and Tucker (1990) | cf.: Kay's (1979) FUG (and other 'unification-based' grammars) |
| Unit | | frame |
| Cohesion | Granville (1983) | |
| Systemic semantics: situation specific | Patten (1988a) | precompiling of knowledge in problem solving (Patten 1988b) |
| functional variation: register | Bateman and Paris (1989) | sublanguages in MT (Kittredge and Lehrberger, 1982); 'micro-worlds' (cf. Winograd, 1972) |
| Metafunctional organization | (in systemic generators to varying degrees) | — |
| textual | | 'focus': Grosz (1978), Sidner (1981), McKeown (1982), McCoy and Cheng (1990) |

| | |
|---|---|
| Context: field | knowledge base domain models |
| tenor | user models (see references under 'user modelling': Section 2.5) |
| Context: situation type | 'scripted' situation (Schank and Abelson, 1977) |
| Generic structure potential | rhetorical schemas (McKeown, 1982) |

## Notes

1. Perhaps the clearest exception is Patten's (1988a) system which draws on systemic theory for both its grammar and its semantics; but his system does not generate extended text so it does not apply a theory of text structuring.
2. This will obviously be obscured if we have not explored the semantic naturalness of grammar; see below.
3. It is helpful to model the ordering in terms of the vertical dimension in an abstract symbolic space.
4. This stratum is graphology in written language; cf. Halliday (1985b).
5. The semantics and lexicogrammar together correspond to Hjelmslev's (1943) content plane and the third to his expression plane. That is, the line of arbitrariness runs between lexicogrammar and phonology but not between semantics and lexicogrammar; lexicogrammar is functionally natural in relation to semantics. This has been taken up again recently — although in a rather more restricted form due to different views of 'grammar' — in work such as that of Jackendoff (1983, 1987, 1990), Langacker (1987), and Talmy (1987). This we characterize as the 'decoding' approach to semantics in Chapter 12.
6. The opening up of semantics in the diagram is meant to indicate that this stratum serves to interface with a multiplicity of uses; see Section 5.10 below.
7. The organization of 'context' is not necessarily a stratal one in the same way as the overall organization of the linguistic system is. In particular, Martin (e.g. 1985) has built a model using Hjelmslev's (1943) notion of *konnotationssprog*, 'connotative language'. A *konnotationssprog* has language as its expression plane.
8. American stratification theory follows European work in this respect.
9. We will return briefly to the concept of metarule in Section 6.1 below.
10. Striking examples of this can now be found in the explicit hierarchies that appear when classifying, for example, lexical rules in HPSG (cf. Pollard and Sag, 1987). We discuss this exciting development briefly in the conclusion as an area where future convergence may be expected.
11. Compare also the syntactic descriptions designed by Bates and Ingria (1981) as a superimposition on their transformational generation grammar for the purpose of controlling the application of phrase structure and transformation rules.
12. In particular, they do not allow for disjunction; nor do they represent simultaneous choice alternatives. Other forms of taxonomic representations

developed in AI can handle disjunctions — frame-based inheritance networks such as NIKL and LOOM (see Chapter 9) — and such networks might well serve as the basis for representing systemic-like grammars (cf. Kasper, 1989b). More recent developments in unification-based formalisms are also expanding their representational capabilities in this direction and so might also be candidates for formal representations of system networks (cf. Emele and Zajac, 1990).

13. Since these are stratally distinct and separated by the line of arbitrariness, there is no necessary correspondence between the two rank scales. In the unmarked case, the English clause corresponds to the tone group, but this is the only correspondence; and there are also marked mappings.
14. A perhaps useful analogy can be drawn here with AI research in vision. Early work based on extremely impoverished sources of input have generally given way to rich input situations where a more sophisticated comprehension system can draw upon many cues in order to recover the meaning of what is being seen (cf. Marr, 1982).
15. It should be noted that there are other dimensions of interest within systemic linguistics that we have not described here, for example: probabilistic systems (Nesbitt and Plum, 1988), evolving instantial systems that are constructed in the course of interaction (Halliday, 1988).

# 6 The theoretical framework in action: generation with a systemic grammar

In the previous chapter we introduced the basic organizational dimensions of systemic-functional theory. Now we present in detail the application of the framework of grammar in the context of computational implementation — in particular in the context of the Penman text generation system and the Kyoto grammars. The Penman project started around 1979/80 and was a continuation of a research effort into text generation led by Bill Mann (KDS: see Chapter 2) and the Kyoto project started in the spring of 1985. The computational instantiation of the theory we describe in this chapter was developed in the Penman text generation project for its grammar component Nigel and was subsequently also applied in the initial construction of the Kyoto grammars.

The Nigel grammar component was the first part of Penman to be worked on: the original version of it was provided by Michael Halliday in the summer of 1980. The framework was close to the version of systemic grammar worked out earlier by Halliday (1969, 1970, 1976b). Although there have been some additions, the basic framework used within Penman has remained the same — for accounts, see also e.g.: Mann (1983b), Mann and Matthiessen (1985), and Matthiessen (1985). The description encoded in the framework was a clause grammar of English consisting of about 80 systems. Since then, we have worked with the help of Halliday and other systemic linguists to extend and revise the clause grammar and add clause complexes, nominal groups, prepositional phrases, and so on. The grammar now consists of 600–650 systems. It is a very large grammar by computational linguistic standards, covering each of the functional regions specified in Section 5.8 above.

The grammars of the Kyoto project — first of Japanese (by Genichiro Kikui, Atsuchi Tabuchi, and Bateman) and later of Chinese (by Li Hang) — also began by following the organization established for Nigel. Thus, our detailed introduction of systemic grammar in this chapter will essentially employ the terminology used within Nigel.

We begin with a detailed description of the basic grammatical resources of a computational systemic-functional grammar — concentrating primarily on the stratum of lexicogrammar and its interface to higher-level strata.

## 6.1 The system network as principle of organization

Within all strata of the linguistic system the principle of choice is crucial. This paradigmatic organization is captured by the construct of the system network, which represents a set of interrelated choices. The stratum of grammar is no exception: it is represented as a large directed acyclic graph whose nodes are choice points, called SYSTEMS. The excerpt from the system network of TRANSITIVITY (including here determination of process type) and MOOD regions of the grammar of English shown in Figure 6.1 will serve as a simple example.

The system network above consists of eight systems, whose names are capitalized. Each system has two or more TERMS or output features representing a grammatical alternation, such as indicative/imperative in the system MOOD TYPE. In addition, each has an ENTRY CONDITION, such as the feature clauses in the leftmost system RANK which serves as entry condition for both the PROCESS TYPE and MOOD TYPE systems. The entry condition may be a simple feature (clause, interrogative) or a complex of features (for example, the disjunction declarative/imperative in the system TAGGING).

Given an algorithm for traversing it (see Section 6.5 below), the system network can be used to generate grammatical *paradigmatic specifications*; for instance, the following paradigmatic specifications, or sets of possible feature selections, can be generated:

clauses: material & indicative: interrogative: wh-

clauses: (relational: intensive & ascriptive) & declarative: tagged

The system network does *not* generate grammatical structures; the 'bare' system network represents a purely paradigmatic grammar and it needs a realization component to produce grammatical structures. The result of each 'pass' through a system network is simply the complete set of grammatical features that uniquely distinguishes that unit from all others that the network describes. These features position the linguistic unit in the paradigmatic space of possibilities defined by the network: i.e., they classify the linguistic unit along many distinct simultaneous dimensions of functional potential so as to uniquely pinpoint the function the unit serves.

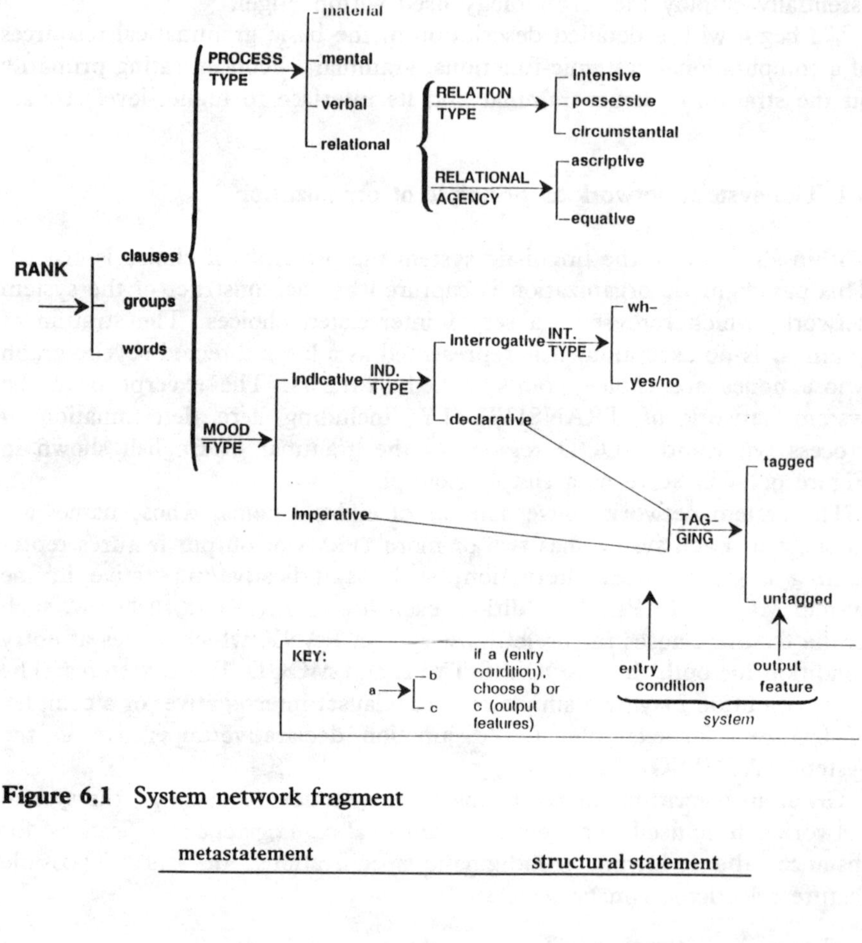


**Figure 6.1** System network fragment

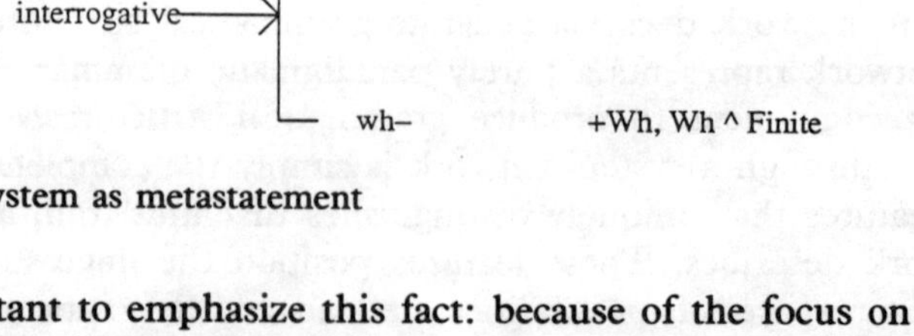


**Figure 6.2** System as metastatement

It is important to emphasize this fact: because of the focus on structure in many approaches to syntax, the system network has sometimes been taken to be a syntagmatic rule formalism comparable to phrase structure rules.[1] If we want to look at the system network from the point of view of structure, it is much less misleading to think of it as a metastatement comparable to the much more recent notion of metarule in Generalized Phrase Structure Grammar (Gazdar *et al.*, 1985); cf. Figure 6.2. That is: the structure fragments Finite ^ Subject (i.e., the grammatical element labelled as Finite is constrained to occur immediately to the left of the element labelled as Subject) and Wh ^ Finite (i.e., the element labelled as Wh is constrained to occur immediately to the left of the element labelled as Finite) are opposed as the alternatives 'yes/no' vs. 'wh-' in interrogative clauses. The notion of 'meta' indicates the relationship between system network and structure; it is a symbolic one, not a compositional one, and realization is necessary to relate the two.

## 6.2 Beyond the system network

Systemic grammars in general, then, have a paradigmatic base. Since the systemic network represents the paradigmatic organization, this means that the system network is the fundamental organizing principle of the grammar. It is also the locus of three additional types of specification which we introduce in detail in the sections following below:

(i) 'alongside': the organization of the other axis, syntagmatic organization, is specified by means of realization statements associated with features. In this respect, the grammar contrasts with one operating by means of independent[2] syntagmatic rules such as phrase structure rules.
(ii) 'above': the organization of the semantic stratum above the grammar is handled by means of choosers associated with systems. In this respect, the model contrasts with one in which the semantic stratum is represented by a global network. This area of the framework is an extension that has been made in the context of text generation.
(iii) 'through': the network has to be interpreted in order to generate and this involves specifying traversal algorithms by which generation may proceed. This is also an area that has only been made fully explicit in the context of computational accounts and text generation in particular.

Realization statements were already part of early systemic-functional grammar (see, e.g., Halliday, 1969); the type of systemic semantics indicated in (ii) was developed in the context of the Penman project, as was the traversal algorithm mentioned in (iii).

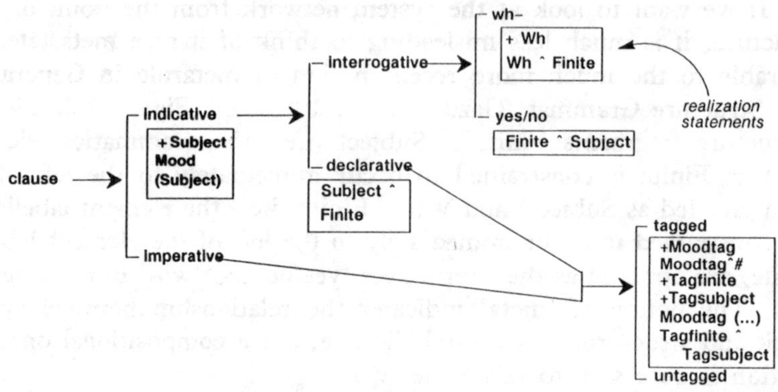


**Figure 6.3** System network with realization statements

## 6.3 'Alongside' the system network: realization statements

Any feature in a system network may have an associated REALIZATION STATEMENT specifying a fragment of syntagmatic organization. The feature constitutes the paradigmatic context for the realization statements associated with it.

### *6.3.1 Addition of realization statements*

Recall the system network presented in Figure 6.1. We can now use it as an example of the paradigmatic base for syntagmatic specifications. Realization statements are written inside boxes in the diagram in Figure 6.3. (We have left out the systems PROCESS TYPE, RELATION TYPE, and RELATIONAL AGENCY from Figure 6.1.)

As noted, a realization statement specifies a structural fragment in the context of a feature of the system network. For example, the feature 'indicative' has the realization statement +Subject, which means 'insert the grammatical function Subject' and ensures the presence of Subjects in indicative clauses. This is the way grammatical structure is handled within systemic grammars of this type; i.e., structure is built up in terms of functionally labelled constituents that are first introduced and then manipulated by a variety of realization statements that are triggered in the contexts of particular paradigmatic environments, as captured by the grammatical features of the system network. All realization statements are specified in the context of systemic features.

Let us now consider realization statements in more detail.

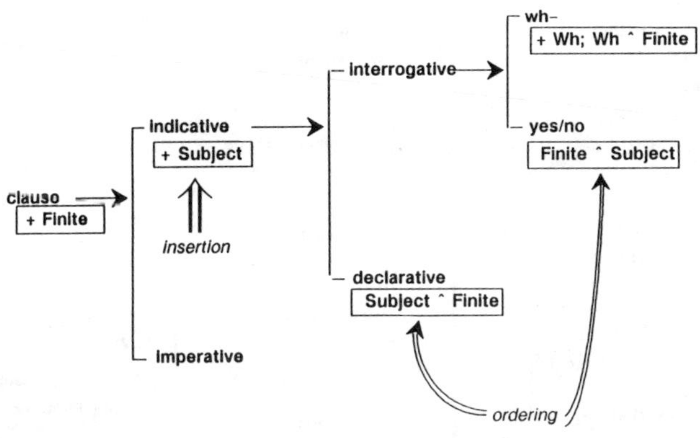


**Figure 6.4** Paradigmatic contexts for realization

### *6.3.2 Paradigmatic conditioning of realization statements*

Realizations are associated with systemic features, their realization CONDITIONS. That is, the context in which a realization is applicable and is applied during generation is defined paradigmatically rather than syntagmatically: a feature in the system network is re-expressed (realized) syntagmatically. For instance, we can look in Figure 6.4 at the paradigmatic contexts in which realization statements involving Subject and Finite are specified. Insertion of the functions (+Finite, +Subject) and ordering of them in relation to one another (Subject ^ Finite, etc.) are stated in different paradigmatic contexts.

The function Finite is inserted in the context 'clause' but it is ordered in the contexts 'declarative', 'yes/no', and 'wh-'. Similarly, Subject is inserted in the context 'indicative' but is ordered in the contexts 'declarative' and 'yes/no'. Insertion and ordering statements thus occur in different paradigmatic contexts. This separation in the specification of structure illustrates a general principle. Realization statements specify 'minimal' aspects of syntagmatic organization; for example:

(i) the presence of a function and its ordering are specified by different realization statements;
(ii) The presence of a function and the nature of its realization are specified by different realization statements; and
(iii) the presence of a function and the identification with other functions are specified by different realization statements.

The example with Subject and Finite illustrates the first observation: the presence of Finite is specified as a realization of the feature 'clause', the

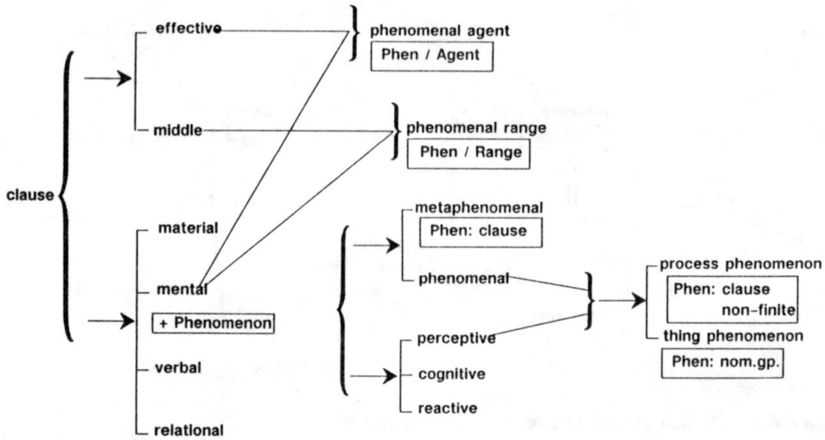


**Figure 6.5** Realizations involving Phenomenon

presence of Subject as a realization of 'indicative' and different relative orderings of the two in the contexts of 'yes/no' and 'declarative'.[3] The other two observations about separate specifications of presence and other properties are both illustrated in the following example involving the Phenomenon (abbreviated as Phen in Figure 6.5) in a mental clause, i.e., the object of perception.

The function Phenomenon is inserted in the context of 'mental'.[4] However, its 'conflation' with Agent or Range and the specifications of how it is to be realized are postponed to more delicate paradigmatic contexts. For example, if Phenomenon is a process, it is realized by a non-finite clause, as in *we saw* <u>*him sign the treaty*</u>. The first feature here is 'mental', since a process of sensing (seeing) is to be represented. That selection opens up two simultaneous options. One is concerned with the type of phenomenon that enters into the senser's consciousness — is it a fact, in which case 'metaphenomenal' is chosen, or an ordinary, first-order phenomenon, in which case 'phenomenal' is selected? The process of him signing the treaty is not a fact (contrast *we saw that he had signed the treaty*); it is a first-order phenomenon. The other option has to do with the type of mental process. The process of seeing is a kind of perceptive process. The conjunction of 'perceptive' and 'phenomenal' constitutes the entry condition to another system, which differentiates between two different types of first-order phenomena. If the phenomenon is a composite configuration of a process plus participants, 'process phenomenon' is selected; if it is a simple phenomenon, 'thing phenomenon' is the choice. The process of him signing the treaty is a composite of a process (signing)

| paradigmatic feature<br>realization condition | realization statement | | syntagmatic result |
|---|---|---|---|
| | realization operator | arguments | |
| declarative | (Order | Subject Finite) | Subject ^ Finite |
| effective | (Insert | Agent) | Agent |
| metaphenomenal | (Preselect | Phenomenon clause) | Phenomenon: clause |

**Figure 6.6** Examples of realization statements

plus participants (him, the treaty), so 'process phenomenon' is selected. The specification of the type of Phenomenon has now become delicate enough to determine how Phenomenon is to be realized, viz. by a non-finite clause — Phenomenon: clause, non-finite. (Whether this clause is infinitival or participial — *him sign the treaty/him signing the treaty* — is a still more delicate decision, which is not represented in the system network above.)

We can note in passing that the example above suggests how the grammar can be extended towards lexical delicacy with systems such as 'perceptive/cognitive/reactive'. It also shows that such extensions are often both grammatically and lexically motivated, which is obscured if lexis and grammar are separated.

### *6.3.3 The form of a realization statement*

Realizations are given as REALIZATION STATEMENTS consisting of one realization OPERATOR and one or more arguments, which are functions or features. The application of a realization statement produces a SYNTAGMATIC RESULT; Figure 6.6 sets this out in more detail. All realization statements have features as realization conditions. The nature of the operator and the type of argument depend on the specific kind of realization.

### *6.3.4 General types of realization statement*

There are two kinds of intrastratal realization,[5] viz. (i) interaxis realization and (ii) interrank realization. Both have a function as the first argument of the realization operator, but in the case of interrank realization, the second

| | **realization statement** | | | **syntagmatic result** — executed at |
|---|---|---|---|---|
| | **realization operator** | **argument** function | **argument** function/feature | |
| (i) interaxis | | | *function* | *current traversal* |
| | (Insert | Agent) | | Agent |
| | (Order | Subject | Finite) | Subject ^ Finite |
| | (Conflate | Agent | Subject) | Agent/Subject |
| | (Expand | Mood | Subject) | Mood (Subject) |
| (ii) interrank | | | *feature* | *subsequent traversal* |
| | (Preselect | Phenomenon | clause) | Phenomenon: clause |

**Figure 6.7** Argument types and cycle of execution

argument is a feature. The specification given by an interaxis realization is executed within the traversal through the grammar in which it occurs. The specification given in an interrank realization anticipates a subsequent traversal cycle and it is not executed until that cycle. These differences are shown in Figure 6.7.

The only realization statement in the figure of which we have not seen an example so far is EXPAND — this provides a means for creating structure *within* ranks of the grammar. The example given in the figure shows the expansion of a clause-level constituent labelled as the Mood to itself contain a subconstituent labelled as the Subject. This is one means of capturing the fact that in certain contexts functions from a single level of structure may group together structurally without necessarily providing a constituent that has full rank status: there is no network that has as its point of entry a slot of Mood.

(i) INTERAXIS realization is directed from systemic feature selections to function structure specifications but not from structure to feature: since the grammar has a paradigmatic base, structures are determined by paradigms. It takes the form of realization statements that specify structure fragments in terms of one or two grammatical functions and are associated with features in the system network. For example, the feature declarative in the system declarative/interrogative has the realization statement (Order Subject Finite) associated with it. If the feature is chosen, the realization statement is executed.

(ii) While interaxis realizations are executed fully within one traversal of the grammar, INTERRANK realizations are preselections of features at a lower rank and these preselections do not become actual selections until the grammar has been re-entered and a subsequent traversal of it has started.

## 6.4 'Above' the system network: choosers and inquiries

Another early need for a grammar that was to function as part of a computational text generation system was to create a framework that provided for semantic control of the grammar in a purposeful way and that could relate it to other parts of the planned generator. In 1981, a sketch of a semantic interface for the systemic grammar, the *chooser and inquiry framework*, or more simply, INQUIRY SEMANTICS, was developed — see further Mann (1983a) and Matthiessen (1981, 1985, 1988b). This interface has now been built up for the whole grammar. One of the side-effects of this work was a presentation of the semantics of English tense using systemic grammar and the chooser and inquiry framework (Matthiessen, 1984); we will use this as an example of generation below. Inquiry semantics is one approach to the semantic stratum; we will compare it with another in Chapter 12.

### *6.4.1 The association of choosers with systems*

Semantic control in Nigel is organized in terms of the grammatical system network: each system has an associated CHOOSER. Choosers are drawn as ovals in the diagram in Figure 6.8; the associations to systems are represented by vertical lines. A chooser is a semantic procedure which knows how to make a purposeful choice among the features of the system it is associated with. It makes the choice by asking one or more questions, called INQUIRIES, thus obtaining the information relevant to the decision. Choosers and their inquiries belong to the semantic interface in Nigel. The diagram in Figure 6.8 is thus an enlargement of part of the Nigel box in Figure 2.2. The double line represents the boundary within Nigel between the chooser and inquiry interface and the systemic grammar.

### *6.4.2 The internal organization of a chooser*

We have seen that choosers are associated with systems in the system network: the global organization of the semantic process of choosing is organized by the grammatical system network. We have also suggested that

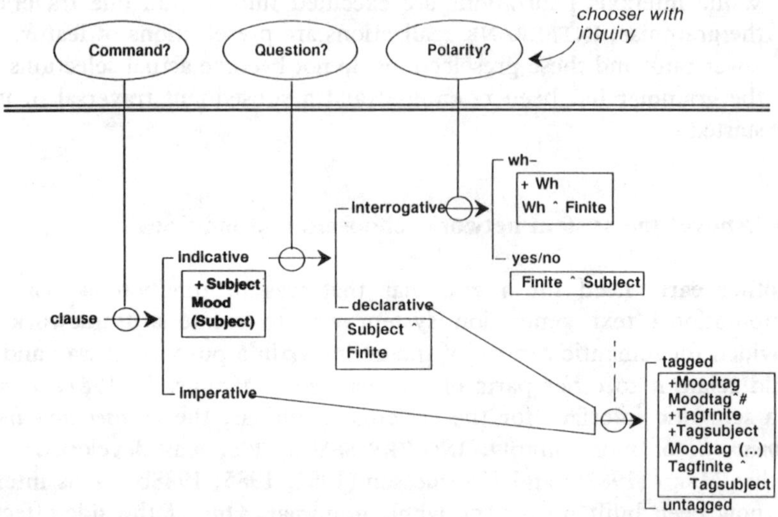


**Figure 6.8** System network with choosers and realization statements

the choosers do their job by presenting inquiries and selecting features in their systems according to the responses. This selection is interstratal realization — preselection from semantics to lexicogrammar. We will now look in some more detail at the internal organization of a chooser.

A chooser is organized as a decision tree. Each node in this tree corresponds to a branching inquiry and the branches that leave the node are the set of possible responses. As an illustration of a simple chooser, let us consider the MOOD TYPE chooser, the first chooser of the MOOD part of the clause network diagrammed in Figure 6.8. It uses the branching inquiry CommandQ to obtain the information needed to choose between indicative and imperative.

The MOOD TYPE chooser contains only this branching inquiry, since it fully determines the possible choices in the system.[6] If the response is COMMAND, the feature imperative is chosen, and if the response is NON-COMMAND, the feature indicative is chosen. Abbreviating the inquiry as (CommandQ MOOD), we can represent the chooser as shown in Figure 6.9. If the response is 'command', the variable Subject is identified with the response to (CommandResponsibleID MOOD) and the grammatical feature imperative is chosen. If the response is 'not command', the feature indicative is chosen.

The inquiry CommandResponsibleID is an identifying inquiry and does not affect the decision tree organization of the chooser. Identifying

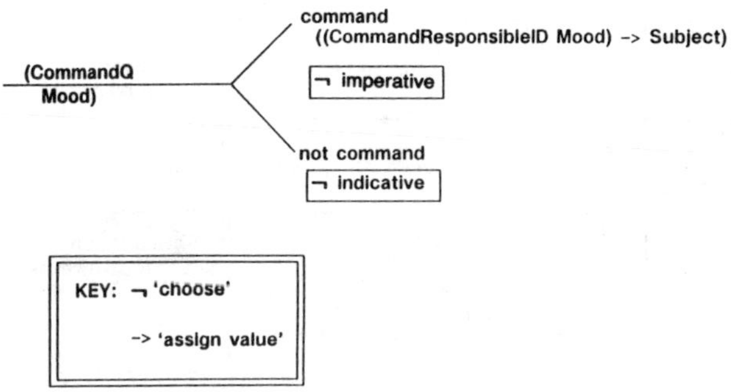


**Figure 6.9** The organization of a chooser

inquiries can occur after a response to a branching inquiry, as in the example, and they can also occur before a branching inquiry is asked. The inquiry CommandResponsibleID serves to give a value to Subject when the response to CommandQ is COMMAND (i.e., in imperative clauses):

What entity is specified as responsible for the realization of the process being commanded by MOOD?

For instance, in the environmental representation of a clause such as *Wash the asparagus carefully*, the addressee would be identified as being responsible for the realization of the process of washing.

We see then that a chooser is organized as a decision tree. The branching points are defined by branching inquiries and the branches by the responses. In addition, a chooser may contain identifying inquiries, occurring before the root of a chooser or embedded under a response branch, and it contains a realization statement, a choose statement, embedded under each terminal branch.[7]

Although most choosers use inquiries to obtain the information needed to make a principled choice, there are choosers without inquiries. They consist of only a choose operator. This choose operator is different from the normal one in that it can be overruled by a preselection within the grammar without a resulting conflict. It is called DEFAULTCHOOSE and is used to specify the feature to be chosen in a system when there is no preselection to identify the feature to be chosen. DefaultChoose is thus a way of specifying a feature as the unmarked or default choice. For example, the chooser of the system PRONOUN CASE is '(DefaultChoose oblique)', which means that the feature oblique is chosen unless a preselection provides the reason for another choice.

The possible components of a chooser are summarized in Figure 6.10. As specified above, the chooser of MOOD TYPE will only select 'imperative'

<table>
<tr><td>branching</td><td>branch</td><td>branching inquiry</td><td rowspan="2">inquiry<br>(upwards)</td></tr>
<tr><td rowspan="3">non-branching</td><td>identify</td><td>identifying inquiry</td></tr>
<tr><td rowspan="2">choose</td><td>Choose</td><td rowspan="2">realization<br>(downwards)</td></tr>
<tr><td>DefaultChoose</td></tr>
</table>

**Figure 6.10** Chooser components

if a command is issued. Assume we also want to account for offers such as *have another piece of cake*; *take my car*; *drop in any time*. One way to include them is to add another branching inquiry, Say OfferQ, to the chooser under the response NON-COMMAND, which gives us a two-branch decision tree. We will meet further examples of complex choosers in Chapter 7 and we will discuss extensions to the simple organization of inquiries presented here in Part III.

## 6.5 'Through' the system network: the generation algorithm

Having dealt in some detail with the system network at rest, we will now turn to the actualization of it. To use the system network and the grammar in general in generation, we need a dynamic model of how to activate the grammar: we need for the computational context an explicit statement of precisely how systems are to be entered, their choices made, and the effects of these choices realized as structure fragments. This model is represented by a GENERATION ALGORITHM, which controls the successive generation of grammatical units. This is concerned with the dynamic organization of a system network in the sense that it defines the *process* of generation rather than the static statement of possibility presented by the network at rest.

### *6.5.1 Overview*

We know what the abstractions — i.e., the ranks, functions, systems, and structures — of the grammar at rest are. The question is what the basic abstractions of a dynamic model are. We have much less experience to fall back on in linguistics. Indeed, this is an area of systemic theory that has

| potential | actualization (process) | actualized (product : recorded states) |
|---|---|---|

**Figure 6.11** The three aspects of generation

been 'targeted' for development (as noted earlier, cf. Martin, 1985; and Halliday, 1985b). All we can hope to do at this stage is point to some of the abstraction we will have to take account of, as we discuss the generation algorithm.

The underlying assumption is that there is a distinction between grammatical resources — the potential — and the process of actualizing the grammar — the generation algorithm: cf. Section 5.9 and Chapter 11. Furthermore, the process will yield products, i.e., new states. The three aspects of generation are diagrammed in Figure 6.11.

There will also be subtasks, or subprocesses, organized in terms of the potential. These will be differentiated according to the various aspects of that potential. Their primary task is to activate the potential and to record the resulting state. They thus refer to the potential but they also operate on resulting states to keep track of the progress made in activating the potential and to change one state into another by adding further specifications. (No records are ever changed other than by the addition of specifications nor are parts of records ever erased.)[8]

In addition to the differentiation of subprocesses according to task, we need to specify how subprocesses are ordered. A number of orderings will be determined inherently in terms of the organization of the potential, such as the partial ordering of systems in the system network, by a producer–consumer kind of logic: producers come before consumers. For instance, features have to be selected before they can be realized. However, the potential underspecifies the ordering of generation processes. For example, while systems are ordered by the system network and have to be entered according to that ordering, they are only partially ordered since they may also be simultaneous — as are PROCESS TYPE and MOOD TYPE in Figure 6.1. above. Furthermore, while relative ordering may be determined, the immediacy of the succession is not. For instance, realization may be immediate (follow immediately after the selection of a feature) or it may be delayed to some later point.

The underspecification of the ordering of generation processes by the potential is not a drawback at all but rather a very important opportunity for parallelism in generation; we discuss this further in Chapter 10 below. The current generation algorithm, however, is a sequential one and we have to impose sequential orderings even where they are not inherently necessary.

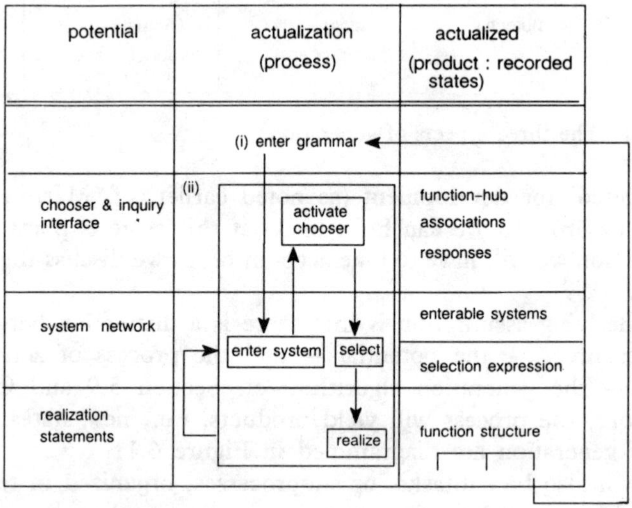


**Figure 6.12** Grammar entry and traversal in generation

We can divide the generation algorithm into two major processes, viz.:

(i) GRAMMAR ENTRY: the grammar is entered for each unit (clause, nominal group, etc.) to be generated; each grammar entry is followed by (ii);

(ii) GRAMMAR TRAVERSAL: the grammatical system network is traversed, which means that systems are entered and features are selected, and in the course of this traversal choosers are activated and realization statements are executed.

The generation process is summarized diagrammatically in Figure 6.12.

When the grammar has been entered (grammar entry: (i)), the grammar traversal is started (ii). The first system whose entry conditions has been satisfied, i.e. all the grammatical features specified in its input condition as required have indeed been selected, is entered, and then its chooser is activated. The chooser obtains the information needed to select one of the features of the system. Once the feature has been selected, any associated realization statements may be executed (either immediately or at some later time as specified by the details of the generation algorithm employed). This process of system entry is repeated and continues until the system network has been fully traversed and all enterable systems, i.e. all systems whose entry conditions have been satisfied, have been entered. When the traversal has been completed, the grammar can be re-entered for each constituent that has been generated.

We will now discuss the basic generation algorithm in some more detail, starting with grammar entry.

### 6.5.2 *Grammar entry*

In order for the grammar to be traversed, it has to be entered first. Each grammar entry leads to one grammar traversal undertaken to develop one grammatical unit of a particular type (a clause, a nominal group, etc.). The general principles determining grammar entry as implemented within the Nigel grammar are as follows.

(i) Grammar entry is *rank-descendant*; it is ordered by the rank scale and proceeds down this scale. The rank-descendant approach contrasts with a rank-ascendant one; the first is 'top–down' and the second is 'bottom–up'. The choice of the rank-descendant approach is quite natural in a functional, clause-based grammar as opposed to a word-based one.

(ii) Another dimension of variability here is that between *breadth first* generation and *depth first* generation; again, this is a design decision of the specification of traversal and is not constrained by the specification of the grammar at the level of detail at which it is specified in Nigel.

(iii) When more than one unit of the same rank is waiting to be developed, the grammar is entered again and again (serially, not in parallel) to develop them in linear sequence from left to right. Note that this is an additional specification, it is not intrinsic to the mechanism that they are developed left to right; as far as the mechanism is concerned they could equally well be realized right to left or in random order. To proceed from left to right is therefore a design decision which can be considered as having theoretical import of its own — before the need to specify the generation algorithm with this kind of precision that came with computational implementation, this kind of theoretical issue was not raised so centrally.

(iv) The grammar is only re-entered after a grammar traversal has been completed; entry and traversal are not interleaved. This means that in the current grammar one traversal of the grammar that has started can never be affected by a subsequent traversal. In fact, the only means of communication between traversals is preselection.

### 6.5.3 *Grammar traversal*

The heart of the grammar traversal is the system entry that controls the traversal of the system network itself. There are two other aspects of the grammar traversal: chooser activation and realization.

*6.5.3.1 System entry* The general bounds on the traversal algorithm are set by the organization of the system network. The traversal has to abide by the partial ordering of the systems of the network. As far as partially ordered systems are concerned, there are two principle alternatives we can adopt for the traversal algorithm:

(i) delicacy-increasing: traversal of systems from least delicate towards most delicate in the system network — what we might also call forward chaining;
(ii) delicacy-decreasing: traversal of systems from most delicate to least delicate in the system network — what we might also call backward chaining.

In general, the traversal in Nigel is delicacy-increasing.[9] Since the systems are only partially ordered, the delicacy-increasing principle leaves the traversal algorithm underdetermined: whenever systems are simultaneous, the system network does not impose any restrictions on the traversal sequence. As long as the computational implementation of the traversal has to be serial (sequential) rather than parallel, the algorithm designed for the traversal of the network simply has to pick one system at random when there are two or more simultaneous ones available (i.e., enterable systems, or, as we shall call them below, *waiting systems*).[10] There are thus two general principles for the traversal algorithm that derive from the system network itself:

(i) proceed towards increasing delicacy;
(ii) whenever there are simultaneous systems available, pick one at random.

*6.5.3.2 Chooser activation* When a system is entered during the network traversal, its chooser is activated. Chooser activation is thus determined by system entry. (The alternative would be to give more independent control to generation at the semantic stratum: see, for example, Chapters 8 and 12.) Within the chooser, the ordering of steps is according to the organization of the chooser tree. (Some operations are left unordered and in a parallel generation algorithm they could be executed in parallel.) Since choosers present their inquiries to the environment, the generation algorithm has to wait until the environment has determined the responses.

*6.5.3.3 Realization* There are two alternative orderings of the execution of realization statements:

(i) immediate realization: as soon as a feature has been selected, any associated realization statements are executed;
(ii) delayed realization: realization statements are not executed until after the traversal of the system network.[11]

The approach of immediate realization is taken in Nigel: when one of the features of a system has been selected by its chooser, any associated realization statements are executed.[12] This has the advantage that any potential problems can be caught immediately, in the context of the system network traversal.

*6.5.3.4 The traversal algorithm in detail* These are the considerations underlying the design of the traversal algorithm and we can now illustrate its application in detail. The traversal algorithm is diagrammed in Figure 6.13. The columns correspond to different 'levels' of processing — chooser activation, system entry and the traversal of the system network itself, and realization. The records of the changing states are presented to the right of the processes. (The boldface numbers in square brackets, [1] through [4], identify opportunities for parallel processing as will be discussed below in Chapter 10.)

The traversal algorithm of the system network starts by *picking one system* from a list of systems whose entry conditions have been satisfied and which are thus waiting to be entered. It does not matter which system is picked from the waiting system list; the result is independent of the order in which the systems are selected and entered.[13] The first system on the list is always the RANK system whose entry condition is satisfied by the feature 'start', which is the root of the system network. The system picked becomes the current system.

The next step is to *enter* the current system. Next, *selection* takes over and one of the features of the systems is selected; the chooser of the system is in charge of selection. The chooser is itself a decision tree with certain additional operations, which is traversed one step at a time until a choice has been made. Once a feature has been selected, any realization statements associated with it are executed, apart from ordering statements, which are more conveniently processed when all the available information has been accumulated.

Next, the traversal algorithm goes through an *entry condition test* to see if any new entry conditions have been satisfied by the choice of the new feature. If there are systems whose entry conditions have been satisfied, they are added to a list of *enterable (waiting) systems*.

Once the enterable systems list has been updated (if necessary), the algorithm *checks the waiting system list* to find out whether it is empty. If

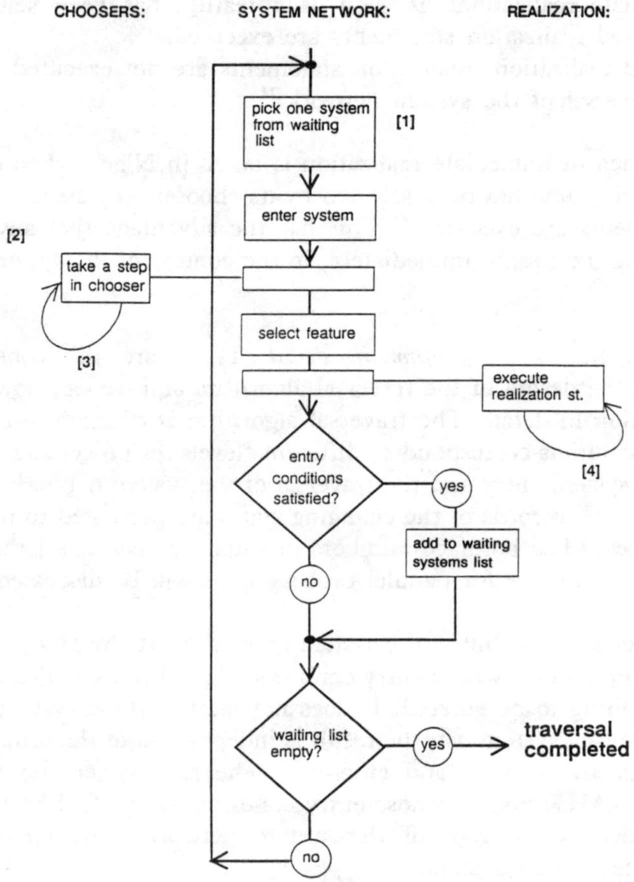


**Figure 6.13** A basic sequential traversal algorithm

it is, the traversal of the system network has been completed: there are no more systems whose entry conditions have been satisfied.

As an illustration, we can consider two consecutive cycles through the traversal algorithm. These cycles are illustrated in Figure 6.14.

Cycle (1): First, the current system (i.e., the system entered) is RANK and the feature clauses is selected. As a result, the systems with clauses as their entry condition, PROCESS TYPE and MOOD TYPE, become enterable and are thus on the list of waiting enterable systems (in boxes in the diagram). Then, the next system to be entered, PROCESS TYPE, is picked and it becomes the current system.

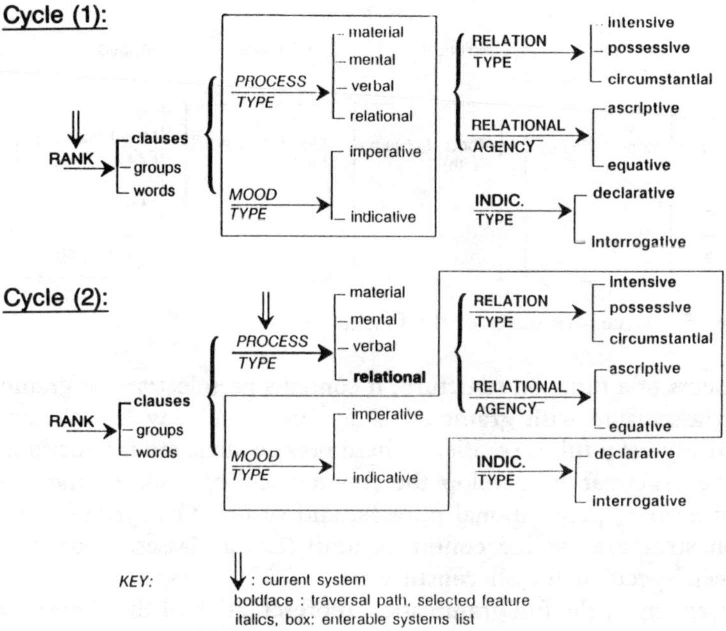


**Figure 6.14** Two successive states of enterable systems

Cycle (2): First, the system PROCESS TYPE is entered and can be marked as entered in the enterable systems list (or removed from the list; the effect is the same). The feature relational is selected. The systems RELATION TYPE and RELATIONAL AGENCY become enterable and are added to the list of enterable systems.

After the selection of a feature, whenever a realization statement such as +Subject, i.e., 'Insert Subject', is encountered associated with the feature selected, the statement is executed and the result is recorded on a 'blackboard'.[14] Since there may be more than one realization statement associated with a feature, the realization execution is repeated until all the realization statements have been consumed.

As the clause network is traversed, new features are selected, and the realization statements associated with these features are activated, the clause structure grows one step at a time on the blackboard; this is shown in Figure 6.15. When the network has been completely traversed — when there are no more unentered enterable systems on the list of enterable systems (i.e., no more waiting systems) — a full description of the clause structure can be found on the blackboard. In addition to the functional

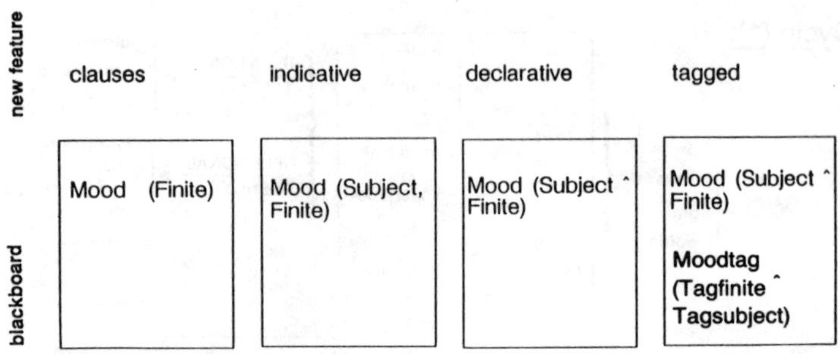


**Figure 6.15** Successive states of the blackboard

constituents of a function structure, it contains preselections of grammatical features associated with grammatical functions and any lexical items that have already been fully specified. These preselections are instructions to re-enter the grammar to develop the function constituents of the clause as nominal groups, prepositional phrases, and so on. The system network to function structure cycling continues until lexical classes or unique items have been specified for all constituents.

As an example, the full grammatical representation of the clause, i.e., the full consequences of the traversal through the grammar network at clause rank and prior to subsequent traversals, for the example:

*the new system is more reliable than the old one isn't it?*

is shown in Figure 6.16. The function structure of this example has three layers, one for each metafunctional component. (Textual: Theme; interpersonal: Mood (Subject ^ Finite) . . . Moodtag (Tagfinite ^ Tagsubject); and experiential: Carrier Process Attribute.) The associated preselections and lexical items are shown below each functional constituent. For example, the constituent Theme/Subject/Carrier has the preselection [nominal group, third, singular]. The generation algorithm will return to the system network to develop this constituent as a nominal group, selecting features that will constrain it to be third person and singular.

### *6.5.4 Moving beyond the basic algorithm*

*6.5.4.1 Parallel generation* The traversal algorithm sketched above is serial. Only one system at a time is entered even though there may be several enterable systems waiting. Similarly, chooser actions and the execution of realization statements are fully sequenced in the traversal algorithm, although they are not intrinsically ordered. In general, there is no linguistic reason why more than one system should not be entered in parallel nor why

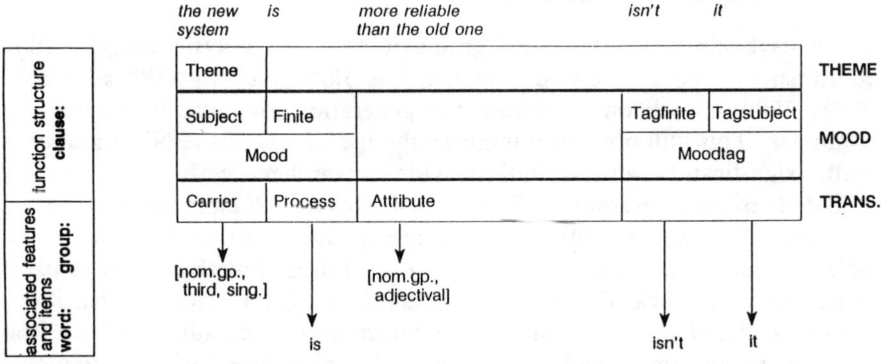


**Figure 6.16** The output structure of an example

actions in the three columns of Figure 6.13 above (the chooser column, the system network column, and the realization column) should not be performed in parallel.

There are, then, significant opportunities for parallel processing. We will return to them in Chapter 10.

*6.5.4.2 Dynamic potential* At the beginning of this section we said that the dynamic model is represented by the generation algorithm. With the basic algorithm defined, we can take a step back now and ask what kind of dynamic model it is, what kind of implications does it have for the linguistic theory of dynamic organization, and how it needs to be extended. We return to these issues in detail in Chapter 11.

## 6.6 Remaining Issues

### *6.6.1 Lexis*

One of the first questions in the design of Penman was how to relate the grammar to a *lexical model*; an early design was presented in Matthiessen (1981). The work on the lexicon for the Nigel grammar has since been carried out by Susanna Cumming (Cumming, 1986). Although it has hierarchic organization, the lexicon is not a systemic one and we will not discuss it here. The possibility of developing a systemic lexis as an addition to the grammar, Halliday's (1961) model of lexis as most delicate grammar, is discussed and exemplified in, e.g., Hasan (1987) and Matthiessen (1990a).

### 6.6.2 *Parsing and understanding*

Since its beginnings, the Nigel grammar has been a systemic generation grammar. A more recent development is Bob Kasper's (1987a, 1987b, 1988, 1989b) work on extending the generation grammar into a parsing grammar. This will obviously increase the usefulness of the Nigel grammar quite significantly and it will provide researchers with a functionally oriented parsing grammar. The initial strategy Kasper chose was to translate the systemic functional grammar into a functional unification grammar, since there has already been a good deal of work on how to parse with that framework. One additional benefit of his translation is that it has shown in detail how systemic functional grammar and functional unification grammar are related and he has identified areas where functional unification grammar needs extending (Kasper, 1987a, 1987b). Current work is taking this further within the context of *classification*-based parsing (Kasper, 1989b) using the knowledge representation language LOOM (MacGregor and Bates, 1987; see also the comments in Chapter 13).

### 6.6.3 *Other languages*

Systemic-functional linguistics has provided effective guidance for some computationally tractable and beneficial partial implementations of the grammatical stratum of the linguistic system of English, and the Nigel grammar is a significant outcome of this. Systemic linguistics also has a long history of application to languages other than English and the Kyoto project has started to bring this into contact with computational work also; the multilanguage generation project being launched at Sydney University is now following this up. This needs to be taken further, both with respect to increasing coverage and development of Japanese and Chinese and to developing computational systemic-functional treatments of other languages. The existence of systemic-functional descriptions of a number of languages, such as is also being pursued by the KOMET project of the German Gesellschaft für Mathematik und Datenverarbeitung in Darmstadt, for example, will be quite important here (cf. Steiner *et al.*, 1990b; Hu *et al.*, 1990).

### 6.6.4 *Components outside of the grammar*

This entire chapter has only considered those aspects of the framework up to and including the informal statement of the semantics of a computational systemic-functional grammar in terms of inquiry definitions. This needs to be taken further if the grammatical resources are to be usable in response to higher or deeper strata of the linguistic system.

To answer the inquiries presented by Nigel's chooser and inquiry interface, Nigel's *environment* needs the information to support the responses to the inquiries. For example, it was necessary to specify the general organization of the *knowledge base*. In 1985, drawing on his interpretation of English grammar, Michael Halliday and Matthiessen drafted a general ideational semantics, known as the 'Bloomington lattice', to be used as a guide for a 'conceptual' taxonomy in the knowledge base. The question addressed was what contextual support the ideational part of a grammar needed in a text generation system. Partial computational implementations of the Bloomington lattice have now been used as aids in modelling a number of domains in the knowledge base, the first being an electronic mail and calendar (correspondence and diary) domain and a navy domain. We will touch on this work and its current relation to the ongoing development of the Penman UPPER MODEL in Chapter 9; see also Matthiessen (1987) and Halliday and Matthiessen (in preparation). However, we need equally to extend the exploration of the organization of the environment to the interpersonal and textual spheres of meaning and so we take this discussion further in Chapter 9 also; this line of development has arisen very naturally in the context of the work on Japanese (e.g., Bateman, 1988; 1990a).

One of the important issues is the use of the knowledge base for planning purposes in generation: Peter Fries has designed a nominal group planner for the Penman system. Previous nominal group planners focused only on the need to identify referents; in contrast, Fries's planner is also sensitive to, for example, text organization; for some discussion see Fries (1987).

When the work on the Penman generator started, there was no general theory of text organization or part of text organization in use in text generation. Generators either did not include any strategies for organizing text or used strategies that, being bound to particular registers, did not generalize in any obvious way to new generation tasks. In 1982, Bill Mann, Sandy Thompson, and Matthiessen began to work on an analytic framework for *text organization* to be turned into a constructive one for text generation. Bill Mann and Sandy Thompson developed the framework into *Rhetorical Structure Theory* (RST; Mann and Thompson, 1987; Mann, 1984; Mann, Matthiessen, and Thompson, 1989) and started to design a constructive version of it with the help of Cecilia Ford (Ford, 1987). A constructive version of RST based on the paradigm of hierarchic planning in AI is now being developed by Ed Hovy (cf. Hovy, 1988a) and has also been extended for use in computational systems (e.g., Moore and Paris, 1988; Scott and de Souza, 1989). While RST is not a systemic theory of text organization in the sense of being a direct continuation of systemic work, it was influenced by the systemic work of Ruqaiya Hasan and Jim Martin. We will return to RST briefly in Chapter 9.

## 6.7 Conclusions and summary

In this chapter we have provided a detailed description of the basic representational resources used in the initial computational instantiations of systemic-functional grammar used within the Penman and Kyoto projects. Although starting from a shared set of representational resources, the two projects differ somewhat in goals and aspirations.

The two principal computational goals of the Nigel research were:

- to provide a framework for writing systemic generation grammars;
- to develop a general purpose, reusable English grammar component for computational use.

The initial principal goal of the Kyoto exploration was:

- to investigate the possibility of providing reusable grammatical resources for Japanese and Chinese — two languages very different both from each other and from English — that could be employed in contexts similar to those envisioned for the resources of English represented in the Nigel grammar. This would then offer a basis for developing linguistically sound, functional characterizations of these languages that could also serve as viable tools for text generation/understanding.

Although our conclusion was that the systemic view of grammar as meaningful choice with structural consequences applies equally appropriately to English, Japanese, and Chinese, and the representational mechanisms required to achieve this are shared, the linguistic organizations required by our treatments of Japanese and Chinese have highlighted the need for certain representational mechanisms that had not been implemented computationally in Nigel. These were found in the non-experiential areas of grammar — i.e., in those regions of the grammar concerned with realizing interpersonal, textual, and logical meanings. They were also consistent with conclusions that were being drawn within the Penman project as experience with more sophisticated linguistic phenomena increased. This led to a further research goal at Kyoto:

- to explore the computational representation and implementation of interpersonal, textual, and logical types of grammatical organization that had not previously received sufficient formalization for use within computational systemic-functional grammars.

In Parts III and IV, we describe these extensions in detail, relate them to extensions equally appropriate for the treatment of English and suggest the need for certain general theoretical extensions applicable to any application of systemic theory.

## Notes

1. This is a type of misunderstanding that goes back to Postal (1964).
2. They are independent in the sense that they are not conditioned by particular paradigmatic contexts. A good deal of the complexity for such grammars then results from the attempts to reintroduce paradigmatic context in a way that respects the syntagmatic organization. In general, we feel that this reverses the appropriate relationship between syntagmatic and paradigmatic organization in natural language.
3. This factorization of realizational consequences now finds certain similarities, of course, with the more recently developed 'immediate dominance/linear precedence' (ID/LP) factorization proposed for phrase structure grammars (e.g., Gazdar *et al.*, 1985: 44f.). Such grammars still typically fail, however, to capture the *paradigmatic* contexts that condition particular ID/LP configurations.
4. Not all mental clauses have an explicit Phenomenon, but for the purposes of the example they do.
5. That is, realization within a stratum. The other major type of realization is interstratal, as between semantics and lexicogrammar. Like interrank realization, it operates by means of preselection (one manifestation of which is the 'choose' operator introduced in Section 6.4.2 below).
6. The chooser would be more complex if it was intended to handle interpersonal metaphors of mood, such as commands expressed as questions. We will only discuss congruent cases in this section.
7. More accurately, each path through the chooser tree has to lead to a choice in the system of the chooser or else the generation process could not run to completion. In addition to the chooser organization mentioned here, there are other chooser operators, notably Pledge; see Mann (1983a). Chooser operators are used to present the two types of inquiry: Ask + branching inquiry; and Identify + identifying inquiry. Since they do not affect the organization of choosers or inquiries, we have chosen to regard them as aspects of the implementation of the chooser and inquiry framework.
8. All choices and their effects are 'indelible' — cf. McDonald (1980) on the importance of this; this was set as a goal for the MUMBLE generator.
9. The delicacy-decreasing direction is used when a feature has been preselected and the path to it has to be computed — so-called path augmentation. This happens when the grammar has been entered but before the system network is traversed towards increasing delicacy: the point of this precomputation is to guide the normal network traversal. We will return to the possibility of using delicacy-decreasing traversal at the lexicogrammatical stratum in Chapter 12.
10. Again, this assumes that there are no extra dependencies of any kind in the network over and above the connections between systems of the network. This may not always be the case; see Chapters 8 and 11.

11. The synoptic tabular specifications given separate from the system network in Fawcett (1980) suggest delayed realization. However, the place where realization statements are given in the synoptic specification can, of course, easily be overridden by the generation algorithm that interprets the grammar.
12. Currently, ordering statements are collected and executed after the traversal of the system network.
13. The order of entry may be constrained because of interdependencies among the choosers of systems; cf. Chapter 8.
14. The blackboard metaphor comes from the HEARSAY system developed to control complex processes (see, e.g., Erman, Hayes-Roth, Lesser and Reddy, 1980); the systemic generator itself is not a HEARSAY control structure, however. Once a piece of information has been added to the blackboard by means of a realization statement, it is available to other processes.

# 7 Two examples of constructive accounts for generation

## 7.1 Introduction

Before proceeding to the extensions that we present in Part III, in this chapter we will give a sense of what can be achieved within the basic framework of systems, choosers, and inquiries as developed and implemented within Nigel and the Kyoto Project and as described in detail in the previous chapter. We will not discuss here issues beyond the presentation of inquiries — i.e., we will not describe the sources of information to which inquiries need appeal.

The grammars of English and Japanese, as the grammars of any natural language, exhibit metafunctional diversification — the ideational, interpersonal, and textual spectrum. Each metafunction engenders a number of grammatical resources distributed across the units of the grammar (clause, groups, words, etc.).

For the first extended example, we have selected from the logical subtype (see Section 5.6.1) of the ideational metafunction in the grammar of English — i.e., from the component of the grammar concerned with the representation of reality. More particularly, we show the construal of time as a combination of serially related temporal points or intervals. For the second example, we have turned to the textual metafunction in the grammar of Japanese — i.e., the component of the grammar concerned with the textual presentation of ideational and interpersonal information. In particular, we show the presentation of process, participants and circumstances in terms of their intended textual salience for the development of a text.

In both cases, our aim has been to provide detailed illustrations concerning the formulation of fragments of grammar in terms of system networks containing grammatical alternatives functionally motivated by appropriate inquiries and to show the interaction of these theoretical constructs. We are not presenting exhaustive linguistic accounts of the areas used for illustration, although the accounts we suggest can be taken to be suggestive for how more detailed treatments might be pursued within this framework.

## 7.2 The treatment of tense in English

The resources of TENSE in English are important both in the representation of temporal relations themselves and in the organization of discourse in terms of temporal relations, for instance in the use of flashbacks and flashforwards. Thus in the following extract from a short Graham Greene biography, the unmarked tense choice is the simple past. The organization of the biography is chronological, so the location of the time related as past with respect to 'now' moves forward in the discourse (represented by circumstances: *in 1904*, *in 1935*, *in 1938*, and so on). However, the text has been organized in such a way that one event is 'dislocated' from the narrative time line and is presented as a flashback providing background information that helps the reader understand why the R.C.C. would commission Greene. To accomplish this, the writer chooses a 'second-order' past tense — one that is past in relation to the simple past (the past perfect of traditional grammar).

In 1935 he made a journey across Liberia, described in 'Journey without Maps', and on his return was appointed film critic to the 'Spectator'. *In 1926* he *had been received* into the Roman Catholic Church and was commissioned to visit Mexico in 1938 and report on religious persecution there.

As this example illustrates, text planning and tense selection interact — a fair challenge for, say, a generator of mini-biographies.

In computational linguistics, again following the ideational bias noted in Chapter 4, tense has also attracted interest more because it is part of the problem of representing knowledge of temporal intervals, temporal relations, the temporal structure of events, and so on. TENSE is one of the areas of English grammar that 'construes' time.[1] As we will show below, it is organized as a logical resource and it construes time serially and relationally: it serves to build up series of temporal relations. But time is also construed experientially, interpersonally, and textually.

By means of experiential resources, it is possible to represent temporal locations (e.g., *tomorrow*, *next year*) and temporal extents (durations, e.g., *for two hours*). Textual time is concerned with conjunctive relations that serve to develop and organize a text (e.g., *then*, *subsequently*, *previously*). The interpersonal metafunction offers an interpersonal alternative to (primary) tense — modality (including usuality); but it also includes interpersonal comments concerned with time, such as earlier or later than expected (*still*, *yet*, *already*).

### *7.2.1 Approaches to TENSE*

There is, of course, a long tradition of interpretations of tense in English, going back at least to the seventeenth century. A good many studies in linguistics have appeared in the last thirty years or so. They include foundational frameworks for interpreting tense (e.g., Bull, 1963; Diver, 1963; Halliday, 1976a; Hornstein, 1977), corpus-based studies (e.g., Wekker, 1976), and explorations of the relationship between the organization of discourse and tense selection (e.g., Schiffrin, 1987). Tense and aspect have also been examined in a typological perspective (e.g., Ultan, 1978; Comrie, 1976; Dahl, 1985). More recently tense and the representation of time have been taken up in computational linguistics. The range of concerns is illustrated in a recent special issue of the *Journal of Computational Linguistics* (Webber, 1988).

All along logicians and philosophers have contributed to the discussion and their work has influenced both linguists and computational linguists; two recent important contributions are Reichenbach's (1947) three-time (S, R, E) framework and Prior's (e.g., 1967) tense logic. It is Reichenbach's framework that has attracted most interest since the latter half of the 1970s. Its major insight is that it makes it quite explicit that tenses represent relations between times. In Reichenbach's framework, three times are always involved, the time of speaking (S), the time of the occurrence of the event being represented (E), and a reference time (R). This basic framework is embodied in Hornstein's (1977, 1981) theory of tense, which has influenced linguists and been taken up in computational linguistics. Unfortunately, Reichenbach's framework misses two fundamental generalizations about the English tense system.

(i) The tenses of the system are not limited to those recognized in traditional grammar, which were taken over by Reichenbach and have then been taken over by others together with his framework. Rather the tense system is serial and allows for more complex tense selections than those traditionally recognized — tense selections such as *will have been going to have been tested* (see Halliday, 1976a, 1980).

(ii) Tense selections do not represent composites of the three-time configurations (S, R, E) posited by Reichenbach but pairs of times. These pairs of related times may constitute links in longer chains. For instance, in *will have tested*, *will* signals a relation between $t_0$ and $t_1$ and *have* between $t_1$ and $t_2$ (see further below).

Both of these generalizations are reflected in Halliday's model of tense in English. This model was originally developed by Halliday and Ellis in the first half of the 1950s.

### *7.2.2 Halliday's model of tense*

We now turn to Halliday's grammatical interpretation of tense in English and sketch its semantics. We will start with the basic assumptions and then show how they can be represented by means of systemic grammar (Section 7.2.2.2) and chooser and inquiry semantics (Sections 7.2.3 and 7.2.4).

*7.2.2.1 Two central assumptions: grammar and semantics* Following Halliday (1976a, 1985a), we will make two central assumptions about the grammatical resources of tense in English. One has to do with the tense opposition and the other with the possibility of repeating selections from the tense opposition:

(i) The tense opposition: Tense in English is a three-term opposition:[2] past (e.g., *built*)/present (*build*)/future (*will build*). This three-term opposition can be interpreted semantically in terms of a precedence relation, <, between two time variables, $t_x$ and $t_y$ — future: $t_x < t_y$; past: $t_y < t_x$; present: neither, i.e., no precedence relation between $t_x$ and $t_y$. These two times may be either moments or intervals; the distinction plays no part in the tense system.

(ii) Seriality: Complex tense combinations can be built up from repeated selections from the three-term opposition. Semantically complex tenses correspond to a series of the time relations mentioned in (i). That is, serial tense is chosen to represent serial time. This second assumption follows from Halliday's interpretation of tense as a logical resource in English.[3]

For example, it is possible to select 'future' and then to select 'past': (future:) *will* (past:) *have built*; or 'future', then 'past', and then 'present': (future:) *will* (past:) *have* (present:) *been building*. As these examples illustrate, what is often called aspect (the progressive and sometimes the perfect) or phase (the perfect) is interpreted as secondary selections from the tense system — secondary tense. It is possible to build up even more complex tense selections; for instance, 'future, past, future, past, present' *will have been going to have been building*. Halliday (1979, 1988) notes that these complex tense selections are more likely in casual speech than in writing, which may explain why they have been overlooked by researchers basing their work on Reichenbach's (1947) three-time framework and the tenses inherited from traditional grammar.

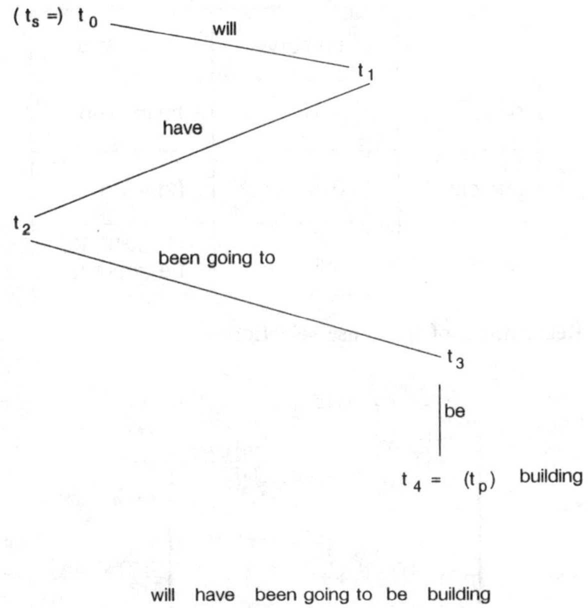


**Figure 7.1** Chain of time pairs

We observed that complex tenses represent chains of related times. Each tense relates one pair in this chain. Any such chain has two end points, the time of speaking ($t_s$, cf. Reichenbach's S) and the time of the occurrence of the Process ($t_p$, cf. Reichenbach's E). These two times are fixed by two different situations — one interpersonal, the situation defined by the interaction between speaker and listener: the 'here and now', and one ideational, the situation that is the part of the speaker's experience being represented through the resources of transitivity. The temporal chains created by tense serve to bridge these two situations. In the simplest case, the two times form a simple pair; but if there are repeated tense selections, the two times are pushed further apart. The selections thus come to serve as a temporal 'bridge' between the interpersonal 'now' and the ideational time of occurrence of the process.

The two time variables, $t_x$ and $t_y$, have new values for each tense selection. The first value of $t_x$ is $t_s$ and the last value of $t_y$ is $t_p$. For example, we can start the time chain built up by *will have been going to be building* as shown in Figure 7.1. The first tense selection, the selection that relates the time of speaking ($t_s$) to another time, is primary tense. Subsequent tense selections are all secondary tense. The realizations are shown in Figure 7.2.

| | primary | secondary |
|---|---|---|
| past | –ed | have –en |
| present | 0 | be –ing |
| future | will | be going to, be about to |

**Figure 7.2** Realizations of the tense selections

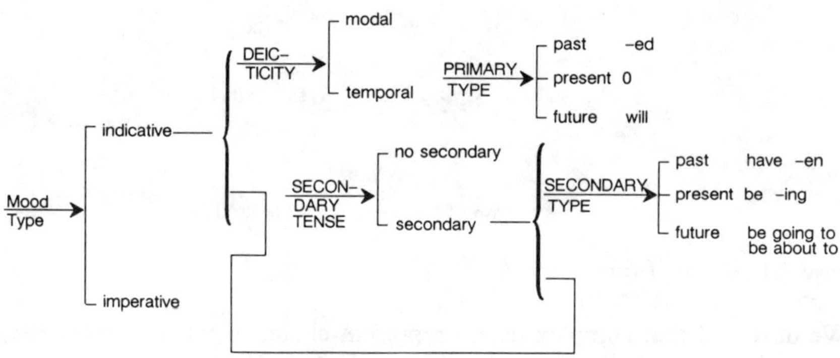


**Figure 7.3** The grammar of tense

*7.2.2.2 Systemic representation of the grammar of tense* We will now consider Halliday's systemic representation of his interpretation of tense and then turn to the representation of the semantics of tense in terms of the chooser and inquiry framework.

The full tense grammar is represented in Figure 7.3. MOOD TYPE distinguishes 'imperative' clauses (*Build another house!*) from 'indicative' ones (*They'll build another house*). It defines the context for the tense systems: only indicative clauses select freely for tense.[4] In indicative clauses, there are two simultaneous systems. DEICTICITY offers two alternative ways of relating a proposition to the here-and-now, either through time (temporal; e.g., *they're building another house now*) or through modality (modal; e.g., *they may be building another house now*). SECONDARY TENSE offers the choice between having a secondary tense (e.g., *they're building houses*) and not having one (e.g., *they build houses*).

Both 'temporal' and 'secondary tense' lead to a three-term tense system, 'past/present/future'. In principle, the two systems diagrammed in Figure

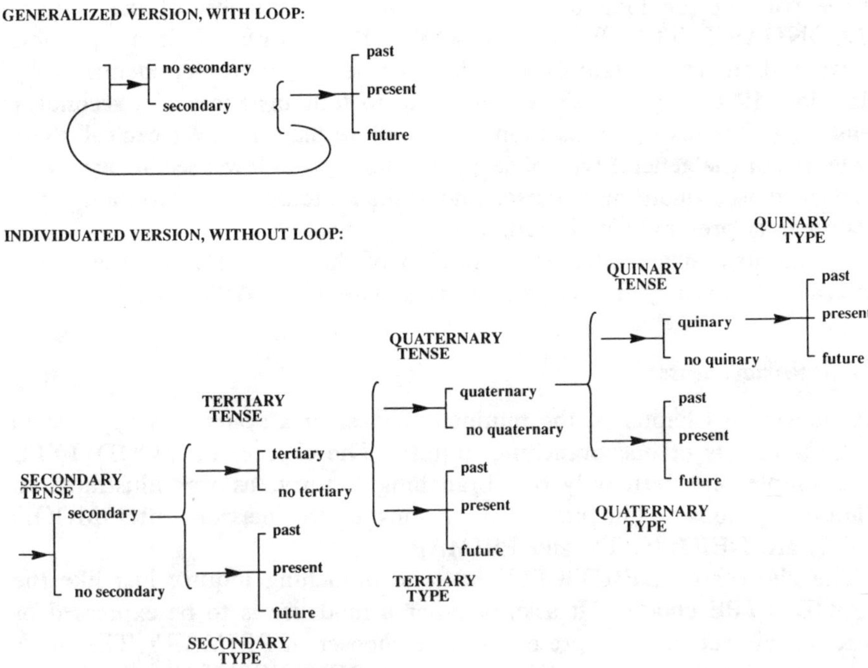


**Figure 7.4** Tense grammar without loop

7.3 are the same, but since the realizations differ and their choosers (cf. below) also differ in some respects, it is convenient to set them up as separate systems. (Alternatively, we could represent them as one system with a disjunctive entry condition — 'temporal/secondary tense'.) PRIMARY TYPE has the realizations past: *-ed*; present: *0*; and future: *will* (+ infinitival verb form). SECONDARY TYPE has the realizations past: *have -en*; present: *be -ing*; and future: *be going to* (*be about to*).

The system SECONDARY TENSE has a disjunctive entry condition, either 'indicative' or 'secondary'. The second possibility simply represents the fact that once a secondary tense has been selected, it is possible to go on and decide to select another secondary tense. The representation suggests that the systems SECONDARY TENSE and SECONDARY TYPE are within a 'partition' in the system network that can be instantiated more than once in the traversal of the system network. The computational model of the grammar we sketched in Chapter 6 cannot handle this type of system, a system type that characterizes the logical metafunction. We will return to the question of how such systems are to be interpreted in Chapters 8 and 11. In the meantime, we will redraw the system network above without the loop by spelling out all the instances of the systems SECONDARY TENSE and SECONDARY TYPE. This is possible because there are certain 'stop rules' for secondary tense, identified by Halliday (1976a, 1985a); there can be up to four instances of a secondary tense in a complex tense selection, but no more than that. We can call these instances of the general type of secondary tense as follows: secondary tense, tertiary tense, quaternary tense, and quinary tense. The resultant tense grammar is presented in Figure 7.4.

Let us now turn to the representation of the semantics of tense in the chooser and inquiry framework, starting with PRIMARY TENSE.

### *7.2.3 Primary tense*

As we saw in Chapter 6, the minimal chooser of a system (as opposed to a gate) consists of one branching inquiry. The chooser of MOOD TYPE is a simple one with only one branching inquiry, as was illustrated in Figure 6.9 above. The next two systems in the network after MOOD TYPE are DEICTICITY and PRIMARY TENSE.

The chooser of DEICTICITY has one branching inquiry just like the MOOD TYPE chooser. It asks whether a modality is to be expressed or not; we will return to it presently. The chooser of PRIMARY TENSE is more complex than the MOOD TYPE and DEICTICITY choosers in that it contains several branching inquiries. The selection of one of the PRIMARY TENSE features expresses the temporal relation between two times, $t_x$ and $t_y$, the first of which is 'now', the time of speaking ($t_s$). We will refer to the primary tense values of $t_x$ and $t_y$ as $t_0$ and $t_1$. The second may or may not be the time of the occurrence of the Process of the clause, depending on whether a secondary tense has been selected or not.

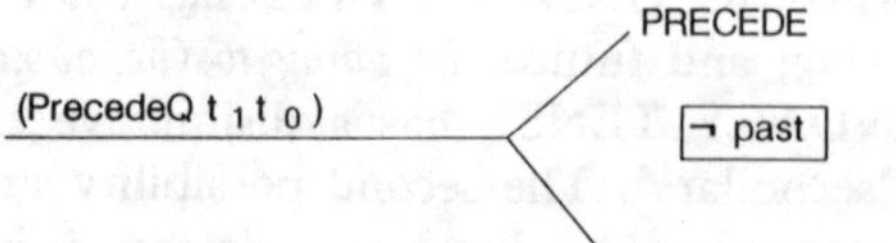


**Figure 7.5** The first inquiry in the PRIMARY TENSE chooser

If $t_1$ temporally precedes $t_0$, the feature past is chosen; if $t_1$ does not precede $t_0$, i.e., if the response is NON-PRECEDE, an additional inquiry, ConditionQ, is presented; cf. Figure 7.5. We can say that this second inquiry is dependent upon (embedded under) the NON-PRECEDE response from the first inquiry; it is only asked under the condition that

NON-PRECEDE is the response. NON-PRECEDE is the INQUIRY PRESENTATION CONDITION for the second embedded inquiry. We can think of it as comparable to a simplex, single-feature entry condition of a grammatical system. However, there is a significant difference. In a system, the entry condition is part of the definition of the system itself. In contrast, the inquiry presentation condition of an inquiry is not part of its definition but is represented by its place of embedding in a chooser. Thus, in the current formulation, ConditionQ does not itself have an inquiry presentation condition, but in the PRIMARY TENSE chooser it has the presentation condition NON-PRECEDE since it is embedded under that response in the chooser tree. We will see that the difference between the two types of condition is significant when we explore the possibility of complex presentation conditions (Chapter 8).

ConditionQ has two responses, the choice depending on whether a logical/temporal condition is being expressed or not:

ConditionQ

Does the situation to be expressed constitute a logical or temporal condition on some other process in the text to which it is rhetorically related, i.e., does it set up — logically or temporally — the possible world in which this other process occurs?

(CONDITION, NON-CONDITION)

If a condition is being expressed (e.g., in a *when*-clause or an *if*-clause), the feature present is selected (as in, *If/When he gets a new job, we will celebrate*). In other words, in the context of CONDITION, no further temporal distinctions are made.[5]

If no condition is being expressed, a further temporal distinction must be made. PrecedeQ is used again, this time with the parameters reversed: (PrecedeQ $t_0$ $t_1$). The positive response to this third inquiry, PRECEDE, leads to the selection of the feature future. The negative response leads to the choice of the feature present. The assumption is that the choice condition for the feature present is that no precedence relation holds between $t_0$ and $t_1$ and at this point in the chooser this information has been obtained, since PrecedeQ has been presented twice. This illustrates the importance of inquiry presentations conditions *within* a chooser: they represent the current state of knowledge when an inquiry is presented.

The PRIMARY TENSE chooser is summarized in Figure 7.6. The fact that (PrecedeQ $t_1$ $t_0$) is the first inquiry about precedence is significant. It means that the reason for choosing the feature past is unaffected by the further distinctions made in the chooser. In contrast, the reasons for

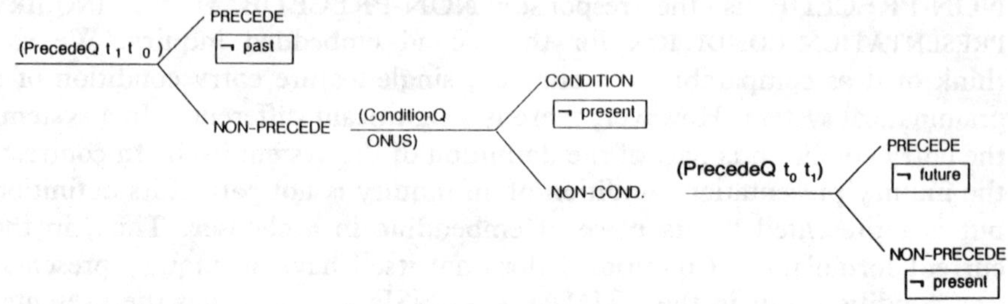


**Figure 7.6** The chooser of PRIMARY TENSE

choosing present and future are not since (PrecedeQ $t_0$ $t_1$) is embedded under ConditionQ: NON-CONDITION.

### *7.2.4 Secondary tenses*

In the area of secondary tenses (secondary tense, tertiary tense, quaternary tense, and quinary tense), there are two types of systems, SECONDARY TENSE and SECONDARY TYPE. Each particular instantiation of these types (secondary, tertiary, etc.) will have the same type of chooser.

In SECONDARY TENSE, we have to decide whether to have an additional tense or not. Roughly, the choice depends on whether we have completed the chain that connects the time of speaking ($t_s$) and the time of the occurrence of the process ($t_p$) or not. If the chain has not been completed, at least one additional tense is needed. If the chain has been completed, $t_y$ is the same as $t_p$, so the chooser of SECONDARY TENSE can simply check

(SameAsQ $t_y$ $t_p$)

The particular value of $t_y$ will depend on the particular instantiation of the secondary tense — secondary ($t_2$), tertiary ($t_3$), quaternary ($t_4$), or quinary ($t_5$). If the response is that the two times are different, the choice is 'secondary'; if they are the same, the choice is 'no secondary'.

If $t_y$ is not the same as $t_p$, the new time to be related to $t_y$ in the temporal chain has to be identified, which is done by means of TimeInRelationID:

What time is to be directly related to the old $t_y$?

The chooser of SECONDARY TENSE is diagrammed for the first instance of this system type in Figure 7.7. SECONDARY TYPE has the same kind of chooser as PRIMARY TYPE with the exception of ConditionQ, since conditionality only affects primary tense. The inquiry PrecedeQ is used to

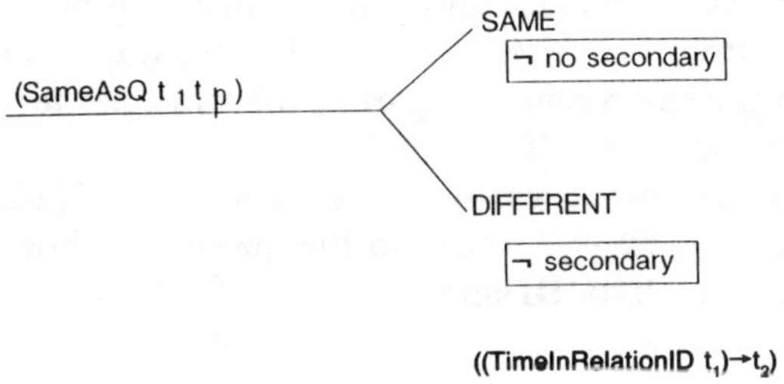


**Figure 7.7** The chooser of SECONDARY TENSE

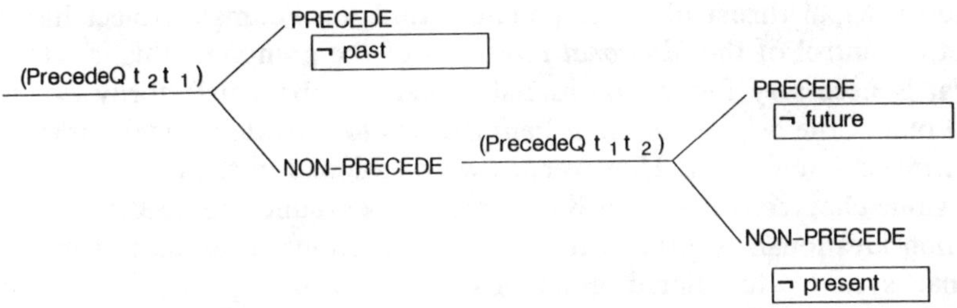


**Figure 7.8** The chooser of SECONDARY TYPE

determine what temporal relation obtains between $t_x$ and $t_y$. The chooser of the first instantiation of SECONDARY TYPE is diagrammed in Figure 7.8.

As in the PRIMARY TYPE chooser, the feature 'present' is selected only after it has been established that neither of the two times being related precedes the other. In the case of secondary tenses, the 'present' option can be further specified as representing time inclusion: $t_2$ in the diagram above includes $t_1$. (It is this characteristic that has led to the interpretation of the secondary present as an imperfective type of aspect.)

### *7.2.5 Conclusion*

We have given a brief presentation of a systemic treatment of tense in English, encoding the semantic interpretation in the framework of chooser and inquiry semantics.

There are certainly special cases of tense uses that we have not discussed, including those illustrated by examples such as *we leave at three tomorrow*; *we're having dinner at eight*. However, the point is that the systemic framework we have discussed in this chapter is powerful and flexible enough to deal with tense. To support the inquiries presented here, the environment will have to handle sophisticated planning of discourse as the opening example from the Greene biography illustrates, but identifying such demands on the environment is part of the strategies for extending the generation system (see Part III).

In addition, we saw that it was not possible to model Halliday's looping logical system directly; we will return to the question of how such systems can be represented in Parts III and IV.

## 7.3 The treatment of textual salience in Japanese

The principal thrust of development within the Penman project has been on the control of the *ideational* resources of the grammar; this is, after all, what is necessary for 'propositional content' to be satisfactorily expressed and one of the original goals of Penman was to provide a widely usable text generation component. However, as we mentioned in the conclusion to the previous chapter, within the Kyoto project we found the need for a variety of non-ideational extensions to the representational resources of computational systemic-functional grammars. One of our principal underlying presuppositions that came to shape our approach to text generation and the development of a grammar/semantics component specifically tailored towards text generation's requirements was, therefore, that an overly narrow interpretation of what is to constitute the 'meaning' of a linguistic expression had been limiting natural language text generation in computational linguistics generally. Often the move to consider text has been based on a simple extension of the notion of propositional content to cover the set of propositions asserted over a text and some of the logical/rhetorical relations holding among those propositions.

This is *insufficient* for generating text because many aspects of text design are sensitive not to 'core' meanings but to the *reasons* for choosing such meanings over any others in the particular context of a text's use. A specification of core meaning therefore omits much information that is crucial for text generation. Although there are now more linguistic approaches which have, at least in principle, accepted this, particularly approaches within the broad range of functional linguistics, the sheer pervasiveness of textually conditioned phenomena has still not been sufficiently appreciated within the generation paradigm.

The recognition of the three metafunctions, among which core semantic content represents just one, helps with this problem immediately. As we saw in the previous chapter, it is only when these three types of information are combined to form single, multiply functionally decomposable structural products that fully specified linguistic expressions result. Thus, since previous grammatical accounts in text generation outside of Nigel have been strongly oriented to the ideational 'layer' of organization, we decided in the Kyoto project to complement this work by concentrating almost exclusively upon *non*-ideational information. When this work is considered in *combination* with existing accounts, therefore, the imbalance that Hallidayan linguistic metatheory would predict for any account that does not respect equally the contributions of the three metafunctions is rectified.

In this further illustration of the application of the basic set of grammatical resources described in the previous chapter, therefore, we will examine a component of Japanese grammar that is concerned with establishing participants' SALIENCE, or PROMINENCE, for a text. The grammatical resources for managing such attributions of salience are rather extensive; indeed, the repercussions of salience-related decisions surface across the entire range of lexicogrammatical potential. In this section, however, we will focus particularly on the appropriate assignment and distribution of the Japanese nominal post-positions. This provides many good examples of the grammaticization of such textual meanings and, further, has long been a source of difficulties and controversies in treatments of Japanese grammar (Kuno, 1973; Shibatani, 1977; Hinds, 1983b; Hinds, Maynard and Iwasaki, 1987; Gunji, 1987; and many others). In particular, we shall present a partial systemic account of the principal uses of the Japanese postnominal particles: *wa* and *ga*.

The following is an extremely simplified example where the particles *wa* and *ga* appear; it is adapted from a text describing an already identified student's lodgings. Here we see the two principal uses of *wa* and a common occurrence of *ga*. We will refer to these sentences below in our examples of generation according to our systemic account of particle selection, motivating the particular selections here accordingly.

(1) *geshuku- wa semai.*<br>
lodgings narrow<br>
The lodgings are small.

(2) *mannaka- ni tsukue- ga atte,*<br>
centre at desk is-and<br>
In the centre there is a desk, and

(3) *sumi- ni tansu- ga aru.*<br>
corner at drawers is<br>
in the corner there is a chest of drawers.

(4) *tsukue-* wa *geshuku-* *no* *mono* *aru-* *ga*
desk lodging poss thing is but
The desk belongs to the accommodation, but

(5) *tansu-* *wa* *oneesan-* *kara* *karita.*
drawers older sister from borrowed
the drawers he borrowed from his elder sister.

Note that we will not describe the linguistic data at issue here in any depth (for more details see: Bateman, 1990a). We will instead simply present some acceptable Japanese clauses, representing the range of particle assignments being addressed, together with a description of the hypothesized textual functions of the particles employed in those clauses. This functional account will then be couched more explicitly making use of the representational resources for grammar that we have so far introduced.

Although there appears to be a great deal of flexibility in particle assignment, the functional orientation of a systemic account requires that we consider this apparent flexibility in the light of the functionality that it provides. A fundamental assumption of systemic-functional linguistics is that variation in language, until proved otherwise, carries functional loads that require description. The basic questions that we are led to ask are therefore:

1. why is any one assignment made over others in a particular context; i.e., what are the criteria for appropriate assignment? What functional load does the assignment carry?
2. precisely what are the limits of the flexibility of particle assignment; i.e., what assignments can and cannot be made?

We will first consider the particle *wa*, and then widen the discussion to *ga*. We will conclude with versions of the segments of a systemic grammar responsible for generating clause structures with nominal groups marked appropriately by each of these particles. We also, as was the case with the treatment of TENSE in the previous section, present a description of the criteria for their appropriate selection as captured by their associated choosers.

### *7.3.1 The 'topic' particle* wa

The particle *wa* offers one of the most often cited examples of a linguistically realized textual distinction. Two principal meanings are typically assigned to its use:

- Topic introduction (e.g., Maynard, 1980; Hinds, 1983a). By means of the particle *wa* some general topic, or framework within which subsequent talk is to develop, is proposed. Examples of two common usages of this type are: (i) a topic is introduced, but taking up that topic and making a statement about it are left to subsequent contributions; this is a common way of asking questions, e.g.:

(6) *ashita* *-wa*
tomorrow- TOPIC
'As for tomorrow . . .?'

and (ii), there is an identification of some topic and then a statement is made about that topic, e.g.:

(7) *ashita* *-wa* *eiga-* *wo* *mi-*
tomorrow- TOPIC movie- OBJECT see-
*ni* *iku*
IN ORDER TO go
'As for tomorrow, I'll go to see a movie'.

In both cases, the entity selected for topic status is typically taken to be already 'known' or 'predictable' in some sense. Thus, a conversation or text is held to have already established some range of possible topics, either explicitly or implicitly, and the selection of one such as the basis for future talk is achieved by marking with *wa*. In our toy text example above, clause (1) exhibits this use of *wa*. It is known that the student's accommodation is to be discussed and that this is now to become the topic of development. Thus, the accommodation *geshuku* is marked with the particle *wa* to realize this textual status.

- Contrast (e.g., Kuno, 1973; Clancy and Downing, 1987). This may be either explicit or implicit in that the entity with respect to which a contrast is being made may either be expressed or not as is required. In these cases, the use of *wa* serves to mark *variations* in, or *restrictions* on, what is established. For example, if discussion is revolving around the comprehension of languages, variations in the applicability of the established predicate *wakaru* ('understand') might be expressed by:

(8) *eigo-wa yoku wakaru,* *nihongo-wa zenzen deki-nai*
English well is understood, Japanese at all cannot
'English is understood well, but Japanese not at all.'

In each case attention is focused upon the predicate being expressed, or rather in this case, upon the *polarity* of that predicate with respect to the particular language being addressed. Referring again to our toy text above, this contrastive use of *wa* is shown in clauses (4) and (5). In (4) ownership of the desk in the student's room is attributed to the lodgings themselves, in contrast to the ownership of the drawers by the sister shown in (5).[6]

In both cases, we can see in action a type of grammatical resource that will receive further attention in Section 9.4 below: that is, resources which manipulate the textual context local to a clause or sentence. Building on the kinds of abstractions that we develop there, one can argue that the two uses of *wa* — topic introduction and contrast — are manifestations of the same phenomena. A topic is introduced relative to some 'method of text development' (very likely embodied in a rhetorical relation as the 'point' of elaboration or sequence) and contrast is just one particular subtype of method of development.

The part of the grammar responsible for the generation of structures of types (6) and (7) is set out in Figure 7.9. Here the principal choice point is called the TOPIC LINKAGE system. This is responsible for the basic organization of a *discourse contribution* — which is taken experimentally to be a linguistic unit of Japanese one rank higher than the clause. The alternatives it presents are between relying upon a former establishment of topic, in which case no use of *wa* is required (grammatical feature 'implicit-topic'), and expressing a topic explicitly (grammatical feature 'explicit-topic'). The latter alternative admits of two further possibilities: either the contribution serves only as a discourse 'setter' which is content to establish the topic and not volunteer further development (example case 6), or that move itself offers further development (example case 7).

While the subnetwork describes the structural possibilities that Japanese provides, this is not sufficient. We also need to specify the conditions under which any of these structural possibilities is to be selected. This is handled by means of appropriate chooser and inquiries. The chooser and inquiry organization for controlling the network of Figure 7.9 is as follows. The two inquiries shown state the questions that need to be asked of the text plan for appropriate grammatical features to be selected.

TOPIC LINKAGE: Does the communicative intent propose a shift of topic?
no: select *implicittopic*
yes: select *explicittopic*
Does the communicative intent involve a statement about that topic?
yes: select *explicitstatement*
no: select *discoursesetter*

Corresponding to the possible answers for these principal chooser inquiries,

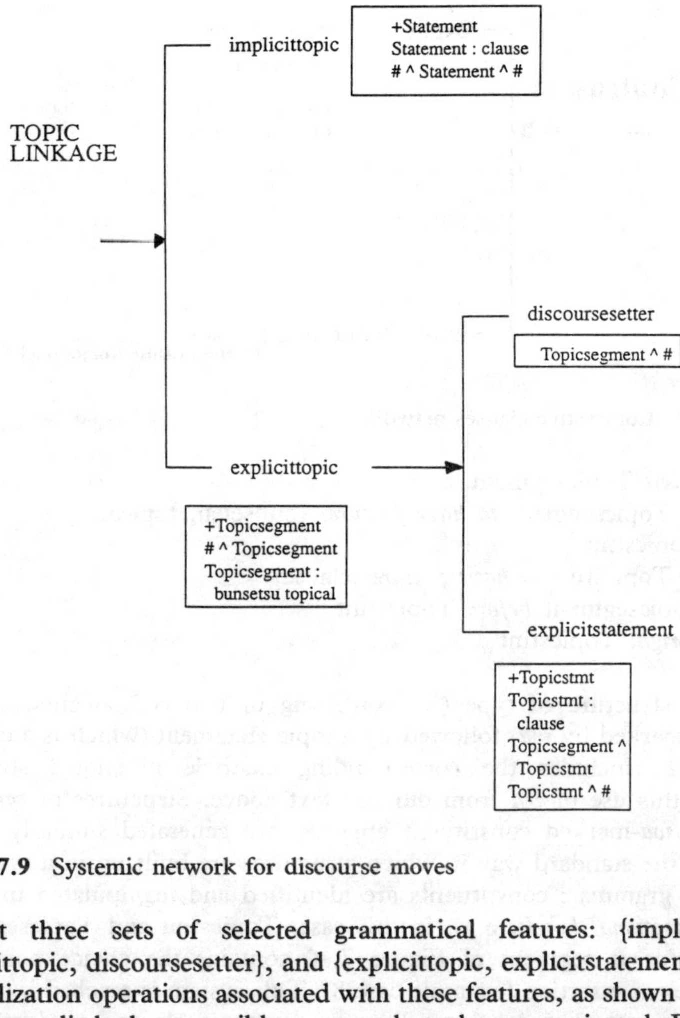


**Figure 7.9** Systemic network for discourse moves

we get three sets of selected grammatical features: {implicittopic}, {explicittopic, discoursesetter}, and {explicittopic, explicitstatement}. When the realization operations associated with these features, as shown in Figure 7.9, are applied, three possible structural results are motivated. For example, given a selection of features {explicittopic, explicitstatement}, which are motivated by the textual semantic distinctions:

Does the communicate intent propose a shift of topic? : YES
Does the communicate intent involve a statement about that topic? : YES

the following realization statements are executed:

*insert* Topicsegment

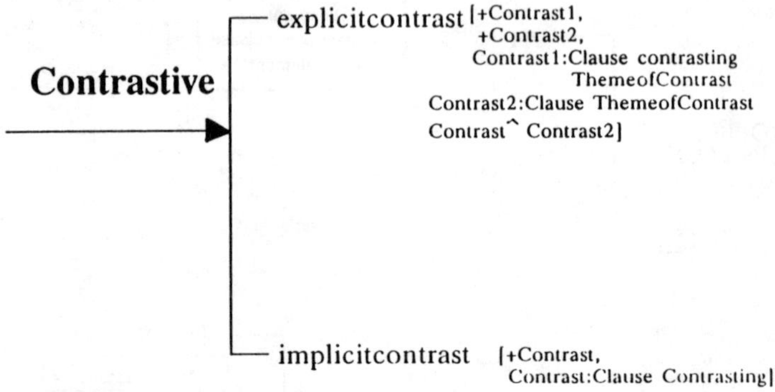


**Figure 7.10** Contrastive clauses network

*order-at-left* Topicsegment
*preselect* Topicsegment *to have features* {bunsetsu, topical}
*insert* Topicstmt
*preselect* Topicstmt *to have feature* {clause}
*order* Topicsegment *before* Topicstmt
*order-at-right* Topicstmt

This is a structure of type (7), consisting of two components, a topic segment (marked by *wa*) followed by a topic statement (which is a clause). Figure 7.15 includes the corresponding example functional structure involving this use of *wa* from our toy text above. Structures of type (6), where no *wa*-marked constituent appears, are generated similarly.[7] This illustrates the standard way in which structures are built up in a systemic-functional grammar: constituents are identified and manipulated in terms of their *functional labels*, e.g., in this case: Topicstmt and Topicsegment.

The grammar segment of Figure 7.10 contains the choice points for contrastive *wa* insertion (example case 8). This system is reached by a path in the grammar that considers how to construct clause *complexes*; i.e., sequences of more than one clause related grammatically. This system is, therefore, one rank lower than the previous system shown for discourse contributions, reflecting the fact that a single topic segment can thematically 'place' an entire clause complex in addition to single clauses. The particular inter-clause relation at issue here is accordingly that of *contrast*: if there is some contrast to be drawn, the grammar sets up a clause which possesses the feature *contrasting*. This is eventually responsible for the insertion of the particle *wa* as the marker of the 'topic/theme' of the contrast being made. All that we need to say about the chooser relevant here, therefore, is that it needs to be able to ask the environment whether a contrast is being drawn or not; it may be noted that contrast is a common rhetorical relationship that text planners already typically support (e.g., Davey, 1978; Mann and Thompson, 1987; Hovy, 1988a); we shall see more of the support that the 'text base' provides for motivating the deployment of textual grammatical resources — of which the rhetorical relationship of contrast is one example — below in Section 9.4. Figure 7.15 includes the functional structure from our toy text that exhibits the realization of contrast.

### *7.3.2 The 'subject' particle* ga

The Japanese postnominal particles *ga*, *wo*, and *ni* are often referred to as 'case' particles, although there is often debate concerning whether this is to be interpreted as grammatical case (e.g., 'Nominative', 'Accusative', etc.: cf. Shibatani, 1977), grammatical relations (e.g., 'Subject', 'Object', etc.: cf. Gunji, 1987; Johnson, 1988), or semantic case (e.g., 'actor', 'goal', etc.). For example, *ga* is usually considered to mark the constituent which, in traditional terms, is appropriately the grammatical *subject* of its clause, *wo* marks either the direct object or the semantic 'goal', and *ni* marks less primary grammatical relations such as that of the 'demoted' subject in passive constructions and occasionally the actor of a process. In this section, however, we focus on the *textual* conditions for the *ga* particle's deployment, suggesting that in main clauses these textual conditions play the decisive role in particle selection. This argues that such particles should not be analysed as primarily marking either surface case or semantic role.

To begin, we can note that the use of the particle *ga* is typically said to pick out an entity that has not yet been 'established' in the discourse. Candidates for marking with *ga* are new discourse entities, entities whose appearance is not predictable or known. Thus, the use of the particle *ga* contrasts with uses of *wa* in that it picks out an entity whose identity has manifestly *not* been established in the discourse — often explicitly so in that a question may have been asked precisely to achieve that establishment. The information organization appropriate for *ga* will therefore be one in which an information 'hole' is addressed and, often, subsequently filled. This is met in cases both where identification is sought, e.g.:

| | |
|---|---|
| *nani-ga* | *ari-masu-ka* |
| what is it that | is there? |
| *nani-ga* | *noma-reru-ka* |
| what is it that | is being drunk? |

and where identification is provided, e.g.:

| | |
|---|---|
| *hon-ga* | *ari-masu* |
| book it is that | is there |
| *biiru-ga* | *noma-reru* |
| beer it is that | is being drunk |

In each case, that the predicate holds is *presupposed*, i.e. it is not a conversational issue, of what it holds *is* at issue and this lack of information calls for marking with *ga*. We can also see that there is a restriction on the use of *ga* according to the grammatical role of the participant as follows. The second of the immediately proceeding questions might also be expressed by:

| | |
|---|---|
| *nani-wo* | *nomu-ka* |
| what-(*object marker*) | is (someone) drinking? |

where the information 'hole' of what is being drunk has *not* been mentioned with *ga* because the form of the verb calls for the constituent *nani* ('what') to be the Goal and Direct Object not the Subject. Thus marking by *ga* must be allowed to be sensitive to both the permissible grammatical or participant-role relationships for the clause and its status as being either established or unknown.[8]

Kuno (1976: 23) further considers *ga* able to serve both as an 'exhaustive listing' marker in which 'X-*ga* Predicate' claims that it is X *and only X* of which the predicate is true, and as a 'neutral description' marker which does not entail exhaustivity, merely new, and possibly incomplete, information.

All of these readings are essentially textual in that they signal aspects of the presentation of information rather than the information itself. Marking of an entity by *ga* must therefore at least be made sensitive to its status as either established or unknown, in addition to any simple consideration in terms of the permissible grammatical relationships for a clause (which, in fact, can also be textually conditioned).

Although this provides an initial set of chooser questions for controlling *ga* and for beginning to set out the conditions under which each reading may be considered appropriate — essentially choosers need to be able to ask the grammar's environment about the participant roles of a constituent and about that constituent's information status — the situation is complicated by the distributions of particle deployment shown in Figures 7.11 and 7.12. Here it becomes difficult to maintain the commitment to *ga* functioning as a subject marker: for example, clauses (10c), (11c), and (12b) all contain two *ga*-marked constituents which cannot both be subject in any traditional

| | | | | |
|---|---|---|---|---|
| (9) | a. | *taroo-ga* | *iku* | |
| | | Taroo | goes | |
| | b. | *taroo-ga* | *mondai-wo* | *toku* |
| | | Taroo | problem | solves |
| (10) | a. | *biiru-ga* | *nomi-tai* | |
| | | beer | there is a wish to drink | |
| | b. | *taroo-ga* | *biiru-wo* | *nomi-tai* |
| | | Taroo | beer | wants to drink |
| | c. | *taroo-ga* | *biiru-ga* | *nomi-tai* |
| | | Taroo | beer | wants to drink |
| (11) | a. | *mondai-ga* | *tokeru* | |
| | | problem | there is the ability to solve | |
| | b. | *taroo-ga* | *mondai-wo* | *tokeru* |
| | | Taroo | problem | can solve |
| | c. | *taroo-ga* | *mondai-ga* | *tokeru* |
| | | Taroo | problem | can solve |
| | d. | *taroo-ni* | *mondai-ga* | *tokeru* |
| | | by Taroo | problem | there is the ability to solve |
| (12) | a. | *hebi-ga* | *kowai* | |
| | | snake | is frightening | |
| | b. | *taroo-ga* | *hebi-ga* | *kowai* |
| | | Taroo | snakes | is frightened of |
| | c. | *taroo-ni (wa)* | *hebi-ga* | *kowai* |
| | | Taroo | snakes | is frightened of |

**Figure 7.11** Contrasting acceptable and unacceptable particle deployments: some acceptable clauses

| | | | | |
|---|---|---|---|---|
| a. | *taroo-ga* | *mondai-ga* | *toku* | |
| | Taroo | problem | solve | |
| b. | *taroo-ni* | *mondai-wo* | *tokeru* | |
| | Taroo | problem | can solve | |
| c. | *taroo-ga* | *biiru-ga* | *nomu* | (Taroo, beer, drink) |
| d. | *taroo-ni* | *biiru-ga* | *nomu* | (Taroo, beer, drink) |
| e. | *taroo-ni* | | *iku* | (Taroo, go) |
| f. | *taroo-ga* | *hebi-o* | *kowai* | (Taroo, snake, frightening) |

**Figure 7.12** Contrasting acceptable and unacceptable particle deployments: some unacceptable clauses

sense.[9] It is also not sufficient for selection of *ga* for the information status of a participant to be new: acceptable clause (11c) and unacceptable clause (a) need not differ with respect to the straightforward information statuses of their participants and yet, in the latter case, it is not possible to have both participants marked by *ga*. Furthermore, many of the acceptable clauses shown in Figures 7.11 and 7.12 largely share their ideational meaning – e.g., (10b) and (10c), (11b) and (11c), (11b) and (11d), and (12b) and (12c). It is thus necessary to tease out how these clauses differ so that the different forms that occur can be functionally motivated; otherwise groups of clause-types such as these remain in free variation with the possible danger that selections will prove inappropriate in particular contexts of use. Speakers do, in fact, deploy these clause-types differently, and it is the role of analysis to uncover what their distinctive properties are: it is necessary to be more explicit about the conditions that govern the appropriateness, or otherwise, of *ga* selection.

Rather than presenting here a more complete analysis drawing upon the situated use of these clauses in texts, for the purposes of the current illustration we will move directly to the conclusions that have been drawn and their systemic representation. We will show how the basic meanings for *ga* given above can be straightforwardly extended to cover, functionally motivate, and control the distributions patterns shown in Figures 7.11 and 7.12. To do this, we make use of the *layered* nature of the systemic-functional view of structure (Section 4.6 above); different functional components of the grammar often operate on sets of distinctively labelled constituents, which are subsequently combined into a single structure by *conflating* constituents whose labels originate from different functional regions. Simple examples of this metafunctional layering were given for English clauses in Figures 5.3 and 6.16 above. Here, we focus on the interaction of two layers of functional organization in the Japanese clause: the *information* layer and the *agency* layer.

Corresponding to previous analyses of *ga* as marking nonestablished status within a text, each use of *ga* is here taken to be compatible with the occurrence of a constituent functionally labelled as News. Additionally, the use of *ga* as an exhaustive listing marker will be taken as a symptom of a constituent functionally labelled as the Focus of the news. Since there is no reason for presuming prior to analysis that these functions will necessarily be realized as a single constituent, cases where two constituents appear marked by *ga*, one marking the News the other the Focus, are readily predictable; clauses (10c), (11c), and (12b) provide examples of this. Furthermore, although the actual situation is more complex, for the present purposes of illustration we will assume that when two *ga*-marked constituents occur, the leftmost *ga*-constituent may be considered the Focus and the second will be simply News.[10]

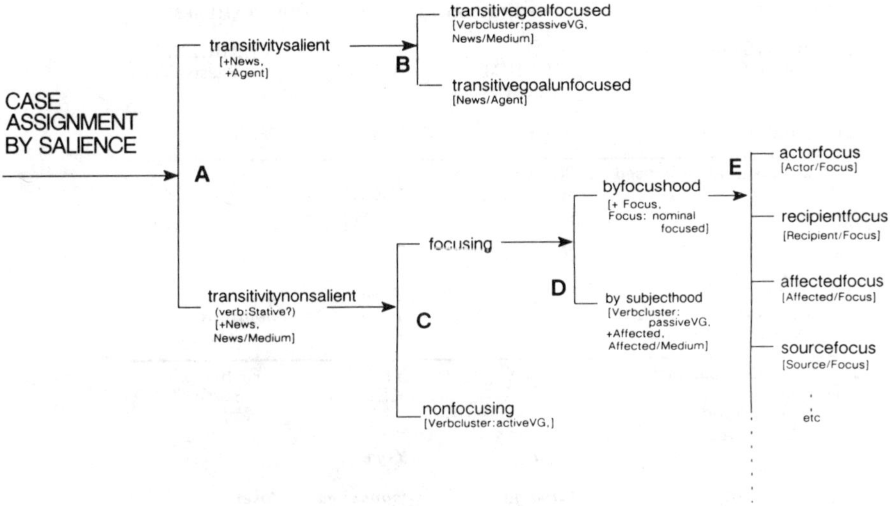


**Figure 7.13** The case assignment by salience network

Given this view of *ga* deployment and evidence concerning the consequences for focusing that various selections of verb forms have — e.g., selection of passive (as in English, although this is not so common in Japanese), and selection of 'desire' forms (the clauses under (10)) and forms that express ability (11) — we can motivate the deployments of *ga* on 'pragmatic' grounds directly without requiring complex particle assignment rules based on surface ordering, structural configurations, or grammatical relations. In addition, accounts such as Gunji's (1987: 193) treatment of particles in terms of adjunction and gapping defined over phrase structures present more an account of grammatical possibilities, *not the motivations for those possibilities* — this he places outside of grammar and semantics proper. In the account here, we integrate the functional motivations directly into the organization of the grammar. The network of Figure 7.13 shows this in terms of the functionally motivated deployment of *ga*.[11] This network is a clause rank network of the textual metafunction.

Figure 7.14 shows examples of the kinds of structures that the network generates — on the lefthand side of the figure are the grammatical features that have been selected, i.e., the path that has been taken through the network, and on the righthand side are the clause structures that these feature selections motivate. The structural results show the two layers of organization (and, additionally, where it is especially relevant, the placement of the transitivity functions ACTOR and GOAL) that combine to determine the particle selection. Simplifying the situation somewhat, we can

| FEATURES | FUNCTION STRUCTURES AND EXAMPLES | | |
|---|---|---|---|
| TransitivitySalient: | NEWS | | VERBCLUSTER |
| TransitiveGoalFocused | MEDIUM | AGENT | PassiveVG |
| | (GOAL) | | |
| i.e. 'pure' passive | X-*ga* | Y-*ni* | VERB(passive) |
| TransitiveGoalUnfocused | NEWS | | |
| | AGENT | MEDIUM | |
| | | (GOAL) | |
| i.e. | X-*ga* | Y-*wo* | VERB |
| e.g. 'X drinks Y' | X-*ga* | Y-*wo* | *nomu* |
| 'X wants to drink Y' | X-*ga* | Y-*wo* | *nomi-tai* |
| 'X is able to drink Y' | X-*ga* | Y-*wo* | *nomeru etc.* |
| TransitivityNonSalient: | FOCUS | NEWS | VERB |
| Focusing: | AGENT | MEDIUM | Stative? |
| ByFocushood: | | | |
| ActorFocus: | (ACTOR) | | |
| i.e. | X-*ga* | Y-*ga* | |
| e.g. (transitive) | *taroo-ga* | *mondai-ga* | *tokeru* |
| | 'It is Taroo for whom the problem is solvable' | | |
| or | *taroo-ga* | *biiru-ga* | *nomitai* |
| | 'It is Taroo who wants to drink the beer' | | |
| but not | *taroo-ga* | *biiru-ga* | *nomu* |
| | ? 'It is Taroo for whom the beer drinks' | | |
| AffectedFocus | FOCUS | NEWS | VERB |
| | AFFECTED | MEDIUM | Stative? |
| e.g. | *taroo-ga* | *hebi-ga* | *kowai* |
| | 'It is Taroo that snakes frighten' | | |
| e.g. | *biiru-ga* | *nomi-tai* | |
| | 'it is beer for which there is a wanting for it to be drunk' | | |
| BySubjecthood | | NEWS | VERBCLUSTER |
| | | AFFECTED | PassiveVG |
| | | MEDIUM | |
| e.g. 'Taroo is rained on' | *taroo-ga* | ... | *fura-reru* |
| NonFocusing | | NEWS | VERBCLUSTER |
| | | MEDIUM | ActiveVG |
| e.g. 'Taroo goes' | | *taroo-ga* | *iku* |
| or | | | |
| e.g. 'A window opens' | | *mado-ga* | *aku* |
| | | *hebi-ga* | *kowai* |
| | 'It is snakes that are frightening' | | |

**Figure 7.14** The structures constrained by the case assignment by salience systems

state that the presence of an information layer function News or Focus is sufficient for marking with *ga*. Figure 7.15 shows the functional structures for our toy text (1)–(5) above, as those structures are defined by the portions of grammar networks shown in Figures 7.9, 7.10, and 7.13. The figure also shows the grammatical features for each structure (the selection

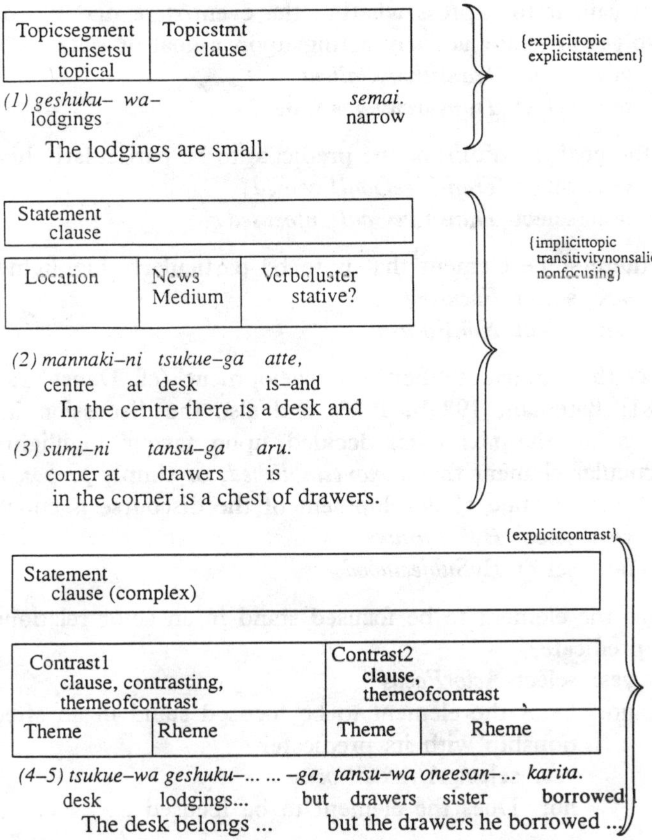


**Figure 7.15** **Functional structures and partial selection expressions for toy text (1)–(5)**

expressions) that are motivated by the grammatical systems we have given.

Although most of the possible combinations involving *ga* and *wa* are covered by the network as given, what is important in the context of text generation is not so much covering the space of grammatical possibilities, but *controlling* those resources that are available. For this, we need to examine the choosers associated with the network. As we saw in the discussion of tense and of the 'topic' particle, each choice point in the grammar network has associated with it a decision based upon the kinds of textual distinctions that the grammatical distinction has been found to be helping to express; these may be set out as follows, respecting the labelling given in Figure 7.13.

A: Is it salient to express whether the event/state under consideration involves an actor actively acting upon a goal or not?
    yes: select *TransitivitySalient*
    no: select *TransitivityNonSalient*

B: Is the goal (medium) of the predicate to be particularly highlighted?
    yes: select *TransitiveGoalFocused*
    no: select *TransitiveGoalUnfocused*

C: Is there some element that is to be particularly highlighted?
    yes: select *Focusing*
    no: select *NonFocusing*

D: Does the pattern of 'thematic development' (cf. Daneš, 1974; Fries, 1981; Bateman, 1985b, 1986; and also the discussion in Part III below on the *text base*) decided upon favour highlighting some particular element that is *nonestablished*, or simply *proposed* as far as the current state of development of the discourse is concerned?
    yes: select *ByFocushood*
    no: select *BySubjecthood*

E: Does the element to be focused stand in an actor relationship with its predicate?
    yes: select *ActorFocus*
    no: Does the element to be focused stand in an affected relationship with its predicate?
        yes: select *AffectedFocus*
        no: Does the element to be focused . . . etc.

We can now contrast those clauses shown in Figure 7.11 that appeared to share ideational meaning to see how they differ; the principal examples were (10b,c), (11b,c,d) and (12b,c). The clauses may be grouped in terms of their grammatical features as follows:

| *clauses* | *grammatical features* |
|---|---|
| (10b), (11b) | {TransitivitySalient, TransitiveGoalUnfocused} |
| (10c), (11c), (12b) | {TransitivityNonSalient, Focusing, ByFocushood} |
| (11d), (12c) | {TransitivityNonSalient, NonFocusing} |

This shows the commonalities and differences between the clauses in terms of their feature selections. Clause (11c), for example, is similar to clauses (10c) and (12b), while simultaneously differing from clause (11d), in that it selects to single out one of its participants as focused and does not grant any particular salience to the transitivity relationship of some agent actively acting upon some medium or goal; clause (11d) also does not grant any salience to a transitivity relationship but does not focus especially on any of its participants. Similarly, clause (10b) differs from clause (10c) in that it grants the transitivity relationship salience while clause (10c) does not. Each of the different clauses that appear to share ideational meaning can now be functionally motivated in this way.

We can now also explicitly *motivate* the particle deployments that we saw in the toy text of (1)–(5), and whose functional structures and feature selection expressions we gave in Figure 7.15, by considering the responses that the environment (text planner, user model, etc. — see Chapter 9) must provide for the grammar's inquiries. When beginning this segment of text, the TOPIC LINKAGE system (Figure 7.9) is entered and the following chooser inquiries are made:

> Does the communicative intent propose a shift of topic?
> Does the communicative intent involve a statement about that topic?

Since the text is now moving on to discuss the lodgings (*geshuku*), the first inquiry receives a positive response; then, since there is text content to be expressed concerning this topic, the second inquiry also receives a positive response. This sets up the structure of contribution (1) with the new topic marked by *wa*. In each of the subsequent contributions, (2)–(5), the first of these inquiries receives a negative response since the topic remains fixed on the lodgings. This sets up contribution structures for (2)–(5) where each consists of a single constituent which is labelled Statement and preselected to be a clause (either simplex or complex).

Thus, when (2) is considered, it is already known to be a topic preserving statement (implicittopic) that is a clause. Subsequently, when traversing the case assignment by salience systems (Figure 7.13), the inquiry:

> Is it salient to express whether the event/state under consideration involves an actor actively acting upon a goal or not? [A]

is put. Since the meaning to be expressed is simply a static attribution of location to an entity, this receives a negative response and results in the selection of the grammatical feature 'transitivitynonsalient'. This leads on to a grammatical system where the inquiry:

> Is there some element that is to be particularly highlighted? [C]

is put. This again receives a negative response since there is no particular reason for highlighting the items of furniture or their locations at this stage in the text: this is simply a neutral presentation of information. This causes the selection of the feature 'nonfocusing' and a structure similar to that of (12d) is constructed, with the item of furniture realized by a constituent functionally labelled as the conflation of News and Medium. This is therefore marked by the particle *ga*. Exactly the same state of affairs holds for contribution (3).

Finally, when the Statement for (4)–(5) is considered, the text planner has decided to express a contrastive relationship between the ownership of the desk (*tsukue*) and the drawers (*tansu*). Thus, the inquiry for the CONTRASTIVE system (Figure 7.10) gets a positive response, selecting grammatical feature 'explicitcontrast'. This constructs a clause complex, with a clause for each part of the contrast to be expressed and the 'themes' of contrast, which are marked by the particle *wa*, realizing the desk and the drawers.

### *7.3.3 Conclusion*

In this section we have given a brief presentation of a systemic treatment of a very restrictive part of the Japanese resources for expressing participants' textual prominence — i.e., that achieved by deployment of the nominal post-positions *wa* and *ga*. We have illustrated the organization of coherent sets of grammatical feature selections by chooser questions, or inquiries, that are specifically oriented to issues of salience. To a significant degree, Japanese post-positions directly indicate the kinds of 'textual saliences' that participants are to be granted in the context of the 'story' that a text tells. According to this view, treatments that attempt to restrict their accounts to clause-internal phenomena, such as grammatical relations or structural position (cf. Kuno, 1973), will be unlikely to be able to *motivate functionally* the full range of particle deployments that can be seen in Japanese and so will not be able to generate *under control* the linguistic variation that different contexts of use require. In addition, the few functional attempts to motivate particle assignment do not have the benefit of a framework of functional organization such as inquiry semantics and this limits their possibilities for expressing functional generalizations. The theoretical link that is established between linguistic structures, inquiries, and components of the grammar's environment provides a natural framework within which previously disparate, or undiscovered, facts concerning the textual control of linguistic constructions can be integrated and generalizations sought.

Now, however, just as was the case with tense, it is necessary to consider the kinds of information that the grammar's environment must support in order to be able to answer the grammar's inquiries. This again will involve rather sophisticated text planning in order to attribute degrees of prominence to participants and events as appropriate for the needs of particular texts. Following the definition of the two grammar fragments

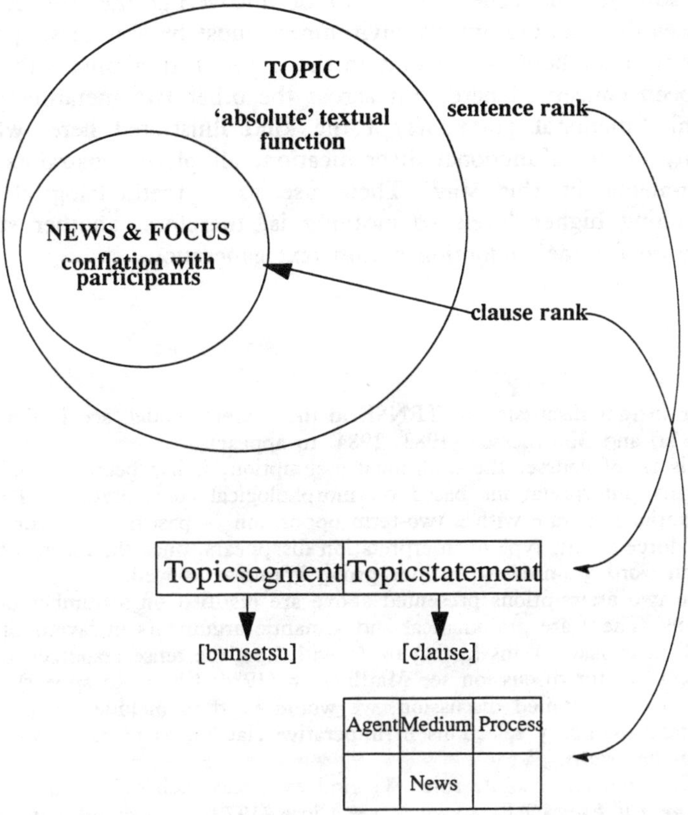


**Figure 7.16** Textual meanings and their realizations for Japanese

shown in Figures 7.9 and 7.10 and their corresponding choosers and inquiries, for example, we have identified two types of textual meanings that must be supported: topicality and contrast. In addition, we know that it must be possible for the text plan to determine whether the text requires an explicit statement about a topic to be made or not. Furthermore, following the grammar fragment shown in Figure 7.13, it is also necessary for the text plan to establish whether entities mentioned in a discourse are known, established, etc. or not. A text planner that does not plan in terms of these features will be unable to control the grammar and inappropriate or unconstrained choices are likely to result. Figure 7.16 shows in diagram form the interrelationship between the kinds of textual meanings that need to be supported and expressed for Japanese and their realization through lexicogrammatical functional structures.

We address this general question of uncovering the information and processes that the grammar's environment must be able to support in the next part of the book — not only in the largely textual area with which we have been concerned here, but across the other two metafunctions also. Systemic-functional grammars of the kind illustrated here, which rely crucially on metafunctional diversification, all place constraints on their environments in this way. Their use as a methodological tool for approaching higher levels of meaning is, therefore, another substantial motivation for their adoption within text generation.

## Notes

1. For further discussion of TENSE in the present model, see Halliday (1976a, 1985a) and Matthiessen (1983, 1984, to appear).
2. This is, of course, the traditional assumption; it has been rejected in structuralist interpretations based on morphological considerations. These interpretations operate with a two-term opposition — past/non-past (present). But the force of this type of interpretation disappears, once the focus is broadened from word grammar to include group grammar as well.
3. The two assumptions presented above are justified on a number of different levels. There are grammatical and semantic arguments in favour of them, as well as considerations having to do with how the tense resources are used in discourse: for discussion see Matthiessen (1984: Ch. 6; to appear).
4. In a more detailed discussion, we would need to include the possibility of certain secondary selections in imperative clauses, as in *be working when the inspection starts*.
5. This is not an absolute rule. We find examples such as *It'll take me an hour before I'll know* (AE, spoken); see Close (1979) for examples in conditional dependent clauses.
6. In this case, the contrast is also additionally realized in a clause combination involving the contrastive clause combiner *ga* — which bears no relation to the nominal postposition we are discussing.
7. Further, *wa*-marked constituents might be admitted by allowing a recursive, looping re-entry of the TOPIC LINKAGE system; we will not discuss this possibility further here — although we do discuss in Parts III and IV some of the problems inherent with using networks with such loops.
8. Although in subordinate clauses the case or grammatical relation marking function of *ga* comes to predominate, yet this can be expected given the restricted thematic and textual options available for clauses that already occupy a subordinate position.
9. Even though these constructions are occasionally referred to as 'double subject' constructions.
10. Kuno (1973: 68) and Gunji (1987) discuss clauses where there is more than one *ga*-marked constituent. We will not consider this detail here; see Bateman (1990a) for further discussion.
11. Figure 7.13 also contains some of the grammatical options responsible for the use of the particle *wo*; for further discussion, again see Bateman (1990a).

# Part III Up to and beyond the limits of the basic framework

In Parts I and II of this book we saw the overall systemic-functional linguistic framework and two similar computational instantiations of some significant aspects of that framework. As we have suggested, and as can be seen in the text generation literature, there is much that can be done within the limits of these systems. To show their existing power, however, is not our main concern here. We are more concerned with showing computational systemic-functional linguistics as another application of systemic-functional linguistics in general. And, following systemic-functional methodology, this requires that applications stretch and feed back into theory development: the theory development–application–theory redevelopment cycle of exchange is crucial.

In this part of the book, then, we present applications where the basic instantiation of the grammar, choosers, and inquiry semantics levels of the theory has not been adequate. In these areas we have implemented extensions to provide the functionalities required. Typically, these developments have been made on the basis of evidence from both English and Japanese, but first implemented with respect to the Japanese system because of its smaller size and manageability. Our discussions will reflect this course of development. They are divided into two chapters: the first (Chapter 8) is concerned with extensions within the level of grammar and semantics, the second (Chapter 9) with developments at the higher levels of organization to which grammar and semantics must be responsive. Both chapters are additionally organized in terms of the three metafunctions.

Subsequently, in Part IV, we concern ourselves with more speculative re-abstractions and theory development motivated by these extensions.

# 8 Metafunctional refinements

## 8.1 Introduction: metafunctional diversity of modes of expression

In the course of extending our grammars and semantics, we found that various *representational issues* arise which can be beneficially interpreted in terms of the differences between the metafunctions. More specifically, Halliday (1979) has shown that each metafunction tends to engender its own mode of organization. For example, the *experiential* subtype of the ideational metafunction engenders the mode of *configurational constituency* — this is typically expressed through constituency configurations such as Actor + Process + Goal, etc. We can make the broad generalization about the computational implementations of systemic-functional grammar discussed in Part II that they are also essentially based on the experiential model of grammatical organization. This means that the structures that are defined by the realization statements are *constituency* structures and the systems in the system network can be represented synoptically (statically).

This experiential mode of organization is a good starting point in computational work, because it is well understood and easy to formalize; in particular, constituency structure has been the focus of most recent work on grammar both within linguistics and computational linguistics. Furthermore, the experiential mode of organization can be used to represent the other metafunctions — up to a point. Thus, interpersonal clause structure in English is represented as a configuration of Mood + Residue, as in Halliday (1985a: Ch. 4), and textual clause structure as a configuration of Theme + Rheme (op.cit., Ch. 3). It is this method of representation that supported the use of the experiential model of grammatical organization throughout Part II. Importantly, however, this use of configurational resources to represent the realization of non-experiential meanings is *only an approximation* and, in this part of the book, we will begin to explore in more detail what it means for a computational account to take into consideration metafunctional diversity in modes of organization. This will of necessity be rather limited, since this entire area of the computational modelling of systemic theory is only just beginning.

The modes of organization engendered by the remaining metafunctions may be described as follows.

- The logical subtype of the ideational metafunction is expressed through INTERDEPENDENCY STRUCTURE — as occurs, for example, in sequences of coordinated units. Halliday introduces this kind of structure thus:

  > We shall interpret the relations between clauses in terms of the 'logical' component of the linguistic system: the functional-semantic relations that make up the logic of natural language. There are two dimensions in the interpretation. One is the system of interdependency, or 'tactic' system, parataxis and hypotaxis, which is general to all complexes . . . (Halliday, 1985a: 193)

We will discuss the logical subtype of the ideational metafunction in Section 8.2 and further discussion is presented in, for example, Martin (1988, forthcoming).

- The textual metafunction is typically expressed through PULSES of prominence and non-prominence — as, for example, in the intonational prominence given to new information, and the linear placing pulse that places thematic information towards the beginning of clauses. We will discuss this metafunction and its expression further in Section 8.3.
- The interpersonal metafunction is typically expressed through PROSODIES that run through a linguistic unit, affecting a range of grammatical feature selections. Examples of this phenomenon include selections of modalization and 'hedging' words running through a clause to indicate that its proposition is tentative; or the expression of identity or nonidentity of a participant or circumstance with the subject by means of the use of reflexive forms. In each case, a particular 'melody' is maintained across a specified domain in the linguistic unit effected. Martin (1990) and Poynton (forthcoming) provide more detail on the expression of interpersonal meanings, while we consider some of the implications for interpersonal modelling within the semantic stratum in Section 8.4.

Importantly, we must emphasize that a typical grammatical unit may make use of *all* of these kinds of syntagmatic organization *simultaneously* to a greater or lesser degree: only the composition of the properties described will provide a 'complete' description.[1]

In addition to distinct modes of organization the metafunctions also tend to create different types of *systems*. This is presented in summary form in the table of Figure 8.1. Finally, for further discussion of this important area of systemic theorizing, see Halliday (1979), Matthiessen (1988a), MacGregor (1989), and Matthiessen and Halliday (forthcoming). A

| *metafunction* | *special system type* | *'structure' type* |
|---|---|---|
| logical | recursive system | interdependency |
| experiential | (normal) | constituency |
| interpersonal | (normal; scalar system) | prosody (potentially amplified) |
| textual | 'situated' system | pulse |

**Figure 8.1** System and structure types according to metafunction

definitive overview of the distinct kinds of modes of organization and their metafunctional motivation is given in Matthiessen (1990c).

## 8.2 Ideational: networks with loops

As we have seen in our description of systemic-functional theory of Part II, an SFG is organized around the dimension of choice; a grammar consists of a network of interconnected and interdependent points of abstract choice between minimal grammatical alternatives. These choice points are called *systems* and are represented by an entry condition, which specifies when the choice is relevant, and a set of possible choice alternatives, called output features. In addition to the kind of network connectivity that we have made use of up to now, however, systemic linguists have found it useful to employ the extended kind of connectivity typically engendered by *recursive systems*. A recursive system is, most simply, a system which uses one of its output features as one of its entry conditions. When represented graphically, this is usually taken to imply a loop that connects a system's feature back to the entry point for that system; this was illustrated in Figure 7.3, where we offered a system for serial tense in terms of linear recursion. Naturally, this can be generalized to include recursive (sub-)networks where the looping back is not confined within a single system.

Even though the inclusion of such systems violates the partial ordering that may otherwise be imposed upon systems of a system network and so complicates the network's formal properties, systemic linguists have nevertheless felt the need to represent linguistic potential using such recursive networks in a variety of areas. Most commonly, these areas share the notion of 'complexing'. Complexing provides a mechanism for building up structures of arbitrary size without resorting to structural embedding. One rather basic motivation, then, for placing recursion in systemic networks is to allow arbitrary long structures with minimal, flat structural bracketing

— thus avoiding the linguistically unmotivated depth of structural recursion's immediate constituency style of bracketing (e.g., Hudson, 1971: 61–2). A rather more significant reason for employing recursive systems, however, is the different principle that is involved in constructing complexes. Complexing creates *dependency* organization rather than constituency organization and is the natural mode of representation for the resources of the logical subcomponent of the ideational metafunction.

A grammatical unit, such as the clause, may participate in a clause *complex* that chains together a sequence of clauses that are in some way interdependent (cf. Halliday, 1985a: 192ff.). Dependency organization attempts to capture a different kind of linguistic patterning to that found in constituency-oriented treatments, one that is more suited to the intricate flow of spoken language. An example of this organization, and the complexity it regularly achieves in natural, spontaneous language is provided by the following extract from a spoken text cited by Halliday:

> but you can't get the whole set done all at once because if you do you won't have any left to use at home, unless you just took the lids in and kept the boxes, in which case you wouldn't have to have had everything unpacked first; but then you couldn't be sure the designs would match, so. . . (Halliday, 1985a: xxiv)

In spoken language, this kind of complexity is the norm rather than the exception; intricate combinations of clauses are managed with no apparent difficulties in production or comprehension. Thus,

> The clause complex is of particular interest in spoken language, because it represents the dynamic potential of the system — the ability to 'choreograph' very long and intricate patterns of semantic movement while maintaining a continuous flow of discourse that is coherent without being constructional. This kind of flow is very uncharacteristic of written language. Since grammatical theory evolved as the study of written language, it is good at synoptic-type 'product' representations, with constituency as the organizing concept, but bad at dynamic-type 'process' representations, which is what is needed for the interpretation of speech. (Halliday, 1985a: 201–2)

The dependency style of organization is intended to capture precisely this sense of a dynamic and ever-changing reassessment of possibilities on the basis of what has gone before and where one wishes to go. Indeed,

> The clauses that go to make up a clause complex such as this one are not embedded one inside another. The speaker does not construct a mental plan of the grammar in advance, like a completed architectural drawing; rather, he sets out on a journey, and each lap of the journey takes him to a point from where he can set out again. One lap may be dependent on another, in the sense that he sets out for point (a) because this is a good way of getting to point (b); but each lap is a distinctive stage in his progress. The grammar (that is, the model of grammar) that is used for interpreting casual conversation needs to represent the clause complex in this fashion,

rather than as a static edifice of structural constituents. (Halliday, 1985b)

A number of areas in the grammar of English have been treated in terms of dependency, including the clause complex, nominal group complexes and tense (Halliday, 1976a). Martin (1988) contains a more exhaustive list of areas that *could* be treated in dependency terms as an alternative mode of analysis, although more as a way of presenting some counter-hypotheses rather than as an argument that they should be so treated in all cases. There are good grounds, then, for allowing the statement of linguistic potential that recursive systems and networks represent. Unfortunately, the recursive system networks of the logical mode of organization have long been known to present theoretical problems: this was one motivation for our non-recursive 'simulation' of the recursive network for tense in Chapter 7 (Figure 7.4). We will argue below, particularly in Chapter 11, that these problems arise from the essentially distinct natures of *synoptic* and *dynamic* modes of linguistic organization.[2] Meanwhile, we will make our way to this conclusion by means of a concrete computational implementation of the theoretical resources required.

One of the earliest attempts to computationally represent a systemic-functional type grammar was that of Henrici (1981/1965). He undertook to provide a fully specified computational algorithm that could produce the set of selection expressions corresponding to any specified grammar network. This task involves recording the output features that are selected, or chosen, during a traversal of a network. He also began to work out in some detail how the structural consequences of these choices, i.e., the *realization statements* associated with particular feature selections, could be interpreted algorithmically in order to build up automatically the structure that the feature selections entail.

However, Henrici's basic algorithm relied upon the network of systems having certain properties, one of which is precisely the partial ordering of systems that excludes the possibility of any feature being used as an entry condition of its own system. This rejection of recursive systems was certainly well motivated; it was already clear that the necessary extension to the algorithm to handle recursive systems was non-trivial. As Henrici notes, 'linear recursion is rather more troublesome' and, although he does make some suggestive comments concerning recursive systems, he concludes that 'further speculative discussion of how these devices might be made to work would at this stage be premature and unprofitable' (Henrici, 1981/1965: 95).

Almost twenty years later the situation had not appreciably changed. Even though the computational implementation of certain aspects of the grammatical stratum of the linguistic system found in Nigel (see Part II) moves far beyond Henrici's implementation, recursive systems are still noticeably absent.[3] It was found, however, in the construction of our Japanese grammars that *not* providing the theoretical resources of linear recursion significantly complicated the accounts we could offer. We therefore took the step of attempting prototype implementations of networks that support recursion and the construction of dependency style syntagmatic organization.

### *8.2.1 Logical recursion in the Japanese verbal group*

The verbal group of Japanese provides a rich domain of morphological, grammatical, and semantic interactions. Many distinct meanings, from all three metafunctions, are typically expressed in the verbal group. Examples include:

- ideational: causation, tense;
- interpersonal: permission, 'passivization', doing favours for others, receiving favours from others, wanting the main process to come about, interlocutor-oriented level of formality;
- textual: discourse subordination.

All of these meanings are expressed in a rather similar way: by the insertion of a morpheme responsible for one of the above meaning contributions. These morphemes all have regular consequences for the morphological form of their neighbours.

In a little more detail, the verbal group in Japanese (VG) is generally constructed by appending a sequence of auxiliary verbs (AUXV) to the main verb; these AUXVs influence the morphology of the word they follow. That is, considering word *a* and word *b* as elements of a VG and assuming that *b* is appended after *a*, then *a* is inflected according to the 'inflection type' which *b* prefers and the 'inflection pattern' to which *a* belongs. For example, in the clause:

| *watashi-* | *wa* | *gakkoo-* | *e* | *iki-taku-nakat-ta* |
|---|---|---|---|---|
| I | -TOPIC | school- | to | go-want-not-past |

'I didn't want to go to school'

the final verb constituent may be decomposed as follows:

```
iki  --  taku  ---  nakat  ----  ta
 |        |           |          |
iku      tai         nai         ta
(go)    (want)      (not)      (past)
```

The past morpheme *ta* conditions the negative morpheme *nai* to have the

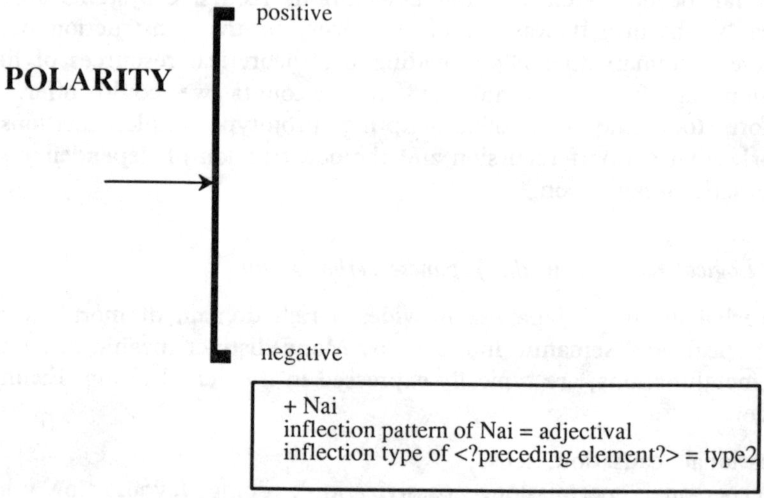


**Figure 8.2** The positive/negative distinction in the verbal group

form *nakat*, the negativity morpheme conditions the 'want' morpheme *tai* to have the form *taku*, and the 'want' morpheme conditions the main verb *iku*, 'to go', to have the form *iki*.

The extensive range and variety of auxiliaries that may be used in Japanese raises the following problem. When constructing VGs of this kind with a systemic grammar in which there are systems which decide whether certain AUXVs are to be added or not, the inflection of each word cannot be identified until the next word is distinguished. In computational implementations of SFG such as Nigel there is no general way to refer to the constituent *preceding* a given constituent. Constituents may only be referenced via their functional labels identifying them as constituent elements of a particular unit; unless some functional label of the constituent actually preceding is already known, therefore, that constituent cannot be referred to. The realization statements of any given AUXV system cannot then refer to the constituents they need to influence.

In the system of Figure 8.2 for example, which decides the polarity ('negative'/'positive') of a VG, consider when grammatical feature 'negative' is selected. This causes the AUXV *Nai* to be inserted into the VG structure. Another consequence of this grammatical feature selection needs to be that the verb component *preceding* this is constrained to have a particular inflection type (in this case, type 2). But this is difficult to realize because there is no functional label available where this constraint can be placed. When this choice is made it is not yet known what the verb

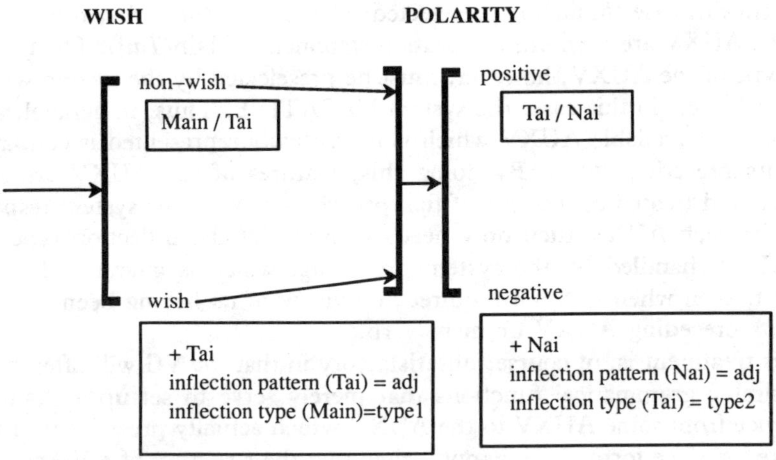


**Figure 8.3** Capturing dependencies in the verbal group

```
Unit of type VERB-GROUP-UNIT denoting READS
structure:

------------------------------------------------------------------------
||      T2          CORE        H1      VC1
||      H2          VC2         H3      VC3
||      H4          H5          H6      T1
||      H7          VC7         H8      VC8
||      H9          VC9         H10     VC10
::                             :CONTENT-VERB     STEM1      INFLECT
::                             :WORD
yomu
```

**Figure 8.4** Functional structure of the verbal group 'reads'

component preceding *Nai* will be. Neither does it suffice simply to collect the features until they are all known for the verbal group and then to attempt the appropriate structure construction: in order to trigger appropriate realization statements it will almost be necessary to enumerate the possibilities — not an attractive option given the range of potential available within the verbal group.

Despite these problems, in our research at Kyoto University we first attempted to construct a treatment of these constructions remaining within the constraints imposed by the mechanisms developed for Nigel. This treatment assumed a default ordering of AUXVs and then tried to link up the systems dealing with them accordingly; this is illustrated in Figure 8.3. If a system decides to add an AUXV (say *tai* by selecting the feature 'wish'), that AUXV's own inflection pattern and the inflection type of its preceding word (in this case 'Main') is preselected; if it is not added, that front word and the AUXV are *conflated* (realization statement: [Main/*Tai*]). The inflection type of the AUXV, however, must be preselected by the system which 'follows'; e.g., in this case, the system NEGATIVE. Thus, in general, any 'potentially' available AUXV which is not actually represented is conflated with its preceding word. By doing this, features of the AUXV are also merged and treated as features of that preceding word. The system responsible for each AUXV then only needs to preselect the inflection type for the AUXV handled by the system preceding, which is guaranteed to be present, even when it is not required, by virtue of its having been merged with *its* preceding AUXV or main verb.

This treatment is, of course, unsatisfactory in that the VG will often have undesirable grammatical functions that merely serve to set up a chain of reference from some AUXV to the AUXV which actually precedes it in the required surface form. It is inappropriate that the structure of a VG should include functions corresponding to 'wish' or 'negative' even though the corresponding surface forms *tai* or *nai* are not represented and their meanings are not intended. Figure 8.4 shows an actual worst case in which no less than twenty grammatical functions were conflated in order to produce a single grammatical constituent *yomu*, 'to read', because no auxiliaries at all were required.[4]

Attempting to cover the range and variety of auxiliaries that may be used in Japanese in this manner therefore pays the price of having a grammar that is over-complex and rather 'tangled' considering the evident regularity of the verbal constituent itself. Indeed, the initial fragment that included this treatment of verbal groups, which is described in full in Tabuchi (1986), altogether consists of around 260 systems and gates, although very few of these systems have had their choosers specified. Even though the grammar fragment was capable of producing quite complex verb phrases and there is no doubt that various optimizations and simplifications could have been made, the basic nature of the complexity involved led us to the conclusion that there would be no real point in extending the fragment further if the same form of organization were maintained. What was involved was the basic notational problem with the current implementation of SFG representational resources. We therefore rewrote the grammar for this area of Japanese, building into our implementation an extension that permitted us to express the *dependency* relationships between the successive elements of the verbal group directly.

To recap, the essential problem for capturing this type of organization by means of the implementation of SFG found in Nigel-style grammars is that there is no way for a system to reference an immediately 'preceding' element of structure without knowing in advance some functional label of that element. This problem is another example of the lag between theory and representation in systemic linguistics that we referred to in Chapter 2; Halliday (1981/1965) has already presented an analysis that may be applied to the kinds of structure that we observe in the Japanese verbal group and our extension to the computational mechanisms available was a move towards incorporating this analysis. Applying the dependency account of complexes to Japanese, a complex verbal group such as:

| | | | |
|---|---|---|---|
| *yoma-* | *seta-* | *morat-* | *ta* |
| read- | cause- | receive- | past |

literally, 'someone received the favour of having someone make someone read', as found in the following clause suggested by Kuno:[5]

| | | | |
|---|---|---|---|
| *Taroo-wa* | *Jiroo-ni,* | *kodomo-ni* | *jibun-no-heya-de* |
| (TOPIC) | (OO1) | child (OO2) | SELF 's room(LOC) |

| | |
|---|---|
| *hon-wo* | *yoma-seta- morat- ta* |
| book(GOAL) | read-cause-receive-past |

(Kuno, 1973: 306)

'Jiroo made the child read the book in his/her own room for Taroo'

may be analysed in terms of Halliday's treatment of HYPOTAXIS as shown in Figure 8.5, where the structure is viewed as a 'chain' of similar elements linked by a *logical dependency* relation. In this case, the dependency runs from right-to-left — the realization is regressive — and is reflected in the influence that each verb part has upon the morphology of the verb part which depends upon it. Although the acknowledgement of this kind of structuring would seem to provide the functional labels necessary for accessing the 'constituent preceding', since it is possible to refer to them in terms of the dependency structure [$\alpha$, $\beta$, $\gamma$, . . .], present computational systemic frameworks do not have any explicit representation for this theoretical possibility. It is commonly assumed that what is required to generate this type of dependency structure is a 'looping' network of the form shown in Figure 8.6 but, despite a long-standing tendency to write systemic grammars using such logical looping systems, no clear formalization of what this is intended to capture has been achieved.

Our current experimental program supports such systems as follows. Previously, single cycles of actualization, i.e., single traversals of the network constituting the grammar, were always taken to be generating a MULTIVARIATE grammatical structure. This is a functional structure of the traditional kind where the constituents receive a variety of distinct

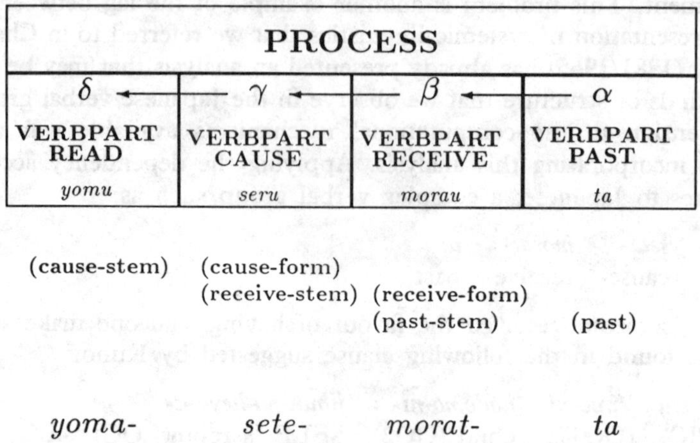


**Figure 8.5** Verb complex analysis in terms of hypotaxis

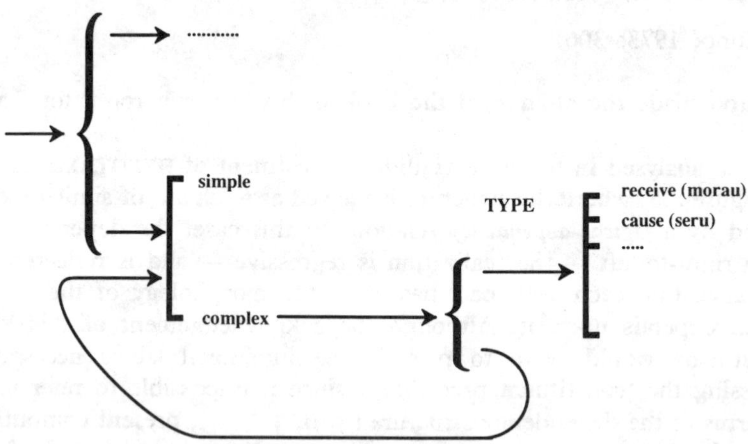


**Figure 8.6** Simple recursive network for the verbal group

functional labels (e.g., Actor–Process–Goal). Importantly, each occurrence of a functional label is unique at its own level of structure; i.e., it has no similarly labelled siblings. Now cycles of actualization may also generate UNIVARIATE grammatical structures which consist of constituents of a *single* grammatical function label repeated any number of times. The former type of structure typically has EXPERIENTIAL functions, the latter LOGICAL functions (e.g., hypotaxis: $\alpha$, $\beta$, $\gamma$, . . .; parataxis: 1, 2, 3, . . .

— cf. Halliday, 1985a) which simply serve to represent the chain of dependency for otherwise similar grammatical elements.

This initial implementation of the representational resources necessary for expressing dependency organization as realizing feature selections made within a recursive network attempted to embody as closely as possible a straightforward 'natural' interpretation of such networks, as generally employed in noncomputational contexts, making use of current computational techniques. This involved both revisions to the interpretations of system networks and extensions to the set of realization statements supported. We will take these two areas of extension in turn and then show an example of actual generation drawing on the resources created.

The principal alteration that needed to be undertaken in the interpretation of a systemic network when allowing the network to contain loops was to permit certain systems to be 'entered' more than once during a single traversal of the grammar. This has the natural consequence that features from such systems may be selected more than once and, worse, that distinct features from any single such system — which would normally be in strict alternation given the standard interpretation of a system — may be selected for a particular traversal. This needed to be made sense of for the extension to work. The most simple way of achieving this was by interpreting the network itself as a 'flowchart' (see, for example, the discussion in Fawcett 1980: 198–200); this, in terms of implementation, amounted to a simplification of the network traversal process since it was no longer considered necessary to inhibit multiple entries of a single system. Unfortunately, although this did provide a mechanism which could, at least, follow a system network as a cooperative linguist would tend to do, it created a number of problems of its own and evaded questions as to the precise *meaning* of multiple feature selections from a single system. We will return to these difficulties in Chapter 11.

Rather more work had to be done for the realization statements necessary to create dependency structures. The realization statements in this area, as is often the case in SFL with its emphasis on the paradigmatic mode of organization, had previously received less attention and precise specification than their rather crucial position warrants. In particular, it was necessary to build in the following property: complexes, or dependency structures, need to be able to grow on demand. This differs from the corresponding multivariate (constituency-style) insertion of an additional grammatical (micro-)function (e.g. Actor, Goal, Locative, etc.) in that dependency functional labels do *not* identify the component. In dependency structures, the *dependency position* is the defining characteristic; for example, a third component ($\gamma$) in a hypotactic dependency chain will typically be constrained by the realization of the second component ($\beta$). The components need receive no further identification of function than their dependency position.

To capture this, two additions were made to the realization facilities of the framework:

- A realization operation for growing a dependency structure was defined; this had two forms: *expandpara* and *expandhypo*, for developing paratactic and hypotactic dependencies respectively. Each application of this realization statement causes a new link in the dependency chain to be grown, as in the $\alpha$, $\beta$, . . . chain shown in Figure 8.5.
- Two *logical* micro-functions were defined: Current and Next. These were deliberately made analogous to the *experiential* micro-functions found in multivariate structures, such as, for example, Actor, Medium, etc. The logical micro-functions, however, need to be interpreted with respect to the *current state of growth* of the dependency chain they are helping define; that is, they always refer to, and relate, the two most 'recent', i.e., most dependent, elements of the chain and are, therefore, essentially dynamic in nature. These naturally change as new elements are grown by further applications of the *expandpara* or *expandhypo* realizations; in particular, what was the Next element becomes the Current element, and a new Next element is created. Note that this removes the need to 'index' elements in order to identify uniquely which element of a chain is being addressed.[6]

Figure 8.7 shows a network for generating basic Japanese verbal groups that uses these network and realizational extensions. The generation of the example shown in Figure 8.5 would then proceed as follows. When the features selected are: {complex, past, complex, receive, complex, cause, simple}, as they need to be for our example, then the following realization statements are executed:

| | | |
|---|---|---|
| Preselect Next | (i.e. $\beta$) | past-stem |
| Preselect Current | (i.e. $\alpha$) | past-form |
| Expandhypo | | |
| Preselect Current | (i.e. $\beta$) | receive-form |
| Preselect Next | (i.e. $\gamma$) | receive-stem |
| Expandhypo | | |
| Preselect Current | (i.e. $\gamma$) | cause-form |
| Preselect Next | (i.e. $\delta$) | cause-stem |
| Preselect Next | (i.e. $\delta$) | contentverb |

That is, first, the feature 'complex' takes us to the TYPE system from which 'past' is selected; then the choice of 'simple'/'complex' is made again so as to re-enter the possible TYPEs. Finally, the looping is brought

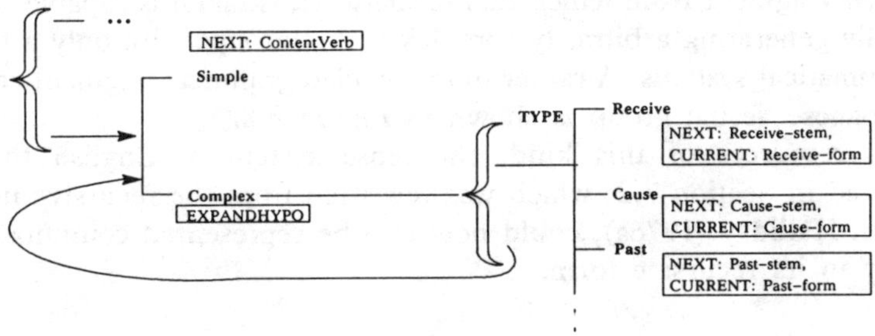


**Figure 8.7** A basic recursive network for the Japanese verbal group

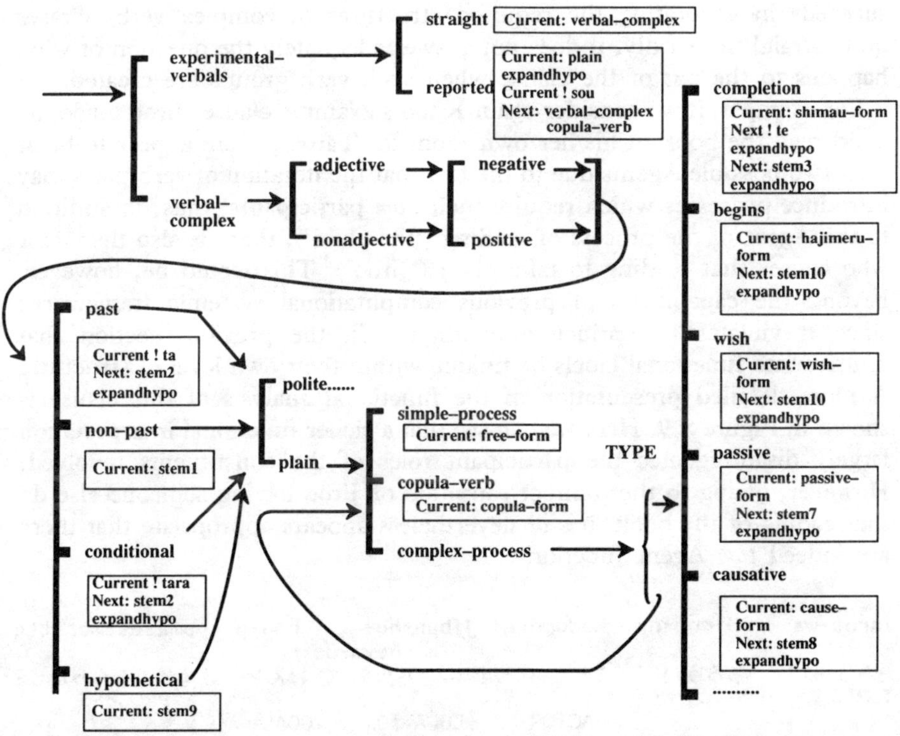


**Figure 8.8** Experimental verbal group network

to an end by the selection of the feature 'simple'. Although this serves to construct the desired verb complex structure, there are a few problems with this network as it stands. It does, however, illustrate the basic idea of constructing complex structures by means of a looping network and the nmar fragment from which this subnetwork is taken is capable of automatically generating arbitrarily complex verbal groups with only a handful of grammatical systems. A rather more detailed grammar fragment covering the Japanese verbal group is shown in Figure 8.8.

With resources of this kind, the tense system of English that was illustrated in Section 7.2, which was rewritten from the recursive network given in Halliday (1976a), could now also be represented computationally directly in its recursive form.

### 8.2.2 *Logical recursion in transitivity: causation*

Although the treatment of verb groups shown in the previous section succeeds in generating the required structures of complex verb phrases quite straightforwardly, it does not answer adequately the question of what happens to the *rest* of the clause when such verb groups are created.

For example, if we consider again Kuno's example clause 'Jiroo made the child read the book in his/her own room for Taroo', there appear to be at least two possible Agents due to the fact that the iteration of verb parts may introduce processes which require their *own* participants; thus, in addition to the Agent of the process of reading ('the child'), there is also the Actor who causes that reading to take place ('Jiroo'). This would be, however, beyond the capabilities of previous computational systemic frameworks since it violates the principle mentioned in the previous section that multivariate functional labels be unique within their own level of structure. A more detailed presentation of the functional analysis of this clause is shown in Figure 8.9. Here we can see that a richer functional interpretation largely disambiguates the participant roles of the constituents involved. However, owing to the indirect causation of Jiroo having someone else do the reading of the book, it still nevertheless appears appropriate that there are indeed *two* Agent functions.

| | | | | | |
|---|---|---|---|---|---|
| Taroo-wa | Jiroo-ni | kodomo-ni | jibun-no-heya-de | hon-o | yomasetemoratta |
| たろう は | じろう に、 | こども に | じぶんの へや で | ほんを | よませてもらった |
| TOPIC | | | | | PROCESS |
| | | ACTOR | LOCATION | GOAL | γ |
| | AGENT.1 | AGENT.2 | | MEDIUM | β |
| | INITIATOR | | | | α |
| BENEFICIARY | BENEFACTOR | | | | |

**Figure 8.9** Functional decomposition of example clause

Similarly, however, Halliday (1985a: 264) suggests the following possibilities for English:

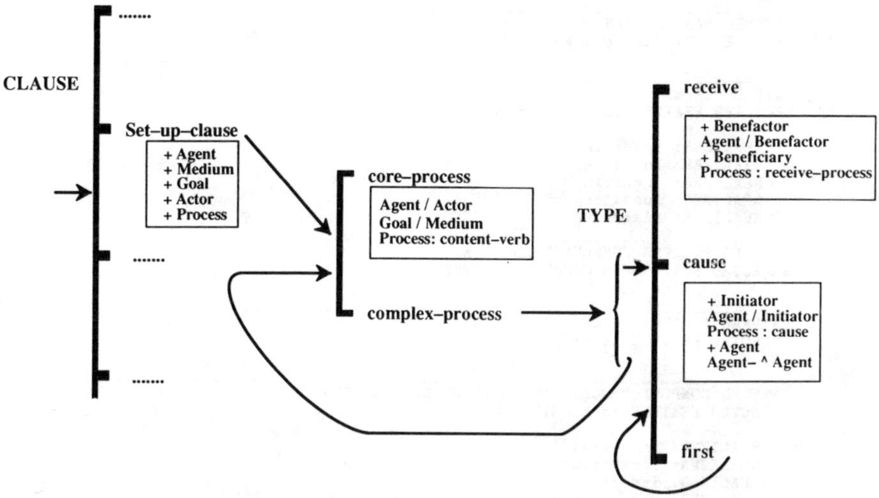


**Figure 8.10** Prototype system for clause structure with hypotactic verb groups

| | | | | |
|---|---|---|---|---|
| Fred | made Mary make . . . . | make | John roll | the ball |
| Initiator | | | Actor | Goal |
| Agent.1 | Agent.2 | Agent.3 . . . | Agent.N | Medium |

where we have an indefinite expansion of the clause by iterating ('make') Causes and their associated Agents. The treatment of these kinds of structure suggests that we acknowledge looping recursive systems together with the generation of multivariate structures also; we could also cite examples from 'serial verb' constructions in other languages where circumstantial transitivity features are realized by dependent verbs. These are therefore termed *experiential* looping systems since they serve to introduce additional experiential functions rather than the logical functions/constituents described in the previous section.

Our present implementation of this process augments realization statements so that repeated requests for the *insertion* of constituents with a particular functional label, when in the context of a looping system, actually cause *additional* constituents with the same label *type* to be added into structure. Thus, if an insertion operation, (e.g.: [+ Agent]), is executed a number of times due to a system being looped through, then a corresponding number of similarly labelled constituents are inserted into structure (e.g., Agent.1, Agent.2, . . .).

The generation of the example Japanese clause that we took from Kuno above therefore proceeds by having a looping system which, for each

```
-------------------------------------------------------------------
ENTERED RANK-SYSTEM
SELECTED FEATURE is CLAUSE

-------------------------------------------------------------------
ENTERED EXPERIMENTAL-CLAUSE-SYSTEM
SELECTED FEATURE is SET-UP-CLAUSE

   REALIZER: inserting       AGENT
   REALIZER: inserting       MEDIUM
   REALIZER: inserting       GOAL
   REALIZER: inserting       ACTOR
   REALIZER: inserting       PROCESS
-------------------------------------------------------------------
ENTERED PROCESS-COMPLEXITY-SYSTEM
SELECTED FEATURE is COMPLEX-PROCESS

-------------------------------------------------------------------
ENTERED COMPLEX-PROCESS-TYPE-SYSTEM
SELECTED FEATURE is FIRST

-------------------------------------------------------------------
ENTERED COMPLEX-PROCESS-TYPE-SYSTEM RECURSIVELY
SELECTED FEATURE is RECEIVE

   REALIZER: inserting       BENEFACTOR
   REALIZER: conflating      AGENT and BENEFACTOR
   REALIZER: inserting       BENEFICIARY
   REALIZER: preselecting    PROCESS for RECEIVE-PROCESS
-------------------------------------------------------------------
ENTERED PROCESS-COMPLEXITY-SYSTEM RECURSIVELY
SELECTED FEATURE is COMPLEX-PROCESS

-------------------------------------------------------------------
ENTERED COMPLEX-PROCESS-TYPE-SYSTEM RECURSIVELY
SELECTED FEATURE is CAUSE

   REALIZER: inserting       INITIATOR
   REALIZER: conflating      INITIATOR and AGENT
   REALIZER: preselecting    PROCESS for CAUSE
   REALIZER: inserting       AGENT.2
   REALIZER: ordering        AGENT.1 before AGENT.2
-------------------------------------------------------------------
ENTERED PROCESS-COMPLEXITY-SYSTEM RECURSIVELY
SELECTED FEATURE is CORE-PROCESS

   REALIZER: conflating      AGENT.2 and ACTOR
   REALIZER: conflating      GOAL and MEDIUM
   REALIZER: preselecting    PROCESS for CONTENT-VERB
===================================================================

Unit of type CLAUSE-UNIT denoting NIL
structure:

-------------------------------------------------------------------
||  BENEFICIARY
-------------------------------------------------------------------
||  BENEFACTOR        INITIATOR       AGENT.1
-------------------------------------------------------------------
||  ACTOR             AGENT.2
-------------------------------------------------------------------
||  MEDIUM            GOAL
-------------------------------------------------------------------
||  PROCESS
::                              :VERB            CONTENT-VERB     CAUSE
::                              :RECEIVE-PROCESS
```

**Figure 8.11** Generation of example clause involving multiple agents

additional auxiliary process inserted into structure that calls for its own participants, inserts a new Agent-function constituent. Any other appropriate participant functions necessary are then conflated with this newly inserted function. A schematic network for this is shown in Figure 8.10, while the resulting trace of its traversal when generating the clause rank structure of the example clause is given in Figure 8.11.

The network consists of two principal systems: one that presents the options of deciding that the core process has been reached, possessing the features: 'coreprocess'/'complexprocess', and one which presents options for additional meanings to be made, e.g., 'receive' and 'cause'. The realization statements of these latter options perform two main functions: first, they set up the participant structure of the clause — i.e., they determine the necessary combination of clause rank participant roles such as Beneficiary, Agent, Initiator, etc. — and, second, they preselect the verb group to have the requisite feature to trigger the insertion of the appropriate morpheme, e.g., for the Process to be a 'receive-process' for example. Once this has been stated, the networks we presented earlier for the verbal group can ensure that a morphologically appropriate verbal group is generated.

The trace of this network's traversal in Figure 8.11 shows the actual output from the Kyoto network traverser. For each grammatical system entered, we are told the grammatical feature that is selected and the realizational consequences of that selection. These correspond exactly to the realization statements specified in the network. Finally, following generation, the structure produced is displayed. In this case we see that a structure of type CLAUSE-UNIT has been generated, which has five constituents — constituents are presented running down the page and conflation of grammatical functions is shown running across the page. In addition, preselections that have been made are shown to the right of the constituent for which they hold; here, only the Process constituent has received any preselections: the features {verb, contentverb, cause, receive-process}.

The remaining structures that this network produces with two or less recursions through the loop are set out in Figure 8.12(a–d); the display format here is again that of the Kyoto system as we have just described it, with the addition of the 'selection expression', i.e., the set of grammatical features responsible for each structure fragment. Additional recursions would call for some feature to be selected twice or more and there appear to be no communicative situations supporting such a selection; the structures generated nevertheless seem more or less appropriate attempts to incorporate the functions that would be required should such recursion ever take place.

(a) Corresponding to the selection expression:
{clause set-up-clause core-process}

```
Unit of type CLAUSE-UNIT denoting NIL
structure:
-----------------------------------------------------------------
|| ACTOR            AGENT
-----------------------------------------------------------------
|| MEDIUM           GOAL
-----------------------------------------------------------------
|| PROCESS
::                            :VERB            CONTENT-VERB
```

(b) Corresponding to the selection expression:
{clause set-up-clause complex-process first receive core-process}

```
Unit of type CLAUSE-UNIT denoting NIL
structure:
-----------------------------------------------------------------
|| BENEFICIARY
-----------------------------------------------------------------
|| ACTOR            BENEFACTOR    AGENT
-----------------------------------------------------------------
|| MEDIUM           GOAL
-----------------------------------------------------------------
|| PROCESS
::                            :VERB            CONTENT-VERB  RECEIVE-PROCESS
```

(c) Corresponding to the selection expression:
{clause set-up-clause complex-process first cause core-process}

```
Unit of type CLAUSE-UNIT denoting NIL
structure:
-----------------------------------------------------------------
|| AGENT.1          INITIATOR
-----------------------------------------------------------------
|| ACTOR            AGENT.2
-----------------------------------------------------------------
|| MEDIUM           GOAL
-----------------------------------------------------------------
|| PROCESS
::                            :VERB            CONTENT-VERB  CAUSE
```

(d) Corresponding to the selection expression:
{clause set-up-clause complex-process first cause complex-process receive core-process}

```
Unit of type CLAUSE-UNIT denoting NIL
structure:
-----------------------------------------------------------------
|| BENEFICIARY
-----------------------------------------------------------------
|| AGENT.1          INITIATOR
-----------------------------------------------------------------
|| ACTOR            BENEFACTOR    AGENT.2
-----------------------------------------------------------------
|| MEDIUM           GOAL
-----------------------------------------------------------------
|| PROCESS
::                  :VERB     CONTENT-VERB    RECEIVE-PROCESS  CAUSE
```

**Figure 8.12 Example structures with multiple agents**

### 8.2.3 *Summary*

In this section we have seen a number of extensions to the basic grammar representational resources concerned with providing the capability of using recursive system networks. These have involved both complexes proper, i.e., combinations of grammatical units related by logical dependencies, and combinations of normal clause functions such as Actor, Agent, etc. In addition, this can be related to treatments of the nominal group in Halliday (1985a), where it is also noted that both experiential and logical organization needs to be represented simultaneously for any given nominal group.

This similarity can be shown thus:

| | *clause* | *nominal group* |
|---|---|---|
| logical: | causation | modification |
| experiential: | configurational transitivity | qualification<br>classification<br>epithetization |

While the resources developed permitted us to generate some new kinds of structures, the consequences of the implementation have not been sufficiently explored. We return to this in Part IV. One aspect that we will follow further there is the *dynamic*, *procedural* nature of the implementations that we have been led to. In the following section, we explore another area where the interpretation of the grammatical resources needs to be made responsive to the dynamic process of generation. This area is drawn from the textual metafunction.

## 8.3 Textual: situated potential for theme selection

We saw in the previous section that an extension of the implementation of the logical metafunction means considering dynamic grammar. In this area, the dynamicity is concerned, more specifically, with system entry: the recursive system is dynamic in the sense that it can be entered more than once in the creation of, for example, a clause complex. We discussed how this type of dynamicity can be approached in computational modelling. When we turn to the textual metafunction, we find that there is another type of dynamicity, one that pertains not to the entry of a system, but to the potential itself (cf. Matthiessen, 1988a: Section 5.2): the potential of a textual system — i.e., even *its set of options* — may, in some sense, vary according to the current context. These systems do not seem to be adequately captured within the simple instantiation of system networks represented in a Nigel-style grammar. In particular, it is again not possible to state the available grammatical options independently of context.

A good example of such a *dynamic* system is that concerned with theme selection. Here the problem is that if we have a THEME system that says it is possible to choose either a Goal, or a Recipient, or a Locative, or a Time, etc. as the Theme, then that system is, in general, wrong because it is only possible to offer the potential of having, say, a Locative as theme *if there is a locative to be expressed in the clause*. Thus, the grammatical alternatives that are available for the theme depend on the circumstances and configuration of participants that are actually available in a particular clause. For instance, the following examples all have different potential sets of Theme candidates:

Sub-sea well-heads are being installed on the Sea-horse field.

Sub-sea well-heads are being installed by Esso on the Sea-horse field.

Sub-sea well-heads are being installed by Esso on the Sea-horse field this week.

Sub-sea well-heads are being installed by Esso on the Sea-horse field this week together with a new emergency system.

The response to this problem in Nigel is to distribute the thematic options in systems that are dependent on logically prior selections of participants and circumstances. So, for instance, the circumstantial systems PLACE, TIME, and ACCOMPANIMENT may all lead to their separate theme systems (SPATIAL THEME, TEMPORAL THEME, etc.). A separate single 'theme system' where all the relevant decisions concerning thematic selection and its realization are grouped is not then possible.

An alternative that offers a way of representing the theme alternatives as a unified set of options within a single grammatical system is to accept a distinction between *abstract* and *situated* grammatical potential. The abstract thematic potential consists of all the possible participants and circumstances; the situated thematic potential is the subset of participants and circumstances licensed in a given clause situation.

This was implemented for the Japanese grammar by making more use of the chooser level of organization. If we have the system fragments shown in Figure 8.13, we only want the option LocationTheme to appear in the THEMATICITY system if ExpressedLocation is selected; otherwise, if UnExpressedLocation is selected then we definitely want the LocationTheme option *not* to appear in the THEMATICITY system because there can be no location constituent in the clause. By extending choosers so that they may

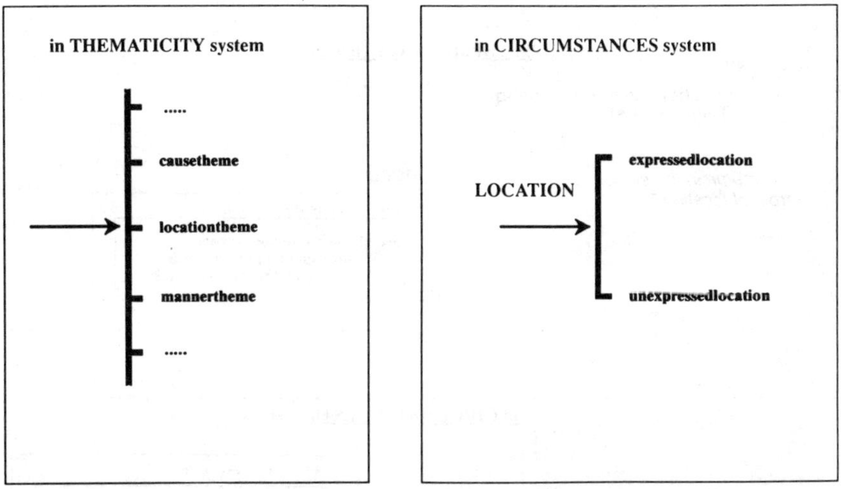


**Figure 8.13** Grammatically independent Theme and Circumstance systems

predetermine the outcome of inquiries that are put by *other* choosers, this effect may be achieved. Figure 8.14 sketches some chooser definitions that situate the options of the THEMATICITY and the CIRCUMSTANCES system in the desired way. These should be read in precisely the same way as the chooser decision trees given in Part II.

If the chooser of the theme selection system has already determined that the Theme is a location, then the grammatical potential of the CIRCUMSTANCES system is restricted so that not expressing the location is no longer a possibility. Similarly, on the one hand, if the CIRCUMSTANCES system has determined that there is a location to be expressed, then the potential option in the THEMATICITY system of having a location is determined to be actually present; if, on the other hand, there is no location to be expressed, then the THEMATICITY system is situated such that the option of a location theme does not appear.

Figure 8.15 shows an example grammar trace illustrating this setting of chooser-inquiry responses to model situation-sensitive dynamic systems; the format is that of the Kyoto system as we described it in the previous section. Here, the location system first determines that there is no location to be expressed. Subsequently, when the THEME system is entered, the possibility of having a location as theme has already been specified to be impossible, i.e., in this actual situation of use to be irrelevant. Therefore the system, in effect, can no longer offer that grammatical option: the actual system used during traversal has been dynamically restricted according to the selections made elsewhere in the grammar.

This mechanism is also of use with the *recursive systems* illustrated in the

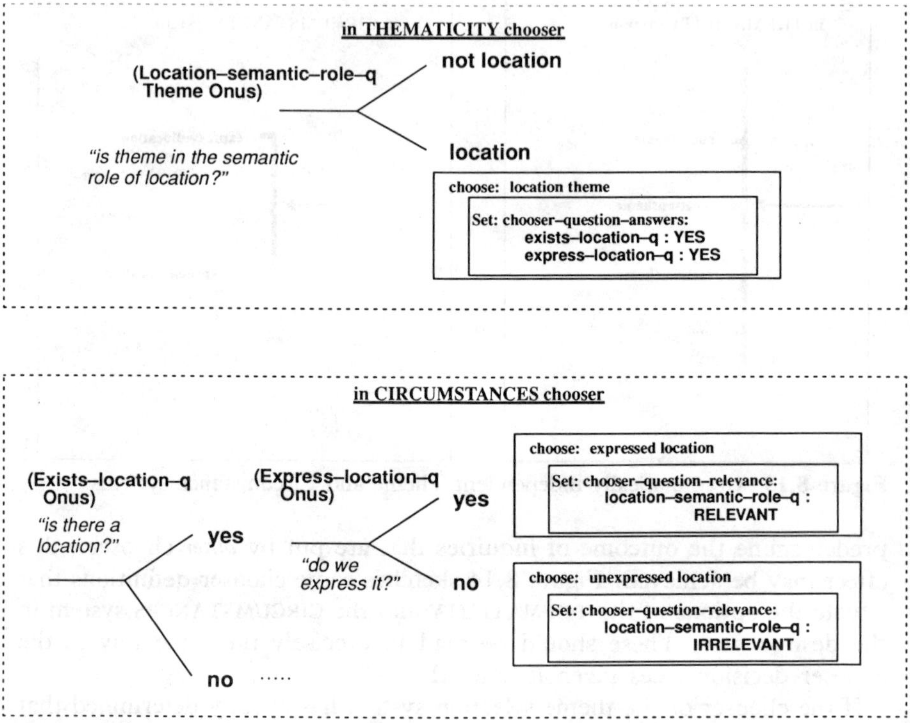


**Figure 8.14** Using extended choosers to situate systems

previous section. When a system is looped through it is necessary to interpret its realization statements relative to that recursion. In addition, it is also necessary to preserve the information of the *order* in which features are selected while looping through a single system since distinct orders may correspond to distinct structures and correspond to distinct meanings. Although we have adopted the option of making the selection expression of grammatical features selected an *ordered* set in order to preserve this information, this in effect interprets the *features* of a recursive system relative to the recursion, i.e., the second selection of a feature 'cause' is now no longer the same selection as the first selection of that feature. A description of this in terms of a distinction between SYSTEM-TYPES and SYSTEM-TOKENS can begin to capture this (cf. Matthiessen, 1988a: Section 5.1). 'Normal' systems would permit only one instantiation as a system-token for each pass through the grammar, whereas recursive system-types would permit multiple tokens. Interpreting features in terms of the particular instantiation of the systems from which they are selected renders

```
------------------------------------------------------------------------
ENTERED LOCATION-SYSTEM
  CHOOSER: inquiring           Has the text plan established a location at
                               which EXISTENCE (PROCESS) in EXISTS (ONUS)
                               holds?
  ENVIRONMENT RESPONSE:        YES
  CHOOSER: inquiring           Provide a symbol for the location at which
                               the process EXISTENCE (PROCESS) obtains:
  ENVIRONMENT RESPONSE:        LOCATION-1
  CHOOSER: associating         LOCATION-1 with LOCATION
  CHOOSER: inquiring           Does the present state of the text plan call
                               for the expression of the LOCATION-1
                               (LOCATION) participant of EXISTS (ONUS)?
  ENVIRONMENT RESPONSE:        NO
  CHOOSER: restricting potential
  CHOOSER: formal inquiry (LOCATION-SEMANTIC-ROLE-Q THEME ONUS)          <--
           constrained to IRRELEVANT
  CHOOSER: selecting feature UNEXPRESSEDLOCATION
SELECTED FEATURE is UNEXPRESSEDLOCATION
------------------------------------------------------------------------
   .......   .......   .......   .......   .......   .......   .......
------------------------------------------------------------------------
ENTERED THEME-IDENTITY-SYSTEM
  CHOOSER: inquiring           Is the constituent LOCATED-ENTITY (THEME)
                               of EXISTS (ONUS) in the semantic relation
                               of actor?
  ENVIRONMENT RESPONSE:        NO
  CHOOSER: inquiring           Is the constituent LOCATED-ENTITY (THEME)
                               of EXISTS (ONUS) in the semantic relation
                               of goal?
  ENVIRONMENT RESPONSE:        NO
  CHOOSER: inquiring           Is the constituent THEME (NIL) of ONUS
                               (NIL) in the semantic relation of
                               location?
  CHOOSER: This inquiry has been restricted to be irrelevant             <--
  CHOOSER: inquiring           Is the constituent LOCATED-ENTITY (THEME)
                               of EXISTS (ONUS) in the semantic relation
                               of receiver?
  ENVIRONMENT RESPONSE:        NO
  CHOOSER: inquiring           What is the semantic role of the element
                               LOCATED-ENTITY (THEME) in the intent of
                               EXISTS (ONUS)?
  ENVIRONMENT RESPONSE:        UNDERGOER
  CHOOSER: selecting feature UNDERGOER-THEME
SELECTED FEATURE is UNDERGOER-THEME
------------------------------------------------------------------------
   .......   .......   .......   .......   .......   .......   .......
========================================================================

Unit of type CLAUSE-UNIT denoting EXISTS
structure:

------------------------------------------------------------------------
||<LOCATED-ENTITY>
||     UNDERGOER       THEME
------------------------------------------------------------------------
||     VERBCLUSTER
::                                  :PLAIN       ACTIVE-VG         VERB
::                                  :ARU-TYPE    VERBGROUP
```

**Figure 8.15** Example of the situated restricting of grammatical potential

them unique and so identifiable.[7] The question which then arises for choosers is how multiple instantiations of a system-type are to be related to the chooser defined for that type.

The most straightforward response to this might be to allow a similar type-token distinction among choosers and to associate with each system-token a corresponding chooser-token. However, some observations we have made on the properties of successive instantiations of chooser-tokens when traversing recursive systems have suggested a possible refinement to this most straightforward approach.

When systems are re-entered it is commonly the case that either the features actually available differ from the full set the system claims are potentially available, or that the manner of choosing among those features differs in some way from that of preceding entries. This is clearly illustrated by considering Matthiessen's (1984) non-recursive rewriting of the tense network, that would be more naturally written as a looping network, that we used as an illustration in Section 7. In this case, the choosers of the second and subsequent systems to be entered are *restricted* versions of the chooser of the first system. Similarly, in the looping systems for the Japanese verbal group described above, where the option of removing the loop is very much less attractive, there are restrictions on the combinations of verbs that may be combined and, again, these restrictions may be expressed by having the *choosers* that are attached to re-entered systems be restricted versions of those attached to the systems entered on earlier iterations through the loop. Our general approach to treating choosers in the context of looping systems is therefore to treat successive instantiations of chooser-types as successively *restricted* versions of the chooser definition.

This may be intuitively justified on the grounds that as the possibilities that a looping system presents are explored further and further via recursion, those possibilities are more likely to become stereotyped and lacking in exceptions than those of the more frequently explored traversals arising from taking fewer cycles. Thus early choosers are more likely to need to take account of additional meaning distinctions, special usages, etc. which may be successively dropped as deeper recursion moves beyond them.

The description of chooser interaction that we gave above provides one way of achieving this behaviour. Above we made reference to the presumed 'dynamic' nature of systems and choosers that involve looping. This may be taken to imply that explicit appeal needs to be made to the generation algorithm for traversing the grammar network. For example, the logical micro-functions Current and Next of Section 8.2.1 do not pick out unique grammatical units: as the network is traversed they are made to pick out different units depending upon the realization statements executed previously during that traversal. Similarly, the distinguishing of features of the same name when selected on different loops through a single system relies upon the generation algorithm preserving somehow their order of selection. As an initial experiment, then, we chose to interpret all systems as essentially 'dynamic' — i.e., *as making essential reference to their position in the generation process as defined by the generation algorithm.*

While the system-type specified in a grammar definition sets out the full range of 'theoretically' applicable grammatical distinctions at its (static) position in the network, when the grammar is traversed, due to the actual communicative situation that holds, only some of those theoretically applicable distinctions may actually be appropriate. This 'situating' of grammatical potential was implemented in terms of the restricted choosers that we described above; i.e., only the grammatical features that can actually be chosen by a situated chooser decision tree are considered to be actually available as choices. This, then, offers a more dynamically manipulable mechanism than one in which a system-type is directly mapped on to an identical system-token. The chooser-token associated with some system-token is restricted such that certain of the system-type's features *may no longer be selected* and then that system-token is interpreted as *no longer offering* those features as appropriate choices. The GRAMMATICAL POTENTIAL of the system-type is then said to have been restricted by the situation of use to produce the actually appropriate SITUATED GRAMMATICAL POTENTIAL captured by the system-token.

The removal of the restriction that chooser actions only operate within their own choosers motivated by these considerations further supports our construction of chooser actions which, when executed, restrict the options available in other choosers — hence, dynamically restricting the grammatical potential that is actually available when the grammar is traversed. The successive restricting of choosers attached to looping systems may then be seen as just another example of the process of dynamically restricting the options presented by a system during network traversal that does not differ from the case of non-looping systems: chooser interaction is simply also occurring between chooser-*tokens* that are created from single chooser-types during the traversal of a recursive system.

The implementation of a general mechanism such as we have investigated here by which the options made in one chooser can influence the options available in other choosers has therefore had several significant consequences. If a system's chooser becomes unable to select certain features then those features are precluded from relevance for the generation of the particular grammatical unit at issue. Thus, a system may in effect be dynamically restricted by choices made elsewhere in the *same* cycle through the grammar. This has suggested not only a means of controlling looping, but also a way of representing some of the 'dynamic systems' which appear to be necessary in several areas of both English and Japanese grammar.

The findings presented above indicate that choosers may 'interact' beyond the local domains determined by the systems they are associated with. This type of interaction is one way of achieving a more global organization of chooser inquiries. We will now turn to the interpersonal metafunction and we will again find evidence for the need for a more global kind of organization of inquiries.

## 8.4 Interpersonal: inquiry networks

As we have seen, the chooser and inquiry interface between the Nigel grammar and its environment is organized by the grammatical system network. This means that the control of the choice is localized to grammatical systems and that inquiries are 'packaged' into choosers. In the previous section, we saw how the local choosers may 'communicate'. We will now take one further step and explore the need for more global organization of inquiries into INQUIRY NETWORKS. This need comes clearly into focus within the interpersonal metafunction in both English and Japanese so we will draw our examples from this metafunction.

### *8.4.1 Problems with local chooser parcels in English and Japanese*

We have seen how information from the Environment is embodied in a chooser tree in the responses under which further inquiries can be embedded, as in the PRIMARY TENSE chooser presented in Section 7.2. The response to a branching inquiry is part of the structure of the chooser that presents it and can thus be used within that chooser. However, it cannot be used directly outside the chooser that presents it. It can be used indirectly. If the response leads to the choice of a grammatical feature and another chooser whose system presupposed the selection of that feature is reached, the response that led to the selection of the feature can, in principle, also be presupposed and does not have to be obtained again.

For example, the chooser of INDICATIVE TYPE determines whether the speech functional value of MOOD is that of a question or not by asking QuestionQ. If the response is 'question', the feature interrogative is chosen and this is the only response that leads to the choice of interrogative. Consequently, the choosers of systems that have interrogative as an entry condition can present inquiries that presuppose the response 'question', as in the chooser of INTERROGATIVE TYPE, shown in Figure 8.16, which presents the inquiry PolarityVariableQ.[8]

However, when a chooser inquiry of one chooser obtains information needed by the inquiry that is part of another chooser and their respective systems are *independent* of one another both choosers have to present the same inquiry. That is, the two systems are grammatically independent — 'compositional' in terms of the system network — but they are not semantically independent or compositional to the same extent. We saw one

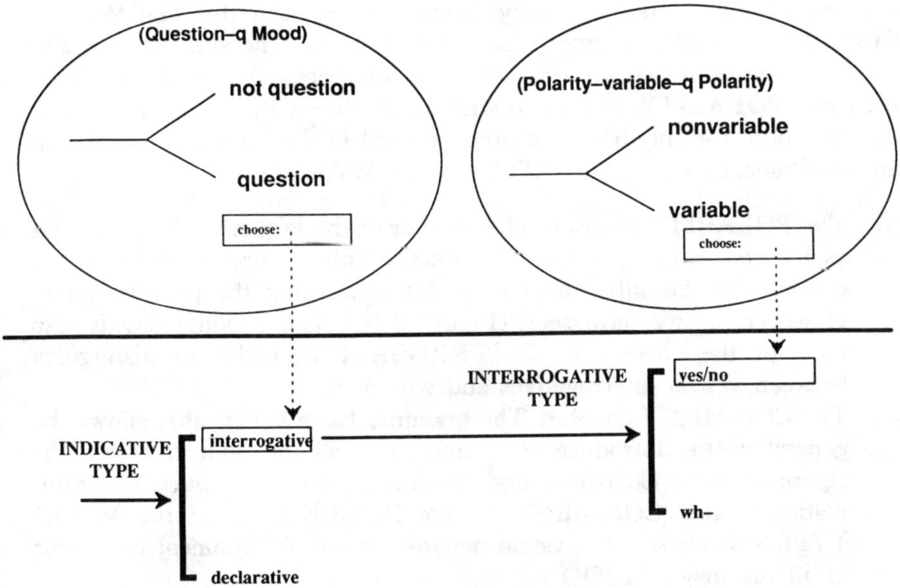


**Figure 8.16** Inquiry responses encoded in grammatical features

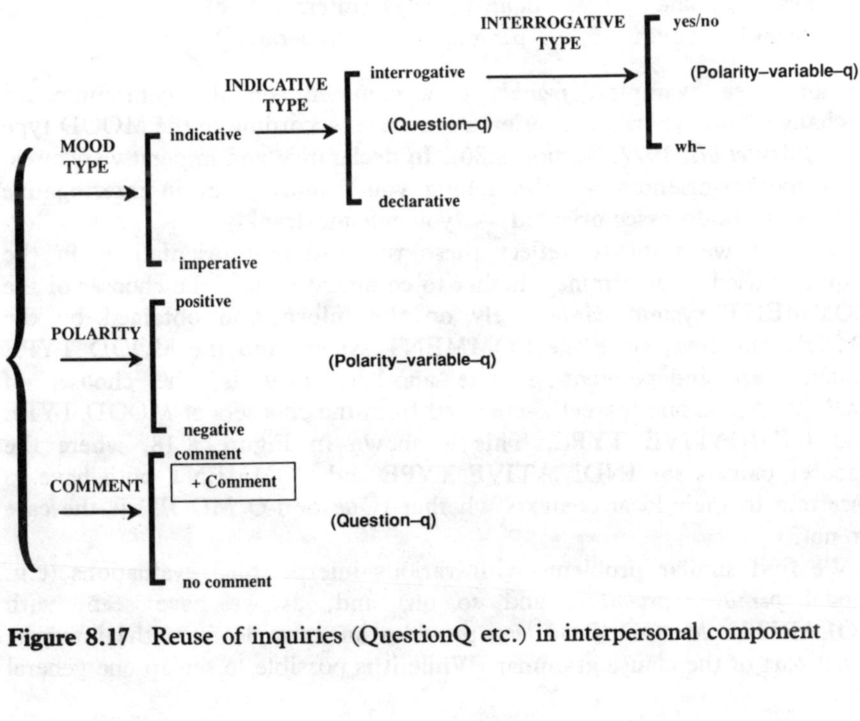


**Figure 8.17** Reuse of inquiries (QuestionQ etc.) in interpersonal component

example of this in the necessary interaction between the THEME and CIRCUMSTANCES systems in Section 8.3 above. The situation can also be illustrated with two systems from the interpersonal part of the clause network, POLARITY and COMMENT, as shown in Figure 8.17; their choosers both use inquiries that are also used in the MOOD systems that are simultaneous with POLARITY and COMMENT.

(i) The POLARITY chooser. The chooser of the POLARITY system has as its first inquiry: PolarityVariableQ. This is used to establish the context for the subsequent inquiries concerning the polarity value. However, as we have seen (Figure 8.16), PolarityVariableQ is also used in the chooser of INTERROGATIVE TYPE to distinguish between yes/no interrogatives and wh- ones.

(ii) The COMMENT chooser. The grammar has a system that allows the generator to introduce a comment on the sincerity of the communicative exchange, e.g. *frankly*, *honestly*, or *sincerely*. Grammatically, this COMMENT system is independent of the MOOD TYPE system; see the system network above. A Comment can occur in all the major MOOD types:

`Frankly, I don't know what you mean by that` (declarative)
`Frankly, what do you mean by that` (interrogative)
`Frankly, never try to please Henry` (imperative)

In all three examples, *frankly* is a comment on the communicative exchange, but, typically, its orientation varies according to the MOOD type (cf. Quirk *et al.*, 1972: Section 8.80). In declarative and imperative clauses, it is speaker-oriented — 'I'm telling you frankly'; but in interrogative clauses it is addressee-oriented — 'you tell me frankly'.

Now, if we want to reflect these two different orientations in the inquiries used to determine whether to comment or not, the chooser of the COMMENT system cannot rely on the information obtained by the MOOD choosers, since the COMMENT system and the MOOD_TYPE systems are independent of one another. That is, the chooser of COMMENT is one 'parcel', separated from the choosers of MOOD TYPE and INDICATIVE TYPE. This is shown in Figure 8.18, where the chooser parcels for INDICATIVE TYPE and COMMENT both have to ascertain in their local contexts whether (Question-Q MOOD) is the case or not.

We find similar problems with various interpersonal evaluations (e.g. modal *perhaps*, *probably*, and so on) and, as we have seen, with POLARITY. MOOD TAG also provides an example from the interpersonal part of the clause grammar. While it is possible to set up one general

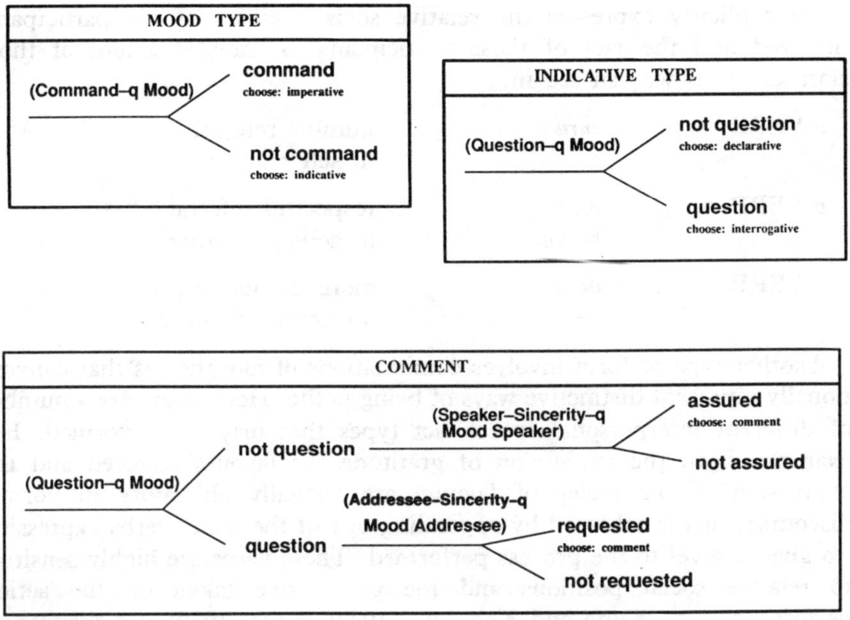


**Figure 8.18** Repetition of inquiries due to chooser tree parcels

grammatical MOOD TAG system whose entry condition is a disjunction of 'declarative' and 'imperative' (see Section 6.3), the chooser of such a system has to distinguish between the two entry contexts as statements and commands. In the case of a statement, tagging is used to request an indication of agreement — the response that does not automatically follow a statement (*They shoot horses, don't they, — Yes, they do.*). In the case of a command, tagging is used to request an indication of willingness to comply with the command (*Shoot horses, will you. — OK, I will.*).

We also find similar problems of inter-chooser dependencies in the interpersonal region of Japanese grammar, where the grammatical expression of various interpersonal relationships is quite common. In particular, the expression of appropriate degrees of humility and respect in references to one's own actions, to those of one's audience, and to those of third parties presents a number of problems that are difficult to address within the Nigel-style implementation of local chooser parcels and inquiries.

A variety of clause forms are regularly employed in Japanese for the expression of interpersonal meanings related to 'politeness'. For example, the 'demotion' of the process information to a nominal-like form preceded by a normal nominal honorific prefix (e.g. o, as in o-*cha*: 'honorable' tea) supported by an auxiliary verb such as *suru*, 'to do', or *naru*, 'to become', often explicitly expresses the relative social statuses of the participants involved and the fact of those participants' acknowledgement of those statuses. This we can see in,

| | | |
|---|---|---|
| *o*-VERB | *suru*<br>do | humble referral<br>to self's action |
| *o*-VERB-*ni* | *naru*<br>become | respectful referral<br>to action of other |
| *o*-VERB | *desu*<br>be | more distant respect<br>for action of other |

Another type of form involves combinations of morphemes that conventionally represent distinctive ways of being polite. Here, there are a number of different interpersonal speech act types that may be performed. For example, both the expression of gratitude for favours received and the expression of the *giving* of favours are virtually obligatory in normal discourse; this is achieved by appending one of the many verbs expressing 'to give/receive' to the process performed. These verbs are highly sensitive to relative social positions and the perspective taken on the action performed (e.g., Kuno and Kaburaki, 1977; Inoue, 1979) and this aspect of their meaning is carried over for the expression of favours done or perceived.[9] Typical combinations also express polite ways of seeking permission for actions; one here modifies the action to be performed by means of the morphemes for causation/allowing, receiving a favour, wishing for, and thinking: a rough literal gloss of this form would be along the lines of 'I think I want to humbly receive from you your allowing me to do X'.

Thus, the following clause forms are also commonly required in normal discourse:

| | |
|---|---|
| VERB-giving | doing a 'favour':<br>respectfully or humbly |
| VERB-receiving | receiving a 'favour':<br>respectfully or humbly |
| VERB-cause-receive-wish-think | deferential seeking of permission |

This by no means exhausts the range of forms that are relevant to discussions of politeness, respect, and humility in present-day Japanese, but it will be sufficient as an indication of the kinds of structures and meanings addressed within the present grammar. It should also be noted that there are different 'dimensions' of politeness involved in the use of these forms; for example, the clause,

| | | | |
|---|---|---|---|
| *yoku* | *kite-* | *kureta-* | *ne* |
| well | come | favour to speaker | tag |

which means 'thanks for coming', is in the *familiar* level of speech form, i.e., it could only be used between people who are on familiar terms. It is nevertheless *still* necessary for the favour being done to be explicitly acknowledged; not expressing it would result in a clause that would often be inappropriate. Our present grammar also treats the range of distinctions that arise along this 'familiar'/'polite' levels of speech dimension but this will not be of concern here.

With politeness forms we are faced with a set of alternative meanings concerning level and type of politeness to be expressed, but these alternatives correspond to no single points of *grammatical* alternation. For example, if the process of reading (*yomu*) is to be expressed but we want to make a selection of politeness-related meaning between a simple respectful reference to another's actions and a more distanced, indirect and reserved respectful reference, then the choice of appropriate *forms* for that process is between

| | | | |
|---|---|---|---|
| *o-* | *yomi* | *ni* | *naru* |
| HONORIFIC | reading | CASE | becoming |

and

| | | |
|---|---|---|
| *o-* | *yomi* | *desu* |
| HONORIFIC | reading | COPULA-be |

While the distinction in meaning may be captured by a simple scale of the 'directness' of the sentence that is appropriate for the particular interactive situation in which it is to be used, there is no grammatical system in the grammar of Japanese that offers a direct choice between these two clause structures. The former structure is similar to the typical use of the verb 'become' as in *x-ni naru*, 'to become X'; the latter is similar to clauses such as *X desu*, 'it is X'. They are not normally, e.g., in contexts not involving this particular contrast of politeness, in grammatical contrast.

It is not then possible to associate a 'politeness' chooser with a grammatical system as is done with the choosers for ideational meanings because there is no *grammatical* system of 'politeness' to which it may be attached. A simple choice between minimal alternatives of politeness can result in radically different grammatical structures that differ by virtue of many features. This may be related to the kind of realization that interpersonal meanings frequently receive, i.e., 'prosodic' realizations which are not locatable by single grammatical feature selections. In this case, the semantic increase in 'politeness' distance (relating to tenor) correlates in expression with the increase of the 'prosody' — 'amplitude'. This we have referred to in terms of the different modes of expression according to different metafunctions at the beginning of this chapter.

The differences in meaning that these alternative politeness-related forms represent nevertheless need to be made available to a text generation system. But this is again problematic due to the local nature of chooser decisions. As long as each chooser determines which grammatical feature is to be selected as appropriate for the context of use from a single point of minimal grammatical alternation, the selection between alternative grammatical choices, or features, that are offered by a *single* grammatical system is the only influence that the chooser of that system is permitted to have on the generation process. This means that politeness of this kind cannot be made available as a controllable expressive resource for a text planner within the chooser framework as it is implemented within the Nigel project.

To sum up, the general problem we have pointed to in this section is that simultaneous systems in a grammatical system network are grammatically independent but may interact semantically. We can mention two symptoms of this semantic interaction:

(i) One symptom is that the choosers of simultaneous systems may need to reuse the same inquiries; this we saw in the English examples where choosers of both the COMMENT system and the INDICATIVE TYPE system used the inquiry *QuestionQ*. This is an indication that possible generalizations at the semantic level are not being clearly represented because of the subordination of the chooser organization to the grammatical organization of the system network.

(ii) Another symptom, as we saw in the Japanese examples, is that grammatically unrelated constructions appear to be in direct semantic contrast.

It is clear, then, that the Nigel chooser tree organization of inquiries is problematic.

As long as these problems are confined to single choosers, we can address them by means of the tree organization — for instance, disjunction can be simulated; but we also find many examples of the need to relate inquiries beyond single choosers. There are at least two possible approaches to this problem:

(i) we can add to the set of possible chooser actions so as to allow choosers to exchange information not only with the environment but also with each other;

(ii) we can abandon the chooser packaging and create a more global inquiry organization.

We saw some experiments involving the first alternative in the previous section in our experiments with situated potential for the THEME systems (Section 8.3). Here, we will explore the second alternative, replacing the assumption that inquiries are organized into decision trees that come in chooser parcels local to each system with the assumption that they are organized more globally into an inquiry network. We will explore this possibility in a number of steps. First, we present a less locally restricted form of inquiry decision tree that was implemented for the treatment of politeness in Japanese (Section 8.4.2 immediately below). Second, we consider the extension of this mechanism to provide a full networking capability (Section 8.4.3). Finally, we return to the possible implications of the availability of such a mechanism in the treatment of English (Section 8.4.4).

### *8.4.2 The Japanese 'politeness' decision tree*

In order to allow full control of politeness phenomena, the following extension was implemented within the context of the computational systemic grammar framework supported at Kyoto. The chooser framework was maintained as a decision tree that selects between minimal points of semantic alternation — however, it is no longer the case that this needs to be held in a one-to-one correspondence with the minimal alternations that the systems of the grammar network represent. The possibility of distinct patterns of organization at the two levels, as would be claimed by systemic linguistics proper for a level of semantic organization (cf. for example, Halliday, 1973, 1984; Hasan 1987ms) and as shown to be necessary in the previous section, is therefore captured.[10] Accordingly, any chooser is permitted to make any number of selections of grammatical features from anywhere in the grammatical network.

This extension made it possible to construct a chooser decision tree that groups together precisely those distinctions in meaning required to ascertain which level and form of politeness to employ. The inquiries of this decision tree are free to ask all the questions related to the aspects of the social relationships of the participants in the speech situation that are necessary without being concerned about where in the grammatical network the consequences of those questions will be felt. This makes that reasoning available in a modular and easily comprehensible form. The result of any particular path through the decision tree is a set of grammatical features that the grammatical product being generated as a whole must bear. This can therefore call for very different structural results to be selected which differ by many grammatical features drawn from many distinct grammatical points of alternation. The present politeness 'chooser', or decision tree, has around fifteen decision points where a distinct inquiry needs to be put to a component of the 'knowledge base' or environment concerned with interaction and interpersonal relationships;[11] it is shown in three parts below, representing the 'politeness discrimination', 'humility', and 'respect' reasoning in Figures 8.21, 8.22, and 8.23 respectively.

An abbreviated example of this decision tree's use is the following. After traversal of the decision tree has already established a number of important facts concerning the text need, including that the actor is the hearer, that the situation is not one classifiable as formally 'official', that there is considerable social 'distance' between the speaker and hearer, among others, the simple semantic distinction glossable in English as

*Is the subject-matter of the process such that additional reserve should be shown?*

is drawn. If the text need is classifiable as requiring a yes-response to this inquiry then the grammatical features: *identifying*, *intensive*, and *special-grammatical-placing* are constrained to appear. If a no-classification is possible, then the grammatical features: *becoming-attribute*, *intensive*, and *special-grammatical-placing* appear. The former set results in clauses with a functional structure of the form:

| | | |
|---|---|---|
| *o-* | VERB | *desu* |
| HONORIFIC | X | COPULA-be |

which, as we have seen, expresses additional distance between the action and its performance as required. The latter set is sufficient to constrain the structure produced to be of the form:

| | | | |
|---|---|---|---|
| *o-* | VERB | *ni* | *naru* |
| HONORIFIC | X | CASE | becoming |

which is the less indirect expression of respect.

Formerly, any such decision tree employed as a chooser would only have been able to call for the appearance of a single grammatical feature; here any number of features may be selected during the decision tree's traversal. Modelling the kind of non-local organization inherent in the expression of politeness would therefore have required numerous decision trees split according to the grammatical organization: this subordinates the semantic organization to the grammatical organization and necessarily obscures the unity of the politeness reasoning process. By allowing the two levels of grammar and semantics their own, not necessarily isomorphic, dimensions of organization it is possible to express the unity and coherence of patterns at either level and to capture the relationship between those levels.

We can now show the generation of an actual utterance exhibiting complex attributes of politeness.[12] The context for the utterance is one of making hotel bookings by telephone. After a negotiation of precisely where, when, and how long the customer is to stay, the person responsible for hotel booking states that he will send the confirmation of the reservation to the customer 'today'. It is worth noting that the 'direct' translation of this statement in terms of its ideational content (perhaps glossable as a very neutral *I will send it today*), such as might be handled by current machine translation systems, would be quite inappropriate in a genuine interactive situation such as the one described. What was actually said was of the following form:

| | | | | | |
|---|---|---|---|---|---|
| *honjitsu* | *hassou* | *sasete-* | *itadaki-* | *tai to* | *omoimasu* |
| today | send/ forward | do-cause | receive humbly | wish | think |

'might I be permitted to send it today?'

During generation the grammar causes the politeness reasoning chooser network to be entered; this performs the classifications shown in Figure 8.19, the humility section of this reasoning may be followed through in Figure 8.22 also.

The grammatical features constrained to appear in this case, i.e., *wishfulness*, *favours*, *cause*, etc., then result in particular predetermined paths being taken through the grammar network. For example, Figure 8.20 shows when the grammatical system responsible for the construction of the functional structure concerned with the expression of causality is entered. This grammatical system offers two alternative grammatical features: one which constrains the structure generated to be an expression of causation and one which does not.

Here, since the grammatical feature *cause* has been constrained to appear by the politeness chooser, no further reasoning needs to be done at this point and the construction of the appropriate structure may proceed directly (via execution of the realization statements associated with the *cause* feature, which call for a variety of operations to be performed on functionally labelled constituents such as Agent, Process, etc.). The trace of Figure 8.20 also contains a number of the other experimental extensions over the computational systemic framework implemented in Nigel that we have discussed in this chapter; for example: the entering of grammatical systems 'recursively' (Section 8.2.1) and the insertion of multiple functions of the same type, as in Agent.1 and Agent.2 (Section 8.2.2).

Similarly preselected grammatical decisions are made for each of the other regions of the grammar responsible for creating the structure required to express the politeness need as determined during politeness reasoning.

```
-------------------------------------------------------------------------
ENTERED SOCIAL-PLACING-REQUIREMENTS-SYSTEM
   CHOOSER: inquiring            Is it possible for the speaker to
                                 identify with the actor of the process
                                 SENDING (PROCESS)?
   ENVIRONMENT RESPONSE:         YES
   CHOOSER: inquiring            Does the relationship (e.g., one of great
                                 social distance) between the current
                                 speaker and the hearer require the
                                 expression of special social positioning
                                 information during the statement of
                                 SENDING (PROCESS)?
   ENVIRONMENT RESPONSE:         YES
   CHOOSER: preselecting feature HUMBLING
   CHOOSER: HUMILITY-REASONING:
   CHOOSER: inquiring            Is the action SENDING (PROCESS) independent
                                 of others, the audience in particular?
   ENVIRONMENT RESPONSE:         NO
   CHOOSER: inquiring            Would the performance of the processing
                                 SENDING (PROCESS) obligate the hearer in
                                 any way? (e.g., to carry for someone, ...)
   ENVIRONMENT RESPONSE:         NO
   CHOOSER: inquiring            Is the process SENDING (PROCESS) of the
                                 kind that a special lexical verb exists that
                                 expresses humility?
   ENVIRONMENT RESPONSE:         NO
   CHOOSER: choosing             POSITIVE-SOCIAL-PLACING
   CHOOSER: inquiring            Is there reason for explicitly making
                                 clear consideration of the other's wishes
                                 regarding the process SENDING (PROCESS),
                                 such as in seeking permission for an
                                 action which may benefit the actor as
                                 much as or more than it does the hearer?
   ENVIRONMENT RESPONSE:         YES
   CHOOSER: preselecting feature WISHFULNESS
   CHOOSER: preselecting feature FAVOURS
   CHOOSER: preselecting feature MODIFIED-PROCESS
   CHOOSER: preselecting feature CAUSE
   CHOOSER: preselecting feature MODIFIED-PROCESS
   CHOOSER: preselecting feature SPECIAL-GRAMMATICAL-PLACING
 SELECTED FEATURE is POSITIVE-SOCIAL-PLACING
-------------------------------------------------------------------------
```

**Figure 8.19** Trace of the grammar's politeness reasoning

This serves to build the structure of the example sentence as an appropriate realization of the distinctions in politeness that were ascertained to be necessary by the politeness chooser inquiries. The remainder of the politeness chooser is shown in Figures 8.21 and 8.23. These trees follow the choosers given above in presenting a tree-like organization of decisions. The decisions themselves, shown at the nodes, are given here in their informal form only. We will return to questions of how these might begin to be formalized in the following chapter. In general, the tree is traversed

```
------------------------------------------------------------------------
ENTERED MODIFIED-PROCESS-TYPE-SYSTEM RECURSIVELY
** preselections overriding: selecting feature CAUSE
SELECTED FEATURE is CAUSE

   REALIZER: inserting         INITIATOR
   REALIZER: conflating        INITIATOR and AGENT.2
   REALIZER: preselecting      PROCESS for COMPLEX-PROCESS
   REALIZER: preselecting      PROCESS for CAUSATIVE
   REALIZER: ordering          AGENT.2 before AGENT.1
------------------------------------------------------------------------
ENTERED MODIFIED-EXPERIENCE-SYSTEM RECURSIVELY
  CHOOSER: inquiring           Is this use of the process SENDING (PROCESS)
                               modified further in some way?
  ENVIRONMENT RESPONSE:        NO
  CHOOSER: selecting feature CORE-PROCESS
SELECTED FEATURE is CORE-PROCESS
   REALIZER: preselecting      PROCESS for SIMPLE-PROCESS
------------------------------------------------------------------------
```

**Figure 8.20** Traversal of the causativity region of the grammar

according to the answers that are received to the inquiries from the environment, until terminal leaves in the tree are reached. Preselections of grammatical features are collected during the traversal. In contrast to the choosers as originally defined in the context of the Penman generation system and as we introduced it in Chapter 6 above, a single decision tree here can now preselect grammatical features from any systems defined in the grammar network within one traversal.

In conclusion, we can note that the implementation of a decision tree that can select features non-locally enabled us to capture semantic organization and distinctions that would have been obscured if the system-bound chooser parcelling had been preserved. The natural question to which this has led us is a consideration of whether an even more network-like organization for inquiries could be usefully implemented. This we turn to in the next section.

### *8.4.3 Towards a network of inquiries*

The next step towards achieving a network of inquiries that we will discuss can be stated as follows:

> *Inquiries are organized in the same way as systems. That is they have presentation conditions that can be either simple or complex and form a network (directed acyclic graph).*

Having already moved away from the Nigel organization with respect to the globality of the organization (local chooser packages vs. global

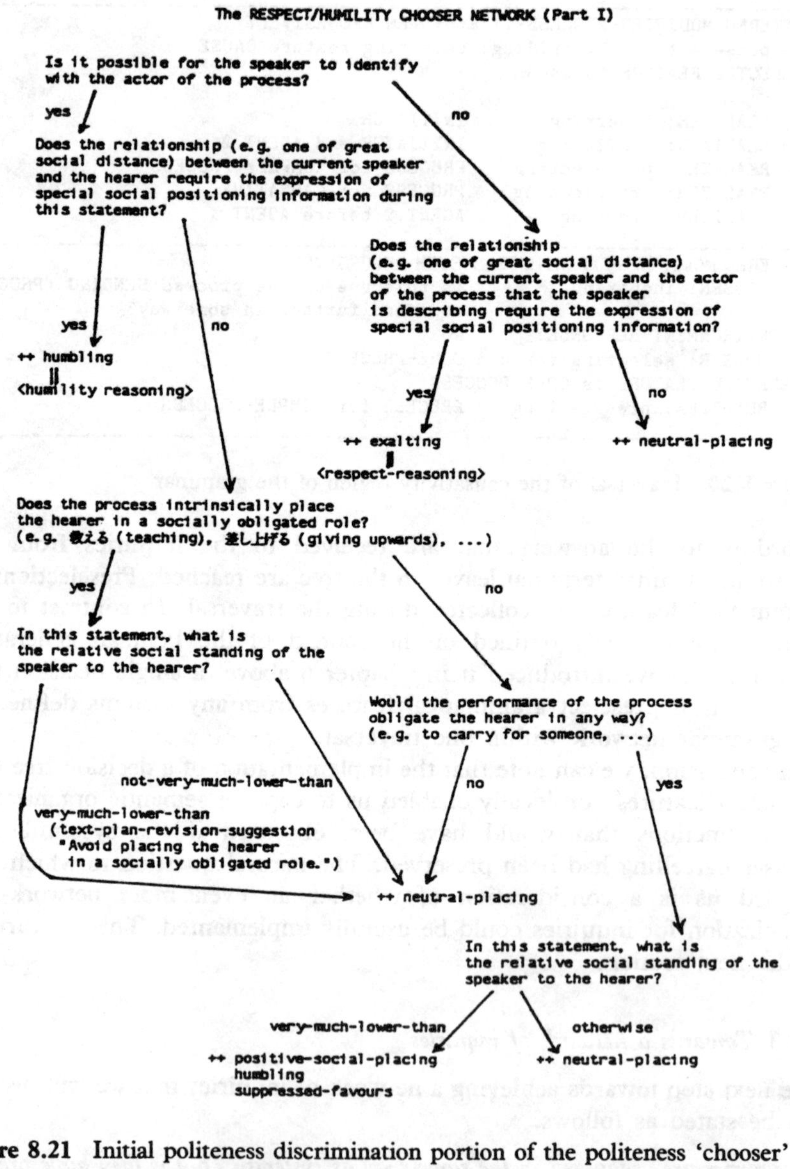


**Figure 8.21** Initial politeness discrimination portion of the politeness 'chooser'

network), this assumption about the organization of inquiries moves us further still from Nigel with respect to the *type* of organization (tree vs. network) of inquiries that we can utilize. This is shown in Figure 8.24.

There are at least two alternative ways of introducing the complex

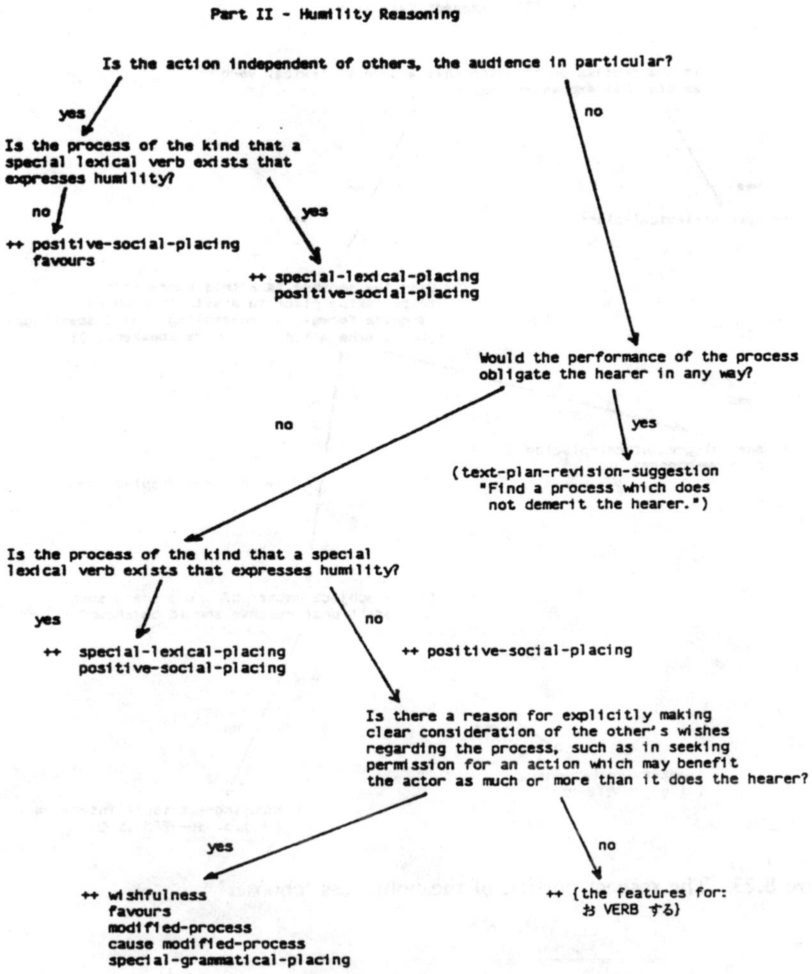


**Figure 8.22** The humility portion of the politeness 'chooser'

inquiry presentation conditions that networking requires:

(i) We can define an *inquiry presenter* that consists minimally of (a) an inquiry presentation condition and (b) a branching inquiry.
(ii) Alternatively, we can think of the inquiry itself as being enhanced with an inquiry presentation condition.

Here, we will follow the second alternative, although there are certain reasons to prefer the first.[13] Inquiries enhanced with presentation

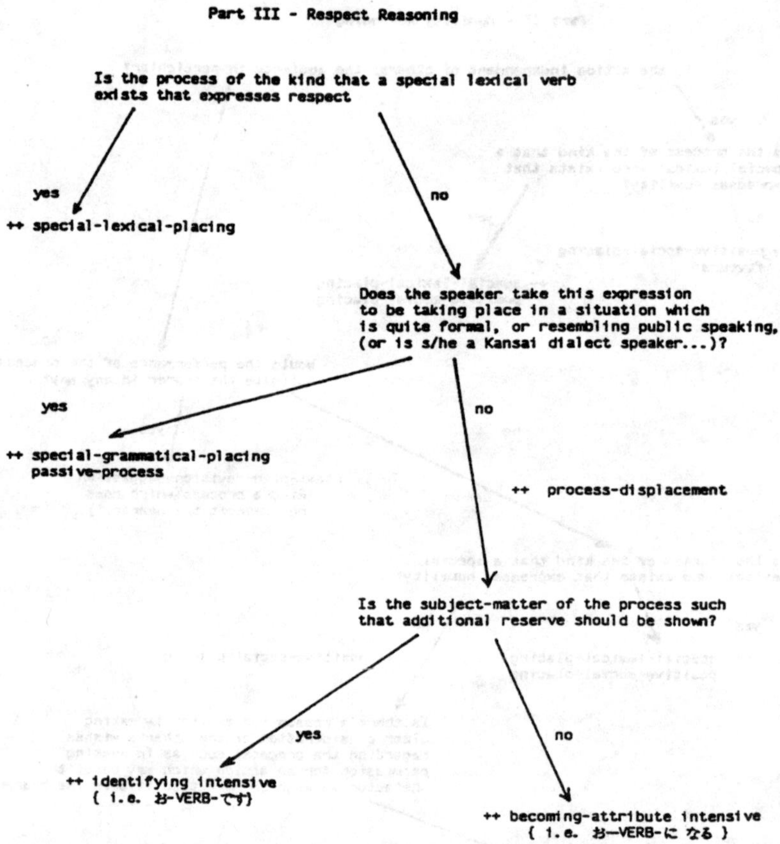


**Figure 8.23** The respect portion of the politeness 'chooser'

| *chooser framework* | *inquiry network* |
|---|---|
| inquiries are organized into decision trees | inquiries are organized into networks |
| decision trees form choosers, local to systems | inquiry networks are not local to particular systems |

**Figure 8.24** Chooser framework vs. network framework

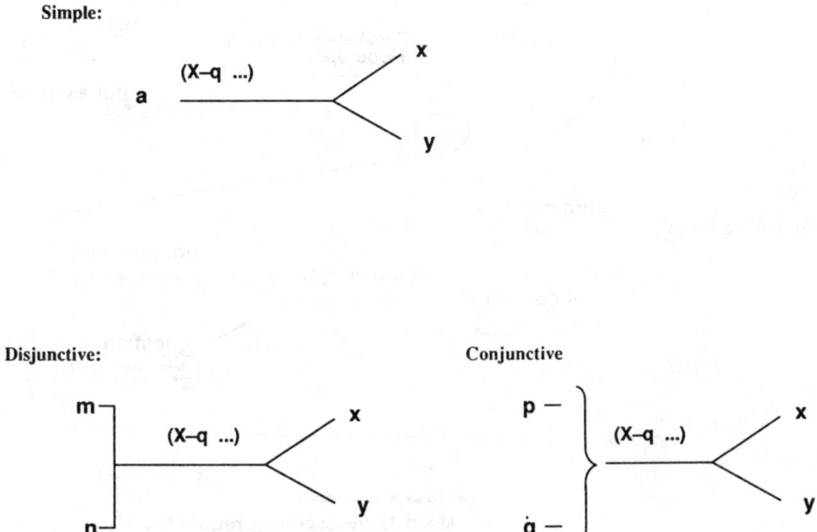


**Figure 8.25** Inquiries with presentation conditions

conditions according to alternative (i) may be diagrammed schematically as in Figure 8.25; a, x, y, etc. in the figure are inquiry responses; X Q is an inquiry.

We can return to the example MOOD and COMMENT (Section 8.4.1 above) for an illustration of the use of a disjunctive presentation condition. A fragment of an appropriate inquiry network is given in Figure 8.26. Here, if the response to the inquiry QuestionQ is 'question', the inquiry AddresseeSincerityQ can be presented. If the response is 'nonquestion' or 'command', the inquiry SpeakerSincerityQ can be presented. Another alternative to present this inquiry is possible, however: the response 'command' to CommandQ would, through the disjunctive presentation condition, also be grounds for presenting the inquiry.

Since the inquiry network is global rather than local to systems, preselections associated with the responses to an inquiry may refer to more than one system in the grammatical system network. Further, preselections of features from different systems may be associated with a single response. This presupposes a generation algorithm that differs from the one discussed in Chapter 6, which is based on the grammatical system network. We will return to this at the end of this section. In the meantime, we will discuss the descriptive consequences of adopting the inquiry network framework for the organization of inquiries.

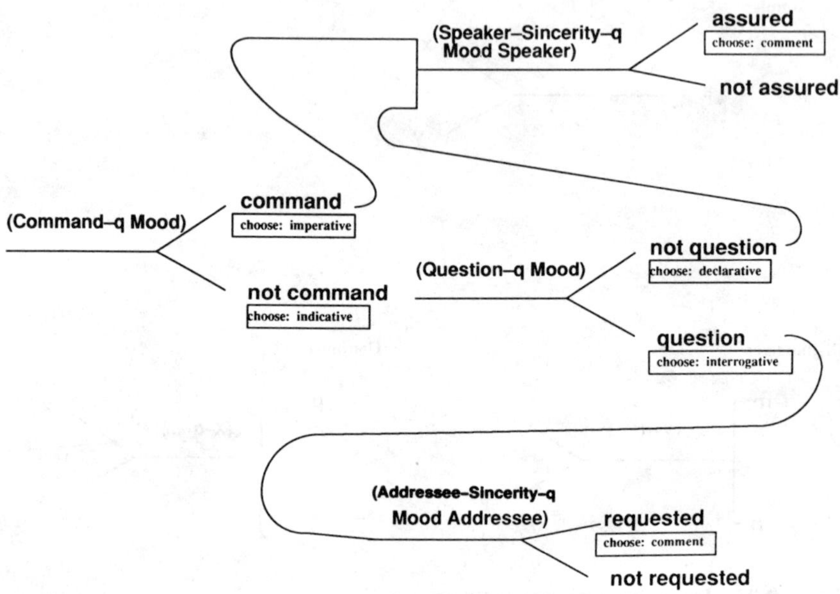


**Figure 8.26** Inquiry with disjunctive presentation condition

The framework changes just proposed are formally simple but they lead to fairly fundamental descriptive consequences. We will consider examples of inquiry networks set up to choose in the clause part of the grammatical system network. We find two major clusters:

(i) An ideational–experiential cluster: inquiries that depend on the identification of the Process 'hub', i.e., the chunk of information in the environment or context of the generation system that contains the experiential semantic specification of the event being described.
(ii) An interpersonal cluster: inquiries that depend on the identification of the Mood 'hub', i.e., the chunk of information in the environment or context of the generation system that contains the interpersonal semantic specification of the role of the linguistic act in its text or discourse.

As we will see in the illustrations below, the inquiry network involves grammatical systems that are simultaneous within each metafunction as well as metaphorical alternations not represented systemically in the grammar (cf. Sections 5.5.3 and 13.1.4). This is summarized in table form in Figure 8.27. Here we will only focus on the interpersonal cluster, leaving the ideational cluster for discussion elsewhere.[14]

| | interpersonal | experiential |
|---|---|---|
| interaction between simultaneous systems | MOOD & POLARITY, TAGGING | PROCESS-TYPE & AGENCY |
| | MOOD & COMMENT | PROCESS-TYPE & CIRCUMSTANCE |
| grammatical metaphor | speech functional metaphors | transitivity metaphors |

**Figure 8.27** Grammatical areas related by inquiry network

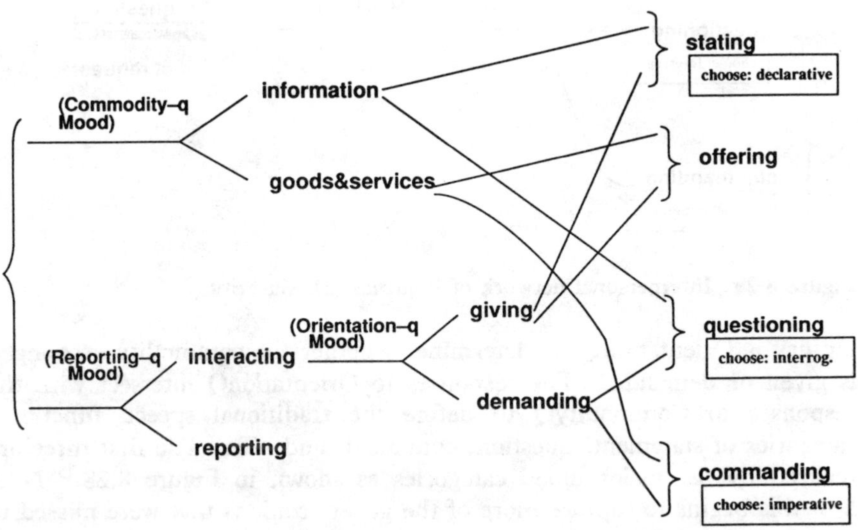


**Figure 8.28** Interpersonal network of inquiries (1)

### *8.4.4 The English interpersonal cluster*

There is an identification of a speech functional hub for Mood early in the network. Once Mood has received its hub association, inquiries requesting information about this hub can be presented. There are two simultaneous inquiries. One addresses the nature of the commodity in the exchange: is it information or is it goods and services? The other determines whether the current part of the exchange is acted out by the speaker (response: 'interacting') or is reported (response: 'reporting'), leading either to direct speech or indirect speech (e.g., *I'm not a crook* vs. *he said he wasn't a crook*).

*(1) Interacting* We will follow up the interacting alternative first. The next

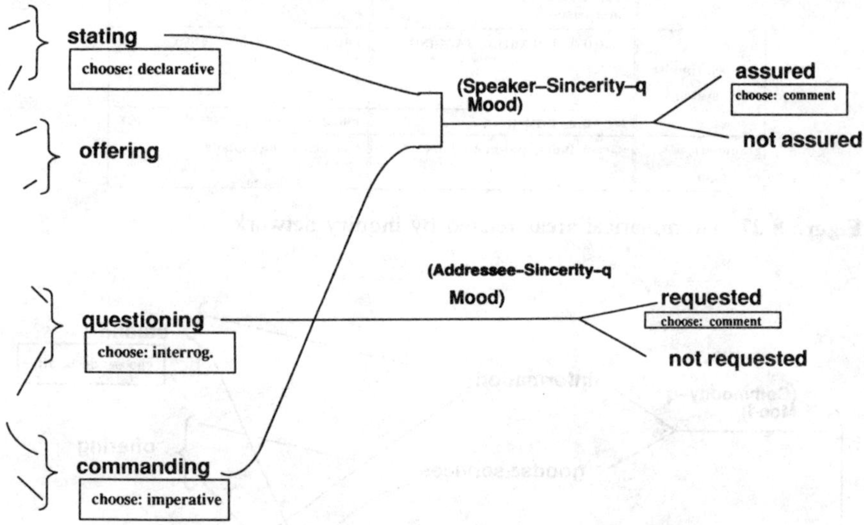


**Figure 8.29** Interpersonal network of inquiries (2): sincerity

inquiry is OrientationQ. It determines whether the commodity exchanged is given or demanded. The responses to OrientationQ intersect with the responses to CommodityQ to define the traditional speech functional categories of statement, question, command, and offer. The first three are realized by the major mood categories as shown in Figure 8.28.[15] Note how this begins to capture more of the generalizations that were missed in our example of Figure 8.17 above.

The disjunction of stating and commanding is the presentation condition of the inquiry concerning the speaker's SINCERITY, SpeakerSincerityQ; the question is whether the speaker's indication of sincerity should be specified. Questioning is the presentation condition of Addressee-SincerityQ; the question is whether the listener is to be encouraged to respond sincerely: see Figure 8.29.

We can also fold POLARITY inquiries into the network. Questioning leads to PolarityVariableQ, which differentiates between polarity questions and other types by ascertaining whether the value of the polarity is variable rather than a fixed value. If it is variable, PolarityBiasQ is presented. In other cases, PolarityValueQ is used to determine the value of the polarity; the notion of 'other cases' is captured in a somewhat awkward disjunction of three responses (giving, commanding, nonvariable): see Figure 8.30.

*(2) Reporting* When we turn to the reporting case, we see how the

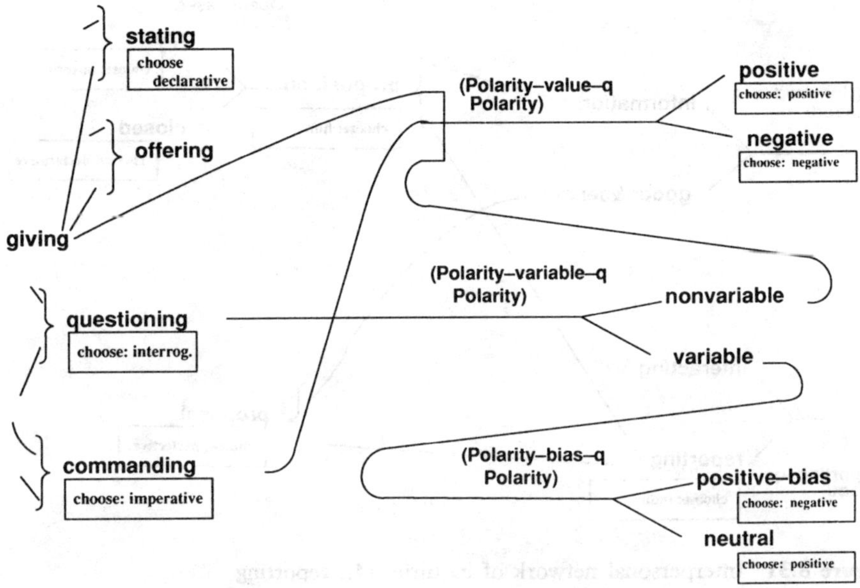


**Figure 8.30** Interpersonal network of inquiries (3): polarity

responses to CommodityQ are again relevant. Reporting and information define the category of proposition and reporting and goods & services define the category of proposal. There is thus no interactive distinction between giving and demanding in the reporting case.[16] Instead, there is a distinction based on the nature of the proposition between open and closed information; if it is open, it includes a variable. These alternatives are set out in Figure 8.31.

We have now set out first approximations to a network of inquiries which provide an interpersonal semantic network. With the support of this network, the exploration can immediately be taken further in a number of directions. One of these is to explore the semantic integration of two components within the grammar: the MOOD and KEY (cf. Halliday 1985b) systems that determine intonation contours and speech act types. Thus, while MOOD and KEY can be set up as simultaneous systems in the grammar and are realized independently of one another, they interact semantically to form speech functional categories that may not be predictable from the combinations of grammatical features: thus, it is beneficial to capture their semantic relatedness directly. This line of development is now under study in new research that aims to add speech capabilities to systemically based generation systems (Bateman and Oshika, 1989; Sefton, 1990; Fawcett, 1990b).

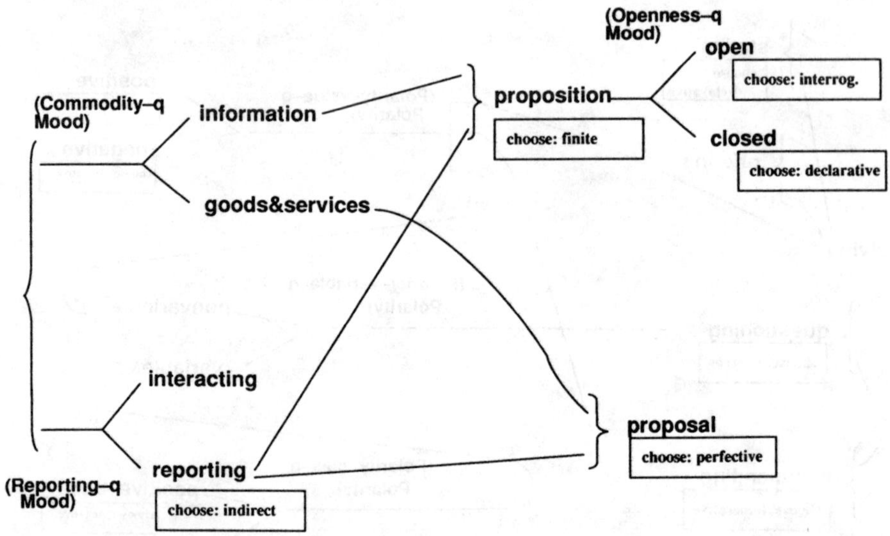


**Figure 8.31** Interpersonal network of inquiries (4): reporting

## 8.5 Summary

At this point, let us pause to summarize briefly. We have explored the metafunctional limits of the 'base line' implementation of systemic functional grammar presented in Part II. These limits are, we suggested, essentially those of the experiential subtype of the ideational metafunction. We have gone beyond this experiential baseline in two ways. (i) We have considered dynamic systems in the context of the local and textual metafunctions – i.e. dynamically enterable systems and systems with dynamic potentials. (ii) We have also gone beyond the local chooser packaging of inquiries and considered more global inquiry networks.

The next step is to go beyond the framework we have sketched so far by moving upwards (stratally speaking). This we now turn to in Chapter 9.

## Notes

1. Thus, we are not arguing, as is occasionally attempted, the superiority of, e.g., 'dependency' over 'constituency' or vice versa. Indeed, such attempts miss one of the more challenging areas of current grammatical theorizing: that is, *how* it

is exactly that syntagmatic constraints of very different natures are able to combine to specify a single grammatical unit. We will not be able to address this issue further here, however.

2. See Martin (1985) for more on the synoptic/dynamic distinction, and Bateman (1989a) for a condensation of some of the points made here.
3. This is also the case in other recent attempts to formalize and make use of SFG-style organizations in computational linguistics. For example, Patten (1988a: 42) provides a brief overview of some of the problems that recursive systems bring for the coherence of the interpretation of the meaning of a systemic network and, while acknowledging that some replacement needs to be found for them since the absence of the functionality they provide weakens the abilities of systemic grammars, excludes them from his account. Also, none of Patten and Ritchie's (1987), Mellish's (1988), and Brew's (1990) explorations into formalizations of limited aspects of the meaning of a systemic network moves beyond basic network notions. One exception to this has been the more recent work of Fawcett and Tucker (1990), where there is some provision for recursion.
4. This figure is an actual output from the Kyoto system; it is read as follows. The symbols of the first four lines T2, CORE, H1, etc. are grammatical functions that co-describe a single grammatical constituent. The symbols following these, and preceded by colons, are the grammatical features preselected for that constituent (content-verb, stem1, etc.). Finally, the symbol in the last line at the left is the lexicalization for the constituent, the Japanese hiragana characters for 'yomu'. Further examples of this output format occur below.
5. The constituent labels OO1 and OO2 refer to 'Oblique Objects', i.e., grammatical constituents similar to Direct and Indirect Objects but participating less centrally. The necessity of the 'receive' morpheme is described briefly in Section 9.3.2 below.
6. In fact, some further experimental properties were built in at this stage, including 'sister' preselection across elements of the dependency chain, differing feature 'percolation' schemes for contained dependency chains, and both progressive and regressive orderings for the complexes as a whole. These will not be discussed here, however.
7. This is in contrast to the treatment of realization statements implemented within the Japanese system. Rather than relying upon an explicit notion of system-token to generate token-specific realization statements, those statements are instead embedded into the process of traversing the network defined by the generation algorithm. Their precise meaning is then, as is the case with chooser restriction, defined by their dynamic position within the traversal process rather than by explicit representation. This is far from an optimal solution.
8. In the figures containing inquiries in this chapter, inquiries are represented by name followed by the letter 'Q', and the grammatical features that they select are represented in the form: choose FeatureName.
9. Thus, for verbs corresponding to the English 'give' and 'receive', there are seven Japanese verbs in common usage and these differ in most part according to the relative social positions of the participants in the giving.
10. This is a general property of stratification in a semiotic system: related options that are dispersed across different contexts at one stratum can be 'brought together' as one choice at a higher stratum.
11. In Chapter 9 below we explicitly introduce this component of the environment

as the *interaction base* and show its relation to two other components of the environment motivated by the ideational and textual metafunctions.

12. The utterance is drawn from a corpus of telephone conversations concerning hotel reservations that is currently being built up by the Language Group of the Advanced Telecommunications Research Institute (ATR), Kyoto, Japan.
13. In particular, the same inquiry may be used in different contexts, calling for different inquiry presentation conditions. This can be handled if different inquiry presenters use the same inquiry.
14. Although in our discussion below of the informational support required for inquiries, we will touch on some details of the organization presupposed by the ideational experiential cluster of inquiries (Section 9.2).
15. In fact, the possibilities for realization are more flexible than we describe. In particular, *grammatical metaphor* (Sections 5.3.3, 13.4.1; Halliday, 1985a; Ravelli, 1985) takes us considerably further than the 'congruent' realizations that we limit our discussion to here.
16. That distinction is 'carried' by the process of the reporting clause — demand/offer, etc.

# 9 Stratal extensions: context as seen from lexicogrammar

In Chapter 8, we moved up to and beyond the limits of the modelling of the theory of metafunctions within the grammar and its semantic chooser and inquiry interface as defined in Part II. We suggested ways of refining the model so that the theory of logical systems and structures and those of the other metafunctions can be represented more faithfully: this involved the internal organization of the chooser and inquiry interface. In this chapter, we will extend the model presented in Part II in another direction; we will move upwards from the grammar and its semantic interface to the higher-level systems that are responsible for responses to the semantic inquiries.

## 9.1 Uncovering contextual organization by projecting from lexicogrammar

The source of responses to the inquiries presented by the chooser and inquiry interface has been identified as the ENVIRONMENT (cf. Sections 2.1 and 6.4). If we just focus on the Nigel component, as we have mostly done until this point, we can treat the environment as a black box. It does not matter how the responses to the inquiries are arrived at, as long as they are appropriate. This independence makes the Nigel component *portable*, which is very desirable. In all of our discussions so far, we have essentially stopped at the level of the inquiry interface: we have stated what inquiries need to be defined, but we have not addressed how those inquiries are to find their answers. Now, however, we want to turn to consider this question in detail. For a fully functioning text generation system, it is necessary to provide mechanisms by which the inquiries can operate automatically.
Although this can be achieved in a number of ways, the path we are going to take here, as is consistent with our general goal of developing

computational systemic-functional *theory*, is to consider the further specification of inquiries and their source of information, the environment, as a further development of systemic-functional theory positioned stratally with respect to our existing development of theory for the lexicogrammar. In fact, when we focus on the overall design of a text generation system such as Penman, the design of the environment becomes a central question. We approach it here from the point of view of the lexicogrammar.

### *9.1.1 The components of the environment in current systems*

By way of background, let us return first to the simple design of a text generator presented in Chapter 2 and our interpretative survey of existing text generators in Chapter 3. According to these designs, we saw that the environment of a computational system typically might contain the following general sources of information:

- the knowledge base;
- the reader model;
- the rhetorical resources and text plans.

Now we can provide some additional structure and motivation to these sources of information since they respond to, or can be assumed to respond to, different kinds of inquiries from Nigel. One way of differentiating inquiries is again by metafunction; e.g., experiential inquiries get their answers from the knowledge base, while textual inquiries appeal to the reader model and the rhetorical resources. However, neither existing reader models nor text planning components have been worked out in a way that is both general and detailed in any generation system: as we have seen, inquiries pose rather fine-grained questions and so make strong demands on their supporting information sources.[1] It will be helpful therefore, to develop a number of *design considerations* that have to be accommodated in the design of the environment of a text generator if it is to support the level of functional detail expected by, for example, Nigel.

To contribute to this development, we will approach the organization of the environment with the linguistic system as our point of departure. This approach suggests a particular way of organizing the environment in the most general terms. The metafunctional view of the design of, and division of labour in, the environment provides a good foundation for thinking about the environment from the lexicogrammatical vantage point. The alternative is to start with some theory of the organization of the environment, such as the ethnographic interpretation developed by Hymes and others or the interpretation of context in terms of higher-level semiotic systems within systemic linguistics (cf. Part I and our discussion of contextualism in Part IV). These approaches — from lexicogrammar and its semantics and from context itself — are not mutually exclusive; on the contrary, we need to pursue both.

### *9.1.2 Approaching the environment from lexicogrammar*

We can take the *grammatical resources* of a particular language as sources of suggestions for how to organize information in the environment. For instance, when we use the Nigel generator, each inquiry can be the basis of a detailed design decision. This design will be considerably more highly differentiated than some general, all-encompassing notion such as 'text-plan'; we have seen examples of some of these fine-detailed decisions that will need to be made in the inquiries shown in the previous chapter and in Chapter 7.

The availability of such an extensive set of suggestions for environmental organization has resulted in a specific methodology for working with the environment. In general, we proceed from a set of inquiries in some particular semantic region and attempt to make explicit the dimensions of organization that those inquiries entail. We then seek methods of representing this abstract level of organization computationally — both as a way of making the result computationally usable and as a means of articulating the theory further. Below, we will provide examples of this methodology in practice for each of the three metafunctions.

Another consideration is the dynamics of selecting and organizing the information to be presented in a text. Here we need to look at the way in which the grammatical resources are used in texts of various types to present information in units of information, in clauses, and so on. Here, however, we will focus on the more static aspect of the organization of information rather than the selection of information to be presented.

We present suggestions for organizing information in the environment that are based on a linguistic approach to modelling and which reflect considerations of how information is organized and classified when it is represented lexicogrammatically in text generation. In other words, we are concerned with the organization of information for the purpose of verbalizing it. As far as the knowledge base is concerned, it is important to emphasize that this is only one of the possible uses of it; it might also be used in reasoning, in planning, and perhaps in the interpretation of sensory input.[2] This is an aspect more salient for the knowledge base than for the other parts of the environment (which we will call the text base and the interaction base). Indeed, for these other components there is less 'competition' from designs not based on language. To the extent that these other components are modelled at all in a text generator, the modelling is usually driven by the need to generate text rather than by any other considerations. Furthermore, it is important to note that the use of language is not restricted to generation or understanding; perception, reasoning, and planning can also be linguistic activities.

Although we will be using lexicogrammar in the exploration, our discussion is not about lexicogrammar. It is about the organization that is above lexicogrammar and is projected on to it in generation. One reason for using lexicogrammar to infer the organization of the components of the environment is that the lexicogrammar of a natural language reflects a theory of that organization. Lexicogrammar reflects a theory of reality (to focus on the ideational metafunction) and this theory is the ideational semantic organization of the system. Or, to put it in non-linguistic terms, it is the conceptual organization we find in the knowledge base of a generation system. Similarly, it also reflects an enactment (and a theory) of (symbolic) interaction — the interpersonal metafunction — and a theory of the nature of information presented in text — the textual metafunction.

Another reason for using lexicogrammar is a practical one: we know a good deal more about lexicogrammar than we know about the organization of other parts. In particular, we have extensive functional accounts of grammar such as those by Halliday, other systemic functional linguists that interpret lexicogrammar as a resource in a communicating system. Systemic linguistics simplifies the move of making use of lexicogrammar in our modelling, because

- the grammar is a functional one; it is 'semanticky' and thus serves to bring out semantic distinctions we need to make. For example, transitivity is interpreted in such a way as to bring out a typology of process concepts as well as a typology of phenomena that can participate in these processes.
- the grammar combines a 'case frame' approach of the kind that has been built into semantic nets with a taxonomic organization (systemic) of these 'case frames' that can be related to the hyponymic taxonomy of a semantic net.
- lexicogrammar is organized in such a way that grammar is related to lexis by delicacy and this corresponds to the move from general to specific that is needed in the knowledge base taxonomy. For example, it is possible to classify lexical concepts such as mixing, beating, adding, and frying (via intermediate steps) under the grammatical concept material process.

The strategy we are using rests on two interrelated assumptions about lexicogrammar and theories of reality:

(i) Lexicogrammar is not arbitrary in relation to semantics. Rather, it is related to semantics in a natural way and it is organized according to functional principles. Under this assumption, it makes sense to use lexicogrammar as a way of exploring the higher-level organization: if lexicogrammar were an arbitrary rule system, we would not be able to make any use of it to explore higher organization and the strategy would make little sense.[3]

(ii) We would not have direct access to reality, but only indirect access through interpretation of it. Ideational semantics is one interpretation of reality; it is the one that is reflected linguistically. There is no a priori conflict between linguistic facts and facts pertaining to reality, but there may be conflicts between the semantic interpretation of reality and other interpretations of reality. For example, according to the system of English semantics, there are conscious beings who engage in private mental processing. An extreme behaviourist might disagree with English and avoid such interpretations; but this would be a conflict between two interpretations of reality, not between linguistic facts (English) and facts of reality (the behaviourist position). Furthermore, what are taken to be conflicts between 'language' and the 'real world' are in fact often conflicts between two alternative perspectives, both of which are embodied in language. One is a congruent interpretation and the other or others are metaphorical ones.[4]

There is an important corollary to this second assumption. When we come across grammatical statements we may have to re-examine them in functional semantic terms to see that the grammar actually embodies an interpretation of reality. In particular, the distributional statements based on grammatical classes that we find in formal approaches to grammar tend to obscure the role of the grammar of a language as an interpretation of reality. For example, if a grammatical account says that verbs of perception take either nominal or sentential complements, this may seem to be only a grammatical observation. In fact, however, it reflects the grammar's 'theory' of perception, a theory of what kinds of phenomena can be perceived, viz. phenomena as well as macrophenomena (i.e., configurations of phenomena); and phenomena as well as metaphenomena (i.e., interpretations of phenomena by language): *she saw the kids* (perception of phenomenon), *she saw the kids playing in the yard* (perception of macrophenomenon), and *she saw that the kids had been playing in the yard* (perception of metaphenomenon).

Similarly, the distribution of *that*-clauses in English may look like a purely grammar-internal affair (as the reference to it suggests it is); however, once we explore a bit further, we discover (among other things) that English embodies an interpretation of reality according to which facts cannot operate on phenomena in the material world (as opposed to the world of consciousness) — cf. Halliday (1985a: Section 7.5).

Having explained why we think the organization of the environment of a text generation system can be usefully approached from lexicogrammar and its semantics, we now turn to the overall organization of the environment that we obtain from this approach.

### *9.1.3 The three bases*

Using a systemic functional theory and the grammar of English as a way of uncovering semantic distinctions as we have just described suggests three perspectives on the environment, one for each metafunction; these we term the ideation base, the interaction base, and the text base:

(i) The IDEATION BASE, which is a theory of natural 'reality' — what one might call a *semanticization* of the world (as a complement to the notion of a conceptualization, since, as we shall see below, we are taking the ideation base to be a *meaning* base rather than a *knowledge* base). This is the part of the environment that supports 'ideation' and hence the ideational component of the lexicogrammar, i.e., a particular interpretation of the world. The phenomena of the world are ranked and are organized into networks — taxonomies of sequences, process configurations, and simple phenomena. They are interpreted as units with a functional type of structure. For instance, process configurations are configurations of a nuclear process (say a process of sensing), participants (e.g. a senser involved in conscious processing and a phenomenon impinging on the senser's consciousness) and circumstances (e.g. a time); they are differentiated into a small number of general types — processes of doing and happening, of sensing, of saying, and of being and having. And so on.

(ii) The INTERACTION BASE, which is an enactment (and a theory) of intersubjective reality and a model of (symbolic) interaction between people and the role relationships they enter into. This is the part of the environment that supports linguistic interaction or exchange and hence the interpersonal component of the grammar, i.e., the speaker's assignment of linguistic role-relationships, the speaker's evaluations, attitudes, and so on. (In some respects, we can think of the interaction base as different interpersonal colourings superimposed on the ideation base.)

(iii) The TEXT BASE, which is a theory of symbolic reality — of information as text. This is the part of the environment that supports the

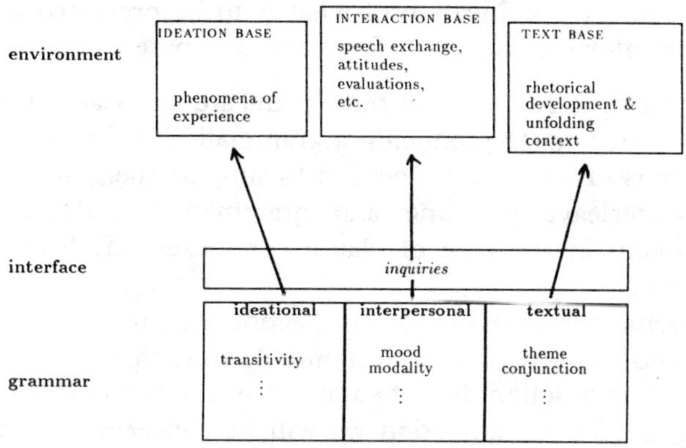


**Figure 9.1** The three bases of the environment as seen from grammar

presentation of information from the ideation base and the interaction base as text in context. The text base includes, among many other kinds of information, a conjunctive component for developing and organizing text in terms of conjunctive relations.

The three bases, shown in relation to the metafunctional components of the grammar (at the rank of clause) in Figure 9.1, obviously suggest the three 'components' of systemic context theory — field, tenor, and mode (cf. Section 5.6.2). However, we maintain a terminological distinction to indicate the different starting points. Ideation base, interaction base, and text base represent a view of the environment from the lexicogrammar, whereas field, tenor, and mode are 'components' of a theory of context and thus reflect a starting point 'outside' language.

The three bases must support the three metafunctions. We can think of this support as being recorded locally in plans for clause complexes, clauses, nominal groups, and so on. Each local plan will contain contributions from each of the three bases. For instance, a clause plan contains the following types of information:

- A configuration that is represented lexicogrammatically in terms of a process, participants, and circumstances. This information comes from the ideation base.
- A speech function of a particular type, with speaker and listener roles specified; possibly also the manner of its performance and assessments of, and attitudes towards, the proposition/proposal of the speech function. This information comes from the interaction base.
- Possibly a conjunctive relation, relating the configuration or speech function to prior text; a specification of what is to be the local context

of presentation; a specification of what is to be presented as unmarked news. This information comes from the text base.

We do not mean to suggest that these plans are necessarily fully specified when the generator starts producing a grammatical unit; rather, the plans specify the kinds of information needed to support the grammar. It is also possible to interleave planning and grammatical realization. This is particularly likely in the case of clause complexes (cf. Section 8.2) and nominal groups.

We will discuss the ideation base in Section 9.2, the interaction base in Section 9.3, and the text base in Section 9.4. In each case, we will see the development of abstraction described at the beginning of this chapter. For the inquiries of each metafunction we will be concerned with:

- abstracting out the kinds of information and support that they require at the semantic stratum of meaning above the lexicogrammar;
- considering the kinds of theoretical and representational resources that this requires.

## 9.2 Ideational: ideation base and general taxonomy

Although the ideation base corresponds by and large to the knowledge base of Figure 2.3 and we will start by briefly reviewing the notion of knowledge base in text generation systems, we also need to make clear why we maintain a distinction between 'knowledge base' and 'ideation base'.

We have said that we are concerned with the organization of information in the knowledge base for the purpose of verbalization. One central question is what the nature of this information is from a stratal point of view. If we take the knowledge base as a given, the information is knowledge. Or, as it has sometimes been called, propositional knowledge or even semantic knowledge. But what is knowledge? If we approach the 'knowledge' base from language, as we are doing here in designing it, the information it contains is MEANING. There has been a considerable degree of uncertainty in this area, as the variation between the terms conceptual net (graph) and semantic net used for the net representing the information indicates.[5] The question of whether the information in the 'knowledge' base is knowledge or meaning might be thought to be mainly a terminological one. However, there are other fundamental consequences as well.

- If the information is meaning, there is no stratal difference between the 'knowledge' base and the (ideational) semantics of the text generator; i.e., there is no difference in abstraction and both deal with the same kind of information. If, on the other hand, the information is knowledge, we should expect there to be a stratal difference.

- If the information is meaning, it follows that the main guide to its organization is language itself. If, on the other hand, the information is knowledge, we should identify other principles for organizing it — e.g., perceptual, psychological, 'logical', neurobiological, etc.

In the remainder of the chapter, we will assume that the information is meaning. It may even turn out to be quite reasonable to interpret knowledge in general as meaning, articulated and differentiated by different semiotic systems. It is important to be aware, however, that this is not an uncontroversial position — especially within the Artificial Intelligence tradition where it would usually be assumed that the information being captured should be treated as knowledge. Such approaches then reject the utility of considering the linguistic input to determining its organization (cf. Weischedel, 1989), a utility that we will be attempting to motivate throughout the remainder of this chapter.

When the domain model for a particular generation task is built, it is already quite common to reflect English LEXICAL SEMANTIC organization in the conceptual organization of the knowledge base (this is reflected in the notion of a *terminological* component or TBox that we will see below; cf. also Quillian's (1967) early conception of the semantic net based on the dictionary). The domain model is thus often a *lexico*-semantic net, a kind of domain-specific thesaurus.[6] However, this approach needs to be generalized; we can take the grammar part of lexicogrammar as well as the lexis part into consideration when we build a knowledge base, so that it reflects not only lexical semantics but also GRAMMATICAL SEMANTICS. This is precisely what has been done for the Penman generator. A general taxonomy has been created under which various domain models can be classified. It draws heavily on an ideational grammatical semantic typology developed by Halliday and Matthiessen (see Halliday and Matthiessen, in prep.) and is based on Halliday's interpretation of English. This abstract typology has come to be known as the 'Bloomington Lattice'.

We can, therefore, be rather more precise about the kind of information that the knowledge base will reflect. The knowledge base will reflect *one kind* of lexicogrammatical semantics: ideational lexicogrammatical semantics, the kind of semantics that deals with ideation. There are two other kinds, interpersonal and textual. They are usually not part of the knowledge base, but we will return to the full functional spectrum of semantics below. In the meantime, we will make a few observations about the linguistic approach in relation to the knowledge base.[7]

There are, then, to summarize, three reasons for using the term ideation base as an alternative to knowledge base.

(i) First, given systemic metafunctional theory, the term ideation base is more precise than the term knowledge base: ideational knowledge is a particular kind of knowledge, differentiated from interactional knowledge and textual knowledge. By calling the knowledge base the ideation base, we indicate what kind of knowledge it is a model of.
(ii) Second, we are not committed to the view that the information that constitutes the ideation base is knowledge; we can also look at it from the vantage point of language as meaning.
(iii) Certain aspects of what may go into a knowledge base (speech act operators, quantifiers, etc.; cf. the ABox described in the next subsection) should not properly be part of the ideation base, but would come from the views taken in the interaction base and in the text base.

### *9.2.1 The notion of 'knowledge base'*

The knowledge base has been the most prominent of the system resources in the environment in work on text generation to date. All generation systems have some knowledge source, even though they may lack a reader model and rhetorical resources. It is the best developed aspect of the environment in text generation systems, and it has also been explored widely outside text generation within computational linguistics and artificial intelligence in terms of knowledge (conceptual) organization. So much so that in the current implemented part of the Penman system, the knowledge base is the only part of the environment to have received substantial implementation so that it can be used in responding to inquiries automatically.[8] However, interest in the past has focused more on the theory of 'knowledge' *representation* than on particular 'knowledge' descriptions,[9] and so here we will reverse the order of our discussion with respect to the methodology we are following: in this area at least, there is a rich variety of representational resources that have been developed. It is thus worthwhile to consider the abstractions required by the ideational metafunction inquiries in the light of these.

*9.2.1.1 Representational resources for knowledge* Many current knowledge representation languages organize a knowledge base according to two kinds of information: general knowledge about concepts organized into a taxonomy, and instantial knowledge about particular situations and individuals.[10] Thus, for example, in the KL-TWO family of representation systems (cf., e.g., Brachman and Schmolze, 1985) there are two components:

(i) the *NIKL component:* concept frames organized into a taxonomic hierarchy of concept types; for example, the concept of forwarding a message in an electronic mail and calendar system belongs in the taxonomy of concept types. NIKL itself exemplifies a common earlier approach to knowledge representation; it belongs to the KL-ONE tradition of knowledge representation (e.g., Brachman, 1978; Schmolze and Israel, 1983) in particular and to the (frame-based) semantic net or conceptual graphs developed in computational linguistics in general.[11] It embodies a notion concept that is a frame of roles and a conceptual taxonomy of the hyponymic kind. It is a combination of so-called semantic nets or conceptual graphs and conceptual frames.

(ii) the *PENNI component:* includes a collection of propositions, whose predicates are concepts in the NIKL hierarchy; for example, the instantial information that Smith forwarded message 63 last Wednesday belongs in the collection of specific propositions.

In related work, Brachman, Fikes and Levesque (1983) identify two components of a similar representational framework, KRYPTON, the *terminological* component and the *assertional* component, and describe them as follows:

> two main components for our representation system: a terminological one (or 'TBox') and an assertional one ('ABox'). The TBox allows us to establish taxonomies of structured terms and answer questions about analytical relationships among these terms; the ABox allows us to build descriptive theories of domains of interest and to answer questions about these domains.

The representation of the TBox is cast in terms of concept frames with associated roles; the frames are organized into a taxonomic hierarchy. The representation of the ABox is cast in terms of a first order predicate logic, with the difference that the predicates are drawn from the TBox. The concepts become one-place predicates and their associated roles become two-place predicates. Brachman *et al.* summarize the organization of KRYPTON as follows:

> Overall, the structure of a KRYPTON system can be visualized as in [Figure 9.2]: a TBox of roughly KL-ONE-ish terms organized taxonomically, an ABox of roughly first-order sentences whose predicates come from the TBox, and a symbol table maintaining the names of the TBox terms so that a user can refer to them.

In this figure, concepts in the TBox are represented as ovals ('doctor' and 'person') and relations between concepts, such as roles ('child'), are represented as small circles with squares within them. The ABox assertion thus corresponds to a proposition that may be loosely glossed as there is a person and a doctor such that the child relation holds between them.

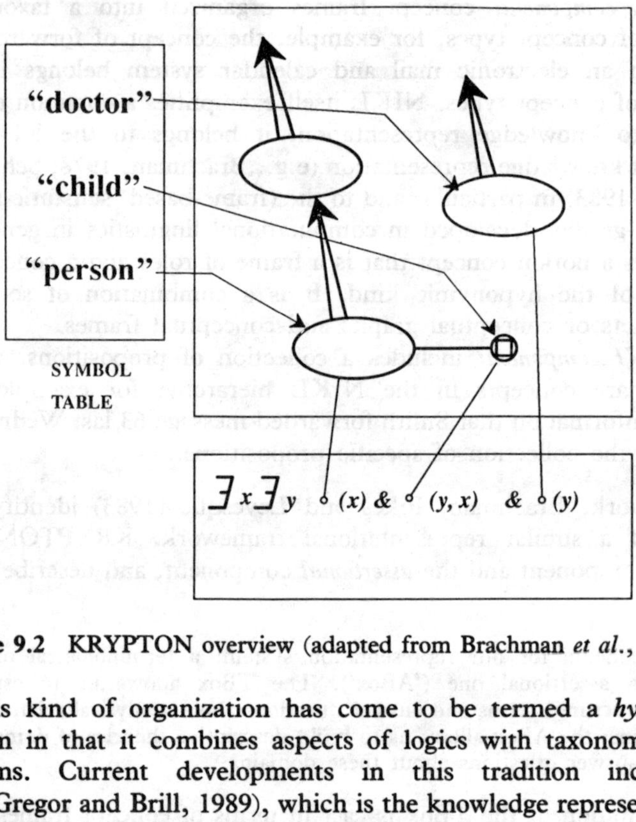


**Figure 9.2** KRYPTON overview (adapted from Brachman *et al.*, 1983)

This kind of organization has come to be termed a *hybrid* reasoning system in that it combines aspects of logics with taxonomic inferencing systems. Current developments in this tradition include LOOM (MacGregor and Brill, 1989), which is the knowledge representation system used presently in the Penman text generator, and the Janus representation language (e.g., Weischedel, 1989) where a taxonomy of general concepts is combined with an intensional logic.

Another way of thinking of the distinction between the TBox and the ABox is as the distinction between *potential knowledge* and actual or *instantial knowledge*. Or, to put it in Hjelmslevian terms, between *system* and *text* (Hjelmslev, 1943), for the TBox contains *knowledge* as *system* and the ABox contains *knowledge* as *text*. Clearly, however, there is more to the ABox than instantiation of TBox concepts, since assertion and quantification are added. Both assertion and quantification are non-experiential in nature in that they typically function to restrict reference possibilities for an interlocutor: they are thus the concern of the interaction base and the text base rather than the ideation base.

*9.2.1.2 Representational resources for the ideation base* Returning now to Nigel, we can describe how the representational resources of the previous section can provide the necessary mechanisms for responding to Nigel's experiential metafunction inquiries. First, we can note that either of the two kinds of components in a hybrid knowledge representation system may serve as the source of inquiry responses. For example, many inquiries are concerned with taxonomic information (as in 'is this process one of doing?'). Other inquiries are concerned with the presence of a particular type of information in a proposition (as in 'is the cause of the process to be represented?'), in which casc the assertional component (or its equivalent) would be the source. We are concerned here primarily with the former.

Above we noted that the PENMAN system relies upon one particular general conceptual taxonomy. This taxonomy draws on the abstract typology developed for English by Halliday and Matthiessen (in prep.) and is often referred to as the UPPER STRUCTURE (or, with respect to the domain models that are defined for particular tasks, the UPPER MODEL) of the knowledge base.[12] The taxonomy is motivated by the particular demands of the grammar's semantics, or inquiries. The experiential inquiries define a set of design criteria for the upper model: if the upper model fails to support a distinction these inquiries require, then the corresponding area of grammatical variation is not controlled.

The notion of frame as we saw it used in the taxonomic organization of, for example, NIKL or the TBox of KL-TWO and later developments such as LOOM, is related to Fillmore's (1968) theory of case frames, which has been an important source of inspiration in work on knowledge representation.[13] One of the differences between Fillmore's case grammar and Halliday's (1967/8) transitivity grammar, however, is that Halliday's theory includes the paradigmatic notion of a system network as well as the syntagmatic notion of a configuration of transitivity functions. That is, in his theory, 'case frames' are paradigmatically organized in the system network of transitivity. In this respect, frame-based nets are closer to systemic theory than to case grammar: frames are paradigmatically organized into a taxonomy.[14] They thus offer a particularly appropriate representation for this component of the ideation base.

As an example, consider the diagram of Figure 9.3, which represents one particular fragment from a Bloomington Lattice type organization:[15] i.e., that the concept 'tell' is a kind of 'saying', which in turn is a kind of 'process.' This kind of taxonomy is organized as a set of *concept units* which are related into a network; these components can be described as follows.

(i) The CONCEPT UNIT. The concept unit has structure; as already suggested, it is essentially like a case frame in the transitivity structure of a clause, with a number of roles (slots) filled by pointers to other case frames. These pointers constitute restrictions on the conceptual values

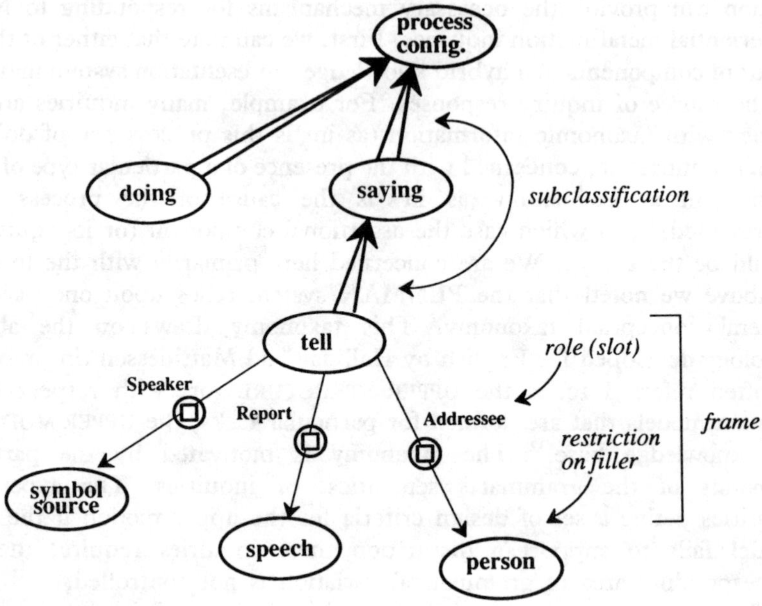


**Figure 9.3** The 'tell' concept frame, role fillers, and superordinate concept

of the role fillers — *value restrictions* on the roles.[16] For example, if we want to define a concept 'tell' as in the diagram above, we would say that it is a kind of saying and that it has three roles, Speaker, Report, and Addressee. For purposes of illustration, we can say that the Speaker role has to be filled by a concept that is a symbol source (i.e., a human, a document, an instrument, or the like), the Report has to be speech, and the Addressee has to be a person.

(ii) The NET. The fragment in Figure 9.3 is part of a large net of concepts such as the 'tell' concept; the concepts are related taxonomically by a general relation of subclassification[17] and they are also related through the restrictions on the fillers of roles. Let us turn to the taxonomic relation first; consider the taxonomy of Figure 9.4, which is an extension of the fragment given in Figure 9.3. (As before, subclassification is represented vertically, but we have left off the arrow heads on the subclassification arrows for the sake of convenience.)

In addition to the 'vertical' organization of the net with its taxonomic aspects, the roles defined on concepts provide a 'horizontal' organization. For example, in Figure 9.3, the Speaker role is restricted to be a symbol source; in the expanded net, the Actor role can be restricted to be a thing

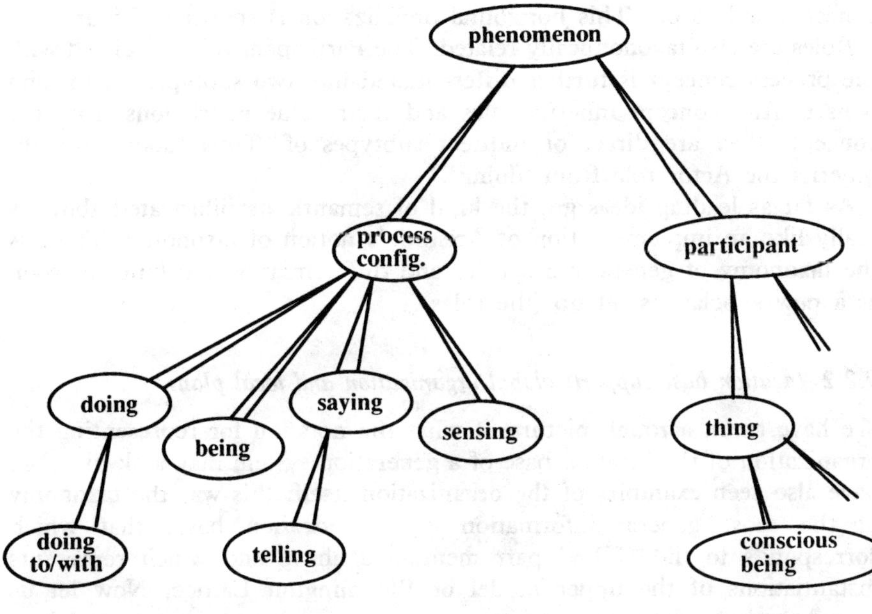


**Figure 9.4** Taxonomic relations in net

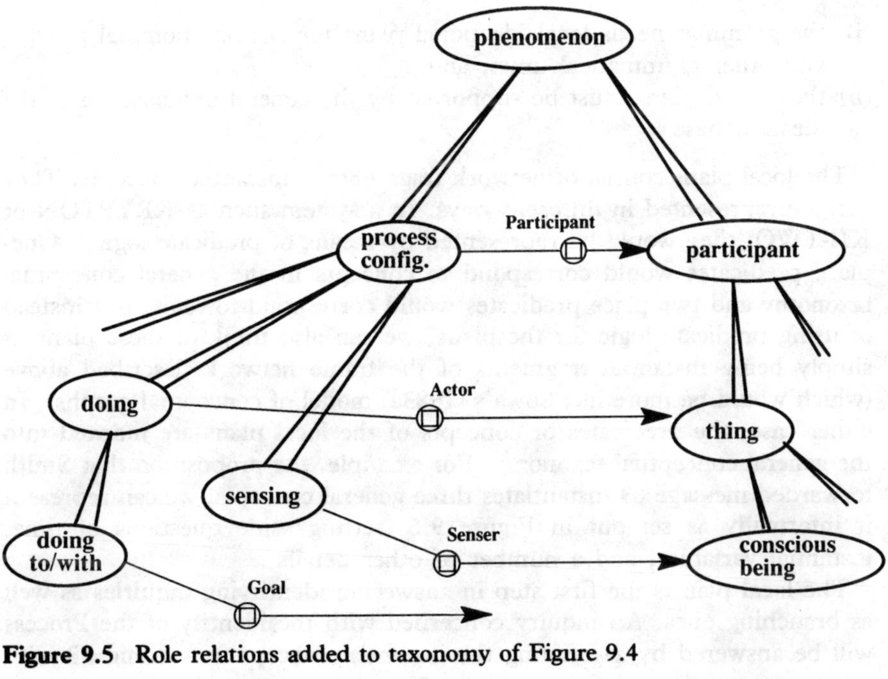


**Figure 9.5** Role relations added to taxonomy of Figure 9.4

concept, and so on. This horizontal organization is shown in Figure 9.5.

Roles are also taxonomically related. The Participant role associated with the process concept is further differentiated into two subtypes. Actor and Senser. Any concept inherits roles and their value restrictions from the concepts they are direct or indirect subtypes of. Thus 'doing to/with' inherits the Actor role from 'doing'.

As far as leading ideas go, the kind of semantic net illustrated above is really like an implementation of Aristotle's notion of taxonomy. There is the taxonomy of genera and species and differentiating attributes as soon as a new subclass is set up (the roles).

### *9.2.2 Ideation base support: global organization and local plans*

We have given a rough picture of what the notation for representing the organization of the ideation base of a generation system may look like. We have also seen examples of the organization itself: this was the taxonomy of the most general information of the ideation base, that which corresponds to the 'TBox' part mentioned above and which represents instantiations of the upper model or Bloomington Lattice. Now let us consider what information the grammar needs to have access to and how it gains that access. We can take this in two steps:

(i) the grammar needs local ideational plans for clauses, nominal groups, and other grammatical units; and
(ii) these local plans must be supported by the general organization of the ideation base.

The local plans consist of network fragments of instantial concepts. They may be represented in different ways. In a system such as KRYPTON or KL-TWO, they would be represented by means of predicate logic.[18] One-place predicates would correspond to concepts in the general conceptual taxonomy and two-place predicates would correspond to roles. But instead of using predicate logic for the plans, we can also think of these plans as simply being instantial fragments of the frame network described above (which would be more like Sowa's (1983a) model of conceptual graphs). In either case, the predicates or concepts of the local plans are indexed into the general conceptual taxonomy. For example, the proposition that Smith forwarded message 63 instantiates three general concepts; we can represent it informally as set out in Figure 9.6 (setting aside questions of time, instantial variables, and a number of other details).

The local plan is the first step in answering identifying inquiries as well as branching ones. An inquiry concerned with the identity of the Process will be answered by associating the instantial concept forwarding#3 with

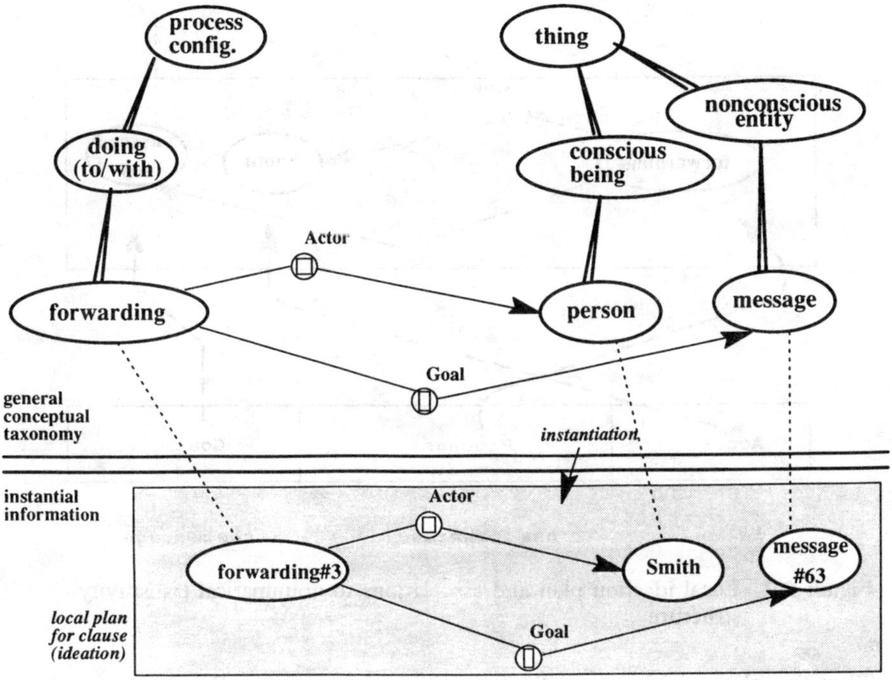


**Figure 9.6** Local plan and general ideation base organization

the function Process. An inquiry concerned with the identity of the Actor of forwarding#3 will be answered by a consultation of the instantial knowledge: the filler of the actor role of the instantial concept forwarding#3 is Smith. Similarly for the Goal: the filler of the goal becomes the instantial concept message#63. Thus we have now reached the stage where the formerly unspecified 'hubs' referred to as the responses to identifying inquiries (cf. Chapters 6–8) can be instantiated as actual concepts from, for example, the ideation base.

For comparability, we can note that this specification of the ideational local plan is isomorphic to one component of the input form that is actually used when generating with the Penman system. This input form is provided by the Sentence Plan Language (SPL) input specification (cf. the Penman Project, 1989; Kasper, 1989a). The SPL-portion corresponding to our current example would be:

```
(forwarding#3 /   forwarding
    :actor        (smith / person)
    :goal         (message#63 / message)).
```

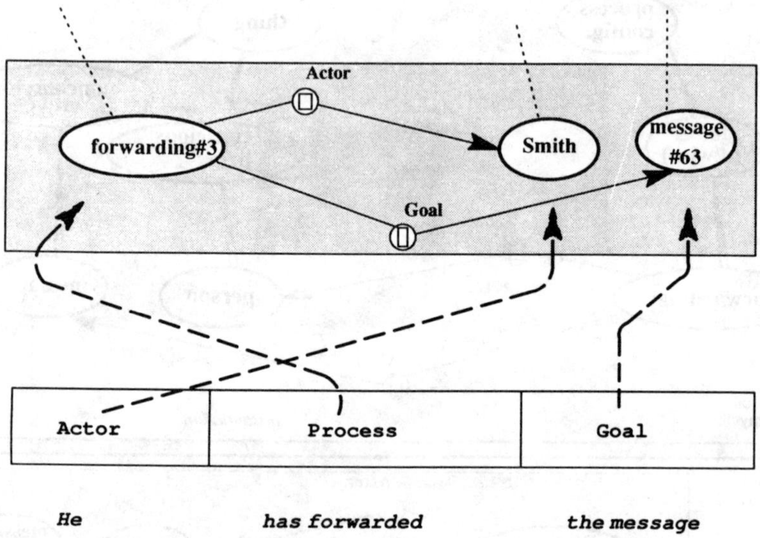


**Figure 9.7** Local ideation plan and associations to grammatical transitivity structure

That is, this would partially constrain the current Penman system to produce the surface string here required. Thus, SPL expressions should be taken as a further format for the specification of local plans as we are describing them here. We will see further applications of the Sentence Plan Language in Chapter 12 below.[19]

Note that in this particular example, the mapping between ideation base roles and grammatical functions (Actor, Goal, etc.) is extremely simple in that it has largely been one-to-one. In general, the relationship between these two strata is far more complex. The determination of the properties of this interstratal mapping forms the basis of much current research (e.g., Bateman, 1990b, 1990c; Halliday and Matthiessen, in prep.).[20] The associations between grammatical constituents and concepts in the local plan are diagrammed in Figure 9.7.

Once an association has been established, taxonomic information from the general conceptual taxonomy is available. For instance, an inquiry concerned with what kind of process forwarding#3 is will be answered by a consultation of the general taxonomy: it is a kind of doing (we have left out the intermediate classes), and this has particular, specifiable consequences on grammatical and lexical possibilities for realization.

The example above illustrates how the ideation base can support ideational choices within a systemic generation grammar such as Nigel. We will not discuss the organization of the ideation base further here (for more detail, see Bateman, Kasper, Moore, and Whitney, 1990; Halliday and Matthiessen, in prep., and Matthiessen, 1987); instead, we will turn to the two other bases in the environment, starting with the interaction base and then moving on to the 'second-order' organizational resources of the text base.

## 9.3 Interpersonal: interaction base and politeness

We have seen that the ideation base is concerned with 'natural reality' – with an interpretation of phenomena, including processes, participants, and circumstances, as well as with sequences of such process configurations. In contrast, the interaction base is concerned with *intersubjective reality*, more specifically with the social interaction between people and their relative social distances. It provides support for decisions within the interpersonal metafunction of semantics and lexicogrammar, that is, decisions concerning mood, modality, attitude and interpersonal comments, person, etc. We have already seen examples of a number of inquiries from this area (in Section 8.4 above, in particular).

While the quantity of computational linguistic work on the generation of interactive discourse is still comparatively small, socially oriented linguistic research on the various interpersonal resources mentioned above has revealed a number of factors that have to be modelled in the interaction base. For instance, Brown and Gilman (1960) discuss the choice of pronouns based on relations of power and solidarity between interactants; Ervin-Tripp (1969) outlines an American address system and shows how choices such as *James/Uncle James/Mr. Cagney* are based on considerations relating to what we might call the social distance between the interactants determined by age, kinship, status, and familiarity. Similarly, but within systemic theory, Poynton (1984) investigates the relationship between the resources of naming and affect (the emotional charge in the interaction), and Burton (1980) shows how the speech functional options that are taken up and accepted or rejected by the two characters in Pinter's *The Dumb Waiter* create and maintain the relationship of unequality between them; cf. also Sinclair and Coulthard (1975) on the different roles adopted by teachers and pupils in class room discourse.

More generally, work within systemic linguistics in this area is concerned with the TENOR of the relationship between the interactants, tenor being one of three major contextual variables. Within tenor, two broad categories can be identified: the SOCIAL DISTANCE between the interactants – hierarchic distance in terms of power and social status (equal vs. unequal, etc.)

and also distance in terms of familiarity (close and regular contact vs. perfect stranger) — and AFFECT (the 'emotional charge' in the interaction).[21] To these aspects concerned with the positioning and 'affective intrusion' of the interactants, we can also add the nature of the interaction itself as an ongoing EXCHANGE: see Halliday (1984) and Berry (1981) in particular. There is, then, especially when we add in the contributions of USER MODELLING from computational linguistics (see Section 12.5 below), a sizeable body of knowledge concerning what kinds of very general information will be necessary in a fully developed interaction base.

We need now to consider the particular kinds of support that the inquiries of the grammar require in order to reveal the organization of the interaction base. For Nigel, these are still rather restricted, although nevertheless present. One can see, for example, the beginnings of a very simple set of interactional turn possibilities in the decisions underlying mood choices and polarity, the possibility of statements of attitudes by interpersonal comments, and a division of the interactants in a communicative situation into those immediately identified with the speaker — realized grammatically as 'first person', those identified with the addressee — realized as 'second person', and others — 'third person'.

We can provide a slightly more detailed illustration of the methodology of abstracting from the informational requirements of the grammar's inquiries to reveal the workings of the environment by returning to our prototype treatments of Japanese — particularly those concerned with politeness that we introduced in Section 8.4.2. As described in Bateman (1990a), the 'grammaticization' of many interpersonal and textual distinctions in Japanese made their treatment rather more central in the work at Kyoto than they have been in the Nigel grammar of English and, one result of this, is the politeness chooser presented in Figures 8.21, 8.22 and 8.23 above. We now take this further and set out the kinds of interpersonal distinctions the inquiries of this chooser require in the interaction base.

### *9.3.1 Interaction base support: local plans*

We begin by developing a specification of the information that needs to be grouped together to support generation. This is equivalent to the 'local plans' described in Section 9.2.2 — but for interpersonal information rather than ideational. The implemented inquiry discrimination network for Japanese politeness makes use of inquiries which[22]

- refer to the 'social distance' between interactants,
- refer to roles with particular social interpretations: e.g., roles of obligation, role of the 'doer' of a process, etc.,

teacher > pupil
customer > salesperson
company head > section head > worker
older > younger
parents > children
out-group > in-group
*senpai* > *koohai*
telephone caller > telephone callee
male > female

**Figure 9.8** Levels in Japanese society

- need to know the general level of formality of the communicative situation as a whole,
- need to know whether particularly sensitive 'subject matter' is at issue.

These can be differentiated more finely by considering the circumstances in which they are used, and the distinctions that those circumstances require to be drawn. For example, we can uncover some of the particular instantiations of 'social distance' by examining the actual roles of speakers and addressees in situations where the inquiries referring to social distance yield determinate responses partially motivating the grammatical forms that are generated. On the bases of such considerations, we can observe a number of differential levels of social status at work in Japanese culture; some of these are given in Figure 9.8. Note that this is by no means a static attribution of status that does not ever change; some of the levels — and the social roles that define them — are very transitory. There is therefore an important element of 'negotiation' involved here, and this dynamism also needs to be reflected in the organization of the interaction base.

Similarly, one can examine the distribution of grammatical forms that indicate that some kind of 'obligation' is at issue, and see how these lead to particular kinds of expectations for how interaction will proceed. Also crucial are accurate estimations of the attitudes of the addressee: this, for example, is necessary in order to know whether some particular subject of discussion requires special treatment or not. Again, both of these types of information, allocation of interactional roles, and the expected attitudes of the bearers of those roles, need to be available in the local interaction plan in order for generation to proceed appropriately.

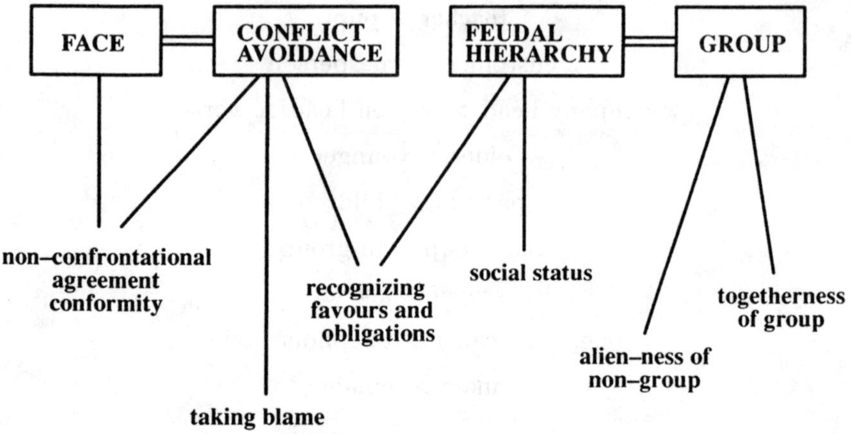


**Figure 9.9** An exploratory social 'upper model' for Japanese

### *9.3.2 Interaction base support: global organization*

This range of information needs more general organization and support just as did the instantial information in the local ideation plans. An initial attempt at such an organization is given in Figure 9.9. This should not, of course, be taken as a 'final' product or research result: its principal function here is to provide an example of the kinds of organization which might be relevant and necessary when putting together an abstract interaction base component for a language such as Japanese. Just as the conceptual hierarchy of the upper model helped with the implementations required for certain of the ideational inquiries, we are appealing here to a similar notion in order to organize our view of what might be necessary when considering the implementations of the interpersonal inquiries. We can expect that a corresponding organization for English would show significant differences — many more probably than would be shown between an ideation base for Japanese and the one for English outlined in the previous section.[23]

Figure 9.9 shows several broad categories of social process: 'face', 'conflict avoidance', 'feudal hierarchy', and 'group'. These, unlike the concepts of the ideational 'upper model' of Section 9.2.1.2, here represent classes of social *strategies* that are pursued by participants in discourse and that define the kinds of social interpretations that are applied to enactments of interaction within discourse. In particular, they are intended to provide foundations for the kinds of interpersonal processes that find realization, through inquiries such as we have seen above, in grammatical constructions.

Thus, for example, the notion of 'face' (cf. Goffman, 1955) — i.e., the preservation of roles and relationships which uphold the self-perceived social status of individuals — is an important motivation for pursuing interactions where agreement is readily offered and non-confrontational responses are preferred. This commonly combines with the general social strategy of 'conflict avoidance' to motivate interactions where agreement and consensus are pursued with frequent indications that listeners are in fact attending to what speakers are saying. Furthermore, the need to avoid, or treat specially, some subject matter as being of a particularly sensitive nature that we saw as an inquiry in the politeness chooser of Section 8.4.2 also respects the requirements of 'preserving face' — in this case, usually the face of others, again as motivated by conflict avoidance.

Additionally, many turns in Japanese interactions are concerned with 'taking the blame' for real, constructed, and imagined events with negative social connotations. For example, it is quite common to begin a Japanese interaction with the utterance,

*senjitsu-wa shitsuree-shimashita*

which, rather literally, means: 'I was rude the other day.' This is particularly used when the speaker was placed in a position of being obligated to the hearer at the time of their last meeting — by, for example, being bought something to drink or eat, or any other favour, virtually no matter how minor. This thus avoids potential conflict that might arise due to the giver of the favour not perceiving sufficient gratitude on the part of the receiver of that favour. This avoidance is taken further in the cases when the speaker is actually explicitly thanking the hearer for a favour. Here it is not sufficient simply to state thanks, it is also necessary to *state* that a favour was done or received. For example, while the utterance,

*tetsudatte-moratte, arigatoo*
help- receive thanks

is an acceptable informal way of expressing 'thanks for your help', the corresponding utterance that omits the explicit morpheme of *receiving* the favour of the help is not possible.[24]

A further source of input that determines the grammatical forms of utterances is provided by the combination of the categories 'feudal hierarchy' and 'group'. The former supports the examples of social levels we saw illustrated in Figure 9.8 above. This category thus motivates the differing forms of language that are considered appropriate for use between interlocutors according to those interlocutors' relative social statuses — examples of these were given in the Japanese examples of Section 8.4.1. This combines with, for example, the strategy of conflict avoidance so as to guarantee that the explicit recognition that a favour has been received or given *also* correctly attributes relative social levels in that process of giving and receiving favours. Thus, in contrast to the informal thanks for help just illustrated, the following would be necessary when more social distance between the interlocutors is to be displayed:

*tetsudatte-itadaite* *arigatoo-gozaimashita*
help- receive (humble) thanks- be (past, humble)

The sole difference between this variant and the previous one is that the forms selected realize the interlocutors' difference in social relationship. By such means, relative social positions and relationships are simultaneously observed and reinforced while furthering the general social goal of peaceful coexistence.

Finally, the notion of 'group' is used to ground the Japanese preference, even in the selection of grammatical forms, for expressing solidarity and involvement with in-group members and the rejection of nonmembers. This is reflected in preference for anaphoric reference over nonanaphoric reference when possible, for interaction strategies that are used to indicate mutual concern for group members, and even in the selection of grammatical forms that express that the group member intends to return to the group whenever an absence, no matter how short, threatens. An example of the latter is the use of complex verbal groups that introduce a verb meaning to 'come' or 'return' whenever the principal meaning being expressed is one of leaving. Mizutani and Mizutani (1987: 143) illustrate this with the following translation for 'I'm going out for a walk':

*chotto sanpo-ni itte-kimasu*
just walk go- come

In this way the speaker defuses the possibly negative connotation of going out, away from the group with the explicit expression of the intention to return.

We can also note, then, a certain similarity between the basis of Figure 9.9. and the strategies for pursuing politeness linguistically given by Brown and Levinson (1987: 102, 131) – especially when we add in the intervening level of detail between abstract characterization and linguistic form suggested by the politeness 'decision tree', or chooser, presented in Figures 8.21, 8.22 and 8.23 of Section 8.4.2. What we suggest here, however, is both a particularly Japanese slant on the organization of social reality portrayed and one which is directly motivated by the functional demands of the (interpersonal) lexicogrammar. Thus, for each of the categories of social strategies offered in Figure 9.9, characteristic patterns of language use can be identified. This means that, during text generation, the inquiries responsible for those patterns can be implemented with respect to this model of the social processes involved in an entirely analogous manner to the implementation of ideational inquiries with respect to the ideation base. These categories can then form the basis of a general characterization of context that includes attributions of 'formality', etc.

We will return to some of the issues concerning context and its relationship to the linguistic system proper in Part IV. It is clear, however, that significantly more work needs to be undertaken for the interaction base – particularly in the area of interaction itself, i.e., the possibilities of conversational turns and rhetorical moves that are supported — to bring it to the level of detail we have seen for the ideation base. This will become increasingly important as sophisticated text generation systems become more involved with producing interactions and taking part in conversation.

## 9.4 Textual: text base and Rhetorical Structure Theory

We have looked briefly at the ideation base as a 'theory' of natural reality and the interaction base as an 'enactment' of intersubjective reality. The ideation base and the interaction base constitute sources of meaning that still have to be presented as *text in context* by a text generation system. The choices about how this is to be done are supported by the text base.[25]

The development of text has been characterized in terms of movement and flow. By nature, the textual metafunction is *dynamic* rather than static like the experiential one: it is concerned with the ongoing presentation of the text. (A 'rose' is a 'rose', but 'it' is not necessarily 'it'!) For example, from a textual point of view, objects are instantiated referents, not classes in an experiential taxonomy. Thus, the textual world view is ever-changing; it changes as the text and its context evolve: what was new becomes old, what was rhematic becomes thematic, was non-identifiable becomes identifiable, and so on. This needs to form an essential property of the text base.

The textual resources of the lexicogrammar include cohesive resources (ELLIPSIS and SUBSTITUTION, REFERENCE, LEXICAL COHESION, and CONJUNCTION) as well as resources that create grammatical structure (THEME, VOICE, and CULMINATION within the clause; and INFORMATION within the information unit). The textual metafunction accordingly demands information about a wide range of distinctions, for example, thematic vs. non-thematic (THEMATIZATION), given vs. new (INFORMATION), and identifiable vs. non-identifiable (DETERMINATION within REFERENCE). These are not, however, part of elaborate taxonomies of textual distinctions.[26] Thus, the textual function contrasts with the experiential one: experiential distinctions concern general classes of experience, such as thing vs. process or doing configuration vs. sensing configuration, whereas textual distinctions *are specific to the text in its context* and their values vary as a text unfolds and the context changes.[27] For example, the textual notion of 'identifiable' means 'identifiable at the current point in the text to the addressee of the text'. And the distinction between near and not near (e.g., *this/that* used to specify how a referent is identifiable) is deictic. What the textual metafunction requires of the text base are procedures for managing the presentation of information as identifiable or non-identifiable, and so on, since distinctions like these are inherently dynamic.

### *9.4.1 Text base support: plans and planning*

The central question we want to raise here is, again, what kinds of demands do the resources of the lexicogrammar make and how these demands can be met. However, the particular focus of these questions is now, of course, the text base. We will address these questions in two ways. First we will sketch the local plans for textual information that the grammar has to be able to consult. Specifying what these plans have to contain is largely a matter of reviewing the inquiries of the choosers of the textual systems of the grammar — just as has been the case for the ideation and interaction bases in the previous sections and as was suggested with respect to the inquiries formulated for the Japanese post-nominal particles used as an example in Section 7.3. Next we will also say something about the harder problem, which is the question of how the text base can produce these local plans.

Local plans are needed for grammatical units to support the inquiries from the various textual resources; we will focus here on plans for clauses. In talking about these plans, we should again emphasize that they need not necessarily be fully specified when the grammar starts developing a clause; rather, the plan represents a *record of the kind of information that is needed* and it may quite conceivably be fleshed out as the demand for information arises. For the purposes of the present discussion we will restrict attention to two principle textual resources of the clause: CONJUNCTION and THEME.

- CONJUNCTION needs a specification of a *conjunctive relation* such as temporal succession or simultaneity, exemplification, and variation to prior text to be expressed (if any); there may be a specification of two relations.
- THEME needs a specification of *contextualization*, i.e., a plan of how to

| TEXTUAL RESOURCE | FIELD IN PLAN | KIND OF SUPPORT NEEDED |
|---|---|---|
| CONJUNCTION | conjunctive relation (to prior text) | RST relation and added delicacy (e.g., subtype of circumstance relation); also: other rhetorical moves (e.g., return to topic, dismissal of point) |
| THEME | context: • textual-conjunctive • interpersonal-modal (etc.) • experiential – circumstantial and participant | continuity and shift in local context, relying on method of development, which correlates (partly) with the point of a rhetorical relation |

**Figure 9.10** Textual resources and required support

contextualize the clause (in relation to what happened up to that point in the discourse). More specifically, the contextualization breaks down into three components: textual — conjunctive (contextualization according to how the clause is related conjunctively to prior text), interpersonal — modal, etc. (contextualization according to how the clause is evaluated modally, attitudinally, etc.), and experiential — participant/circumstantial (contextualization according to some aspect of the process configuration). In English, Theme is realized by order, in particular, the Theme element is placed leftmost in the clause.

The fields in the textual plan that these resources relate to are summarized in Figure 9.10. We have also noted the kind of support needed in the text base to produce the plan specification to be discussed and exemplified.

### *9.4.2 The text base resources producing the plans*

How can the text base produce these kinds of local plans for clauses; to what extent do they rely on the same abstractions and on text plans developed more globally (for the whole text or sizeable spans of it)? As a way of getting started, we will begin with the following simple approximation. To create the local plans, the text base will need two kinds of abstractions:

(i) It will need a model of how the text is developed by *relating spans of text* rhetorically; and
(ii) it will need a model of different *textual statuses* (as context, as identifiable, as news, etc.) within these messages.

The two are clearly related: the relationship to what precedes affects the textual status of what follows and the need to manipulate textual statuses affects the way in which relations are built up.

The question is now what frameworks are available to help us explore these models. In the case of the ideational resources of the grammar, there is an existing 'technology' for representing the information to appeal to — e.g., the various forms of knowledge representation we saw in Section 9.2. above. There has already been a fair amount of research devoted to the problem of representing 'knowledge' and so, when we began the design of the ideation base, we drew on this work. Although there is no comparable body of work on the technology of representing textual information, there have been some relevant explorations in two particular areas in computational linguistics:

(i) RHETORICAL STRUCTURE: the relational structure of a text, identifying the relations by which one span of text can be related to another rhetorically, thus developing the text — this is the concern of the Rhetorical Structure Theory (RST) mentioned briefly in Chapter 2 and in Section 6.6.4; and
(ii) FOCUS SPACES: contexts of topical continuity that succeed one another in the development of a text, with the possibility of interruptions and dependencies — in the work of Grosz (1977), Sidner (1978, 1979, 1981), Grosz and Sidner (1986) and Reichman (1985); e.g., Grosz's (1978) notions of focus, focus spaces, and focus shift (cf. McKeown's use of this in her TEXT system, mentioned in Section 3.3.3) and cf. Grimes's (1982) linguistic interpretation of this work in terms of context spaces, a development of his earlier notion (Grimes, 1975) of staging. Focus spaces have been represented as partitions of semantic networks (for partitions, see Hendrix, 1978, 1979; for their use to represent focus spaces, see Grosz, 1977, 1978).

The second notion needs extending to cover what is often called *information flow* in the development of text: we have to take account of a variety of *textual statuses* — thematicity, identifiability, newsworthiness, etc. Focus covers just one aspect of this.

Let us start by introducing those aspects of Rhetorical Structure Theory needed in the subsequent discussion. We will then introduce the treatment of 'focus'.

*9.4.2.1 Rhetorical Structure Theory* RST is an approach to the study of text organization that is being developed within the Penman project (cf. Chapter 2; Mann and Thompson, 1987; Hovy, 1988a, 1990) and elsewhere (e.g., Moore and Paris, 1988, 1989; Scott and de Souza, 1989). It gives us the resources for describing a text in terms of its 'rhetorical structure'. A text is interpreted as being structured by relations, so-called rhetorical relations: two spans of text enter into a rhetorical relation such as elaboration, cause, circumstance, or motivation. The relation is (typically) asymmetric; one of the spans is nuclear and the other has a satellite status. The difference between the two spans, the nucleus and the satellite, is a matter of centrality or nuclearity; related notions have been used in tagmemic work and work influenced by tagmemics, e.g., hypotaxis (Grimes, 1975) and nucleus–margin (Pike and Pike, eg., 1982). The relational mode of structure contrasts with the constituency mode of structure most commonly used in linguistics; it is closer to the logical mode of interdependency structure introduced in Sections 8.1 and 8.2.[28]

A rhetorical relation is characterized in terms of (i) the conditions on its use (what Mann and Thompson, 1987, call constraints) and (ii) its intended effect.

(i) The conditions may apply to either text span entering into the relation or to their combination. They identify the conditions under which the rhetorical relation is applicable. For example, a relation of motivation is only applicable if the listener is not motivated to comply with the request or accept the offer given in the nuclear span of text.
(ii) The effect identifies the function of a rhetorical relation in terms of the intended end-result — the intended effect on the listener. For instance, the relation motivate relates a motivational satellite to a nucleus and its (intended) effect is to increase the listener's willingness to comply or accept. It is important to note that rhetorical relations are characterized in contextual terms, more specifically in terms of the listener's mental states, rather than in lexicogrammatical terms: a text is not seen as a concatenation of sentences.[29]

Each span of text entering into a rhetorical relation may in turn be organized into spans related rhetorically; i.e., there may be, and typically is, internal nesting. This provision for internal nesting can give a structure of considerable depth. We can see this as the hierarchic organization of text, but it is important to keep in mind that this 'hierarchy' created by internal nesting is very different from the hierarchy of rank-based constituency. In addition to the nucleus–satellite type of relations, RST also identifies multinuclear relations such as contrast.

As an example of an RST structure, we can consider the analysis of the

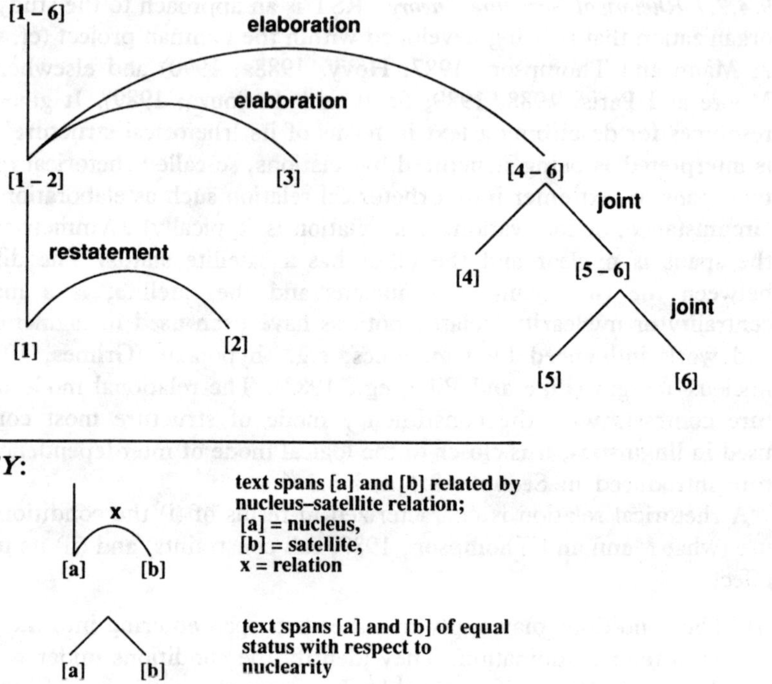


**Figure 9.11** RST analysis of bats report

following grade school report on bats, taken from Martin and Rothery (1981).

[1] The bat is a nocturnal animal. [2] It lives in the dark. [3] There are long nosed bats and mouse eared bats also lettuce winged bats. [4] Bats hunt at night [5] they sleep in the day [6] and are very shy.

The RST analysis of the bats report is given in Figure 9.11. Text spans [4–6] and [3] elaborate text span [1–2]. Internally, [4–6] is organized in terms of joints and [1] is related to [2] by restatement.

*9.4.2.2 Textual statuses and information flow* Taking the notion of information flow seriously, we can explore the possibility of modelling that flow by means of a series of 'snapshots' or informational states that correspond to different kinds of textual statuses. The flow is then represented by the movement or shift from one of these states to another. The first question is how to represent one of the informational states. We noted above that a conceptual network can be partitioned into spaces to represent various types of non-experiential information. Partitioning can also be used to represent textual statuses. We can see this as a reflection of the second-order nature of the textual metafunction. That is, one way of representing this aspect of the text base is to partition the ideation base differentially according to the textual statuses the entities there are to receive.

Textual status can be seen as the general notion of which focus is one subtype.[30] Grosz (1978: 230, 233) characterizes focus in task oriented dialogues as follows:

> A focus representation is developed that highlights those items in the knowledge base . . . that are relevant at a given point in a dialog and included mechanisms for changing focus as the dialog progresses . . . The most crucial requisite of a focus representation is that it differentiate among the items in the knowledge base on the basis of relevance. By highlighting those items that are relevant to the current discourse, the focus representation enables the system to access more important information first during its retrieval and deduction operations. The representation of focus presented here is based on segmenting the knowledge base into subunits. Each subunit, called a focus space, contains those items that are in focus of attention of the dialog participants during a particular part of the dialog. This segmentation is structured by ordering the spaces in a hierarchy that corresponds to the structure of the dialog.

Grosz and Sidner (1986) generalize from task-oriented dialogues to discourse in general. They characterize focus in terms of one of three aspects of discourse structure. These three aspects are linguistic structure (the organization of the discourse into discourse segments), intentional structure (the purposes that organize the discourse), and attentional state. The third is concerned with focus:

> The third component of discourse structure, the attentional state, is an abstraction of the participant's focus of attention as their discourse unfolds. The attentional state is a property of the discourse itself, not the discourse participants. It is inherently dynamic, recording the objects, properties, and relations that are salient at each point in the discourse. The attentional state is modeled by a set of *focus spaces*; changes in attentional state are modeled by a set of transition rules that specify the conditions for adding and deleting spaces. We call the collection of focus spaces available at any one time the *focusing structure* and the process of manipulating spaces *focusing*.

The relative salience of entities in focus spaces and the shift from one focus space to another during the development of the discourse are modelled by a *stack* of focus spaces. A stack is a data structure that implements the notion of 'last-in-first-out'; it has the property that the means of access to the information that the data structure contains is restricted to either adding a new element or retrieving the *last* element that was added. These operations are termed 'pushing' and 'popping' items on to and off of the stack respectively. As a discourse develops, focus shifts can be represented by pushes on to and pops from this focus stack.

Grosz and Sidner's account provides a good deal more detail and sophistication. We will not discuss it further here: the general point for present purposes is that we can think informally of textual statuses as being represented by partitions of the ideation base. These partitions can then be stacked and the 'flow' of textual information is modelled as operations on these stacks.

*9.4.2.3 The relationship between RST and textual statuses* One central question is how the information flow just discussed is effected in the development of a text: what leads to a change from one informational state to another? One can attempt to provide answers in terms of various abstractions such as paragraph structuring, goal (purpose) structure, and rhetorical structure.[31] Throughout the discussion, we will explore the extent to which RST lends support to and organizes informational changes in textual statuses. There have already been some direct and indirect indications that RST is relevant in this regard. Basically, an RST analysis specifies the relations that organize the text; but at the same time, it also indicates a partitioning of the text — and, by implication, its context — into spaces such as the two distinct ones providing elaborations, or contrasts, etc.

This aspect is of interest in the consideration of how the RST structure provides a way of organizing the contexts in which textual statuses and the strategies for presenting them are determined; for example:

- Fries (1981, 1987) has shown that Theme in English is selected to bring out the *method of development* of a span of text; we will see in a moment that 'method of development' correlates well with rhetorical organization.
- Fries (forthcoming) illustrates how the Culminative element of a clause may be chosen to relate to the 'purpose' or point of a particular span of the rhetorical structure of a text — giving a connection to the textual status of INFORMATION.
- Fox (1987) points to correlations between the choice between a pronoun and a nominal group with a lexical noun as head and the rhetorical organization of expository texts — giving a connection to the textual status of REFERENCE.
- Hovy and McCoy (1989) discuss a model in which preferred 'focus' status is explicitly used to guide selection of rhetorical organization — establishing a more appropriate *bidirectional* relationship between textual statuses and transitions.

We will illustrate this interlocking of textual statuses and transition in more detail by looking at the particular relationship between thematicity and rhetorical development.

The notion of 'method of development' of a text indicates the general kind of textual organization that is selected around which to organize that text. Methods of development include organizations that are temporal (as in the example above), spatial, lists, general to specific, object to attributes, object to parts, and compare and contrast (cf. the rather less differentiated schemata for 'thematic progression' proposed in the work of, e.g., Daneš, 1974). Often a clause is contextualized by indexing into this method by which the text is developed: that is, the context in which the clause is to be understood, which is usually specified by the resource of THEME, may include the way in which it develops the text. In such cases, Themes are selected to guide the listener or reader through the text by indicating the method of development: the selection of a particular *type* of Theme will serve to inform the listener or hearer of the *type* of organization which is being used to construct the text. The process of contextualization is here, in a sense, 'anaphoric': the local context of the clause is set up in relation to the preceding discourse context.[32]

There is good evidence that this method of development is embodied in the rhetorical organization of the text as it is stated in terms of RST. This is true, of course, of conjunctions, which are natural Theme candidates; but it is also true of participants and circumstances when they specify *the 'point' of a rhetorical relation* — the point of contrast, instrumental enablement, sequence, elaboration, and so on. This can be seen clearly with *sequence*, where the temporal specifications providing the points of a sequence provide natural Themes. For instance:

The French revolution resulted in a major shake-up among the European powers *and* in 1796 the Dutch were easily supplanted by the British who also managed to subdue the kingdom of Kandy and became the first European power to control the whole island. Until 1802 the British administered Sri Lanka from Madras in India *but* in that year it became a Crown Colony *and* in 1818, three years after the incorporation of Kandy, a unified administration for the entire island was set up. In 1832 sweeping changes in property laws opened the doors to British settlers — at the expense of the Sinhalese who did not have clear title to their land, in British eyes. *Soon* . . . (Wheeler)

Similarly, in the following span of text, we see a movement in two phases and, again, the textual statuses assigned by the thematic options exercised are conditioned by the textual transition, which is one of contrast. Both phrases begin with marked thematic prominence, i.e., marked themes, and the Themes (underlined) serve to identify the points of that contrast.

[nucleus 1:] In his mind he is another 'Carlos the Jackal,' the international terrorist who has kidnapped, killed and still runs free.
[nucleus 2:] *But* in reality Mehmet Ali Agca, the man who shot the pope,

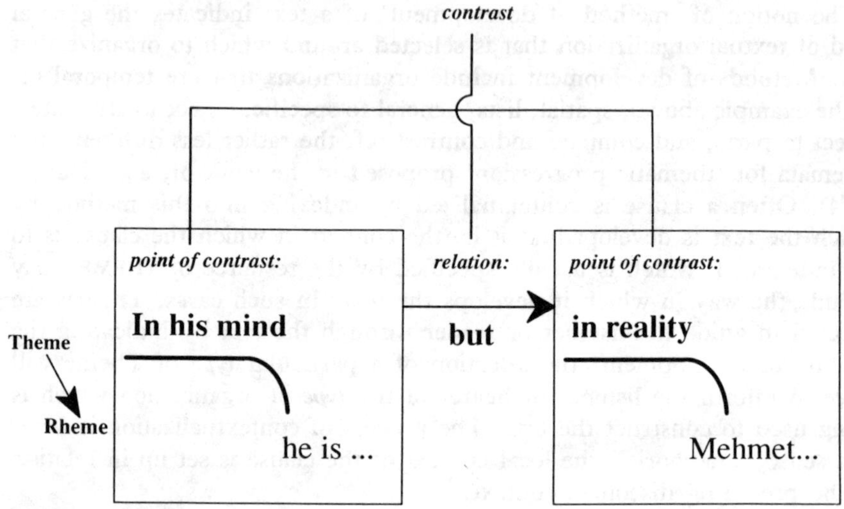


**Figure 9.12** THEME and CONTRAST bringing out contrast

now lives isolated under close surveillance in Ascoli Piceno Prison outside Rome.

There are thus two aspects to the contrast: one is the relation of contrast itself — 'but'; the other is the pair of points of contrast within the contrasting messages — 'mind' vs. 'reality'. These are two ways of marking the contrast, by marking the relation of contrast and by foregrounding the points of contrast; this is shown diagrammatically in Figure 9.12.[33]

In the following case, the text is organized by means of two *elaborations* of a nuclear subspan and the Themes identify the points of elaboration.

> [nucleus:] Last month's devaluation of the peso created an absolute mess for business in both countries. [elaboration 1:]
> On the Mexican side, supermarket shelves were stripped clean of basic necessities by Americans who found their dollars worth three times as many pesos as they were a year ago. [elaboration 2:]
> On the American side, merchants whose lifeblood is Mexican patronage were left standing beside silent cash registers.

The Themes here are locative because the locations are the points of elaboration. In general, however, whatever serves as the point of elaboration may be thematic. In texts that define or describe an object, e.g., in entries in dictionaries and encyclopaedias, the organization is often centred around the object being defined or described. After it has been introduced, the

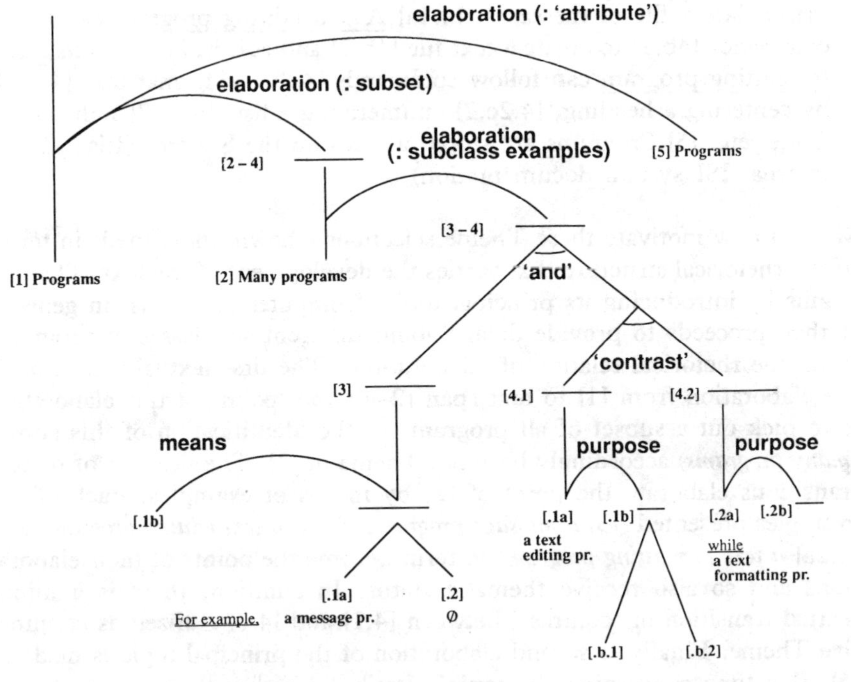


**Figure 9.13** RST analysis of the program text

class it is a subtype of is mentioned, its attributes are identified, and subparts are specified (cf. McKeown, 1985; Hasan, 1978). Theme is likely to be the object itself throughout the text; in descriptive texts, the Theme is often also the 'topic' or 'subject matter' of the description and, further, the Themes are likely to be default ones, i.e., they are likely to be Subjects. For instance:

> [nucleus:] A return to Latin nomenclature for graduation honors at UCLA has been approved by the Legislative Assembly . . . [elaborations:] Summa Cum Laude designates graduates in the top 5 percent of their college. Magna Cum Laude designates the next 5 percent, and Cum Laude the next 10 percent.

As a final example, consider the RST analysis of the following text as shown in Figure 9.13.

> Program. [1] Programs issue instructions to the computer. [2] Many programs process files. [3.1a] *For example*, a message program can, [3.1b] by following your commands, create and send a message [3.2] and

manipulate a file of messages. [4.1a] A text editing program can follow commands [4b.1] to create a text file [4b.2] and edit it, [4.2a] *while* a text formatting program can follow commands [4.2b] to format text [4.2c.1] by centering a heading, [4.2c.2] enumerating a list, [4.2c.3] italicizing a name, etc. [5] Programs are stored as files on the System. (Lisa Moses, internal ISI system documentation)

We can now motivate these Theme selections (shown underlined) in terms of the rhetorical structure that carries the development of the text. The text begins by introducing its principal topic: 'computer programs' in general. It then proceeds to provide details about different subclasses of programs using the rhetorical relation of 'elaboration'. The first textual transition is the elaboration from [1] to text span [2–4]; the 'point' of this elaboration is to pick out a subset of all programs – the identification of this subset (*many programs*) accordingly becomes Theme of [2]. The next set of textual transitions elaborate the point of [2] by means of examples. Each of the examples presented ([3] *a message program*, [4.1a] *a text editing program*, and [4.2a] *a text formatting program*) in term become the points of their elaborations and so also receive thematic status. In addition, there is a minor textual transition of 'contrast' between [4.1] and [4.2] realized as conjunctive Theme. Finally, a second elaboration of the principal topic is made in [5], this time concerning the topic's attributes rather than its subclasses. Nevertheless, as the point of that elaboration, the class itself (*programs*) again receives thematic status.

The method of development of text, as realized through the resources of THEME, is often a consequence of the rhetorical organization that the text base pursues during text development. The transitions between partitions motivated rhetorically redistribute thematic statuses accordingly. Transitions between information states such as have been observed in text linguistics in work such as Daneš (1974) and others may thus be linked with rhetorical relationships. This provides an initial organization for the text base which incorporates information flow as an integrated consequence of rhetorical development.

## 9.5 Summary

We have seen in this chapter a general movement in abstraction beyond the inquiries that form the semantic interface for the grammatical stratum. Section 9.2 showed this movement for the ideational component of the grammar – motivating the construction of an *ideation base* using the computational tools of knowledge representation; Section 9.3 described the similar construction of an *interaction base* to support the interpersonal component of the grammar; and Section 9.4 raised some issues for the construction of a *text base*, corresponding to the textual component of the grammar. In each case, the same procedure was followed: the inquiries as defined within the grammar provide an initial set of requirements for the contents and processes of information management that need to be provided to support those inquiries. This support shows metafunctional differentiation: the three distinct areas of inquiries require contents and processes of rather different natures, reflected in the rather different kinds of organization proposed for the ideation, interaction, and text bases.

We can also relate this general increase in abstraction to a central area of concern in text generation development: i.e., the need to provide *control* of the language generation resources.[34] The more abstract and 'semantic' the level of interaction between a text generation system and its supporting environment becomes, the more manageable those resources are. One needs, for example, to determine general text goals, topics, methods of development, etc. and the finer linguistic detail of particular clause constructions, referential strategies, etc. can be determined within the generation component itself. Future work in text generation can be expected, therefore, to centre rather crucially on the kinds of areas and levels of abstraction that we have here motivated in terms of systemic-functional theory.

Finally, we have now described both a reasonably complete implementation of the lexicogrammar and its chooser and inquiry semantics (Chapters 6–8) and the ways in which the environment can support responses to those inquiries (this chapter). This is sufficient to understand every component of the generation process within Penman and related systems, from the initial specification of a demand for expression down to the selection of realization statements for the construction of the final string. In order to be able to see all of these components in operation, therefore, we give in Appendix II an (abbreviated) annotated trace of the Nigel grammar and its inquiries during the generation of a clause. The interested reader will be able to follow each of the stages we have described as they are brought into play during generation.

## Notes

1. This has sometimes been misinterpreted as a drawback, or failure, of the design — for example, McKeown and Swartout (1987) refer to the large number of inquiries that need to be responded to in order for Nigel to generate even a single clause as presenting a problem for use of the generator. While this would indeed be the case if one were to use Nigel at the level of inquiry responses, the

more appropriate view is one of the inquiries providing a semantic interface to higher levels of linguistic abstraction. Control of the generator should then proceed in terms of these higher levels of abstraction directly. This chapter describes both how this functions and some of the details of these higher levels of abstraction. In addition, in Chapter 12 below, we will see that context can sometimes also offer further direct constraints. It is, then, essential to see the complexity of the account at the inquiry interface level more as a reflection of the necessary complexity of the grammatical stratum rather than as an indication of the work that some user might need to perform in order to use the generation system.

2. For instance, in a current application of Penman, the same knowledge base is used to support presentation of navy information by means of verbalization and by means of tables and maps controlled by menus. The control of the presentation of information by means of menus favours the object-centred representations, leading to the equivalents of grammatical metaphors, where events and activities are represented as if they were attributes of objects — verbally: *ship A is on exercises*; *ship A has a rendezvous with ship B*; and so on. At the same time, it has to be possible to produce wordings such as *ship A will rendezvous with ship B*. The knowledge base must support these varying demands.
3. We can compare this strategy with the assumption of a non-arbitrary relationship between syntax and semantics that can be seen in approaches such as Langacker's (1987) 'Cognitive Grammar' and Jackendoff's (1983, 1987, 1990) approach to 'conceptual relations'. One of the ways in which we can distinguish the approach here from theirs is in the functional and metafunctional organization of the lexicogrammar that we take as evidence for semantic organization: the *breadth* of functional diversity inherent in metafunctional organization is not foregrounded within the theories of grammar assumed by Langacker and Jackendoff.
4. For this point, compare Halliday's (1987) analysis of Bohm's (1979) complaint that natural language forces us to view reality in terms of things rather than in terms of processes. Here there is a 'conflict' between the reifying metaphorical mode of the language of physics and the congruent mode of spontaneous casual conversation.
5. Arguably, natural taxonomies have been based on the categories of language in any case, from the early days of Aristotle's typology of categories, used, e.g., in later pre-modern logic and in Wilkins's (1668) Essay. But it is better to be perfectly explicit about exploring the model of natural language.
6. An account of a knowledge domain will contain two components: the general domain model just mentioned and instantial facts (asserted) about the domain — cf. the distinction between TBox and ABox that we describe below.
7. The strategy of considering what the lexicogrammatical demands for support are is somewhat analogous to what happens when we take our demands to an expert who provides services. If I wanted to build a house, I would take my wishlist to a builder, but since I'm not an expert at all myself, it is very likely that he or she would take the lead and make demands on me for information — information I would never have thought to supply since my view of the house would be as a place to live, not as a thing to build.
8. Although there are simple text base models for pronominalization, these are as yet still rather rudimentary.
9. Exceptions in two different traditions include work by Schank and others of the

'Yale School' in AI on e.g. scripts and primitive acts (Schank and Abelson, 1977); and work by Hobbs and others at SRI on common sense knowledge (Hobbs, 1986).

10. These two kinds of information tended to be mixed in earlier semantic (conceptual) nets — see e.g Woods (1975) and Brachman (1978) on the need to keep them separate.
11. In computational linguistics, there are a variety of approaches to knowledge representation. The two major techniques can be called logic based and conceptual (semantic) net based. The two techniques may often be inter-translatable (cf., for example, Scragg, 1976), but they have been used for different purposes: as we shall see, semantic nets are often used to represent the knowledge potential whereas predicate logic is often used to represent instantial knowledge. Here we will concentrate on conceptual (semantic) nets. For some overviews of knowledge representation, see e.g., Charniak and Wilks (1976), Barr and Feigenbaum (1981: Ch. III), Sowa (1983a), and Brachman and Levesque (1985).
12. A number of domains have been classified under the upper model to date: an electronic mail and calendar domain (Sondheimer *et al.*, 1984), a navy domain (Hovy, 1990), a LISP programming domain (Moore, 1989), a domain of digital circuits (Paris, 1990), and an abstract classification of process and object types used in machine translation from German to English (Bateman, Kasper, Schütz, and Steiner, 1989). Further classification is in progress.
13. In addition, the notion of frame is a very general one that has been used for a long time in various disciplines (cf. the notion of a structured unit in Halliday, 1961). See, for example, the short overview presented in Tannen (1979), who, however, does not mention any of the work in the Malinowski–Firth–Halliday tradition.
14. This closer relationship between systemic networks and the classification schemes of current knowledge representations is being taken further in work such as that of Mellish (1988) or of Bob Kasper (1989b) where the knowledge representations themselves are being examined as possible representational tools for systemic networks.
15. We will be describing more the Bloomington Lattice in abstract here (cf. Halliday and Matthiessen, in preparation), rather than any particular implementation of the upper model as it is currently being used in the Penman system. The organization there is being constantly extended and tested and the interested reader is referred to the relevant reports for discussion of that development and of the accompanying theoretical issues (e.g., Bateman, 1990c). A more or less complete description of the upper model as it was being used in the computational context of Penman in 1989/90 is available as Bateman, Kasper, Moore, and Whitney (1990).
16. Cf. the notion of a two-cell tagmeme in Tagmemic theory (Pike and Pike, 1982). The value restriction is comparable to the notion of preselection in Systemic theory.
17. This corresponds to the ordering of systems in a system network in delicacy. One major difference between the system network and such a NIKL-type taxonomy is that the former is feature-based and the latter is unit- or frame-based.
18. We can assume that the binding quantifiers have been abstracted out, as they are in the Penman system. In previous versions of the system, the logical form

corresponded to two graphs, the so-called verbalization graph, a set of predicates and the relations they enter into, and the quantification graph. The verbalization graph was partitioned by the quantification graph. For further details, see Nebel and Sondheimer (1986). Transitivity inquiries were answered by means of the verbalization graphs, while determination inquiries were answered by means of the quantification graph. In the current system, the verbalization graph is replaced by the dependency organization expressed in the Sentence Plan Language (Kasper, 1989a) input specification, and the quantification information is expressed by direct response to inquiries.

19. With the extent of the non-experiential information that we are concerned with in a multifunctional grammar such as Nigel, there is so much more than simple instantiation of general classes and assertion of quantified statements to be expressed, that Penman cannot at present use the limited representational resources of an ABox as the complete input specification. The SPL interface language allows the specification of information for the interpersonal and textual components also. Although our aim is to allow the SPL to present the combined set of local plans drawn from each metafunction (cf. Section 9.1.3 above), because of the early stages of development of the corresponding interaction and text bases, this is often achieved directly in terms of inquiry responses. This is described in detail in the Penman documentation (Penman Project, 1989) and need not concern us here. This approach sacrifices the ability to carry out automatic reasoning on the input representation for breadth of expression and ease of control of the generator. We assume that reasoning would normally be carried out at a higher level in the system.
20. There are also interesting questions of implementation here: at present the PENMAN system is in the process of moving from an older procedural implementation of inquiries and their access to the local plans and general taxonomy to a revised declarative implementation in terms of the LOOM knowledge representation language. The information content of these implementations, i.e., the definitions of the mappings is not, in general, being changed in this reimplementation, however.
21. General discussion can be found in Halliday (1978), Halliday and Hasan (1985), and Martin (in press: Ch. 7).
22. There is also a further kind of inquiry in the Japanese politeness chooser: these need to know if particular lexical forms are available for respect, humility, etc. This points to a rather different area of concern — i.e., the interaction between grammar, semantics and lexicon. The lexicon remains one important component of the linguistic system that we have not concentrated upon in this book: it has not been well developed in the context of computational instantiations of systemic theory, although this will clearly need to change. See, for example, Matthiessen (1990a), Fawcett (1990) for some first moves in this direction.
23. This issue is considered briefly in the context of machine translation in Bateman (1989b).
24. See Mizutani and Mizutani (1987: 123) for more on this issue, and for a very readable overview of the principles underlying Japanese politeness in general.
25. A more extensive discussion of the text base can be found in Bateman and Matthiessen (to appear); descriptions of the textual resources in more depth are given in Halliday (1985a: Ch. 3) and Matthiessen (1990b), and an account of their semantic correlates appears in Martin (in press).

26. Although there is interesting structure of a limited kind; cf. for example, Prince (1981) on the many subtypes of 'giveness' and Meteer (1989) for a classification of certain textual statuses. Also, CONJUNCTION draws on an elaborate taxonomy of rhetorical relations, but these relations are not unique to the textual metafunction and can be coded experientially as well.
27. This is not to deny that instantial experiential meanings can be developed in the course of a text; see Hasan, Ch. 5, in Halliday and Hasan (1985) and Fries (1982).
28. Extending the analogy, we can note that hypotaxis corresponds to nucleus–satellite relations and parataxis corresponds to multinuclear relations.
29. RST is not a theory of conjunction, which has consequences when we ask how to support CONJUNCTION by means of RST.
30. It has long been emphasized that it is necessary to separate various kinds of textual meanings such as theme and information; see Halliday (1967/8) and Fries (1981), who contrasts Halliday's account with treatments that have failed to distinguish these meanings; cf. also Grimes (1975: 273) on this point.
31. Grosz and Sidner (1986) outline an account according to which focusing structure is 'parasitic upon intentional structure, in the sense that the relationships among [discourse segment purposes] determine pushes and pops' on to and from the focus stack mentioned earlier. It would take too much space to review their account and how it might relate to RST and other relevant work. In any case, they do not try to account for the range of lexicogrammatical textual resources discussed here or in Bateman and Matthiessen (to appear), but concentrate on the interaction between their model and a much less differentiated category of 'cue words'.
32. Although we should not, however, equate the notion of contextualizing with the development of the text. There are occasions when the contextualization provided by Theme may involve factors other than the method of development. For instance, in instructional texts, the means used in a procedure is a natural thematic candidate, although this category seems to be rare as Theme in texts in general (as compared to, e.g., spatial and temporal themes). Thus, in the following example, the method of development is made explicit through the thematic conjunction (*meanwhile*), but in addition the instrument of mixing is set up as the context:

    Reduce heat to simmer and cook for 25 minutes. *Meanwhile*, with a blender or beater, mix: [list of ingredients]. (Cadwallader)

    Similarly:

    When the fat is smoking hot, drop spoonfuls of the mixture into it and cook until brown. *Then*, with a slice or palette-knife, turn the fritter over and cook on the other side. (Highton and Highton)

33. We can note the similarity here to the strategy pursued for contrastive *wa* in Japanese that we described in Section 7.3.
34. For example, see Bateman (1990c) for a discussion of the particular computational manifestation of the ideation base used within the Penman system — the upper model — and its relation to similar attempts in other generation systems to achieve ideational higher level control.

# Part IV Future directions for computational systemic-functional linguistics

## 10 Parallelism

### 10.1 Nature of generation algorithm: reasons for parallelism

In Section 6.5, we sketched a systemic generation algorithm for repeated entries and traversals of the grammar. We showed how the paradigmatic organization of the grammar guides the generation algorithm: the major part of the algorithm is the traversal of the system network. The generation algorithm accomplishes the task of allowing the grammar to be used in text generation. However, we can now turn to the generation algorithm and ask both how well it reflects systemic theory and whether it can be improved from a computational point of view. The crucial factor here is the sequential nature of the algorithm. All the steps are executed in strict sequence, which means that even when the potential does not impose an ordering on specifications, an ordering has to be imposed on the actualization (execution) of these statements. The alternative would be parallel processing.

There are two important reasons to explore the possibility of a parallel generation algorithm. First, it would be a better model of the systemic theory. Consider a theoretical observation made by Halliday (1978: 134):

> a linguistic system is not a progressive specification of a set of structures one after the other, ideational, then interpersonal, then textual. The system does not first generate a representation of reality, then encode it as a speech act, and finally recode it as a text, as some writing of philosophical linguistics seems to imply. It embodies all these types of meaning in simultaneous networks of options, from each of which derive structures that are mapped onto one another in the course of their lexicogrammatical realization. The lexicogrammar acts as an integrator, taking configurations from all components of the semantics and combining them to form multilayered, 'polyphonic' structural compositions.

Thus, while Halliday's framework works well in a sequential implementation, its design characteristics make it an important candidate for parallel implementation. Simultaneity is emphasized and all sequential orderings are purely intrinsic to the organization of choice within the grammar itself. There are no extrinsic rule orderings created artificially because of the nature of the formalism. Moreover, the framework can be fully realized only in a parallel implementation. We will consider the theoretical opportunities for parallelism presently.

Second, parallel processing promises to increase the computation speed, itself a significant issue as the size and number of our grammars and semantics grow.

## 10.2 Opportunities for parallel processing

Systemic theory determines the opportunities for parallel processing in text generation as follows.

### *10.2.1 Grammar traversal*

Let us consider a traversal of the grammar first; opportunities for parallel processing arise (i) within the system network itself; (ii) across strata; (iii) across axes; (iv) within systems; and (v) within choosers. These possibilities can also be seen in the flowchart specification of the traversal algorithm given in Figure 6.13 above.

(i) Within the system network itself: simultaneous systems. The organization of the system network brings out the simultaneous 'strands' from the different metafunctions, e.g., transitivity and mood as shown in Figure 6.1 above. In addition, there are also simultaneous systems within these different metafunctional regions (e.g., AGENCY and PROCESS TYPE within transitivity). In the sequential generation algorithm presented earlier, a list of enterable systems waiting to be entered is maintained. In a parallel generation algorithm, it is not necessary to keep systems waiting. Since a system can be entered when its entry condition is satisfied, all systems on simultaneous strands in the system network can be entered in parallel. Consequently, the traversal of the system network is parallel, breadth-first traversal.

If this type of parallelism is exploited, the time needed for a traversal of a system network is only the time spent traversing the strand that reaches the highest degree of delicacy (i.e., the longest path through the system network), instead of the total computation time as with the sequential traversal algorithm.

(ii) Across strata: stratal simultaneity. Semantic and lexicogrammatical representations are kept separate. The only relative ordering is association of a particular chooser with a particular system: the chooser cannot be activated until its system has been entered and the processing of the system is not complete until its chooser has selected one of its output features. However, systems and choosers that are not associated with one another can be processed in parallel.[1] Any realization statements associated with a feature can be executed as soon as the feature has been selected, even if the chooser still has one or more identifying inquiries left to present. This issue clearly relates to questions of the degree and kind of 'interleaving' between realization and planning phases of text generation that are currently of concern in the text generation community (cf. Section 2.4; Hovy *et al.*, 1988; Emele *et al.*, 1990a).

(iii) Across axes: simultaneity of choice and realization. Since the logic of choice embodied in the system network and realization statements are represented separately, the traversal of the system network can proceed in parallel with the execution of realization statements. In particular, as soon as one of the output features of a system has been selected, any associated realization statements can be executed at the same time as the systems dependent on the feature selected are explored. It is important to note that this kind of parallelism would not be possible if choice and realization were merged into one representation rather than factored into independent representations.

(iv) Within systems: simultaneous realization statements. Since the only ordering in the grammar is the one embodied in the system network, any collection of realization statements associated with a feature is unordered and the statements can be executed in parallel. For instance, a given function can be ordered and preselected at the same time.

(v) Within choosers: simultaneous chooser operations. The operations of a chooser can be parallelized. For instance, if a chooser presents two inquiries that are independent of one another, they can be processed in parallel.

From the point of view of computational speed-up, the first kind of parallelism in the traversal is undoubtedly the most important.

### *10.2.2 Grammar entry*

The sequential generation algorithm enters the grammar to generate one unit at a time. For instance, if a clause has five constituent elements, the grammar will be entered five times in sequence to develop these elements. Whenever one grammar traversal has been completed, the result is a unit consisting of one or more elements of structure, for example, a clause consisting of a process and a few participants and circumstances. If there is more than one element to be realized grammatically, there is an opportunity to process these in parallel: the grammar can be entered in parallel for all the elements.[2]

It is also possible to explore the possibility of combining parallelism with overlapped grammar entries. For instance, in a clause such as *on thousands of acres, cattle, sheep, and horses are pastured*, it might be possible to start developing the prepositional phrase serving as the Theme (*on thousands of acres*) while the traversal of the clause is still in progress. However, in the present model of the grammar, such an approach could easily run into problems. First, there is no way of easily determining when all the relevant preselections have been accumulated, which is the point at which the grammar can be entered to develop a new element. Second, the framework is not set up to specify the Theme before the rest of the clause. It is possible that this points to the need for a more dynamic model of the grammar.

There are many exciting possibilities that could be pursued with respect to increasing the degree of parallelism that is supported within a computational instantiation of a systemic-functional model of language. The discussion begun here is taken further in Tung, Matthiessen and Sondheimer (1988). Also, some of the formalization possibilities that we point to in Chapter 13 could serve as the basis for organizing the linguistic resources at the implementational level in a way well suited to supporting the extensive opportunities for parallelism that we have sketched here.

## Notes

1. There may be certain cases where the chooser of one system has to wait until the chooser of another system has presented an identifying inquiry. Many of the results and algorithms being pursued currently for complex process control and data flow would therefore be relevant and necessary here, were a serious parallel implementation making use of the possibilities described in this chapter to be attempted.
2. If the elements are processed in parallel, it is, of course, no longer possible to process them in a left-to-right sequence for the sake of reference. Consequently, reference has to be planned based on linear sequence rather than the temporal sequence of successive grammar entries.

# 11 Dynamism

## 11.1 Recursive systems: some conceptual problems

In Part III, we presented a number of extensions of the basic framework given in Part II that were concerned with the *dynamics* of the generation process. In particular, we discussed how systemic networks containing loops, i.e., 'recursive' networks, could be provided in order to generate dependency structures (Section 8.2). These resources were subsequently illustrated at work in a number of areas of Japanese grammar and were found to be rather simple and appealing ways of expressing required regularities. However, this approach also exerts a rather high cost on the internal coherence of the implemented framework as a whole. This arises as a consequence of certain conceptual difficulties with the straightforward view of what is involved in recursive systems that our initial implementation, in fact, only serves to clarify, not resolve.

In this chapter, we will focus on these difficulties. First, we present a summary of the problems raised and, then, in the next section, turn to consider their solution anew. We will describe the problems centring on three points: what grammatical systems mean and when they can be entered; what the grammatical features mean; and what the realization statements associated with those features mean. These central issues in the representational resources provided by computational and noncomputational grammars are all 'problematicized' by the move to consider network recursion.

In Section 8.2.1, we removed a restriction of the basic framework that a grammatical system could only be entered once during any particular traversal of the network. This permitted recursive systems — i.e., grammatical systems whose entry conditions can be satisfied by grammatical feature selections that are dependent on those systems already having been entered and having selected grammatical features — to be entered whenever their entry conditions were satisfied, no matter how often this occurred within a traversal cycle. However, this needs further clarification. There is no constraint that the entry conditions for any system can only be met by a single unique traversal of the network; for example, in the simplest case, if a grammatical system has as entry condition a disjunction of two grammatical features:

$$f_1 \text{ or } f_2$$

then the situation may arise where both of these features are independently selected. But then, if a recursive system can be entered multiply, then perhaps a 'normal' system should *also* be entered multiply when it has multiply satisfied entry conditions — that is, if both features $f_1$, $f_2$ have been selected, is this to count as a single satisfaction of the entry conditions or two?

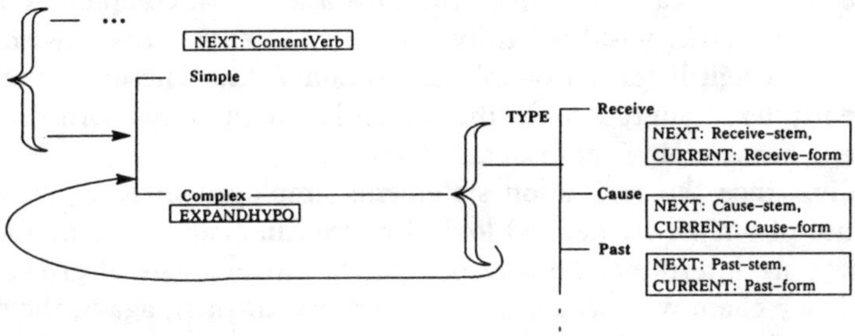


**Figure 11.1** The basic recursive network for the Japanese verbal group (repeated from Figure 8.7)

Without some formal distinction between recursive and non-recursive systems, multiple system entry is difficult to avoid without *ad hoc* apparatus. Furthermore, the *order* of system entry begins to be important: for example, in the Japanese verbal group example depicted in Figure 8.7 — repeated here as Figure 11.1 for convenience — following on from the feature Complex are two possibilities which, in a standard network, would be considered as parallel, or *simultaneous*: these are the TYPE system options, giving the types of component meanings which can be composed in a Japanese verbal group, and the loop back to the 'simple'/'complex' alternation. Now, however, unless the mechanism is complicated elsewhere to compensate, for example, by indexing all features according to the number of times their systems are entered, we need to consider the system TYPE *before* going on to consider the further selection of 'complex'/'simple'. Otherwise, there would simply be a stacking up of selections of the feature 'complex' without the prerequisite accompanying selections from the TYPE system. It is essential that the order of system entry is preserved during this process in order for the realization statements also to be activated in the right order. Thus, systems that previously would have been intrinsically unordered now need to have their order of entry considered explicitly.

Second, grammatical features have traditionally been used to identify the minimal points of grammatical alternation that define a particular grammatical entity. When recursive systems can select features that would normally be considered to be in complementary distributions for a single grammatical entity, the meaning of the selection expression needs to be reconsidered: it is now possible, for example, for a grammatical unit simultaneously to possess features *X* and not-*X* if these are selected on subsequent passes through a given recursive system that has these as possible outcomes. In addition, the ordering of the selection expression is now significant, as is again clear from the Japanese verbal complex example — *cause to wish* {cause, wish} is hardly equivalent to *wish to cause* {wish, cause} — and the English tense example of Section 7.2.2. These are themselves sufficiently large alterations in the semantics of the basic formalism as to require a considerably more detailed account.

Finally, since the realization statements employed in recursive systems make use of our newly defined logical micro-functions, Current and Next, and these are interpreted with respect to the current state of growth of the dependency chain with which they are concerned, then, again, the order of execution of those realization statements becomes crucial. Their order of execution must now follow the order of selection of their associated features.

Most of these changes in the semantics of the formalism are in violation of an awareness in current computer science and computational linguistics that procedurally oriented definitions of processes are to be avoided in favour of declarative definitions. At present, within Nigel, realization statements are best interpreted as constraints that are placed upon the final structural product of grammar traversal. They can be 'applied' in any order; order of processing is not a significant issue. This has the advantage of avoiding directionality in a grammar — theoretically permitting both generation and analysis with a single representation of the grammar — and, furthermore, appears more in line with what is intended by SFL theory as presented by Halliday (1978). Our moves away from this in the extensions made in Section 7.1 re-emphasize a procedural, flowchart interpretation of the grammar network at the cost of the declarative, direction-neutral statement that has been achieved in Nigel; this can be seen in the necessity to preserve *ordering* across all three areas of the formalism — system entry, selection expressions, and realization statements. This weakens the framework as a whole and needs to be considered rather critically.

## 11.2 Making the interpretative process explicit

In our description of the implementations of both the basic framework in Part II and our initial extensions to handle recursive networks in Part III, we have been implicitly relying on a 'straightforwardness' or 'naturalness' of those implementations. This was, in fact, making oblique reference to precisely the flowchart interpretation of networks since it is this interpretation that still largely reflects the way a cooperative linguist might choose to interpret a system network: that is, rather than interpreting the interdependent possible feature selections that a network defines as a set of constraints that hold simultaneously, it is possible to 'walk through' the network following connections and making choices. While perhaps adequate for simpler networks and an informal understanding of the resources involved, in this section we consider in more detail what is involved in providing an interpretation of a systemic network computationally. We will proceed from the general computational notion of *data structures* and then relate the specific data structure of a computational systemic network to this.

In computation, information is generally stored within 'declarative data structures'; examples of this are:

- lists — (a b c d);
- association lists, such as might be used to build a bilingual dictionary — ((table Tisch) (dog Hund) (girl Mädchen));
- trees, such as representations of linguistic structures;
- rules, such as Prolog clauses — `a :- b,c; d.`;
- logical expressions — $a = (b \wedge c) \vee d$;
- and even simple numbers, such as 1 or 3.14159.

What makes these declarative representations of information into *representations* is that there exists a process called the *interpretative process* that knows how to make sense of them. Without this process, the structure has no meaning computationally — the machine does not 'know' what can be done with the structure and its contents and so does not 'know' what it means. This has to be provided by the interpretive process: the meaning of computational representations lies entirely in the interaction between data structure and interpretive process (cf. Smith, 1978).

When represented computationally, systemic networks are just another kind of data structure. We need to give 'meaning' to that data structure computationally in precisely the same way as we do for any other data structure. We need to define an interpretative process that interacts with the network data structure to give rise to the behaviour and properties that we desire such a network to possess. As long as this behaviour matched the interpretation that a linguist would provide, as was the case above with the 'flowchart' interpretation for single non-recursive networks, the properties of the computational interpretative process itself did not attract very much attention. As long as the network definitions in terms of which we work have the properties that we require, there is no need to consider the interpretative process that gives them those properties.

The interpretative process always needs to be present, however. This is one of the consequences of choosing a computational mode of expression for theory development. The process of interpretation needs to be made as explicit as what is being interpreted. For example, a simplified interpretive process possible for a network of the Nigel-type, without linear recursion, is set out below. This provides a *traversal algorithm* for the network, i.e., a specification of how the system network is to be interpreted, of how the connectivity of the systems of the network constrains the features that may be selected and the structures that may result. The algorithm itself relies on and maintains the following kinds of information: a definition of the connectivity of the network, a list of the features that have been selected (initially empty, or better, some distinctive feature sufficient for triggering entry of the first system of the network) called the *selection expression*, and a list of the systems whose entry conditions have been satisfied, called the *enterable systems list*.

1. Add all the systems whose entry conditions are newly satisfied (i.e., the necessary features are present in the selection expression) to the enterable systems list;
2. If the enterable systems list is empty, then traversal is finished and we may stop;
3. Alternatively, enter all the systems on the enterable system list and reset the list to empty;
4. Make the choices of features required from those systems (by some means, e.g., probabilistically, by preselection, or by chooser);
5. Add these features to the selection expression;
6. Perform (or mark to be performed) the realization statements associated with these choices of features;
7. Repeat from step (1).

This is only one way of setting out more explicitly the steps that are involved in interpreting a network. It is similar to the flowchart for network traversal given in Figure 6.13 of Section 6.5. Here, one first looks for the systems that we could enter given the features that have already been selected; then, one makes the additional selections of features from these systems (usually one system at a time, which gives the interpretation its flowchart flavour, although, as we saw in Chapter 10, this need not necessarily be the case). These selections may have further effects on which systems may be entered. Finally, one performs any entailed realization statements. This entire process is repeated until all possible systems have been entered.

While this kind of algorithm is almost appropriate for simple networks, it does not allow for recursive systems. Moreover, we have now seen that the simple extension suggested in Section 8.2 above of relaxing the condition in (1) so that systems may be entered more than once raises certain difficulties for the semantics of the representation. Therefore, since the networks that such a traversal algorithm supports do not seem to have the properties we desire for networks involving recursion, it becomes relevant to examine more critically the simple traversal model implemented hitherto. We will show first how alterations to the algorithm give rise to networks with different properties, i.e., that may employ differing representational resources. This will highlight just how crucial a role the appropriate consideration of the traversal/interpretation algorithm for a systemic network can be. We then return to the question of recursion in particular.

## 11.3 Extending and controlling the system network traversal algorithm

We consider briefly here two aspects of the interaction between a traversal algorithm and a system network definition. The first illustrates how the traversal algorithm defines the properties of the system networks that it supports. The second shows where the need to influence the meaning of the traversal algorithm has been implicitly recognized and attempted previously.

### *11.3.1 Co-selection constraints and markedness conventions*

Martin's (1987) discussion of the meaning of systemic features raises several kinds of systemic network configurations that differ from those of the straightforward Nigel type introduced in Part II. One example of this is the specification of 'co-selection constraints' that already move away from the direct flowchart interpretation of a network.

Figure 11.2(a) shows a paradigm for nasality and voice for English plosives taken from Martin (1987). The absence of an entry for both nasal and voiceless can be represented in terms of *markedness* conventions that state additional constraints on the selections of features from a system network. Thus, Figure 11.2(b) shows two simultaneous systems annotated with a negative markedness constraint that prevents the application of the

| | nasal | non-nasal |
|---|---|---|
| voiced | /m,n,ŋ/ | /b,d,g/ |
| voiceless | — | /p,t,k/ |

(a) Nasality and voice for English plosives (Martin, 1988b:21)

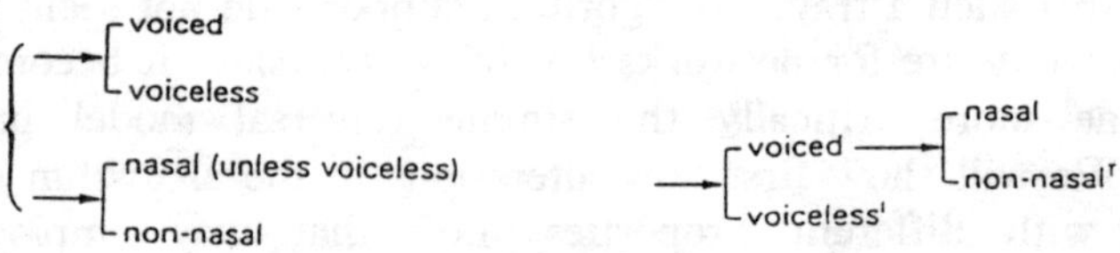


(b) Negative marking (c) Positive marking

**Figure 11.2** Example paradigm showing markedness constraints on co-selection

alternation nasal/non-nasal in the context of a selection of voiceless. Alternatively, Figure 11.2(c) shows a similar way of capturing the hole in the paradigm making use of Martin's suggested formalism for positive marking.[1]

The networks of Figure 11.2(b) and (c) embody a number of claims: most important are the explicit representation of the *lack* of possible alternation when the feature voiceless occurs, and the necessary connection that is set up between features and 'reflexes in form'. It only makes sense to consider the feature non-nasal selected when voiceless has been selected, given that the corresponding realization of that feature is required even when there is no choice involved. In all cases, however, it has become inappropriate to view the network as reflecting a flowchart in which system interconnections may be simply followed in order to reveal the feature choices that need to be made. The inter-system constraints imposed by markedness need to be considered *in addition* to the connections of the network.

We can provide system networks that allow this behaviour as part of their representational resources by extending the basic traversal algorithm given in the previous section as follows:

- After selection of features, before step (6):
  For all features just selected, find any features that participate in

positive markedness relationships with other features . . .
— If there are none: continue with step (6)
— If there are some: add the markedness-related features to the selection expression,
perform (or mark to be performed) any associated realization statements, continue with step (6).

A straightforward extension to the traversal algorithm can therefore alter considerably the properties and functionalities of the network-types that an implementation supports. Moreover, traversal algorithms necessarily build a variety of assumptions and limitations into the possible systemic networks that they accept — e.g., that realization statements can be performed in any order. Since the interpretative process defines the meaning of the data structure it interprets, this is a necessary consequence of *any* traversal algorithm. This needs to be seen as an important *benefit* of the computational framework because such limitations can now be considered explicitly in their own right and be 'designed' appropriately.

### *11.3.2 Network rewirings*

Martin (1987) also draws up a set of criteria for justifying on formal grounds whether a feature should appear in a network or not. Given such a set of formal motivations for features, it is possible to imagine situations where network *connectivity* is required but explicit *grammatical features* are not. This contrasts with the case shown in the previous subsection where we had grammatical features required without the traditional connectivity.

One way of modelling negative and positive marking, for example, is to employ a network 'rewiring' involving *gates*, a representational resource developed for Nigel. A gate is a degenerate system that offers no choice, simply a single feature with associated realization statements that are to be performed when the entry condition of the gate — which can be as complex as desired — is met. An example of a gate wiring away a case of possible co-indexing is shown in Figure 11.3(a); this and other examples may be found in Martin (1987: 27–9).

However, network connectivity and rewiring are actually providing *semi-explicit instructions to the traversal algorithm*. This can be seen particularly clearly in Figure 11.3(b) where realizationally unmotivated features (go and //) are replaced entirely by network connections. Since the network connections are only interpreted by the network's traversal algorithm, rewirings of this form are attempting to control that algorithm from within the confines of the system network definition: a rough gloss of the instructions being given would be to extend the definition of systems and of step (4)

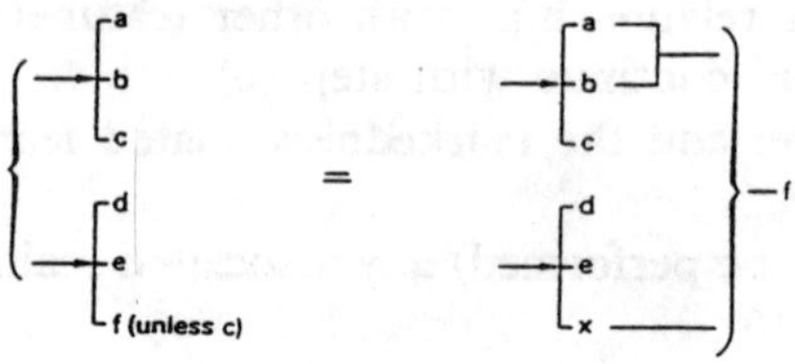


(a) Using a gate

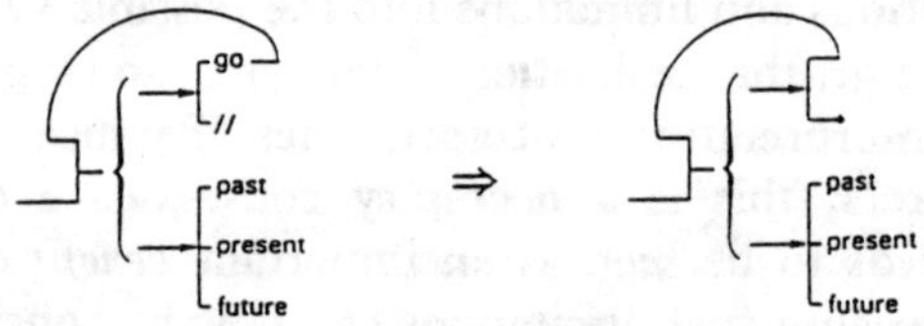


(b) Using pure wiring

**Figure 11.3** Examples of network rewiring (Martin, 1987)

of the traversal algorithm so that it is possible to add systems to the enterable systems list directly without placing features in the selection expression. Since the extension of the traversal algorithm given above permitted a similarly limited control by way of providing the representational resource markedness constraints, both extensions can be seen to reflect the need to gain more explicit control of the traversal algorithm by which networks are interpreted and followed.

## 11.4 Re-abstraction: the dynamic dimension of linguistic potential

We have seen how redefining the traversal algorithm can have the following consequences:

- The conditions for considering a paradigmatic choice applicable can be made more complex.
- The consequences of a feature selection can become more complex.
- The interpretation of a system can become more complex.
- Explicit reference can be made to the process of interpreting and traversing a network.

This provides sufficient representational power to approach the problem of recursive systems.

What is crucially involved when a recursive system is looped through is the conception of moving from one context to another, where the first context constrains, but does not determine, the moves that can be made. This can be seen particularly clearly from our introduction to dependency with respect to spoken language and clause complexes at the beginning of Section 8.2. This can be modelled within the interpretation process by treating recursive systems as explicit points in the network traversal where 'contexts' for exploring subsequent linguistic potential are established. The notion of re-entering a system then corresponds to repeatedly opening up a given area of linguistic potential at the same point within the overall linguistic context, while simultaneously and systematically constraining that potential differently for each invocation.

Thus, as in the example of the Japanese verbal group of Section 8.2.1 (repeated in Figure 11.1 above), a similar area of linguistic potential is opened up each time round the loop: that is, each time the alternation 'simple'/'complex' is activated, the linguistic potential represented by the TYPE system becomes available, as well as a possible further activation of the complexity decision. However, the fact that certain choices have been previously made in these systems can constrain the choices that are made subsequently; free selection of arbitrary morphemes is not permitted in the Japanese verbal group. For example, once the feature 'past' has been selected it is not possible to continue looping through the TYPE system: this morpheme can only appear verbal complex finally.

Clearly, this kind of detail cannot be specified within the synoptic description alone, or even centrally. Information concerning the current state of traversal — including the feature selections that have been made, the preselections/constraints that are already in force, the structure fragments that have been composed, etc. — needs to be saved and used as the basis for further traversal should the recursive system be re-entered. Moreover, it is necessary to relate the products of generation created in each 'traversal space' to one another appropriately, i.e., they need to be connected as interdependent elements of a dependency chain. This calls for a rather more sophisticated extension of the interpretation of the synoptic network and the traversal process than we have seen so far.

It is important, however, to consider the extension of the interpretation algorithm in a theoretically motivated way. This can be seen by expanding the scope of our discussion from the lexicogrammar for a moment. Just as the descriptive resources of co-selection/markedness constraints and network rewirings can be viewed as interacting with the process of network traversal, we can find similar examples of interaction at other levels of the linguistic system also. For example, Ventola (1983, 1984, 1987) explicitly presents flowcharts that are intended to add a dynamic and negotiated level of detail to the achievement of generic structures in the domain of service encounters,[2] and Martin (1985) adapts this technique and offers a level of negotiated, dynamic control, again in flowchart form, to Berry's (1981) exchange structure network. Now, a similar step needs to be taken with respect to the traversal of the grammar network in order to achieve a more sophisticated control strategy for constructing dependency organizations. But these flowcharts are entirely unconstrained: it is unclear what may and may not be placed within them.

This is a significant problem because it is equivalent to allowing an arbitrarily complex traversal/interpretation algorithm as the interpreter for a network definition. It also, since the traversal algorithm is what gives meaning to that network, is equivalent to opening up the possible meaning of that network arbitrarily far. Unless we can find means of constraining the statements that can be made at the interpretation algorithm level, therefore, we severely undermine the meaning that our networks have.

The work reported here strongly suggests, from the formal requirements of representing the kinds of meanings at issue, that we accept the distinction between synoptic and process linguistic descriptions that Martin (1985) offers. However, we need to consider the dynamic dimension of linguistic description and theory as just that, i.e., as a dimension of *linguistic description and theory* that has its own rules and regularities. This provides two importantly distinct yet inextricably linked fundamental dimensions of linguistic theorizing, each of which adds its own kind of organizational resource. However, it is crucial that the dynamic dimension be as representationally constrained and theoretically motivated as is the synoptic account of system networks. As an initial experiment, then, we suggest that we explore the following for the lexicogrammar. Rather than allowing arbitrary flowchart operations, we should constrain what can appear in the dynamic description along the same lines as the synoptic description: i.e., as a network of possibilities. In contrast to the synoptic description, however, these possibilities are to have particular dynamic consequences that require formalization in their own right. What this might mean for clause complexes is shown in Figure 11.4.

At the synoptic level, the account is simplified considerably since the dynamic aspect has been removed. Then, for the dynamic level of control that guides the application of the synoptic resources, instead of a flowchart we place the clause interrelationships previously represented by a supposedly synoptic clause complexity network. The point of interaction between the dynamic complexing potential and the synoptic clause potential is marked by joined stars. When such a point of potential complexing is encountered in the actualization of the synoptic network, the traversal process knows that it may repeatedly utilize the currently available

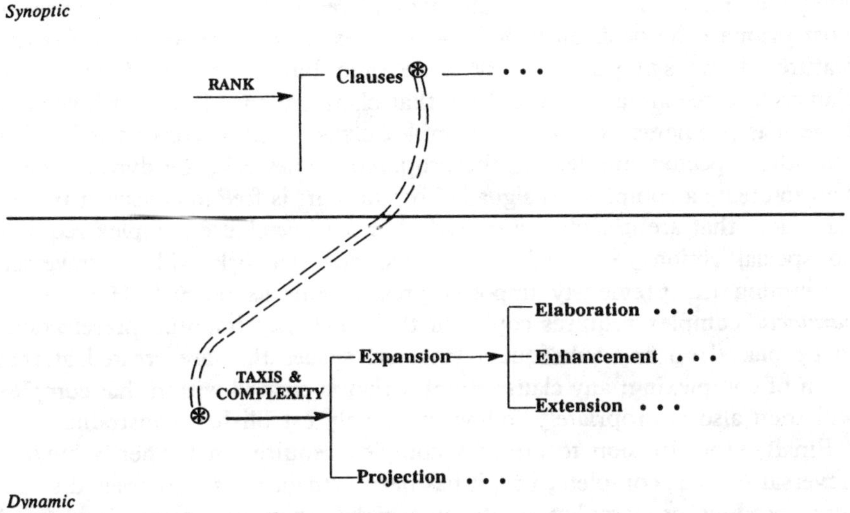


**Figure 11.4** Factoring synoptic and dynamic potential in the clause complex

linguistic potential if required and so saves a copy of the current 'state' of the traversal process. The question '*Are there grounds for complexing?*' is then also set up.[3] Whenever this question receives a positive response, the connected dynamic potential network is activated. The function of this latter network is to determine the particular relationship that holds between two interdependent clauses in the complex being constructed. In terms of the interpretative process, this may be viewed as constructing a particular relationship between two traversal spaces in terms of patterns of constraint between the features that are selected in one space and those that are selected in the other.

A number of different types of dynamic constraints between traversal spaces are conceivable. For example, the logical micro-functions Current and Next that we introduced in Section 8.2 could be used to impose feature selection constraints on the current traversal space and the next (although the explicit use of realization statements such as *expandpara* or *expandhypo* has been absorbed back into the interpretation of the star joining the synoptic and dynamic networks); or different paths through the dynamic potential network could establish differing co-occurrence constraints between synoptic features of the two spaces of the form:

if $\text{feature}_a$ is selected in $\text{space}_i$,
then $\text{feature}_b$ must be selected in $\text{space}_{i+1}$.

In addition, the explicit availability of traversal spaces permits a more adequate treatment of complexing when preselections/constraints already exist prior to the decision to form a complex. For example, if the Clauses feature of the synoptic network is selected but there are 'downstream' clausal features already selected for that clause, then a framework such as Nigel has problems as soon as a complex clause is to be constructed rather than the expected simplex. In the proposed framework, the dynamic decision to create a complex, as signalled by the star, is free to construct traversal spaces that are *already constrained*. A *hypotactic* clause complex requires no special action to be taken: the synoptic network will be traversed consuming the previously imposed preselections as normal. However, a *paratactic* complex requires copies of the previously imposed preselections to be placed on any subsequent traversal spaces that are created at that point of complexing; any clause simplex that is created within that complex will then also appropriately follow previously established constraints.

Finally, the decision to create a complex requires that when a current traversal space is complete, i.e., it has been actualized as a completed structural product or complex in its own right, then that space is chained together with a new, dependent space that has had an appropriate set of constraints already imposed upon it, including the areas of synoptic potential that are available for development. The resulting chain is then spliced into whatever 'structural' context was in force when the complex initiating star was first encountered. The result of network traversal, or actualization, is then an ongoing chain of clauses that are related by dependency, and a set of constraints on what may follow — rather than a closed structural product as was the case previously.

In short, then, the dynamic potential network is to be understood as providing an account of the relationship-types that may hold between the distinct traversal spaces that occur for each element of the clause complex, while the actual creation and maintenance of these spaces would be handled by a mechanism implemented for the synoptic and dynamic networks' interaction. The potential for complexing is simply marked in the synoptic network by attaching a star to a feature; this is to be interpreted by the extended traversal algorithm as a place where distinct traversal spaces may be spawned. Clearly, the dynamic network itself now needs to be considered more carefully, the possible constraints that may be imposed between traversal spaces need to be articulated, and the precise interaction of the dynamic network with the traversal mechanism needs to be made explicit. This, and the technical details of the mechanism loosely suggested here, need to be made active topics for further research.

## 11.5 Summary

We have tried over a sequence of computational implementations to arrive at both a satisfactory definition and the ability to use *recursive grammatical systems*. Each of these have been clearly identified as presenting significant representational problems for many years. We have argued that such systems should be placed at intersections of fundamentally distinct synoptic and process dimensions of organization. Previous, synoptically centred accounts were prevented from adequately characterizing what was involved because of placing too great a functional load on the synoptic description alone. We have now also suggested how a computational implementation of systemic functional grammar requires a modularization of description ideally suited to attacking the processual account of grammar as well as the synoptic in that it makes fully explicit the 'execution strategy', or interpretative process, that is necessary for the synoptic network description to 'make sense' computationally. This must be considered an equally crucial area for theoretical development and *linguistic* inquiry as the synoptic description. The computational embodiment of the theory therefore stands to help this area of theory development considerably by making available the dynamic process of the interpretation of a network as an explicit object of study in its own right.

## Notes

1. Martin also notes a third markedness constraint, developed by Hudson (1973), called *conditional* marking, and a constraint that interacts with realization rules, called *derivational* marking, developed by Hudson (1974). We will not discuss these explicitly here although they could be treated in a similar fashion.
2. This shows a striking similarity to a move in computational approaches to text planning where a notion of text schemata is now being augmented with a level of goal-related, planning information (Paris, 1990).
3. Note that this question may be asked at various times, for example, at the beginning of traversal of the synoptic component or at the end. It could also be implemented as a simultaneous process that is active throughout the traversal of the synoptic network. All of these possibilities become available for exploration and theoretical development once theory and implementation are linked.

# 12 Contextualism

## 12.1 Context

The last two chapters have dealt with process-related issues. We will now problematize another aspect of the application of systemic theory in text generation — stratal organization and functional variation. We started our exploration of issues in text generation at the level of lexicogrammar and we discussed and illustrated the addition of a grammar-based semantic interface — the chooser and inquiry framework (Chapters 5 and 6). We then extended the view from grammar and projected upwards from it in our investigation of the organization of the environment of a text generation grammar (Chapter 9). In this chapter, we propose to shift the viewpoint from grammar to context. We will focus on one issue in particular, viz. the repertoire of different contexts of use. We will project downwards from context on to the linguistic system and ask how to handle the functional variation in the linguistic system that reflects the diversity of uses in different contexts.

In particular we will address two models of the influence that context may have on lexicogrammar and semantics — i.e., of the influence of *register* that we introduced in our overview of text generation systems in Chapter 3 and defined further in Section 5.10. We will consider 'register settings' in terms of:

- customizing semantic systems according to context;
- preselecting inquiry responses according to context.

## 12.2 Semantics from above and from below: 'encoding' and 'decoding'

The kind of chooser and inquiry semantics we have used throughout this book represents one of two possible approaches to the semantic stratum;

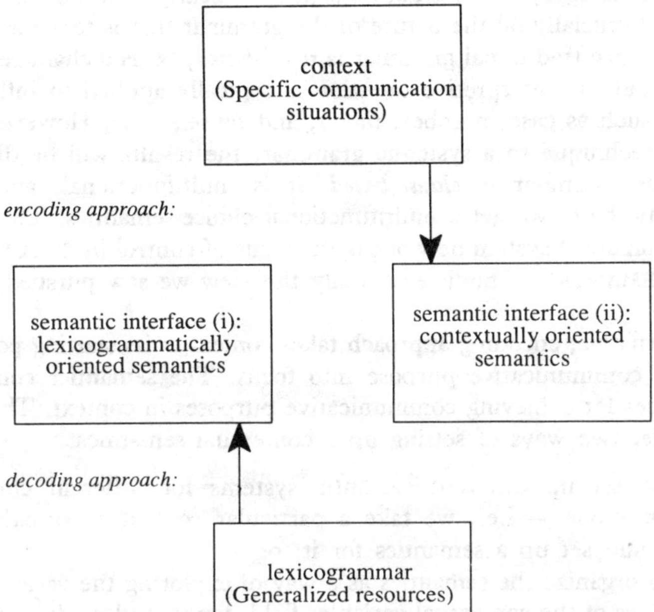


**Figure 12.1** Approaching semantics from above and below

there are two stratal approaches for exploring the organization and categories of semantics.

(i) We can explore semantics from below, starting with lexicogrammar — what might be called a DECODING or interpretative approach, since it works by decoding or interpreting lexicogrammar in semantic terms.
(ii) Alternatively, we can explore it from above, from outside the linguistic system — what might be called an ENCODING approach since it looks at semantics as an encoding strategy and explores how contextual categories are encoded semantically.

Crucially, the two directions pertain to the *design of the semantics*, not to the direction in the flow of control.[1] These relationships are depicted in Figure 12.1.

Thus, we can explore semantics from below, starting with lexicogrammar. This technique was used in ancient Greece; it is the technique of traditional grammar. It also survives in interpretative semantics in modern linguistics. The basic question is 'what is the interpretation of the grammatical category x; what does x signify?' Clearly, the semantic results will depend crucially on the nature of the grammar that is taken as a starting point. Since traditional grammar is *word-based*, 'x' is a characteristic of the word and the interpretive question is typically applied to inflectional categories such as case, number, mood, and tense/aspect. However, if we apply the technique to a systemic grammar, the results will be different, because the grammar is *clause-based*, it is multifunctional, and has a paradigmatic base: we get a multifunctional choice-semantics. The system in the grammatical system network is the locus of control in CHOOSER AND INQUIRY SEMANTICS. This is essentially the view we saw pursued in Part III.

The alternative, encoding approach takes context as its starting point and brings the communicative purpose into focus. The semantics constitutes the strategies for achieving communicative purposes in context. There are, in principle, two ways of setting up a contextual semantics:

(a) we can set up different semantic systems for different contextual configurations — i.e., we take a particular context of situation as a given, and set up a semantics for it; or
(b) we can organize the semantics as a way of exploring the various possible values of the contextual variables field, tenor, and mode — i.e., the semantics is set up to identify (aspects) of the context of situation.

Here, however, we will only describe the first alternative rather briefly, before turning to the question of how observations about register can be captured together with the chooser and inquiry type of semantic interface as it was defined in Part II.

## 12.3 Motivation for approaching from above

There are at least two basic types of motivation for exploring and writing context-based semantic systems: bridging and compilation.

### *12.3.1 Bridging*

The orientation towards context serves to bridge the gap between linguistic categories and higher-level categories. Within sociology, Halliday's concept of semantics is motivated partly because it can act as an interface between language and the rest of the social system. Turner (1973: 195) comments:

[Halliday's meaning potential] should enable researchers to integrate sociological concepts and linguistic concepts. The sociological theory identifies the socially significant meanings. Once these are specified, their grammatical and lexical realizations are also capable of specification.

Within computational linguistics and AI, it is possible to make similar observations: situation-specific semantic systems may serve to relate non-linguistic categories to linguistic ones.

### *12.3.2 Compilation*

Furthermore, a situation-specific semantics can be seen as a set of strategies developed to deal efficiently with the specific, limited set of communication problems inherent in that context of situation. We can find this consideration in computational linguistics and AI. Patten (1986, 1988a) has shown that the approach of situation-specific semantics can be motivated in AI terms as well as in linguistic terms. Patten treats text generation as problem solving and shows that there is a striking similarity between the AI problem-solving framework and Halliday's systemic approach to language. The similarity is all the more interesting because the two traditions have developed independently of one another.

The lexicogrammatical system network can be seen as the space of interrelated alternatives for solving a communicative problem. There are different ways of searching the system network for appropriate feature selections. One way is to traverse the network from left to right and to reason about each systemic alternative by means of choosers (cf. Figure 6.13 above). Patten (1988b, and Patten and Stoops, 1990) argues that it is potentially costly to do this kind of reasoning from basic principles. Another way is to rely on a strategy that has already been developed for a particular problem ('compiled knowledge') and this is what Patten takes a situation specific semantics to be. That is, for a given register there is a particular semantic strategy for traversing the lexicogrammatical system network. If we are faced with a novel generation task which does not correspond to a recognized register, only then do we have to revert to basic principles.

### *12.3.3 An example: a semantics of control in a regulatory context*

Let us consider what has become the standard example of the semantics of a particular register. Assume that we are building a generator for mother–child control, the situation Turner (1973) did sociological research on, Halliday (1973) uses as an example of sociological semantics, and Patten (1986) takes over for text generation.[2] The situation is the following (Halliday, 1973: 65):

[A] small boy has been playing with the neighbourhood children on a building site, and has come home grasping some object which he has acquired in the process. His mother disapproves, and wishes both to express her disapproval and to prevent him from doing the same thing again.

The question is what her linguistic strategies are. The answer lies in the semantic system network; most generally, she can threaten or warn her son. Other comparable contexts of socialization are instructional, imaginative, and interpersonal; cf. Bernstein (1971: 198).

The two basic regulatory strategies are threatening (with punishment or restraint) and warning (about what will happen to the child or the child will cause to happen). Examples of texts include

threat

```
if you do that again I'll smack you
Daddy'll be cross with you
you do that again and you'll get smacked
```

warning

```
you'll get hurt
you'll get your feet wet
you'll tear your clothes
```

The semantic network consists of systems like threat/warning, physical punishment/mental punishment/restraint on behaviour, and so on. Part of the semantic system network discussed in Halliday (1973: 81) is given in Figure 12.2 (only the category of threat is further elaborated in delicacy).

One of the claims of this type of 'semantic' network is that semantic features are realized by preselections of grammatical features. For example, the semantic feature 'threat' is realized by selection of the grammatical feature 'declarative'. In general, delicate grammatical features are preselected and the less delicate features they presuppose can then be chosen automatically by moving from right to left by backward chaining in the system network rather than by explicit preselection, as outlined above in Section 6.5. This method makes good use of the 'logic' of the lexicogrammatical system network and, as shown in Figure 12.3, contrasts with the 'increasing delicacy' direction of grammar traversal.

(The features from the more delicate systems, reachable from the feature 'threat' are realized not by mood selections but by selections in transitivity and voice. Given a specific situation such as the regulatory one, we can expect this kind of integration in the situation-specific semantics of meta-functional considerations.) The interface to lexicogrammar is organized from above, from the semantic stratum. This kind of approach is, in

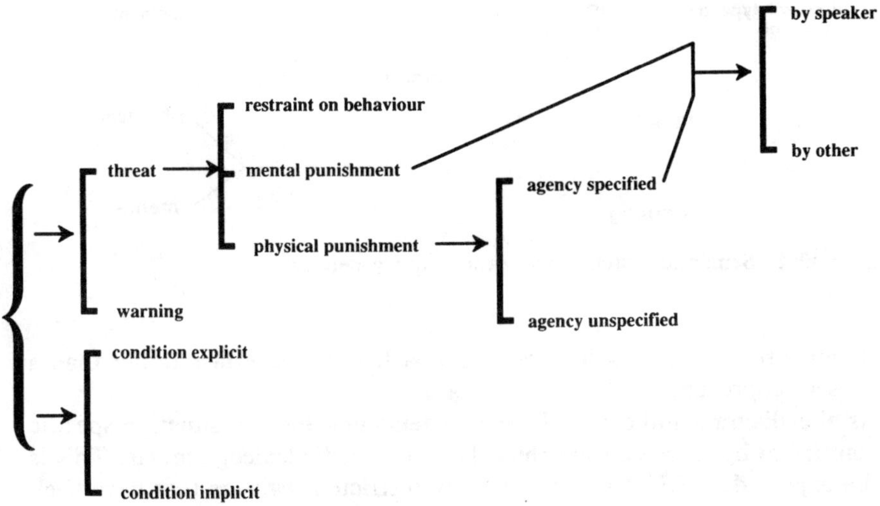


**Figure 12.2** Fragment of regulatory semantics

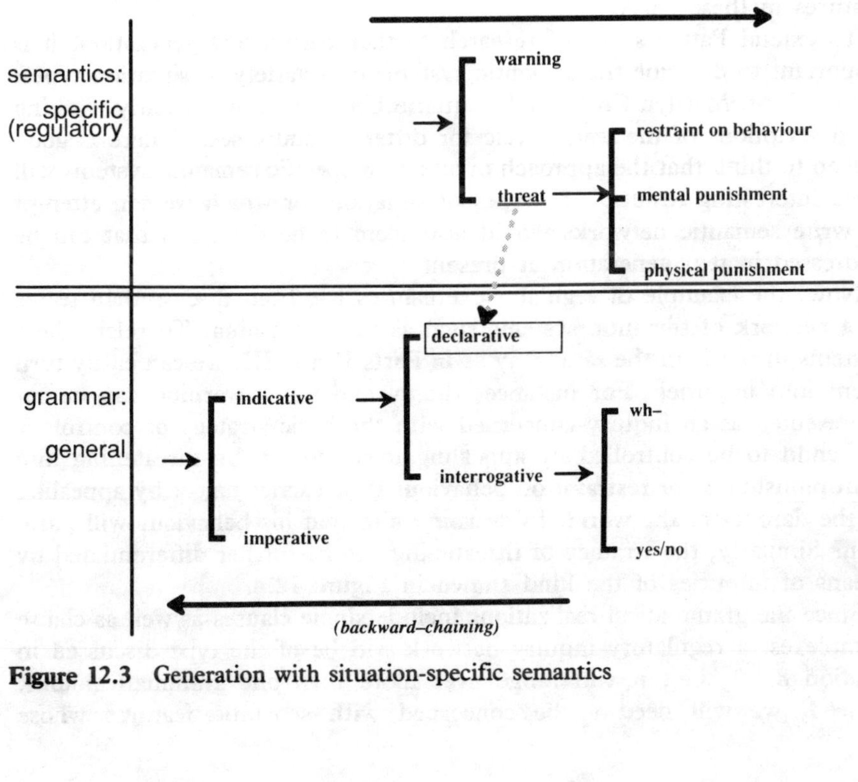


**Figure 12.3** Generation with situation-specific semantics

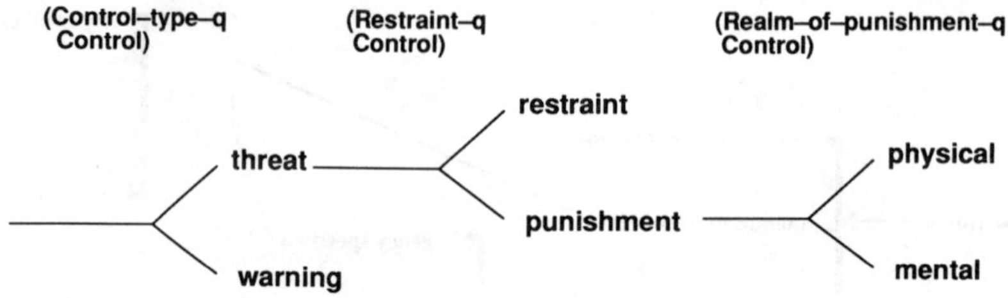


**Figure 12.4** Semantic system network as inquiry network

Halliday's terms (p.c.), a 'charger' approach to the interface rather than a 'chooser' approach.

As the diagram indicates, there is a tendency for the situation-specific semantics to be more delicate than the non-specific lexicogrammar. This is to be expected, particularly in the fairly restricted registers that have been attempted in text generation: only a restricted subset of the lexicogrammatical resources will be employed and the semantics can simply 'turn off' certain parts of the grammar by never preselecting grammatical features in these parts.

To extend Patten's line of research further within text generation, it is important to describe the semantic systems of a variety of situation types; for instance, Marilyn Cross, at Macquarie University, is currently working on descriptions of the water cycle for different addressees. There is good reason to think that the approach of situation-specific semantic systems will yield interesting results. The types of situation for which we can attempt to write semantic networks would also seem to be the types that can be addressed in text generation at present.

Now, the example of regulatory semantics has been discussed in terms of a network of semantic systems such as threat/warning. To relate these systems upwards in the same way as in Parts II and III, we can easily turn them into inquiries. For instance, the system threat/warning can be re-represented as an inquiry concerned with the basic strategy of control: is the child to be controlled by appealing to authority, by threatening him with punishment or restraint on behaviour if he carries on; or by appealing to the dangers of the world, by warning him that his behaviour will harm him? Similarly, the strategy of threatening can be further differentiated by means of inquiries of the kind shown in Figure 12.4.

Since the grammatical realizations include single clauses as well as clause complexes, a regulatory inquiry network will be of the type discussed in Section 8.4.3, i.e., it will range over more than one grammatical unit. Indeed, we will need to be concerned with semantic features whose

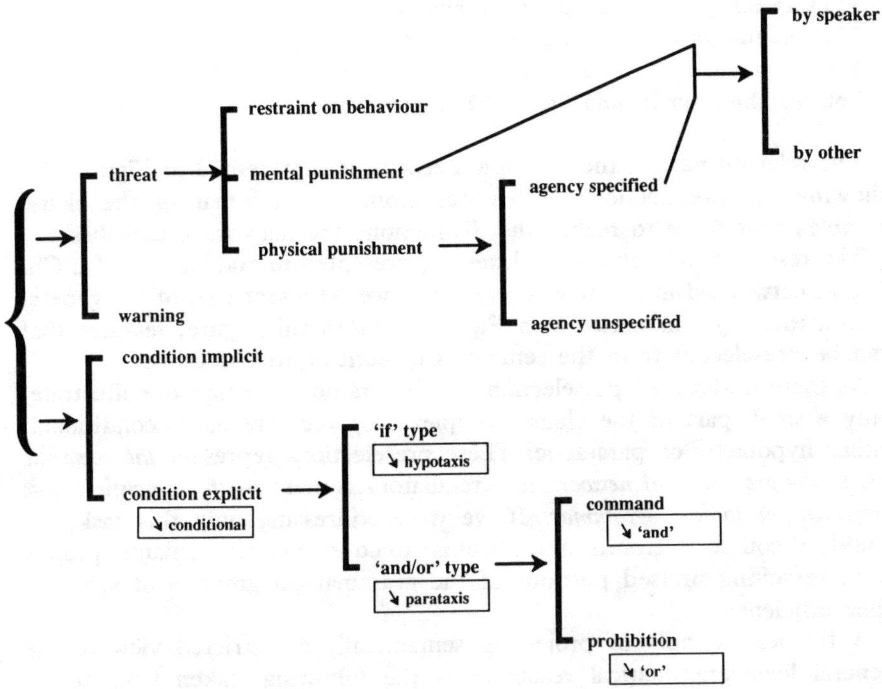


**Figure 12.5** Semantic network with clause complex preselections

influence may extend over considerably larger spans of text — see Matthiessen (1990d) for discussion.

## 12.4 The 'image' of lexicogrammar from semantics

The preselections of lexicogrammatical features in a semantic network such as the one for control represent an 'image' of the lexicogrammar for a particular register. That is, while the semantics draws on the general lexicogrammar, it employs only specific parts.

To see in some more detail what the projection of the semantics on to the general grammar is like, let us consider the grammar of the clause complex, again using the example of regulatory semantics. The resources of the clause complex come into play when the condition under which the threat or warning operates is made explicit, as in the following examples (Halliday, 1973: 77):

```
I'll smack you if you do that again
I'll smack you if you go on doing that
You stop doing that or Daddy'll smack you
You do that again and Daddy'll smack you
```

The relevant part of the semantic network is represented in Figure 12.5 showing the preselections of features from the grammar of the clause complex that serve to realize the distinctions the network establishes.

The resources of clause complexes are presented in Halliday (1985a: Ch. 7) and networked in Matthiessen (1990b); we represent part of the general grammatical system network in Figure 12.6. In this figure, features that can be preselected from the semantics of control are underlined.

As these underlined preselections in the grammatical network illustrate, only a small part of the clause complex resources are used: conditional, either hypotactic or paratactic. These preselections represent *the semantic use of the grammatical network* in a regulatory context — *the semantic image projected on to lexicogrammar*. If we were addressing only this task, we could, of course, customize the grammar to cover only the semantic projection, removing unused portions of the grammar on grounds of space or time efficiency.

A further example of projecting semantically a restricted view of the general lexicogrammatical resources is the following, taken from tense. Here the problem is that a generalized semantics of tense does not relate to particular uses of tense nor to specific contexts of use, leaving a gap in the account. The approach taken in traditional grammar was to list uses for each grammatical category and we can, of course, try to capture these lists in a tense chooser by defining inquiries corresponding to the various categories of use. One of the problems with this approach is that it gives us a fragmented picture with lists of uses for each separate tense; it fails to give us a systemicized account that can relate the *system* of tense to particular contexts of use. It also fails to show whether particular uses of different tenses are related in any systematic way. This issue is taken up for tense in English in Matthiessen (to appear) and further in some detail for French in Caffarel (1990).

Other mechanisms are possible and should be pursued as we determine more finely the precise functionalities required of this level of interaction. For example, if we want to capture particular registers in a model that operates with chooser and inquiry semantics, we can explore the possibility of characterizing registers in terms of *predetermined sets of responses to inquiries*. As a final detailed example of the computational development of theory, therefore, we present a particular approach to achieving this latter mode of control that has been attempted in the context of the Penman system.

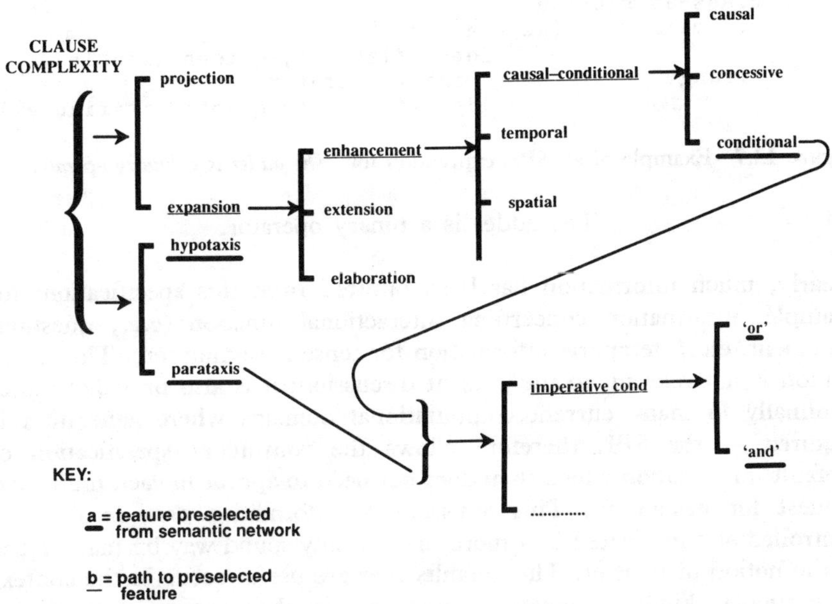


**Figure 12.6** Semantic image projected on to grammatical network

## 12.5 Modelling contextual control and register via inquiries

As we have seen in Part III, Penman/Nigel generates English in response to an input specification, expressed in the Sentence Plan Language (SPL) (cf. Section 9.2.2; Kasper, 1989a), that imposes constraints on the language that the Nigel grammar will produce. This specification includes both ideational content, as mediated by the *upper model* conceptual inheritance hierarchy (Section 9.2; Bateman, Kasper, Moore, and Whitney, 1990; Bateman, 1990c), and constraints on interpersonal and textual presentation, mediated by responses to Nigel's own semantic interface, the *choosers* and *inquiries* (Section 6.4; Mann, 1983a).

A simplified example of an SPL specification is shown in Figure 12.7; here we can see a number of combined domain and upper model types (*class-ascription*, *binary-operator*, *adder*), some Nigel inquiry responses (e.g., *:identifiability-q notidentifiable* for the nominal group region of REFERENCE), and the participant roles that the combined model defines for a process of type *class-ascription*, i.e. *:domain* and *range*.[3] This particular expression is responsible for making Nigel generate the clause:

```
(p1 / class-ascription
      :domain      (A2 / adder
                         :identifiability-q identifiable)
      :range       (B1 / binary-operator
                         :identifiability-q notidentifiable))
```

**Figure 12.7** Example of an SPL expression for: *The adder is a binary operator*

The adder is a binary operator.

Clearly, much information has been omitted from this specification; for example, information concerning interactional function (e.g., question, statement, etc.), temporal information for tense reasoning, etc. This information is not relevant to the present discussion; it is also provided rather minimally in many current computational domains where generation is required — the SPL therefore allows the convenient specification of 'default' information which then does not need to appear in each individual request for generation. This omission of information can, in fact, be controlled and motivated in a more theoretically sound way by making use of the notion of register. The defaults that are useful occur in the context of particular kinds of language use, i.e., in the context of particular registers.

The structure generated by the grammar can be controlled completely from the SPL input specification. Therefore, as an initial experiment in introducing register variation into the generation process, Bateman and Paris (1989) constructed a component that is responsible for constructing SPL from a domain-specified input in a way that is sensitive to a definition of the prevailing register. This component employs two distinct mechanisms corresponding to the differences required between experiential and logical control of the grammar (cf. Section 8.1):

- a definition of a *sub-grammar* that automatically constrains the language generated to exhibit features required for a given register;
- a definition and ranking of *register terms*.

The first, corresponding to the control of experiential variation, is largely equivalent to the mechanism illustrated above for regulatory semantics (Section 12.3.3) and implemented computationally by Terry Patten (Patten, 1988a); the latter is new and corresponds to logical variation. The influence of these mechanisms on the generation process is schematized in Figure 12.8.

This architecture has been pursued with respect to a particular task and computational domain — one provided by the Digital Circuit Diagnosis (DCD) instantiation of the 'Explainable Expert System' (EES). EES

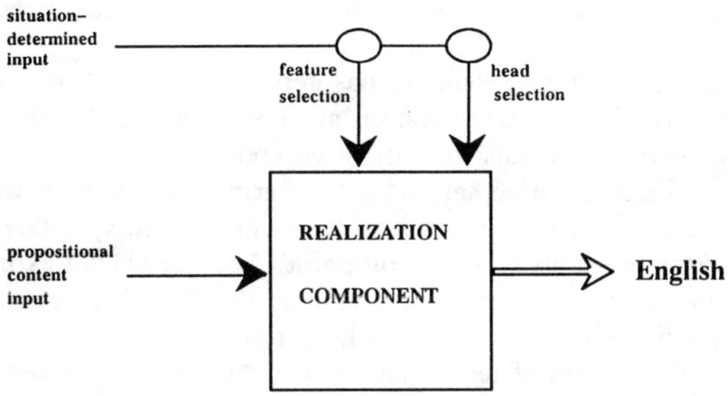


**Figure 12.8** Inputs to the generation process

(Swartout and Smoliar, 1987) aims automatically to produce expert systems which are capable of explaining their reasoning, the decisions they make, their terminology, and the concepts constrained in their knowledge base. In this framework, therefore, an expert system includes an extensive quantity of support knowledge for providing explanations of the system's reasoning. Explanation for expert systems is an important application for natural language generation as these systems are most useful and trusted when they can explain their behaviour, justify their conclusions and describe their knowledge.[4] Typically, such systems are used by people of widely differing expertise and requirements. There is thus a strong need for techniques that constrain the generation of natural texts flexibly and appropriately.

All of the expert systems being developed within EES are expected to support interactions with at least three different types of users: system developers, domain experts, and students using a system as a tutoring aid. Although these groups will need to be refined (by breaking them down into several groups) and added to as the systems are used further, these three were considered for the initial study. They can be described more fully thus:

Group 1: System developers who want to make sure that the knowledge base is correctly represented and that the system is working properly.
Group 2: End-users who want to follow the system's reasoning, but who do not know much about expert system technology (or even about computer science). These users are not necessarily expert in the domain of digital circuit diagnosis either.
Group 3: Very naive users trying to get acquainted with the domain, or learn about digital circuits and digital circuit diagnosis.

Language needs to be generated appropriately for the needs of each of these groups.

Samples of the text that Penman has generated for each of these groups when controlled for register variation are given below. We show two sets of examples here, each consisting of three texts corresponding to the three user groups. Each of these sets was, furthermore, generated with respect to the *same* domain system input: i.e., the same content specification within the DCD system was used as starting point. Another way of expressing this is to say that at some level of abstraction, the 'field' information of the situation remains constant across each text set.

The first set consists of texts that answer the question 'What is a faulty system?':

> A system is faulty, if there exists an O in the set of the output terminals of the system such that the expected value of the signal part of O does not equal the actual value of the signal part of O and for all I in the set of the input terminals of the system, the expected value of the signal part of I equals the actual value of the original part of I. [Sample text (1a): System developers]
>
> A system is faulty, if all of the expected values of its input terminals equal their actual values and the expected value of one of its output terminals does not equal its actual value. [Sample text (1b): End-users]
>
> A system is faulty, if its inputs are fine and its output is wrong. [Sample text (1c): Naive users]

The second set consists of part of the definition of a digital circuit system as maintained in the DCD knowledge base:

> For all I in the set of the input terminals of the system, there exists a CI in the set of the input terminals such that there exists a C in the set of the components of the system such that the C has an input terminal such that the CI is connected to the I. [Sample text (2a): System developers]
>
> All of the system's input terminals are connected to an input terminal of one of its components. [Sample text (2b): End-users]
>
> The input terminals of the system are connected to its components's input terminals. [Sample text (2c): Naive users]

We will use the particular implementation of register control defined with respect to the DCD expert system to illustrate more concretely the mechanisms provided. We will first explain the control mechanism for achieving control of logical variation, and then describe how experiential variation may be controlled using the available capabilities of the PENMAN SPL input specification.

### *12.5.1 Mechanism for logical variation*

Logical variation is made sensitive to grammar-external control by defining an ordered set of *register terms*. These are linked both to the domain's input specification (examples of this are shown in Figure 12.11 below) and to the conceptual hierarchy of the combined upper model and subordinated application domain model. The former guarantees that domain requests for expression will be recognized; the latter guarantees their expressibility in English by Nigel. Their appearance in a register specification makes them available bases on which to construct grammatical units, and their ranking influences the *logical* order in which they will be selected for expression in the generated English. The higher they are ranked, the sooner they will be picked up by Nigel; they will hence tend to occur at higher positions in the constituent tree that is generated than those which are ranked lower. Since Nigel generates in terms of functional organizations of heads and modifiers, this amounts to a differential realization of concepts as heads and modifiers according to their ranking in the register specification. The selection of precisely which terms will be heads at which level in the constituent tree has also been shown elsewhere to significantly influence the form of expression of information — for example, in the computational work of Meteer (1990), Iordanskaja, Kittredge, and Polguère (1990), and Jacobs (1988), as well as in linguistic work such as Ravelli (1985) and Halliday (1985a). In previous computational work, however, this had not been made available as a *decision*, or meaning resource, that was under generator control — typically, the logical organization of generated clauses has followed rather directly that of the presumed experiential content. By making head selection responsive to a register definition, we begin to gain control of this important source of linguistic variation.

Presently, these rankings have been defined as shown in Figure 12.9. The first definition establishes the relative importance of entities and relations according to the language used by the first group of users expected to use the DCD expert system, system developers, the second according to the language of other end-users, and the third according to the language required by inexperienced users. They show the available heads and their relative rankings for the registers used to generate the text examples given above; the first specification is responsible for the (a) texts, the second for the (b) texts, and the third for the (c) texts. These rankings were determined by examining corpora of the texts desired or produced by members of the various user groups and observing the preferred head-modifier

```
(define-register-terms *register-for-system-developers*
  ((*mode*  (RHETORICAL-RELATIONS ifthen iff and or))
   (*field* (RELATIONS exist forall not equal object-relation-ascription
                       material-property-ascription signal-part connected-to)
            (OBJECTS expected-value actual-value value signal
                     output-terminal input-terminal system variables)
            (OBJECT-MODIFIERS input-part output-part part-of))
   (*tenor* nil)))
```

---

```
(define-register-terms *register-for-end-users*
  ((*mode*  (RHETORICAL-RELATIONS ifthen iff and or))
   (*field* (RELATIONS not equal connected-to material-property-ascription)
            (OBJECTS expected-value actual-value value signal
                     output-terminal input-terminal system)
            (OBJECT-MODIFIERS exist forall input-part output-part part-of))
   (*tenor* nil)))
```

---

```
(define-register-terms *register-for-naive-users*
  ((*mode*  (RHETORICAL-RELATIONS  ifthen iff and or))
   (*field* (RELATIONS  material-property-ascription connected-to )
            (OBJECTS  output faulty input system)
            (OBJECT-MODIFIERS input-part output-part part-of))
   (*tenor* (EVALUATION fine wrong))))
```

**Figure 12.9** Experimental head status definitions used for the DCD registers

statuses of the concepts expressed. ‘Paraphrases’ across distinct user groups often appeal to different head-modifier organizations even when the concepts are largely shared. Furthermore, this selection of heads is neither random nor unsystematic. The higher the status of the head to which a component of the input is assigned, the higher the ‘significance’ of that component in the language generated. Particular language-using situations highlight certain entities and relations between those entities at the expense of others. This variation needs, therefore, to be controlled during generation by a register-driven mechanism.

The register term definitions achieve this control by stating that the terms labelled RHETORICAL-RELATIONS are, whenever possible, to be selected from the input as heads around which to generate language prior to those labelled RELATIONS, which are in turn to be selected prior to those labelled OBJECTS, etc. We can see then that, whereas in the register for system developers the relations *exist* and *forall* are given high ranking, they are given the lowest ranking in the register for end-users. As a consequence, the quantifiers appear as salient high ranking heads in the language user group 1, but as lowing ranking heads and ‘modifiers’, e.g., as determiners, in the language of user group 2. This means that although quantifiers still appear in end-user texts, they are attributed with rather less

```
(define-type-attributes faulty-system
 :defining-conditions: ((and (E (o in (output-part self))
                                 (not (equal (expected-value (signal-part o))
                                             (actual-value (signal-part o)))))
                              (A (i in (input-part self))
                                 (equal (expected-value (signal-part i))
                                        (actual-value (signal-part i)))))))
```

**Figure 12.10** Defining conditions of a DCD `faulty system`

```
register term and:      "(and !assertion#1 !assertion#2)"
input constituents:     and, assertion1, assertion2

register term exist:    "(E (!variable-symbol in !set-valued-expression) !assertion )"
input constituents:     exist, variable-symbol, set-valued-expression, assertion
```

**Figure 12.11** Patterns linking register terms *and* and *exist* to the input specification language

'prominence'. This differential attribution of prominence is shown in the following scheme:[5]

| | | | |
|---|---|---|---|
| text (1a): | for all | ↔ | subject matter as topical circumstance; e.g.: 'for all I . . .' |
| | exists | ↔ | existence predicate + conditional; e.g.: 'there exists an O . . .' |
| text (1b): | for all | ↔ | nominal group, determiner *all*; e.g.: 'all of the . . .' |
| | exists | ↔ | nominal group, indefinite determiner; e.g.: 'an input-terminal . . .' |
| text (1c): | for all | ↔ | nominal group, plural; e.g.: 'inputs' |
| | exists | ↔ | nominal group, singular; e.g.: 'output' |

Moreover, whereas the term *variables* is available in the register for system developers, it does not occur in the register for end-users; this prevents it from being selected as the basis for a linguistic expression in its own right. Register terms and ranking define, therefore, how terms appearing in the domain are to be realized *linguistically* in a given register and do not need to respect those terms' statuses as domain or upper model conceptualizations.

The interaction of register term definitions and the generation process by means of constructing differing SPL specifications for a given domain input operates as follows. Given an input specification such as that shown in

Figure 12.10 — which is, in fact, the DCD representation underlying the first set of example texts above (1a,b,c) — and a particular register specification, the program searches the list of register terms for the highest ranking available head whose pattern matches the structure of the input. The recognition of terms in the input specification language is defined using structural patterns that may be matched against the input. Patterns are expressed in terms of the *input* syntactic categories (specified by the EES formal definition language) that define the constituents of the input at that level. In the register for system developers, for example, one of the highest ranking allowable heads is the rhetorical relation *and*; the pattern for this 'rhetorical relation' is shown in Figure 12.11. This pattern matches the top level of input structure (Figure 12.10) and so offers an appropriate head for describing the input. Accordingly, an SPL term is constructed that:

1. specifies the register term found, namely *and*, as an appropriately ranking head,
2. places the remaining input constituents in appropriate modifier relationships. These relationships are drawn from the upper model definition of the type of the head which, in this case, are *conjunct1* and *conjunct2*.

This gives rise to the SPL fragment shown in Figure 12.12.

```
(a1 / conjunction   :conjunct1  <spl constructed for assertion1>
                    :conjunct2  <spl constructed for assertion2>)
```

**Figure 12.12** Constructed SPL fragment

This process is then applied recursively for each constituent, namely *assertion1* and *assertion2*, searching for permissible lower ranking heads. Both assertions in the definition of a faulty system are quantifier expressions. (The pattern for *exist* is also shown in Figure 12.11.) Such expressions have a structural decomposition in terms of the quantifier type, the variable to which the quantifier applies, the variable range and the assertion about that variable. Therefore, for both *assertion1* and *assertion2*, patterns for predicate calculus quantifiers (*exist* for *assertion1* and *forall* for *assertion2*) match and so the quantifiers may form heads at the next level in structure. The SPL is then grown accordingly, and the process recurses.

If no applicable head from the active register matches the input constituent at some level, the intrinsic structuring of the input is used to select where to search next for an applicable head. Elements of the input that are not allocated to heads at that level are retained for possible consumption later in the process. Examples of this can be seen in the differential treatment of variables and relation-types in the two registers. Whereas variables may become heads in the system developer register and are expressed as noun phrases, there are no heads corresponding to variables in the end-user register and so they do not appear in the English of that register. Similarly, some relations types, such as `signal-part`, do not appear in the end-user register and thus are not consumable in the construction of SPL for the generation of the English in that register.

### *12.5.2 Mechanism for experiential variation control*

The second type of mechanism constructs specified sub-grammars by constraining particular grammatical features to occur in the clauses generated; this is the mechanism appealed to exclusively by Patten (1988a). We currently implement this type of constraint in terms of SPL *default environments*, within which the theoretically available grammatical alternatives are restricted to some specified subset. Default environments consist of a set of Nigel inquiries and the responses those inquiries are to be given if they are needed during generation. By predisposing inquiry responses, areas of the grammar as a whole can effectively be removed from consideration so that the alternatives they offer no longer appear relevant. This is equivalent to the dynamic construction of a sub-grammar. An example of a default environment activated when the system developer register is in force is shown in Figure 12.13.

```
(defspl-default high-precision :posture-of-existence-q posture
                               :selection-particularity-q particular
                               :register-q notdistinguished
                               :deictic-part-q notpart
                               :possessor-modification-q nopossessor
                               :empty-number-q nonempty
                               :empty-gender-multiplicity-q nonempty
                               :extension-precedence-q precedes)
```

**Figure 12.13** Experimental definition of grammar constraints

The sub-grammar created by Figure 12.13 has the following properties:

- processes of existence will be lexicalized by the word *exist* rather than some more neutral work (such as *be*, as in *there is a book*) (`:posture-of-existence-q`);
- when possible, selection of a member of a set will be made using specific expressions, e.g., *one X* rather than *some X* (`:selection-particularity-q`);
- since variables are generally referred to in the singular, the distinction between *all* and *every* is neutralized for variables (`:register-q`);

- 'de-emphasizing' expressions such as the possessive modifications of *X's Y* are avoided in favour of the more equal emphasis of *Y of X* (`:deictic-part-q` and `:possessor-modification-q`);
- pronominalization is not attempted (`:empty-number-q` and `empty-gender-multiplicity-q`);
- and the order of conjuncts and disjuncts in the input will not be altered in the output by thematic planning of any kind (`:extension-precedence-q`). Compare, for example, texts (1a) and (1b) in this regard: text (1a) follows the order of the internal expert system definition shown in Figure 12.10, with the 'outputs' mentioned before the 'inputs'; in text (1b) these mentions occur in a different order since some experimental notions of thematic organization and text flow articulated within Penman have been permitted to apply.

This sub-grammar is therefore oriented to language that is precise and explicit, and which possesses the linguistic features observed for the user group of system developers as described above.

### *12.5.3 Limitations of the implementation*

The mechanisms constructed permit us to take single specifications of propositional content from the DCD system — i.e., specifications that involve predicate-calculus internal definitions of digital circuits and their components — and control the generation process automatically according to the register specification that is in force to produce variations such as those illustrated in our example texts. This has involved a preliminary linguistic analysis of the language types required, isolating the dimensions along which the language required differs according to user type, and experimental implementations of some of the constraint processes required to control the generation procedure. Although this has allowed us to isolate some of the problems to be faced and has provided detailed direction for further development, these experimental solutions are limited both in generality and capability. For example, we can immediately draw attention to the following problems:

- the two mechanisms of experiential and logical control combine to give some of the behaviour we require, but there is no formal connection between them;
- the definition of register terms can appear *ad hoc*;
- there is no explicit differentiation of treatment across the experiential, interpersonal, and textual metafunctions.

To conclude this brief description of how the beginnings of register-related control can be achieved with the kind of architecture we have described for the Penman instantiation of systemic-functional grammar, we will set out the directions for future development that are necessary to meet these particular problems.

We can relate the problems to one another by reiterating once again a point that we made in the previous chapter: i.e., that the computational implementation of systemic-functional grammar found in Nigel is based exclusively on the model of constituency — i.e., on an *experiential* model of linguistic phenomena. Thus, the experiential, interpersonal, and textual dimensions of variation have not been differentiated, and the logical has been forced outside of the grammar component altogether — it only takes affect by altering the entire input specification to the grammar, i.e., the SPL. We can also note that at the level of the definitions of the registers themselves, there has been a large divergence from the normal representational resources of system networks and realizational consequences — as explained in our introduction to the baseline framework in Part II, the network organization is not to be restricted to grammatical organization: the conception of paradigmatically organized systems of contrasts is assumed to be applicable to all strata of the linguistic system, register and situations included. Thus, there are two principle further developments to be pursued in this area of computational instantiations and development of systemic theory:

- respecting more the *differences* in nature across metafunctions, while simultaneously respecting their *similarity* as co-existing organizational forces on the system networks of the grammar;
- developing further the similarity in organization to be expected between registers and other strata of the linguistic system — i.e., constructing resources for register specification that follow the lexicogrammar in admitting a paradigmatic, or network-like organization.

Research in both of these directions has already begun — both explicitly within the computational systemic paradigm and within computational linguistics more generally.

The *differences* between the natures of the metafunctions has now surfaced in, for example, Hovy's (1988b) distinction between 'restrictive' and 'prescriptive' planning for the text generator PAULINE that we described in Section 3.3.4 above. Prescriptive goals, i.e., goals which can be planned in advance, be achieved, and then forgotten, correspond largely to the ideational metafunction; restrictive goals, i.e., goals that need to be continually oriented towards during generation and which cannot be achieved once and for all and be forgotten, are largely interpersonal. Also, the different nature of the logical metafunction has manifested itself very clearly, as we have noted, in its necessary placement *outside* of the Penman system, chooser, and inquiry framework.

The *similarities* between the metafunctions as co-determinants of grammatical form is now also being addressed, for example, in the attempt to bring this logical organization and variation back alongside the other metafunctions shown in Bateman (1989b). This work seeks to separate the logical organization generated by the grammar and the structural organization specified within the SPL, so as to allow independent variation of logical organization by inquiry control just as is followed for the other metafunctions.

The second direction has, of course, been the standard approach taken to register within systemic linguistics proper. This is illustrated most concretely in work such as that of Hasan (1978, 1987). It is now also being followed computationally in a continuation of the work presented in this section. Bateman and Paris (1990) describe this research effort in more detail: it plans to make more contact with standard systemic accounts of register — such as that of Hasan — and to provide a computational basis for articulating those accounts further. This involves development of a theoretical apparatus for specifying registerial constraints to permit a tighter connection between the register definition and the existing components of the generation system — such as the domain knowledge, the text planners, and the grammar — and includes a suggestive specification of a register network. This planned work will also attempt integration and reinterpretation of all the possibilities for interaction with context that we have seen in this chapter and which are under active development elsewhere within systemic linguistics.

## Notes

1. Encoding and decoding are thus not to be equated with generative and interpretative semantics, for example. Both generative and interpretative semantics are essentially decoding in that they reflect the categories of grammar rather than contextual categories. For a more extensive discussion of the two approaches, see Matthiessen (1990d).
2. We might undertake this project to test the model, possibly as a pilot for future work. The computer would simulate the mother. In other text generation situations, such as expert system explanation, the computer's social role is more likely to be that of a computer.
3. The entire process of constructing combined upper and domain models, and providing SPL input to Penman, is described in detail in the Penman documentation (The Penman Project, 1989).
4. See Paris (1990a) for further interesting discussion of this relationship between

explanation and generation.

5. In addition, in both the (a) and (b) texts, the relative scoping of the quantifiers is realized by *thematizing* the constituent containing the realization of the wider scoped quantifier; this connection between quantifier scopings in logical form and surface ordering has been frequently noted in computational accounts; e.g., Hobbs and Schieber (1987).

# 13 Conclusion: towards new states of the art

In this book, we have tried to present a reasonably complete account of:

- the application of a linguistic theory in one significant area of NLP, i.e., text generation;
- the feedback that that application has brought for theory;
- and further directions of joint theoretical development/computational modelling that this has supported.

To this extent, the book has been autobiographical: recounting our own experiences in this cycle of theorizing, implementation, re-theorizing. This style of development we regard as neither accidental nor arbitrary, however. It is our belief both that the development of linguistic theory is significantly enhanced by the challenge of computational representation and that the functionality of resulting NLP computational systems will be similarly enhanced by their foundation on firm linguistic principles. We have tried here to illustrate, therefore, something of the range of issues and the depth of their treatment that the approach to understanding natural language offered by computational systemic-functional linguistics demands. We have presented some detailed examples of work in grammar and its corresponding semantics and have sketched some of the deeper semantic and contextual accounts to which this leads.

This direction of development is also a methodological commitment. It is essential that work on, for example, situation, ideology, inter-textuality, education, language teaching, etc. — all central areas of current work in non-computational systemic-functional linguistics — does not lose its foundation in the concrete realizational resources of grammar and lexis. Thus we always take the lexicogrammar as our foundation in computational implementations of theory. This direction of development in the move towards computational systemic-functional linguistics is shown graphically in Figure 13.1.

Given our stance towards developing systemic-functional linguistics by

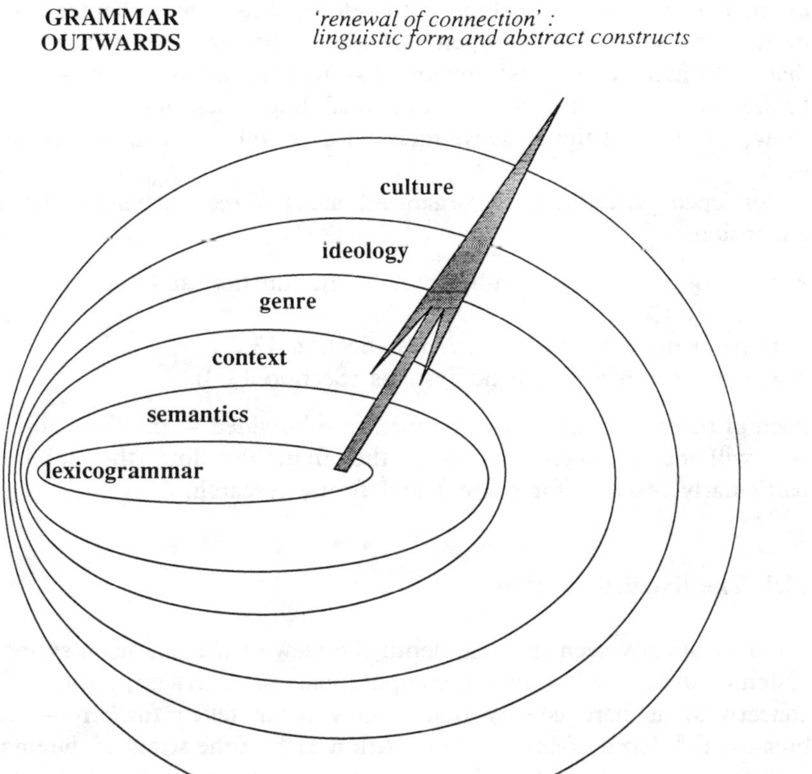


**Figure 13.1** Methodological development in SFL

building further upon the less abstract strata of the linguistic system, it is clear that we still have far to go. In fact, we are still at the very *beginning* of our long-term task of understanding the forms and functions of natural language. Furthermore, it should not even be taken for granted that our understanding of the strata that have been addressed — in most detail, of course, grammar — has achieved the status of a sound and comprehensive body of knowledge. There is certain to be substantial evolution even in our views of grammar.

We cannot predict what these new forms of linguistic descriptions and explanations will include. What we can do, however, is set out reasonably completely how the field of computational systemic-functional linguistics as a whole is moving towards them — mostly based on, or co-extensive with, the development of the field we have presented from our own perspective in this book. To 'conclude', therefore, this final chapter offers a multifaceted, future-facing open parenthesis that provides pointers to work that is, in many cases, just beginning – which areas will form the basis of future computational systemic-functional linguistics only the future will show, but most of the areas we mention here will have contributed in some way.

Our open parenthesis is organized along three partially independent dimensions:

- the linguistic system: substance, form, function and their interactions (Section 13.1);
- implementations and formalisms (Section 13.2);
- the move across linguistic systems (Section 13.3).

Each of these may, of course, be further subdivided – the first most of all. We will begin, therefore, with the first, detailing the subdivisions particularly relevant for current and future research.

## 13.1 The linguistic system

We have already seen in some depth the view of the linguistic system that systemic-functional linguistics, computational or otherwise, posits. Of more concern to us here is how that is now being taken further – both in breadth and depth of explanation. Within each of the strata of the linguistic system with which we have been concerned, important extensions are now being pursued. Furthermore, we can note again the preference for a methodological directionality:[1] as the expressive potential of lower strata increases, there are corresponding higher-stratal repercussions. Thus, in order to gain increased functional capabilities, the system needs also to have correspondingly increased expressive possibilities to support those capabilities. We can see this concretely here both in the repercussions of widening the modes of language available to the computational model on the requirements in grammar ('substance' on 'form') and in the repercussions of widening the computational account of grammatical organization available on the functions that motivate that organization ('form' on 'function'). In addition, as the complexity of the information available at each level or stratum grows, so do the requirements on the mappings and relationships *between* strata. Each of these areas will be a locus of extensive development.

### *13.1.1 Substance*

While traditionally text generation has been concerned with written text, there is now a more concerted effort in the community at large to consider spoken text. This requires the application of speech synthesis technologies that are capable of producing, as an end product, the actual physical speech signal that carries spoken text. There are, in fact, now a large range of so-called 'text-to-speech' devices commercially available. These devices take a computer-internal representation of a text and produce a spoken version of that text. However, even though these devices are often claimed to be capable of delivering speech of very high 'intelligibility' — better than 90 per cent is a commonly presented figure (cf. Klatt, 1987; Pratt, 1987) — it nevertheless remains the case that they produce speech that sounds unnatural and hard to listen to.

One reason for this limited performance is that text-to-speech systems do not attempt to produce functionally motivated intonation, even though high-quality speech synthesis requires appropriate intonation patterns to be enforced. Thus, current research in speech synthesis attempts to provide such patterns as required by the meaning of the text being generated (e.g., Danlos, Laporte, and Emerard, 1986; Davis and Hirschberg, 1988; Houghton and Pearson, 1988; Davis and Schmandt, 1989; Fawcett, 1990). While this requires significantly improved accounts of the interactions of abstract pitch contours or sequences on phonological specifications in order to produce the level of pitch, duration, and intensity control necessary for speech synthesis, it is also clear, however, that there needs to be accounts of the *functions* of intonation. This is completely analogous to the accounts of the functions of syntagmatic organization already offered by the stratum of grammar. Thus, we can see that the expansion of expressive resources to include the spoken mode of language of necessity requires a similar expansion in the use of those resources made in the strata above.

### *13.1.2 Form*

Driving appropriate intonational selections from an extended specification of the grammar has a rather long history in systemic-functional linguistics. Halliday (1967b), for example, details around forty points of connection between the clause grammar and choices that require realization in intonation. Work of this kind has been begun by Robin Fawcett in the COMMUNAL project (Fawcett, 1990a, 1990b) and, in the second half of 1990, also by Robin King and Julie Vonwiller at the Electrical Engineering Department at Sydney University. In addition, the question of interfacing abstract specifications of intonational realization that might be made by an extended system of the Nigel-type with actual input to speech synthesisers is also addressed in, for example, Sefton (1990). Areas of the grammar where there is already need for intonational realizations include: restrictive vs. non-restrictive relative clauses and mood selections. Other work has also emphasized points of connection between intonation and grammar/semantic interpretation, e.g., Jackendoff (1972) on focus-presupposition organization and the scope of negation. In general, however, we can expect a systematic extension of the grammar to be necessary in order to support the full range of intonational variation that is functionally relevant to the grammatical stratum.

A further area that is also addressed in Sefton (1990) is the extension to consider even the form of *written text* more systematically: i.e., to move towards a genuine *graphology* parallel to phonology. Here we can expect more directly functional control of styles of characters, fonts, and type-setting conventions that are used in many cases to augment the written mode of language use in the face of the lack of the options more typically provided by phonology.

As we noted in Section 6.6.1, the organization of lexical information is one important area that we have not addressed in this book. Here, again, we are beginning to find more detailed computationally tractable suggestions for dealing with lexical delicacy, lexical collocation, and the kinds of textual meanings, or perspectives, to which particular lexical choices can give rise (e.g., Matthiessen, 1990a; Tucker, 1988; Sinclair, 1987; Wanner and Bateman, 1990). This work is sure to become more prominent as the coverage of our grammars and semantics increases.

There is also current work that is re-examining grammatical organization — particularly the accounts of syntagmatic organization that have been proposed in the systemic literature and which we have seen in our discussions throughout this book. We suggested in Section 8.1 that it would be beneficial to widen our treatments of syntagmatic organization to include the kind of metafunctionally motivated diversity represented syntagmatically by constituency, interdependency, pulse, and prosody: this would be one way of dealing with a perceived lack of detail at the syntagmatic level that we will return to in Section 13.2. Others are attempting to address this lack of detail by exploring possible combinations of the paradigmatic organization offered by systemic-functional grammar with the syntagmatic accounts found in distinct theoretical approaches: these latter include an exploration into the use of Tree Adjoining Grammars (McCoy, Vijay-Shanker and Yang, 1990) for structural realization, the increasing use of dependency relationships for representing syntagmatic organization (O'Donnell, 1990), and an ongoing general appraisal (Steiner, 1990; Teich, 1991) of the resources of syntagmatic organization with reference to the approaches found in 'information-based' accounts of grammar (cf. Shieber, 1986).

Then there is work that is considering the nature of grammar itself. The view of grammar that is represented within system networks of the type we have presented in this book can be seen, following Halliday, as a three-way compromise: they need to be responsive to the functional demands made upon them from above, they need to organize the regularities in realization that they motivate below, and they need to be internally consistent as networks. This three-way responsibility leads to networks where there appears to be a combination of several kinds of grammatical features: some are more formally motivated, others more functionally; Martin (1987) provides useful discussion of the range of 'meanings' that features may carry. In response to this, there have also been moves to construct system networks where the meaning of the features is more uniform or homogeneous. For example, in the systemic model proposed by Fawcett (1980) and implemented within the COMMUNAL project (Fawcett, 1988 and 1990; Fawcett and Tucker, 1990), the features are claimed to be at the semantic level and to be motivated by functional *and* formal criteria; although whether or not this is a significant complication is not yet clear. In contrast, the grammar networks underlying Steiner and Reuther (1989) and made partially explicit in Teich (1989) move in the direction of trying to motivate their features on purely formal criteria, i.e., on the concrete realizational classes that the network supports. This reduces, in theory, the complexity of the realizational relationship between network and syntagmatic representation, but may accordingly complicate the relationship between the strata of context and the grammar. It has not yet been demonstrated whether or not either of these moves leads to an improved factorization of the difficulty of the task of linguistic description.

It may even be the case that the basic organizational principles of our networks will change or be substantially augmented. For example, we have already seen in Chapter 11 that there is evidence that we need to give much more theoretical attention to the dynamic dimension of the linguistic system: this represents, then, one such dimension of augmentation. In addition, there has always been a significant body of systemic work that holds that language is essentially a *probabilistic* phenomenon and that system networks, if such are drawn, should represent this. Such work is also perhaps arguably closer to providing accounts of the essential *variability* of the linguistic system – i.e., the basic fact that the linguistic system is constantly evolving and that the resources available to a language community change over time, even within single texts. Work in this area includes: Nesbitt and Plum (1988), Halliday (1988, forthcoming), and others.

Another, more radical, dimension of possible change is to consider system networks not solely in the terms of taxonomy or 'typology' that we have seen, but also additionally in terms of *topology* (Martin and Matthiessen, 1990). This has been suggested as a very general theoretical device for accounting for apparent variations in how one might want to draw up the typologies represented in a system network that occur when different criteria for generalization are employed. Thus, as Martin and Matthiessen illustrate with respect to the ideational example of process types:

> There are parameters along which behaviourals resemble material processes and other parameters along which they resemble mental and relational ones. Depending on which parameters are taken as criterial at primary delicacy, behaviourals can be grouped with materials or with mentals and verbals but not both. The criteria deployed at primary delicacy thus become thematic for the description. They act as its point of departure and circumscribe the agnation which can be established. In typological work, all points of departure foreground some criteria and background others. With phenomena such as behavioural processes this means that some agnation must be lost in the process of classification. The typology is limited in just this respect. (Martin and Matthiessen, 1990: 23)

Indeed, it is very likely that this is the basis for the main differences between the system networks proposed for process types that we have seen in this book — which all derive from Halliday (1985a) — and alternatives such as those of Fawcett (1980) and Steiner and Reuther (1989). Adding the topological perspective may well provide the theoretical mechanisms necessary for reconciling these views.

### *13.1.3 Function*

In order to describe some of the current and near-future work concerning the strata of lexicogrammar, semantics, and context, we will again employ the usual metafunctional breakdown of phenomena. Chapter 9 showed how some of the necessary organization of this stratum can be inferred from the possibilities of expression supported by the strata of form. Here we simply mention some approaches that are uncovering further details of that organization.

IDEATION BASE. There is an increasing awareness in the computational community generally, that a 'conceptual' ontology of some kind is necessary to organize the knowledge with which a computational system must operate. More recently, it has also been argued that perhaps the best motivation for such an ontology is essentially linguistic (Skuce and Monarch, 1990). This was, of course, the methodology that was appealed to throughout Chapter 9 and, in particular, in the construction of the 'upper model' shown in Section 9.2. This area is, therefore, one in which we can expect to see very much more work – both from the side of systemic linguistics (most notably here: Halliday and Matthiessen, in preparation), from other schools of linguistics, and from computation (a survey of some of the possible correspondences here is attempted in Bateman, 1990c).

TEXT BASE. Text planning is one of the most active areas in current text generation work and a number of groups are pursuing the development of new planning components building both on the experiences of computational work on planning in the past and on more of the accounts of text already extant in systemic linguistics (e.g., Hasan, 1978; Martin, in press). We also have seen in Chapter 12 how text planning is being made ever more responsive to the context of situation; this is a trend that will certainly continue.

INTERACTION BASE. As indicated in Section 9.3, this area of computational modelling is only just beginning. Relevant systemic linguistic work includes the work on exchange structure of Berry (1981), Bateman (1985b) and Ventola (1987). Some new accounts are also already finding computational implementations in the COMMUNAL system (e.g., Fawcett, van der Mije and van Wissen, 1988).

### *13.1.4 Interstratal relations*

As the complexity and breadth of each of the modelled strata of the linguistic system steadily increases, the specification of the relationship between those strata becomes similarly more complex. The interstratal relationships we have shown in this book are: the relation between paradigmatic grammatical feature selections and syntagmatic organization (realization statements: Sections 6.3, 8.1 and 8.2.1), and the relation between paradigmatic grammatical feature selections and the semantic abstractions supported by the environment or context (choosers and inquiries: Sections 6.4, 8.3 and 8.4; and contextual preselection: Section 12.5).

We have, however, illustrated only the most straightforward manifestations of these interstratal relationships. In particular, we have only discussed *congruent* realizations where a given semantic configuration motivates a corresponding grammatical configuration. The relationship between strata is further complicated by the mechanism of *grammatical metaphor* (Halliday, 1985a: Ch. 10), mentioned above in Sections 4.4 and 5.5.3. Grammatical metaphor is the mechanism by which the fact that given semantic configurations motivate *sets* of grammatical configurations is theoretically organized as a further resource for linguistic expression.

There are many types of linguistic variation of this general kind — the control of many of which still lies beyond what we can achieve systematically with current text generation techniques. Halliday, for example, offers the following illustration of metaphors of *transitivity*, where essentially the same 'content', at some level of description, is re-expressed with very different process and participant role structures:

> instead of *Mary saw something wonderful*, I may choose to say *Mary came upon a wonderful sight*, where the process has been represented as a material process *came upon* and the perception has been turned into a 'participant' *a sight*. Or I may say *a wonderful sight met Mary's eyes*, with the process of perception split up into Actor *a sight*, material process *meet* and Goal *eyes*; and Mary represented simply as the possessor of the eyes. These are all plausible representations of one and the same non-linguistic 'state of affairs'. (Halliday, 1985a: 322)

Such cases of transitivity metaphors are complex and raise important questions of the 'perspectives' that it is possible to take on states of affairs and how these are to be represented within knowledge representation systems and by a corresponding increase in the complexity of the relationship between, e.g., the ideation base and the grammatical features selected.

Two types of grammatical metaphor which are beginning to be controlled are *rankshifting* and *complexity* metaphors. In these cases, a given semantic configuration may show systematic and functionally motivated variation in its realization at the level of the structural *ranks* of the grammar — i.e., clauses, groups (nominal, verbal, adverbial and prepositional), words, and morphemes — and the possibilities of *complexing* at each of these ranks — i.e., forming combinations of units of any rank organized in terms of dependency. Both of these possibilities need to be decided on when generation of a grammatical unit is undertaken. Thus, for each meaning to be expressed, grammatical decisions must first be made not only as to the *rank* of the grammatical unit that will be used but also to the *complexity* of that grammatical unit. This, rather than being an automatic consequence of the type of semantic unit in question, is instead a kind of variability that is employed as an expressive resource of the linguistic system.

A very common example of a rankshifting metaphor is 'nominalization', where what is semantically an event and would, congruently, be realized as at clause rank is instead realized as a nominal group. A more complex example is the following. Consider the semantico-logical relation of *extension* (Halliday, 1985a: 207): very generally, this relationship 'extends' one meaning by adding something new to it. Thus, if there is a demand to express the relationship that 'extends' the meaning expressed, e.g., by 'Hellenistic philosophy' to include the meaning expressed by, e.g., 'mystical eastern traditions', as we might want in the context of expressing a meaning such as 'the unification of Hellenistic philosophy and mystical eastern traditions', this can potentially find expression through each of the *ranks* of the grammar (in the case of rankshifting metaphors) and as either a *simplex* or *complex* grammatical unit (in the case of complexity metaphors):[2]

- Simple clause with accompaniment complement:
  *Hellenistic philosophy was united with the mystical traditions of the east*
- Extending nominal group complex:
  *Hellenistic philosophy and the mystical traditions of the East were united*
- Extending adjectival group complex within simple nominal group:
  *The Hellenistic and Eastern mystical traditions were united*

etc. Each of the possible realizational variants need to receive appropriate functional motivations so that they can be controlled during the text generation process.

This very important area of theory will add significantly to the flexibility of the language that it is possible for text generators to generate. An initial attempt to show this flexibility in action is presented in Bateman (1989b, 1990b).

## 13.2 Implementations and formalisms

It is important to emphasize that theoretical abstractions (such as grammatical systems, system networks, realization statements, grammatical functions, etc.) and the descriptive categories that instantiate these in the accounts of particular languages can be represented in a variety of ways. Thus a systemic grammar may be represented in terms of, for example, the formalisms of Functional Unification Grammar or LOOM (cf. further below) — although any such representation does, of course, constitute an *interpretation* of the theory.

Implementations and the formalisms for *representing* theoretical abstractions applied in those implementations have not, however, been focused upon in this book. One good reason for this is that until very recently (and some would argue even still) there has not been a sufficiently well-developed articulation of the *properties* of the linguistic theory descriptions and entities available to warrant a consideration of the formal mechanisms of their representation. Whether or not this is the case, two broad areas have motivated closer attention to the implementations of systemic-functional theory and the formalisms that are available as representational resources for the linguistic theoretical constructs required:

1. Grammatical phenomena that are clearly beyond the representational capabilities of the mechanisms for constructing structure defined within the Penman system; some of these we have seen (Chapter 8) and further descriptions are given in Matthiessen (1988a, 1990c), Steiner (1990) and Teich (1991).
2. Grammar *directionality* — parsing vs. generation.

With the exception of certain of the Kyoto experiments and the extensive computational implementation of the syntactic principles developed in Fawcett (1980) provided in the COMMUNAL system (Fawcett and Tucker, 1990), there have not yet been many computational extensions in the first area. These may be expected in the near future, but will in any case depend on the results being obtained in the second area, to which we now turn.

In this book, we have concentrated throughout on the task of text *generation*, i.e., the construction of texts on the basis of distinctions initially specified at some higher level of abstraction, such as some configuration of communicative goals with respect to a specification of relevant knowledge. However, the question has naturally arisen — as we mentioned briefly in Section 6.6.2 above — as to whether the substantial computational representation of linguistic resources that have been developed over the course of the Penman and Kyoto projects could also be of use for the 'reverse' task, i.e., that of parsing and text understanding. Constructing a grammatical resource the size of, for example, the Nigel grammar, is a major undertaking and so it would clearly be practically beneficial if this work did not need to be repeated when the 'directionality' of application of the resource is changed from generation to analysis. Note that this is not possible given the implementation of the Penman system as we described it in Chapter 6 — and, indeed, nor with any of the extensions to the framework that we have mentioned in Parts III and IV. The Penman system was only envisaged to be a text *generation* system and, as such, had the *directionality* of interpretation of its grammatical system networks hard-wired into its traversal algorithm (Section 6.5).

Since the Penman system was originally designed, however, there has been a general move within computational linguistics to *declarative* representations of information which do not make commitments to processing questions such as directionality of interpretation. It was, a logical move, therefore, when Kasper (1987a, 1988) began to explore the possible representation of systemic networks within such a declarative formalism: the Functional Unification Grammar (FUG) formalism proposed by Kay (1979). Although Kasper found it necessary to extend the basic representational resources offered by FUG in a number of ways, the essential result of this work was that it was indeed possible to convert, almost fully automatically, the specification of a system network used by the Penman system into an FUG representation which could, then, serve as the basis for a sentence parser. Thus, it was suggested that it was, indeed, theoretically possible to use a single systemic grammatical description for both generation, as we have described in this book, and for analysis.

That this proved possible should not be considered a surprise. Note that although we introduced and described systemic-functional grammar in Chapter 6 in terms of its use for generation, there was nothing intrinsically generation-oriented in the grammar fragments themselves. If the grammatical systems of the networks are interpreted as statements of the grammatical feature co-occurrence possibilities, then there is clearly no particular directionality present. This interpretation also supports the 'rightward', backward-chaining use of the system network made by Patten (1988a) that we saw in Section 12.3 or in the 'path augmentation' that supports preselection in Nigel. Furthermore, as far as systemic theory itself is concerned, the statement of linguistic resources that it presents should, indeed, be neutral with respect to its direction of interpretation: 'realization' between strata is not a directed relation; nor is the increase in delicacy internal to system networks a directed process of choice. Both are nondirectional statements of co-occurrence possibilities (cf. Halliday, 1978, forthcoming).

Although an interesting experiment in itself, the translation of the Nigel grammar into the Functional Unification formalism did not provide a usable parser, however. The grammar did not seem to bring to bear sufficient constraints to resolve potential structural ambiguities in the input strings and this has been used as one of the main pieces of evidence to support the claim, mentioned in the previous section, that the syntagmatic specification of a systemic grammar is underspecified. Certainly one significant contributing factor to the lack of success in resolving ambiguities, however, is the fact that the Nigel grammar places much information outside of the system network and in its semantics, i.e., in the choosers and inquiries and in the relations that hold between the constructs in the ideation, interaction, and text bases. The FUG translation was only applied to the grammar network, and so these additional possible sources of constraint were removed.

The parser was, however, also extremely slow. But, again, part of the cause of this problem was that the FUG translation did not even preserve all of the information available in the grammatical network definition itself. In particular, the hierarchical information created by the connectivity of the network was not preserved, resulting in a less than optimally constrained set of possible grammatical feature co-occurrences to be checked with every parse.

In response to both of these inadequacies of the FUG translation experiment, Kasper has begun a new round of experimentation that seeks both to include a non-directional statement of the chooser and inquiry semantics and to recapture the organizing principle of the systemic network. To achieve this, Kasper (1989b) represents a systemic grammar not in a simple unification framework, but in the form of the multiple inheritance hierarchies supported in modern knowledge representation languages such as LOOM (MacGregor and Brill, 1989; cf. Section 9.2). The usefulness of this move relies on a technique developed within knowledge representation called *classification*, which is formally rather similar to unification. This technique makes it possible to deduce, given a partial class membership description, a maximal class membership description that satisfies both the class–subclass relationships specified in the inheritance hierarchy and the original partial description. Thus, if some linguistic entity is known on some grounds already to be, e.g., a clause that has the features 'perceptive' and 'middle' (cf. the network fragment in Figure 6.5), then the classification process can deduce that that clause must necessarily also belong to the class of clauses that are 'mental' and 'phenomenal range' and, furthermore, will also attempt by using the explicit representation of the choosers and inquiries, to determine which of the possible compatible grammatical features 'metaphenomenal'/'phenomenal' are appropriate given any available semantic information present. Substantial experiments with this technique are still to be performed but the outcome will certainly be interesting.

A parallel development to this move to represent systemic networks using classification techniques has arisen from the increasing use of *subsumption lattices* in more structurally oriented feature-based linguistic theories such as Head-driven Phrase Structure Grammar (HPSG: Pollard and Sag, 1987). There, the representational resources of functional unification are enhanced by introducing *types* which group theoretical meaningful combinations of features together. A type thus has much of the representational capability of a 'frame' (cf. Section 9.2) in knowledge representation, while the subsumption lattice provides the capabilities of the inheritance hierarchy. The nondirectionality of implementations of grammar based upon this notion of 'typed unification' has been demonstrated by Emele *et al.* (1990b). This therefore promises also to be a useful representation mechanism for systemic networks and the possibilities of this are under investigation: Bateman (1990d) presents a discussion of the appropriateness overall of this particular line of development within computational systemic-functional linguistics, and Bateman and Momma (1991) describe a first nondirectional representation of all of the strata that we have described in this book in the typed feature structure (TFS) unification formalism of Emele and Zajac (1990).

By these means attempts are now being made to find a representational formalism that enables a single statement of grammar, semantics, and their interconnections to be used as a common resource in generation, understanding, and also, as we mention in the following section, translation. Whether it will then still be necessary to augment the resources of syntagmatic description in a way that draws significantly on results from outside of systemic theory remains, however, unclear at this time.

This move to a nondirectional interpretation of linguistic information strengthens the general division we described in Chapters 2 and 4 between the *resources* of linguistic information and the *processes* of that resource's application, while beginning to apply more linguistic input to the specification of those processes — e.g., by insisting on a process that respects the nondirectional properties of the realization relationship. It is very important to emphasize, however, that the nondirectional interpretation make *absolutely no claim* that understanding and generating are 'psychologically' the same task. Nor does the claim that understanding and generating are distinct tasks necessarily have an impact on the value of nondirectional statements of linguistic resources. What this theoretical stance means is that there is assumed to be a common resource, the linguistic system, which has certain properties which hold regardless of what the system is being used for. For example, that a clause will be classified as meaning one of four types of processes, and that each of these will have determinate semantic category correlates, is posited as *a fact of the linguistic resources themselves*. The possible relationships between psychological processes and such a resource constitute another set of issues entirely. This position also does not rule out the possibility that *some* properties of the linguistic system will *not* be expressable independently of whether a language user is generating or understanding (or translating). These properties, however, do not fall under the phenomena that we have been concerned with providing accounts for in this book.

## 13.3 The move across linguistic systems

Another dimension of development that is now beginning to gain strength, and which has been heralded in this book, is the application of computational systemic-functional linguistics across languages: firstly, by means of *co-generation*, i.e., the parallel generation of texts in different languages, and, subsequently, drawing on the non-directionality of new formalisms, in the context of full *machine translation* across languages. This direction also, of course, feeds back into theoretical development elsewhere: what, for example, will experiential ontologies from different languages look like? —

will generalizations be possible? What degree of commonality can there be across the other strata of the linguistic system? etc. See, for example, Bateman (1989b) and Bateman, Matthiessen, Nanri and Zeng (1991a,b) for discussion.

Perhaps a logical extension here, although also pursuable independently, is the further move to consider possibilities for expression not across distinct linguistic systems, but across distinct *semiotic systems* altogether — another established research area within systemic linguistics (e.g., O'Toole, in press; van Leeuwen, 1986). In certain respects, this area is already becoming of increasing interest in the computational context. To the extent that distinct semiotic systems can carry similar kinds of meanings, there is naturally the possibility of considering them as alternative choices of representation: as, for example, the distribution of information across text and diagrams, maps, tables, etc. (cf. Arens and Hovy, 1990). As text generation moves to consider *multimodal* information presentation, the quest for generalizations that can hold across semiotic systems becomes ever more relevant.

## 13.4 Final words

Perhaps curiously for a book on text generation, as a final word we probably need to note that, given the increasing orientation to nondirectional linguistic accounts that we described in Section 13.2, it is unlikely that 'generation' systems as such will continue to be constructed. This does not mean, however, that text generation as a field of research will end. As we described in Chapter 3, text generation addresses a very different set of issues and concerns to those traditionally addressed in the parsing community. These issues and concerns — and we have seen many of them in this book — need to be addressed and it is important that they remain. Thus, we will very likely see more of the issues addressed in text generation gradually becoming applicable to analysis also, resulting in significantly deeper analyses than have been possible hitherto. Text generation and parsing will then surely move together as fields of research, but the motivations, theories, and organizations of the more abstract strata of the linguistic system will be based on the foundations that have already been and continue to be laid within text generation in general, and, we believe, within systemic-functional text generation in particular.

Systemic-functional linguistics posits that language is a multi-dimensional semiotic space (Halliday, forthcoming). Within these terms, we can consider all the possible future directions we have described in this chapter as an exploration and opening up of the dimensions of that space. The space is quite large: so we had better take along an as extensive a map of the territory as we can find. We hope that we have in this book given something of a sense of how systemic theory functions as such a map and, even more, how this can now make more of the dimensions of the semiotic space of language accessible to computational investigation.

## Notes

1. A directionality which, in fact, has important similarities with the development of language by children; see Halliday (1975) and Painter (1984).
2. These three possibilities restrict attention to clausal realizations of the predicate 'unify'; the original specification used above, i.e, 'the unification of Hellenistic philosophy and mystical eastern traditions', is itself a further rankshifting metaphor — although here the meaning being metaphorized is the 'unification' and not the relationship of extension.

# Appendix I: Glossary of systemic and computational terms

Linguistic theories and traditions usually differ with respect to their scope — e.g., whether they consider all of language in context or, more narrowly, some subsystem(s) such as phonology or syntax, the basic assumptions about language they make, the basic conceptions of language they favour (e.g., as resource or as rule system), the perspectives they take (e.g., cognitive or social), the most central question they ask about language, their approaches to answers, their theoretical abstractions, etc. Linguistic theories are, in effect, systems of interrelated assumptions, theoretical categories, and so on. Differences between theories have to be understood in terms of the theoretical systems rather than just in terms of the items or elements that enter into relations in the systems.

One aspect of a theory is certainly its technical vocabulary; and theories differ in their terminologies. This glossary is therefore intended to explain systemic terms and to relate systemic and non-systemic terms;[1] it is an aid in metalinguistic translation, i.e., in translation between the systemic metalanguage and other metalanguages. It is necessary to do this, but at the same time it is important to recognize that glossaries can be misleading and even intellectually harmful: a theory cannot be *reduced* to its technical terms. A glossary is based on items — the terms glossed — and this tends to foreground the items at the expense of the system or network of relations they are part of. A technical vocabulary is not a list of items; it is a network of relationships. So if we pick out one vocabulary item, say Goal (systemic), and gloss it as Patient (non-systemic), we have lost the fact that Goal is just one part of one theoretical model of transitivity and Patient is part of another model and they are not systemically equivalent although they may be applied analytically to the same constituents of a clause in a large number of examples. We state this here, explicitly, so that it is clear why it is not possible, even after providing this glossary, to go through the preceding text and replace the systemic terms by other, perhaps more familiar, terms which seem more or less equivalent. Most of the preceding chapters have attempted at length to reveal the system within which the systemic terms explained here take on their full meaning and function.

Furthermore, although there are significant points of contact between the systemic tradition and Indian and Chinese linguistics (e.g., in the theoretical foregrounding of prosodies and syllables), the 'translations' between the systemic tradition and other traditions in this glossary are concerned with Western traditions — more specifically traditional grammar and those originating in the United States. Thus, there are only a few items from the Prague School, while Glossematics, continental structuralism, current French functionalist approaches, the various German traditions, and so on are left out entirely. Also, it should be noted that the main focus is on the level of lexicogrammar (= syntax + morphology + lexis) rather than phonology, semantics, and context, although some central terms in these areas are included. We make these exclusions and restrictions not as an attribution of linguistic importance nor in terms of relative relatedness of different theoretical traditions — clearly the Prague school, its forerunners, and other functional traditions would by this latter criterion provide the most obvious points of comparison. It is rather the case that within text generation, and computational linguistics in general, the most common theoretical borrowings from linguistics remain at the present time rooted in accounts originating in the United States. It is, therefore, particularly relevant in the context of concern of this book to relate to this tradition.

The following symbols and conventions have been used throughout this book and the glossary to follow.

In grammatical systems: systemic features are written all in lower case (often in single quotes; sometimes in square brackets), e.g., 'indicative' [indicative]; system names are written all in upper case, e.g., POLARITY. Combinations of features (for example in selection expressions) are sometimes more finely described in terms of systemic disjunction (/) and systemic conjunction (&). In the realizations of grammatical, semantic features, etc., the following symbols are used (cf. Section 6.3):

| *symbol* | *description* |
|---|---|
| / | Conflation |
| + | Insertion |
| : | Preselection |
| :: , ! | Lexical preselection |
| () | Expansion |
| ^ , > | Strict ordering |

The realization statements using these operators are generally written within boxes attached to the appropriate systemic features in networks, or following the symbol for realization '\' (sometimes '⌐' – note that this is never used for negation in the book).

Grammatical functions are written with an initial capital letter and the rest in lower case, e.g.: 'Actor' (Section 5.7).

Finally, interdependency relations between members of a complex are represented by '→'. '$\alpha$' and other small Greek letters represent elements of hypotactic interdependency structure. '1' and other Arabic numerals represent elements of paratactic interdependency structure (Section 8.2).

**Glossary of terms**

**algorithm:** stepwise specification of how to perform some task. For instance, a recipe is an informal algorithm for making a dish. At the level of grammar, we have to specify a parsing algorithm or generation algorithm to use the grammar in a computational system: see Section 6.5.
**ATN:** Augmented Transition Network: a recursive transition network, augmented with conditions under which arcs can be selected and actions to be taken if they are selected; conditions may refer to and actions may manipulate registers. ATNs have usually been used to represent parsing grammars, but also occasionally to specify generation grammars, as in Simmons and Slocum (1972) and Goldman (1974). More recently, McKeown (1985) has used the ATN formalism to represent text structure: cf. Section 3.3.3.
**backward chaining:** In AI, direction of inference, particularly in a production system: working from actions to conditions of actions. In the context of a system network, it entails working from right to left, from more delicate to less delicate. In particular, the entry condition of a system is inferred to hold from the selection of one of its features. See Section 12.3.3 on the use of backward chaining in Patten's (1988a) systemic, semantically driven generator.
**case role:** See: transitivity functions.
**category:** In systemic theory, category is the principle kind of construct or abstraction; the categories of the theory of grammar are units, functions, classes, and so on (cf. Halliday, 1961). This contrasts with the use of category in formal grammar, which is more usually reserved for the concept of *phrase* category. The systemic term for this is the traditional term *class* (as in word class).
**chooser and inquiry framework:** A framework for making semantically motivated grammatical choices. Each system in the grammatical system network is equipped with a chooser. It is organized as a decision or discrimination tree, where the branches are defined by inquiries. The

chooser presents an inquiry at a time to the *environment* of the grammar and its chooser and inquiry interface; the response constitutes a branch in the decision tree of the chooser. The chooser of a system will select one of the system's terms after asking one or more inquiries. See Section 6.4 for an introduction, Sections 7.2 and 7.3 for examples, and Section 8.4 for some possible extensions.

**circumstance:** Generalized transitivity function in the clause, which consists of a process, participants involved in it, and attendant circumstances which include Locative, Extent, Cause, Manner, Matter, Accompaniment, and Role. Participants tend to be more centrally involved with the process than circumstances, which are consequently said to be attendant or more peripheral.

**class:** The systemic term for the term *category* in formal grammar. It generalizes the traditional notion of word classes and thus applies to morphemes, groups, phrases, and clauses as well as words. The least delicate classes are sometimes called primary classes and further differentiations are secondary classes.

**clause complex:** Halliday's (1981/1965, 1985a) term for a combination of clauses related paratactically or hypotactically but not through embedding; the mode of combination is the mode of organization of the logical subtype of the ideational metafunction — i.e., interdependency (see Sections 8.1 and 8.2). For example, clauses combined through coordination form a clause complex. The term clause complex corresponds roughly to the non-systemic term *clause combining*, except a clause complex never involves embedding and 'clause combining' may include embedding (i.e., constructions where one clause serves as a constituent in another unit as if it were a group/phrase or word).

**cline:** Introduced in Halliday (1961), in opposition to a hierarchy of discrete terms, as a continuum along a single dimension with potentially infinite gradation. 'Cline' might be glossed as scale, except that this term has a special technical sense, particularly in early systemic linguistics.

**cohesion:** The textual lexicogrammatical resources for expressing relations within text without creating grammatical structure. The cohesive resources include reference, substitution/ellipsis, conjunction, and lexical cohesion. The term cohesion is also used in non-systemic literature, sometimes in direct reference to systemic work on cohesion (particularly, Halliday and Hasan, 1976), sometimes more loosely to refer to the 'textness' of a text.

**collocation:** Non-structural, lexical relation between lexical items, measured as the likelihood of their co-occurrence in text. For instance, *regret* and *deeply* collocate.

**complex:** Complex of grammatical units of any rank or class, potentially lineally recursive; complexes include *coordination* (extending complexes)

and *apposition* (elaborating complexes).
**conflation:** Realization operator used to specify the identity of two functions, as in Agent/Subject. Corresponds to what is sometimes called *assignment* in non-systemic work (as in function assignment). See Section 6.3.
**congruent:** The 'literal' as opposed to the metaphorical realization of meaning: the congruence between semantics and lexicogrammar (Halliday, 1985a: Ch. 10). See Section 5.5.3 for grammatical metaphor and cf. Section 8.3 for interpersonal examples.
**context:** Context of culture; context of situation. Higher-order semiotic systems above the linguistic system. Context spans field, tenor, and mode. (In earlier writings, context was used for what is now called semantics.) The term context is also used widely in non-systemic literature, sometimes in the systemic sense, sometimes not. Frames, schemas, and scripts within cognitive psychology and AI are similar to situation and situation type in many respects. The notions of context of situation and context of culture originate with Bronislaw Malinowski, an anthropologist working in the first half of this century. Doing field work in the Trobriand Islands, he came to recognize and argue for the importance of context in the interpretation of text. His work on context was further developed within linguistics first by Firth and then by Halliday and others. For an introduction and relation of context to the linguistic system proper, see Sections 5.5 and 12.1; for a discussion of how to 'uncover' contextual categories viewed as the environment of a systemic generator, see Chapter 9.
**data structure:** Information to be interpreted and used by processes in a program. For instance, a system network is a data structure that can be interpreted for parsing as well as for generation (cf. Section 5.9 and see Section 6.5 for the generation interpretation of the system network).
**declarative:** A representation of information that does not commit to any particular way of processing the information. 'Declarative' contrasts with 'procedural'. A procedural representation embeds the information in particular ways of using it. Thus, a declarative representation is neutral between parsing and generation, whereas a procedural representation would be either a parsing procedure or a generation procedure. cf. the discussion of synoptic and dynamic in Section 5.9.
**delicacy:** The scale from general to specific. In a system network, delicacy corresponds to the ordering of systems from left to right by means of entry conditions. (Sections: 5.7.2 on paradigmatic organization; 6.5.3 on the traversal algorithm.)
**domain:** Knowledge domain: computational linguistic notion comparable to the systemic notion of a particular field (see Section 5.5.4). A domain model is the model of a particular domain of knowledge in the knowledge base.

**entry condition:** The condition under which the options specified by a system are available; that is, in terms of the traversal of the system network, the condition under which the system can be reached. An entry condition is a simple feature or a complex of features. See Section 6.1 for the description of the entry condition, Section 6.5.3 for the role of entry condition in system network traversal and Section 8.1 for entry conditions in logical systems.
**environment:** The resources of the generator 'above' the grammar and its chooser and inquiry interface — the ideation base, the interaction base, and the text base: see Chapter 9.
**Exchange:** Metaphor for talking about the fundamental organization of dialogue and the context in which the speech functions are used. The interactants in a dialogue engage in a symbolic exchange of meanings. For instance, one interactant may move the dialogue forward by demanding information, thus assigning himself or herself the role of 'questioner' but also assigning the addressee the complementary role of intended 'answerer'. (See Section 8.4 on the interpersonal cluster of inquiries, and Section 9.3 on the interaction base.)
**experiential:** One of the two subtypes of the ideational metafunction. It is the resource for representing experience. Its mode of organization is constituency and its typical organizational units are configurations of a process, participants and circumstances. It corresponds (more or less) to what has been called functions of Darstellung, representation, denotation, cognitive content, propositional content, semantics. (Sometimes these non-systemic terms include the other subtype of the ideational metafunction, the logical metafunction, sometimes not.) See Sections 8.1, 9.1, and 9.2.
**feature:** The label for a term in a system; it can be semantic, lexicogrammatical, or phonological. For instance, in the system 'indicative/imperative', there are two terms, the features 'indicative' and 'imperative' (Section 6.1). 'Feature' is also used widely in non-systemic literature — extensively in phonology and lexical semantics and increasingly in grammar, in particular in Generalized Phrase Structure Grammar, Lexical Functional Grammar, and Head-driven Phrase Structure Grammar. Although these now attempt specification of theories of features, their use has not entailed the systemicization of features found in systemic accounts. More recently, however, features are increasingly organized into subsumption lattices (as in Head-driven Phrase Structure Grammar) which begins to approximate the organization of features found in systemic accounts; this similarity is discussed in depth in Bateman (1990d).
**field:** Field of discourse; one of the aspects of context (Section 5.5.4). The field is the social activity relevant to a text; it includes the traditional notion of subject matter. It may be similar to certain uses of the term domain in computational linguistics.

**forward chaining:** In AI, direction of inference, particularly in a production system: working from conditions of actions to actions. In the context of a system network, it entails working from left to right, from less delicate to more delicate. In particular, moving from the satisfaction of a system's entry condition to the selection of one of its terms (see Section 6.5.3).
**frame:** A unit — typically a conceptual or semantic unit — structured as a configuration of slots (roles) to be filled by other units. For instance, a meal can be represented as a frame with slots for the various courses. Similarly, a car can be represented as a frame whose slots are its subparts. Knowledge representation systems making use of frames are called frame-based (see Section 9.2).
**types of function:** (i) micro-function: functionally defined constituent; e.g. Subject, Actor, Theme. (ii) macro-function: language use in early child-language, before use and metafunction have become differentiated. (iii) metafunction: generalized functional principle of linguistic organization. There are three metafunctions — ideational (experiential + logical), interpersonal, and textual (Section 5.6).
**function structure:** A function structure (or structure for short) is made up of a configuration of grammatical (micro-)functions such as Actor, Subject, and Theme. Each function may be realized by either a set of grammatical features or a set of lexical features. The grammatical feature set constitutes a preselection of features that have to be chosen when the grammar is re-entered to develop a function further. For example, the function Actor may have the associated preselection 'nominal group', which means that once the structure of the clause of which Actor is a constituent has been fully defined, the grammar is re-entered and Actor is developed as a nominal group (cf. Section 6.5). The term function structure is used inside and outside systemic linguistics. It always refers to a configuration of functions, but in certain non-systemic theories there may be only one functional layer. In systemic theory, function structure is contrasted with syntagm (Halliday, 1966). In Lexical Functional Grammar, there is a similar contrast between function structure (f-structure) and constituent structure (c-structure).
**generation:** Construction (synthesis) of linguistic units such as clauses or text. A generation grammar is thus a grammar for constructing clauses, clause complexes, and so on (in response to some semantic specification). Note that a generation grammar is not the same as a generative grammar; the latter is generative in the mathematical sense of the term and is, in theory, neutral with respect to generation and parsing.
**Generic Structure Potential (GSP):** GSP is Hasan's (1978; Halliday and Hasan, 1985) term for a statement of the resources for structuring a particular type of text. 'Generic' is related to genre: the structure defined

for a particular genre such as a type of service encounter, a type of advertisement, or a nursery tale. 'Potential' refers to the fact that a given generic structure potential specifies the set of possible structures for a defined genre. Hasan's GSP is formally similar in most respects to McKeown's (1982, 1985) later notion of rhetorical schema (see Section 3.3.3). There are also similar but genre-specific constructs such as narrative structure. Matthiessen (1988c) presents a detailed comparison of GSP and rhetorical schemas.

**goal:** The projected purpose or end state of an action or a sequence of actions to be undertaken. A goal or a set of goals is the input for planning (cf. Section 2.1). In the context of text generation, goals are specified as the mental states to be attained in the reader (listener) after having read (heard) the text to be produced. Note that this is quite a different sense to that employed in the use of Goal as a functional label in systemic function structures.

**grammar:** The term has the traditional sense in systemic theory. That is, it includes syntax as well as morphology, the two simply having different domains on the grammatical rank scale. Grammar is taken to be the most general part of lexicogrammar, the resource for expressing meanings. The other part of lexicogrammar is lexis (vocabulary). In linguistic work influenced by Chomsky, however, grammar is the model of the overall linguistic system: it includes semantics and phonology as well as syntax (and morphology).

**grammatical metaphor:** See: *congruent*.

**group:** Group is the rank between clause rank and word rank: groups function in clauses and are composed of words. A group is in many respects a group of words or a *word complex*: words enter into logical structure to form a group. This aspect of the group explains the difference from the *phrase*; a phrase does not have a logical (univariate) structure but rather an experiential (multivariate) structure: the structure of the prepositional phrase is like a miniature of the clause, viz. Minorprocess: preposition + Minirange: nominal group. In the terms of Bloomfield (1933), we can say that groups are endocentric and phrases are exocentric. If groups were only word complexes, we would not need them as a separate rank; there is more to them than logical structure. The degree to which other metafunctions contribute to their structuring depends on the class of group: cf. Halliday (1985a: Ch. 6).

Outside systemic linguistics, the distinction between group and phrase is not usually made; *phrase* is the usual term for both (cf. noun phrase, verb phrase, and prepositional phrase). While the nominal group of systemic linguistics is comparable to the noun phrase in formal grammar (although they are interpreted in terms of different types of structure), the verbal

group is not equivalent to the verb phrase; the verbal group is a purely verbal construct (i.e., concerned with verbs and their combination) while the verb phrase is roughly the predicate of traditional grammar and logic.
**hub:** A hub is the term used within generation systems of the Penman type for entities in the *environment*. It allows us to talk about responses to identifying inquiries without making any commitments concerning particular representations of semantics. See Section 9.2.2.
**hypotaxis:** One of the two types of logical interdependency (see Section 8.1), the other one being parataxis (Halliday, 1981/1965, 1985a: Ch. 7). Hypotaxis is interdependency where the interdependents are of unequal status — dependency. The traditional term subordination does usually not differentiate hypotaxis and embedding (rankshifted clauses). The term hypotaxis is also used outside systemic linguistics, but not necessarily in the same sense.
**ideational:** One of the metafunctions: language as ideation. It comprises two modes of 'ideating', the logical and the experiential. It corresponds roughly to non-systemic terms such as Darstellung, representational, (semantic) content, prepositional content and semantics. While ideational is often equated with semantics outside systemic linguistics, it is treated as a metafunction in systemic linguistics and applies to grammar as well as to semantics. See Sections 5.6, 8.1, and 9.2.
**interpersonal:** One of the metafunctions (see Section 5.6; cf. Sections 8.3 on interpersonal inquiry networks and 9.3 on the interaction base): language as interaction. The resources for establishing and maintaining the relationship between speaker and listener. It combines Bühler's conative and expressive functions, which are simply different orientations (towards addressee and speaker) within the interpersonal metafunction in the linguistic system (cf. the notion of inter-act in entry on speech act).
**interdependency:** One of the modes of syntagmatic and paradigmatic organization found in systemic theory (Halliday, 1979; see Section 8.1). The others are: constituency, pulse (period), and prosody.
**KEY:** Interpersonal region, with the information unit as point of origin. It includes those speech functional distinctions not expressed by MOOD systems in the clause and realized by TONE selections at the level of phonology (falling vs. rising pitch and many elaborations of this basic distinction).
**knowledge base:** (i) Organization of information pertaining to particular domains of knowledge as well as highly general knowledge (called ideation base here for greater precision; see Section 9.2). (ii) Also used in the more general sense of 'resource' used by processes in a computational system (see Section 2.1). In this sense, the grammar (syntax + morphology) of a system is a knowledge base used by generation or parsing processes.

**knowledge representation:** Notation for representing 'knowledge', such as a semantic (conceptual) net, frames, or some form of logic (e.g., predicate calculus); cf. Section 9.2.
**lexicogrammar:** The combination of grammar and lexis (vocabulary); the resources for expressing meaning as wordings. Outside of systemic linguistics, grammar and lexis are almost always treated as distinct modules (cf. Section 5.6.3) and lexis is modelled as the lexicon (though the lexicon also includes lexical semantics and phonological information).
**logical:** A subtype, together with experiential, of the ideational metafunction (see Sections 5.6 and 8.1). (The term is also used widely outside systemic linguistics in the sense of pertaining to logic.) This is the metafunction providing the resources for creating clause complexes and other complexes, for representing serial time by means of serial tense, and so on.
**machine translation:** Translation from one language (the source language) to another (the target language) or several others by means of computer, either completely automatically or semi-automatically. There are various methods. For instance, the translation may involve only representations in the source language and the target language; or it may operate in terms of an interfacing representation (an 'interlanguage' or 'interlingua'). See Section 13.3. for references.
**metafunctions:** The highly generalized functions language (at the levels of semantics and lexicogrammar) has evolved to serve and which are evidenced in its organization. Halliday (1967a, 1968) identifies three metafunctions, the ideational, the interpersonal, and the textual. The ideational metafunction can be further differentiated into the experiential and logical subtypes. Ideational grammar is often treated as semantics outside of systemic linguistics, while textual and interpersonal grammar are dealt with partly under the heading of pragmatics. Metafunction differs from function in the sense of use, which is a way of employing the linguistic resources from an external point of view, not reflected in the organization of the system itself. See Section 5.6.
**mode:** One of the components of *context*. It represents the role played by language in the speech interaction, including the medium (spoken, written, written to be spoken, etc.) as well as the rhetorical mode (expository, instructive, persuasive, etc.). Mode is a second-order category in the sense that it is brought into existence by the existence of language itself. See Section 5.5.4. (The term mode is also used in other ways in linguistics, for example, as the name of the distinction between *realis* and *irrealis*.)
**Mood:** Interpersonal clause function, in the interpretation of the English clause as interaction. It typically includes Subject and Finite, but may also include modal adjuncts (more specifically, mood Adjuncts).

**MOOD:** Interpersonal clause region; the grammaticalization of speech function in the clause (accompanied by KEY in the information unit). Also used outside of systemic linguistics. (Note that mood is also used for morphological categories such as the subjunctive.)
**multivariate:** A type of structure: the functions of a multivariate structure stand in different kinds of relation to one another. For example, the functions of the transitivity structure of the clause all have different values — Actor, Process, Goal, Locative, and so on. Contrasts with univariate. See Section 8.1.
**network:** A relational type of organization; a graph. Examples include discrimination networks, the networks of stratificational theory, and system networks. In systemic theory, a network is specifically a system network.
**parser:** A component consisting of a lexicogrammar and a parsing algorithm with the ability to assign grammatical interpretations to incoming strings of words. The process of using such a component for the recovering of grammatical description is called parsing: a parsing algorithm uses a grammar and a dictionary to perform the analysis. For discussions of systemic parsers, see, e.g., Kasper (1988, 1989b), O'Donnell (1989b), Bateman and Momma (1991), and Winograd (1972, 1983); also Section 13.2.
**path augmentation:** The computation of the path from a preselected feature in a system to the root of thc system network, i.e. of the path that leads to the feature (see Section 6.5).
**phrase:** Like groups, phrases constitute the rank intermediate between clauses and words. However, unlike groups (*q.v.*) they are not logically structured groups of words, but rather more like miniature clauses. In non-systemic work, phrase is often the common term for both group and phrase (no distinction is made).
**planning:** Activity in response to a goal undertaken in pursuit of that goal. Planning is one of the major research areas in AI and text planning (cf. Section 2.1) is one application of AI planning techniques.
**POLARITY:** The term for the system 'positive/negative' and for the region including this system (cf. Section 8.3.4). Often simply called negation outside systemic linguistics.
**potential:** The representation of what a language user can do, as in meaning potential = what he/she can mean. It contrasts with actual, what he/she does (i.e., potential vs. actual = can do vs. does). The actual is the actualization of the potential (see Sections 5.9 and 6.5).
**preselection:** Selection of a feature before it is actually encountered; preselection takes place from one stratum to the stratum next below or from one rank to the rank next below (allowing for the possibility of rankshift); see Section 6.3. Preselection is partly similar to various feature

spreading conventions, as used e.g. in Generalized Phrase Structure Grammar.
**problem solving:** Problem solving, as developed in AI, involves identifying solutions applicable to some problem and choosing among the solutions. Patten (1988a) models systemic text generation as problem solving (cf. Section 12.3).
**procedural:** A procedural representation embodies knowledge of the linguistic resources (grammar, semantics, etc.) in a program for generation or understanding; for instance, there is no separation between a grammar and the program used to run the grammar in generation.
**rank (scale):** A hierarchy of units such as clause–group/phrase–word–morpheme or tone group–foot–syllable–phoneme (see Section 5.8). The rank scale reflects the basic realization patterns. Functions of the units at one rank are realized by units at the rank below. For example, clause functions are realized by groups/phrases and group functions are realized by words. In non-systemic work, the term *level* is sometimes used. (The term rank was used in a different sense in Jespersen's writings.)
**realization:** Term in linguistics in general for a symbolic relationship between content and expression; also expression, coding, etc. Realization and mutation have been contrasted (cf. Gleason, 1965) as basic principles underlying grammatical theories. Systemic grammar is realizational (cf. Sections 5.5, 5.7, and 6.3) whereas transformational grammar is mutational.
**realization operator:** Together with one or more operands, a realization operator makes up a realization statement (see Section 6.3). Realization operators include Insert, Conflate, Expand, and Order. See realization statement.
**realization statement:** A specification of a structure fragment, such as the presence of a function or its ordering in relation to another function, stated as a reexpression of a systemic feature or a combination of features (see Section 6.3). A realization statement consists of one realization operator and one or more operands. For example, the statement (Conflate Subject Agent) consists of the conflation operator Conflate and the operands Subject and Agent, which are grammatical functions.
**register:** A variety of language determined by a particular set of values of the context; it is determined by what the speaker is doing socially. The principle controlling variables are field (of discourse) — type of social action — tenor (of relationship between speaker and listener) — role relationships — and mode — symbolic organization. The notion of register is a generalization of the traditional notion of *genre*; it is also akin to the Prague School notion of *functional dialect*. Registers can be identified at different degrees of delicacy or specificity. For example, we can identify a

particular register as written instruction in how to prepare food — a recipe in a cookery book — or more delicately, as written instruction for an American public in how to prepare Thai food. (The term register is also used in several other senses in linguistics.) See Sections 3.2, 5.10, and 12.5.
**resource:** (i) Functional interpretation of language as strategies for making meaning (see Section 5.4); contrasts with formal interpretation of language as set of rules. (ii) In computational linguistics, declarative (synoptic) specification of data used by process (procedures) — cf. Section 2.1.
**Rhetorical structure theory:** Theory of text organization developed within the Penman project (Section 9.4). It interprets text as being organized relationally. A rhetorical relation is typically asymmetric, related two spans of text, a nucleus and a satellite. The spans of text related rhetorically may have internal organization. A rhetorical relation is defined in terms of the conditions for using it and its intended effect on the addressee. Rhetorical relations correspond partly to *conjunctive relations* (e.g., Martin, in press.).
**scale:** Introduced in Halliday (1961) as the general term for rank, exponence (later, realization), and delicacy. (The term scale is also used widely outside systemic linguistics in the sense of cline.)
**schema:** This term has been used in a number of ways in cognitive psychology, linguistics and AI. It is often used to refer to, in systemic terms, a configuration of elements within a situation type, but interpreted as a cognitive construct (cf. Section 9.2). Often used in the same way as frame.
**script:** This term was introduced into AI by Schank and Abelson; it is associated in particular with Schank's Yale School of AI. A script is a conventional sequence of actions for achieving some purpose. So, for instance, there are scripts for a visit to a restaurant and for a fishing expedition. The idea of script is broadly related to situation type in systemic theory. Broadly speaking, Schank and Abelson responded to the same type of concerns Malinowski had when he introduced his theory of *context* (context of culture and context of situation; Malinowski, 1923). For instance, Malinowski pointed to the impossibility of interpreting text without reference to context, including problems in translation.
**semantic net:** One form of knowledge representation (cf. Section 9.2). A semantic net consists of arcs and nodes. The nodes are typically meanings and the nodes meaning relations. For instance, a node might represent an action and the arcs (pointing to other nodes) would be the participants (say actor and goal) involved in the action.
**semantic roles:** See: *transitivity functions*.
**stratification:** Organization of a symbolic system into different orders of abstraction or levels (strata; cf. Section 5.5). A symbolic system has to be stratified into at least two levels.

**stratum:** A system or a particular order of abstraction in language: semantics, lexicogrammar, and phonology are the three strata in Halliday's version of systemic theory. Strata are related through (interstratal) realization; for instance, semantics is realized through lexicogrammar. The earlier term in systemic linguistics (taken over from Firth) was *level* (as in Firth's levels of analysis); since level was used in other senses in non-systemic linguistics, the equivalent term stratum was taken over from stratificational linguistics. See Section 5.5.
**system:** A system is the central category for representing paradigmatic organization at any stratum – phonological, lexicogrammatical, or semantic. It consists of (i) a statement of a choice between two or more *terms*, represented by *features*, and (ii) an entry condition, which specifies when the choice is available. The entry condition is a simple feature or a feature complex; these features are terms in other systems. Because of their entry conditions, systems form *system networks*. Each term in a system may have one or more realization statements associated with it. See Section 6.1.
**tenor:** One of the components of context (see Section 5.5.4). The role relationship between the interactants in a speech situation. It includes relations of formality, power, and affect. Tenor influences interpersonal choices in the linguistic system. For instance, the strategy chosen for issuing a command depends largely on the tenor of the relationship (cf. Section 9.3).
**text:** As a systemic term, text refers to a semantic unit; it is a stretch of language functioning – doing a job – in context. Note that a text can be either spoken or written.
**text generation:** Automatic construction (synthesis; encoding) of text. The starting point is some specific need for text and the end product is a wording represented graphically or phonetically.
**text plan:** A specification or blueprint for a text to be generated, giving, e.g., the sequences of units to be generated and the rhetorical relations they enter into.
**text understanding:** Automatic analysis (decoding) of text. The starting point is a string of words represented graphically or phonetically and the end product is some kind of semantic or conceptual representation, in some form that allows the text understanding system to reason and draw inferences.
**textual:** One of the systemic metafunctions – the resources for presenting information as text in context (see Sections 5.6, 7.3, 8.2, and 9.4). It includes the resources of theme, information, conjunction, substitution-ellipsis and reference. This area of meaning includes the notions developed within the Functional Sentence Perspective (FSP) of the Prague School, particularly something like the Theme ^ Rheme structure in English.
**Theme:** Textual clause function: the point of departure of the clause as

message. It sets up the local context for each clause. This local context often relates to the method of development of the text: the Theme is selected in such a way that it indicates how the clause is related to this method and contributes to the identification of the current step in the development (Section 9.4). The term *theme* has an entirely different meaning in formal grammars (as does the term *thematic roles*) — particularly in Government and Binding theory: this has nothing to do with the long tradition of work on theme in Prague School linguistics and other functional traditions.

**transition network:** Network representation of a finite state machine. The network consists of nodes and arcs; the nodes represent states and the arcs represent transitions between arcs. Recursive transition networks and augmented transition networks are extensions of the basic transition network.

**transitivity functions (roles):** The functions in the experiential structure of the clause — its transitivity structure (clause as representation): process, participants, and circumstances. Outside of systemic linguistics, *case roles* and *semantic roles* have been used for different but related interpretations of the same area of language. One difference has to do with the level (stratum) at which these roles are posited: in systemic theory they are at the level of grammar, whereas outside systemic theory they are nowadays usually treated as part of (lexical) semantics. In systemic theory, there are correlates at the semantic level; but both semantics and grammar are needed in the interpretation of transitivity, for instance to handle grammatical metaphor in this area. Another difference in the theoretical status of case roles or deep cases vs. transitivity functions is that inventories of the former are often taken to be universal where the transitivity functions presented in e.g. Halliday (1985a: Ch. 5) are not.

**unification-based grammars:** A family of grammars where there is a clear separation between data structure specifying grammatical information and procedures for using these data structures. Grammar is interpreted as a set of data structures and these are brought together, e.g., in the specification of a sentence, by means of an operation of *unification*. Grammar is here seen as a set of descriptions and using the grammar means unifying (combining) these partial descriptions to produce more complete descriptions.

Unification is largely comparable to the notion of union in set theory, but there are differences; see, e.g., Kay (1979). It is a procedure for combining specifications: the unification will be successful as long as the specifications are not mutually exclusive but will fail if they contradict one another. In his survey of unification grammars, Shieber (1986) includes Martin Kay's Functional Unification Grammar, Bresnan and Kaplan's Lexical Functional

Grammar, and Gazdar *et al.*'s Generalized Phrase Structure Grammar. He does not discuss Systemic Functional Grammar, but it also belongs with this family of grammars (cf. Winograd, 1983, on feature and function grammars; Kasper, 1988, on the intertranslatability between Systemic Functional Grammar and Functional Unification Grammar; and Section 13.2).

**unit:** Units are ordered by the rank scale (of a particular stratum) and are structured. The systemic notion of 'unit' is, in many respects, comparable to the AI use of the term 'frame' (cf. Halliday's (1961) description of a meal).

**univariate:** A type of structure, opposed to multivariate. In a univariate structure, each function stands in the same relation to the others. For example, as we build up a coordinate structure, each new element is related to the previous simply as the 'next' link in the coordination chain: Tom [Next:] Dick [Next:] Harry [Next:] Sue [Next:] and Hellen. There are two types of univariate structure, hypotactic structure and paratactic structure. See Sections 8.1 and 8.2.

**word:** In systemic linguistics, the next to lowest rank on the rank scale in e.g. English (cf. Section 5.8.1). In systemic theory, morphology is simply word grammar, i.e., the grammar of units of a particular rank, but it is not separated from 'syntax'.

**wording:** The term is taken from 'folk linguistics'. Wording is the output of lexicogrammar to be realized phonologically or graphologically: the combination of 'words' (i.e., lexical items) and structure.

## Note

1. For terms in systemic linguistics, see de Joia and Stenton (1980) and the glossary at the end of Halliday and Martin (1981).

# Appendix II: Annotated trace of generation with the Nigel grammar

This appendix contains extracts from an annotated 'dribble file' created when actually running through the Nigel grammar. It gives some indication of the range of information that is typically required during generation. More specifically, the trace gives a very concrete sense of the operations that are performed while the grammar is generating — this should clarify the discussions in, for example, Chapter 7 onwards, where all the mechanisms that we describe should be seen as functioning in the context of generation of the kind we illustrate here. In addition, where it has been thought useful, the responses given for certain inquires are explained in more detail; however, for reasons of length, only the pass through the grammar for clause rank is mentioned, and even here, we have abbreviated the later stages once the general principles are clear.

The sentence being generated is: *Whom was the third message sent?* This was selected on the basis of its being short and yet a normal clause without much internal structure. It is not, however, a straight declarative clause so as to add some interest.

In the trace, the information produced by the Nigel system is in a teletype-like typeface and the responses the system received from the environment are underlined. This is all information that one can obtain directly from the Penman system as it is generating. Our annotations to this trace are printed in italics.

## The trace

*Once the system has been requested to produce a sentence, it begins thus:*

```
Starting on bundle:
(-TOP-)
```

```
((PRESELECT -TOP- NIL))
Currently constructing a constituent associated with hub: EG25
Given preselections are: NIL
Preselections after path augmentation are:
NIL
```

*Generation begins by selecting a particular constituent to realize, in this case the very top constituent, identified by the pseudo function 'TOP', informing the user of the preselections that hold for that constituent, in this case there are none, and identifying the knowledge base entity that is about to be interrogated in order to drive the generation, i.e., 'EG25'. This is all done by the chooser associated with the very first grammatical system to be entered: the RANK system; the options that this system offers are 'clauses/groups/words' as shown in Figure 6.1 of Chapter 6.*

```
  System RANK associates hub EG25 with ONUS as CONCEPT
```

*The first step of generation is to make the knowledge base entity that is to be realized in English accessible to the grammar's choosers. This is achieved by means of placing an appropriate entry in the 'function association table': in this case the required knowledge base entity is associated with the special grammatical function 'ONUS'. All subsequent inquiries that need to find out about the knowledge base entity 'EG25' that is to be expressed may then proceed indirectly by using the function 'ONUS' as a parameter.*

```
System RANK is firing from system *TOP-LEVEL*
because of the feature START.

Possible Systems: (RANK)
Entering: RANK

>> Entering System RANK
Entering Chooser RANK-CHOOSER
  SPEAKER-ID: What concept represents the speaker of EG25?
 Environment's answer to Nigel is PC
 System RANK associates hub PC with SPEAKER as CONCEPT
```

*This inquiry interrogates the knowledge base for a pointer to the required speaker of the utterance concerning EG25. The response is the hub name 'PC', which is subsequently associated with the grammatical function SPEAKER. Subsequently, if any inquiry needs to find out information concerning the speaker of the clause at issue, a reference to the function SPEAKER will serve, via the function association table, to get to the right portion of the interaction base.*

```
HEARER-ID: What concept represents the hearer or hearers of EG25?
Environment's answer to Nigel is READER
System RANK associates hub READER with HEARER as CONCEPT
```

*And similarly for that portion of the interaction base that represents the intended hearer; in this case, the knowledge base entity known as READER is made accessible to the inquiry process by association with the grammatical function HEARER.*

```
EXIST-SPEECH-ACT-Q: Does EG25 have its own illocutionary force?
Environment's answer to Nigel is SPEECHACT
```

*This asks whether or not the entity to be expressed includes a statement of illocutionary force; i.e. whether or not it contributes to the text on its own — this is used to distinguish between, say, clauses, which do contribute on their own, and nominal groups and the like, which do not.*

```
Chooser RANK-CHOOSER chooses feature CLAUSES.
```

*The chooser has now drawn sufficient distinctions to be able to select the appropriate grammatical feature from its system; i.e. the grammatical feature 'clauses'. In this case, however, there remains some housekeeping work and initialisations for the chooser to do, so control does not return immediately to the grammar network.*

```
SPEECH-ACT-ID: What is the concept which is the speech act aspect
of EG25?
Environment's answer to Nigel is EG25ACT
System RANK associates hub EG25ACT with SPEECHACT as CONCEPT
```

*Once it is known that the entity to be expressed possesses its own function as a speech act, i.e. its own illocutionary force, it becomes relevant to know what that function is. This inquiry extracts this information from the knowledge base, (in this case the information is held in the portion of the knowledge base picked out by the hub name EG25ACT, returned as a response, and is made accessible to the grammar by means of association with the grammatical function SPEECHACT).*

```
POLARITY-ID: What concept represents the polarity of assertion or
occurrence of EG25ACT?
Environment's answer to Nigel is EG25POLARITY
System RANK associates hub EG25POLARITY with POLARITY as CONCEPT
```

*A speech act is generally performed with respect to some information; this inquiry seeks out the portion of the knowledge base that represents the polarity of that information.*

```
System CLAUSE-CLASS is firing from system RANK
because of the feature CLAUSES.

Possible Systems: (CLAUSE-CLASS)
Entering: CLAUSE-CLASS
```

*Now the work in both chooser and system has been completed and so the next system may be entered. As was the case with the initial entry into the grammar, the generator again reports upon the systems that are enterable (the selection of the feature 'clauses' above may have led on to a whole set of applicable systems — although in this case there was only one such system, CLAUSE-CLASS) and the one that is actually selected for consideration at this time. (N.B. Since this trace is drawn from the full Nigel grammar, the actual systems differ from those shown in, for example, Figure 6.1, which was pruned for expository reasons.)*

---

```
>> Entering System CLAUSE-CLASS
  Entering Chooser CLAUSE-CLASS-CHOOSER
  PROPOSITIONALNESS-Q: Is the speech act EG25ACT one which has a
  propositional parameter?
  Environment's answer to Nigel is PROPOSITIONAL
  Chooser CLAUSE-CLASS-CHOOSER chooses feature CLAUSE.
```

*This system's chooser was able to make a selection of grammatical feature on the basis of just a single inquiry to the knowledge base. Speech acts are considered to take arguments, typically the informational content in some sense of the act that is being performed. The inquiry here asks whether that content is something that could be true or false, and so should appear as a full clause, or not, in which case it might be a call, an exclamation, a greeting, etc. Here it is propositional.*

```
System CLAUSE-ELLIPSIS is firing from system CLAUSE-CLASS
because of the feature CLAUSE.

Possible Systems: (CLAUSE-ELLIPSIS)
Entering: CLAUSE-ELLIPSIS
```

---

```
>> Entering System CLAUSE-ELLIPSIS
  Entering Chooser CLAUSE-ELLIPSIS-CHOOSER
    ANSWER-Q: Is the speechact EG25ACT an answer, i.e. a response
    statement, to a question?
  Environment's answer to Nigel is NONANSWER
  Chooser CLAUSE-ELLIPSIS-CHOOSER chooses feature FULL.
```

***Another simply made choice — here the inquiry is concerned about the type of speech act that EG25ACT represents. If it is a response to a question then there may typically be ellipsis with respect to the information already expressed in the question; here, however, it is not to be treated as a response and so a full clause without ellipsis is to be created.***

```
System DEPENDENCE is firing from system CLAUSE-ELLIPSIS
because of the feature FULL.
System CLAUSE-COMPLEXITY is firing from system CLAUSE-ELLIPSIS
because of the feature FULL.

Possible Systems: (CLAUSE-COMPLEXITY DEPENDENCE)
Entering: CLAUSE-COMPLEXITY
```

***Here for the first time more than one system is enterable on the basis of the features that have been selected; both CLAUSE-COMPLEXITY and DEPENDENCE may appropriately be entered at this time. One of these is selected (see Section 6.5.3).***

---

```
>> Entering System CLAUSE-COMPLEXITY
  Entering Chooser CLAUSE-COMPLEXITY-CHOOSER
    MULTIPLE-PROCESS-Q: Does expression of EG25 represent a
    multiplicity of related processes rather than a single process?
  Environment's answer to Nigel is SINGLE
```

***This inquiry is concerned with whether the portion of the knowledge base named EG25 corresponds to a single event, concept, state, etc. or a collection. This determines whether a single clause is produced or a 'complex' of clauses related in some grammatically specifiable way.***

```
    PROCESS-ID: What concept is the process aspect of EG25 i.e. the
    one which governs the main verb?
  Environment's answer to Nigel is EG25PROCESS
  System CLAUSE-COMPLEXITY associates hub EG25PROCESS with PROCESS
  as CONCEPT
  System CLAUSE-COMPLEXITY associates hub EG25PROCESS-PS with
  PROCESS as MODIFICATION SET
```

***These inquires first extract the portion of the knowledge base that represents the information concerning the principal 'process', understood in a very broad manner subsuming both static and dynamic relations, of the portion of the knowledge base being expressed (EG25). This is made accessible to the generation process by means of relevant associations with the grammatical function PROCESS. Subsequently, the semantic classification of the process required by***

*the PROCESS-TYPE system (Figure 6.1) will operate with respect to this grammatical function; cf. Section 9.2.2.*

REFERENCE-TIME-ID: What concept represents the time of occurrence or the restricted portion of the time of occurrence of EG25PROCESS which this mention of it has in view?

Environment's answer to Nigel is <u>EG25TIME</u>

System CLAUSE-COMPLEXITY associates hub EG25TIME with EVENTTIME as CONCEPT

SPEAKING-TIME-ID: What concept represents the current time, the time at which EG25ACT is generated?

Environment's answer to Nigel is <u>NOW</u>

System CLAUSE-COMPLEXITY associates hub NOW with SPEAKINGTIME as CONCEPT

***Having identified the processual information of the knowledge to be expressed these inquiries then seek out some of the temporal relations involved. The first establishes the time at which the process itself holds, the second the time at which the speech act is performed. The first is made accessible via the grammatical function EVENTTIME, the second via SPEAKINGTIME. These then provide the basic information for the choosers and inquiries that are illustrated in Section 7.2 for the treatment of tense.***

Chooser CLAUSE-COMPLEXITY-CHOOSER chooses feature CLAUSE-SIMPLEX.

***And the chooser can then make its selection of grammatical feature in its system.***

System TRANSITIVITY-UNIT is firing from system CLAUSE-COMPLEXITY because of the feature CLAUSE-SIMPLEX.
System MOOD-UNIT is firing from system CLAUSE-COMPLEXITY because of the feature CLAUSE-SIMPLEX.
System LEXICAL-VERB-TERM-RESOLUTION is firing from system CLAUSE-COMPLEXITY because of the feature CLAUSE-SIMPLEX.
System CONJUNCTION is firing from system CLAUSE-COMPLEXITY because of the feature CLAUSE-SIMPLEX.
Possible Systems: (CONJUNCTION LEXICAL-VERB-TERM-RESOLUTION MOOD-UNIT TRANSITIVITY-UNIT DEPENDENCE)
Entering: CONJUNCTION

***After this selection a whole set of systems become enterable, but selection proceeds on the same basis as before. This information will not be given in the listing from now on, neither will the information concerning which systems follow from the selection of a feature, and the system that is actually entered.***

```
>> Entering System CONJUNCTION
  Entering Chooser CONJUNCTION-CHOOSER
    CONJUNCTIVE-RELATION-Q: Does EG25 specify expressing a rela-
    tionship between the clause being created and one or more
    clauses of prior text?
  Environment's answer to Nigel is NONCONJUNCTIVE
  Chooser CONJUNCTION-CHOOSER chooses feature NONCONJUNCTED.
```

***i.e., does the text plan specify that this clause should be shown as related to the clause preceding or not. This is an example of the textual inquiries of the kind illustrated in Sections 7.3 and 8.3.***

```
>> Entering System DEPENDENCE
  Entering Chooser DEPENDENCE-CHOOSER
    ENTIRENESS-Q: Does EG25ACT represent the entire speech act or is
    it part of a larger one?
  Environment's answer to Nigel is ENTIRE
  Chooser DEPENDENCE-CHOOSER chooses feature INDEPENDENT-CLAUSE.
```

```
>> Triggering gate INDEPENDENT-CLAUSE-SIMPLEX
  Chooser INDEPENDENT-CLAUSE-SIMPLEX-CHOOSER chooses feature
  INDEPENDENT-CLAUSE-SIMPLEX.
```

***By now some gates have been rendered eligible for entry by the features that have been selected. Gates are like systems but do not allow a choice of feature; they are used to group entry conditions and to avoid repetition of realization statements.***

```
>> Entering System MOOD-TYPE
  Entering Chooser MOOD-TYPE-CHOOSER
    COMMAND-Q: Is the illocutionary point of the surface level
    speech act represented by EG25ACT a command, i.e. a request
    of an action by the hearer?
  Environment's answer to Nigel is NOCOMMAND
  Chooser MOOD-TYPE-CHOOSER chooses feature INDICATIVE.
```

***The MOOD-TYPE system is also one of those that appear in Figure 6.1. The 'surface level' in its inquiry simply serves to make explicit the fact that Nigel is not concerned with generating 'indirect speech acts'. If the type of speech act to be generated is a request or a command then it will appear in the most direct form that expresses that. Our discussions of the choosers and inquiries of the interpersonal metafunction in Section 8.4 and their environmental support in***

*Section 9.3 would attach to this part of the grammar if we were to extend Nigel's capabilities in this regard.*

---

```
>> Triggering Gate FINITE-CLAUSE
  In FINITE-CLAUSE, Realizing: (INSERT MOOD)
  In FINITE-CLAUSE, Realizing: (EXPAND MOOD FINITE)
```

*Here the first realization statements have been performed. That is, the grammatical feature selections that have been made so far sanction these constraints being placed upon the grammatical output that is to appear for this cycle through the grammar. Because the grammar has established that the speech act involved is an 'indicative' clause, it is known that the clause must have a finite verb.*

---

```
>> Entering System DEICTICITY
  Entering Chooser DEICTICITY-CHOOSER
    MODALITY-Q: Does the specification EG25PROCESS specify a
    property - inherent or imposed - which constrains the actualiza-
    tion, i.e., occurrence, of this process?
  Environment's answer to Nigel is NONMODEL
    TEMPORAL-DEFINITENESS-Q: Does EG25PROCESS have a definite
    existence, possibly hypothetical, in space and time?
  Environment's answer to Nigel is DEFINITE
  Chooser DEICTICITY-CHOOSER chooses feature TEMPORAL.
  In DEICTICITY, Realizing: (INSERT TEMPOO)
  In DEICTICITY, Realizing: (CONFLATE TEMPOO FINITE)
  In DEICTICITY, Realizing: (OUTCLASSIFY FINITE REDUCED)
```

*Following the establishment that the text plan does not require that the process appear modified in any modal kind of way, the definiteness of the process's existence in time is ascertained. Since it is definite the chooser selects a feature which results in several more constraints concerning the expression of tense and temporal relations upon the structure being generated.*

This should be enough to see the detailed principles of operation of the grammar, choosers, and inquiries during generation. Now, rather than giving the full trace, we will simply list the realization statements that are constrained to apply by the responses to the inquiries. The full trace is given as an example in the appendix to the Nigel Manual part of the Penman documentation (Penman Project, 1989). This list is still quite long, since it is the *complete* specification of clause-rank structure for the example clause as defined with the 1990 version of the Nigel grammar. Each constraint also identifies the grammatical system where the constraint was decided upon.

| | |
|---|---|
| In POSITIVE-FINITE, Realizing: | (OUTCLASSIFY Finite negative) |
| In PRIMARY-TENSE, Realizing: | (CONFLATE Finite Tempo0) |
| In PRIMARY-TENSE, Realizing: | (INFLECTIFY Finite pastform) |
| In FINITE-INSERT, Realizing: | (INSERT Finite) |
| In INTERROGATIVE-TYPE, Realizing: | (INSERT Wh) |
| In INTERROGATIVE-TYPE, Realizing: | (ORDER Wh Finite) |
| In INTERROGATIVE-TYPE, Realizing: | (CONFLATE Topical Wh) |
| In TOPICAL-INSERT, Realizing: | (INSERT Topical) |
| In TOPICAL-INSERT, Realizing: | (EXPAND Theme Topical) |
| In TOPICAL-INSERT, Realizing: | (ORDERATEND Topical) |
| In THEME-ORDER, Realizing: | (ORDERATFRONT Theme) |
| In TRANSITIVITY-UNIT, Realizing: | (INSERT Predicator) |
| In TRANSITIVITY-UNIT, Realizing: | (INSERT Process) |
| In TRANSITIVITY-UNIT, Realizing: | (INSERT Lexverb) |
| In TRANSITIVITY-UNIT, Realizing: | (CONFLATE Lexverb Process) |
| In TRANSITIVITY-UNIT, Realizing: | (EXPAND Predicator Lexverb) |
| In TRANSITIVITY-UNIT, Realizing: | (INSERT Voice) |
| In TRANSITIVITY-UNIT, Realizing: | (EXPAND Predicator Voice) |
| In PROCESS-TYPE, Realizing: | (CLASSIFY Process doverb) |
| In AGENCY, Realizing: | (CLASSIFY Process effective) |
| In PASSIVE-PROCESS, Realizing: | (CLASSIFY Voice be-aux) |
| In PASSIVE-PROCESS, Realizing: | (OUTCLASSIFY Voice negative) |
| In PASSIVE-PROCESS, Realizing: | (INSERT Voicedependent) |
| In PASSIVE-PROCESS, Realizing: | (INFLECTIFY Voicedependent edparticiple) |
| In LEXVERB-VOICEDEPENDENT, Realizing: | (CONFLATE Lexverb Voicedependent) |
| In DOING-TYPE, Realizing: | (CLASSIFY Process disposal) |
| In RECIPIENCY, Realizing: | (INSERT Beneficiary) |
| In RECIPIENCY, Realizing: | (PRESELECT Beneficiary nominal-group) |
| In COMPLEMENT-BENEFICIARY, Realizing: | (INSERT Obliquecomplement) |
| In COMPLEMENT-BENEFICIARY, Realizing: | (PRESELECT Obliquecomplement oblique) |
| In COMPLEMENT-BENEFICIARY, Realizing: | (CONFLATE Beneficiary Obliquecomplement) |
| In SUBJECT-INSERT, Realizing: | (INSERT Subject) |
| In MEDIUM-INSERT, Realizing: | (INSERT Medium) |

```
In GOAL-INSERT-CONFLATE, Realizing:          (INSERT Goal)
In GOAL-INSERT-CONFLATE, Realizing:          (CONFLATE Goal Medium)
In GOAL-INSERT-CONFLATE, Realizing:          (PRESELECT Goal nominal-
                                             group)
In MEDIUM-SUBJECT-CONFLATE, Realizing:       (CONFLATE Medium Subject)
In MOOD-SUBJECT-EXPANSION, Realizing:        (EXPAND Mood Subject)
In NOMINATIVE-SUBJECT, Realizing:            (PRESELECT Subject
                                             nominative)
In FINITE-VOICE, Realizing:                  (CONFLATE Finite Voice)
In SINGULAR-FINITE, Realizing:               (INFLECTIFY Finite
                                             singular)
In SINGULAR-FINITE, Realizing:               (INFLECTIFY Finite third-
                                             person)
In FINITE-SUBJECT, Realizing:                (ORDER Finite Subject)
In WH-FUNCTION-III, Realizing:               (CONFLATE Wh Oblique-
                                             complement)
In WH-INTERROGATIVE-NOMINAL, Realizing:(PRESELECT Wh
                                             interrogative-nominal)
```

After passing through all the above-mentioned systems (and several others not reported here because they did not have their own realization statements attached), the cycle concerned with generating the clause rank structure is complete. The complete list of grammatical features selected during this cycle through the grammar was the following (partially ordered from most delicate to least delicate)

```
(lexical-verb-term-resolution wh-interrogative-nominal wh-
oblique-complement nonassertive no-wh-subject finite-subject
nonwh-subject no-temporal-location no-temporal-extent no-
spatial-location no-spatial-extent nonrole do-needing-verbs
singular-finite finite-voice real nonplural-subject nominative-
subject mood-subject-expanded medium-subject-conflated goal
medium-inserted subject-inserted explicit-interrogative-subject
indicative-noninteractant noncomplemented complement-
beneficiary nonagentive-medioreceptive benefactive recipiency
dispositive lexverb-voicedependent passive-process nonagentive
effective-material effective material nonmatter nonmanner
noncause nonaccompaniment transitivity-unit theme-order topical-
insert unmarked-positive wh interrogative no-secondary finite-
inserted past positive-finite positive temporal finite-clause
indicative noninternal-subject-matter independent-clause-
simplex independent-clause mood-unit nonconjuncted clause-
simplex full clause clauses start)
```

The constraints that have been specified on the structure by collecting together the realization statements are then:

```
1: Function structure:

  ((TOPICAL WH BENEFICIARY OBLIQUECOMPLEMENT)
   (VOICE FINITE TEMPOO)
   (SUBJECT GOAL MEDIUM)
   (VOICEDEPENDENT LEXVERB PROCESS))
```

This describes the completed clause rank, or level, of constituent structure generated by this pass through the grammar network. It states that there are four main constituents and each of these is composed of several grammatical functions. The four constituents correspond to the embedded lists, thus:

```
Constituent  Component grammatical functions
    1        (TOPICAL WH BENEFICIARY OBLIQUECOMPLEMENT)
    2        (VOICE FINITE TEMPOO)
    3        (SUBJECT GOAL MEDIUM)
    4        (VOICEDEPENDENT LEXVERB PROCESS)
```

If we were to continue without performing any further realizations, i.e., traversals through the grammar, then the following would be the result of generation:

```
   Realized as:

   (TOPICAL+WH+BENEFICIARY+OBLIQUECOMPLEMENT ''was''
    SUBJECT+GOAL+MEDIUM ''sent'')
```

This structural result is in the standard form that is produced following generation when there remain cycles through the grammar that need to be undertaken in order to complete the generation process. In this case, constituent 2 (Voice Finite Tempo0) and constituent 4 (Voicedependent Lexverb Process) have already been assigned lexical items and so there is no need to elaborate them further grammatically. The remaining two constituents need to have their own passes through the grammar to determine their internal structure.

One can also tell that further cycles are needed because in the 'realized as' line not all constituents have been replaced by lexical items; two constituents remain unrealized. The information given for these constituents consists of the preselections that have been declared to hold for those constituents. The next stage in generation is to re-enter the grammar for cycles responsible for each of the two outstanding constituents. Essentially

**the same process as has been shown here takes place and so this will not be shown. The entire generation process ends with no lexical gaps in the structure produced and no constituents with preselections on them calling for grammar re-entry. If we had done this then the following would have been produced.**

```
  Realized as:

  (''whom'' ''was'' ''the'' ''third'' ''response'' ''sent'' ''?'')

Generated string:
Whom was the third response sent?
```

**This structure can also be presented in graphical form as shown in Figure AII.1. This is the standard graphical form of display provided by the Penman system. Conflation of functions is represented horizontally by separating functions by '/'.**

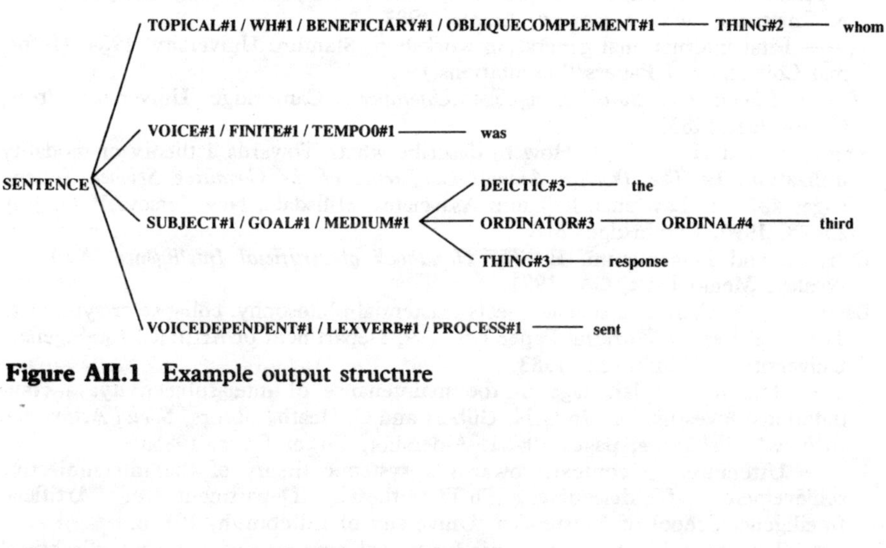


**Figure AII.1** Example output structure

# Bibliography


Abeille, A., Bishop, K., Cote, S. and Schabes, Y. A lexicalized tree adjoining grammar for English. Technical report. University of Pennsylvania, August 1989.

Agre, P.E. Dynamic structure of everyday life. Technical Report AI-TR 1085, MIT, Cambridge, MA, October 1988.

Appelt, D.E. TELEGRAM: a grammar formalism for language planning. In *Proceedings of the Eighth National Conference on Artificial Intelligence*, pages 595–9, Karlsruhe, West Germany, August 1983.

——— First international generation workshop; Stanford University, 1984. (Informal Collection of Papers/Presentations.)

——— *Planning Natural Language Utterances*. Cambridge University Press, Cambridge, 1985.

Arens, Y. and Hovy, E.H. How to describe what? Towards a theory of modality utilization. In *The Twelfth Annual Conference of the Cognitive Science Society*, pages 487–94. Lawrence Erlbaum Associates, Hillsdale, New Jersey, 1990. July 25–28, 1990, Cambridge, MA.

Barr, A. and Feigenbaum, E. *The Handbook of Artificial Intelligence*. Addison-Wesley, Menlo Park, CA, 1981.

Bateman, J.A. Cognitive science meets existential philosophy: collapse or synthesis? Technical Report Working Paper No. 139, Department of Artificial Intelligence, University of Edinburgh, 1983.

——— The role of language in the maintenance of inter-subjectivity: a computational investigation. In G.N. Gilbert and C. Heath, editors, *Social Action and Artificial Intelligence*, pages 40–81. Aldershot, Gower Press, 1985a.

——— Utterances in context: towards a systemic theory of the intersubjective achievement of discourse. Ph.D. thesis, Department of Artificial Intelligence/School of Epistemics, University of Edinburgh, 1985b.

——— Text planning for a systemic-functional grammar of Japanese. Technical report, Department of Electrical Engineering, Kyoto University, Kyoto, Japan, 1986.

——— Aspects of clause politeness in Japanese: an extended inquiry semantics treatment. In *Proceedings of the 26th International Conference on Computational Linguistics*, pages 147–54. Buffalo, New York, 1988. Association for Computational Linguistics. Also available as ISI Reprint Series report RS-88-211, USC/Information Sciences Institute, Marina del Rey, CA.

——— Dynamic systemic-functional grammar: a new frontier. *Word*, 40 (1/2): 263–86, 1989a.

——— Upper modelling for machine translation: a level of abstraction for preserving meaning. Technical Report EUROTRA-D Working Papers, No. 12, Institut für Angewandte Informationsforschung, Saarbrücken, West Germany, 1989b.

——— Uncovering textual meanings: a case study involving systemic-functional resources for the generation of Japanese texts. Presented at the Fourth International Workshop on Natural Language Generation. Santa Catalina Island, CA, July, 1988. In C.L. Paris, W.R. Swartout, and W.C. Mann, editors, *Natural Language Generation in Artificial Intelligence and Computational Linguistics*. Kluwer Academic Publishers, Dordrecht, July 1990. 1990a.

——— Finding translation equivalents: an application of grammatical metaphor. In *13th International Conference on Computational Linguistics (COLING-90)*, Volume II, pages 13–18, Helsinki, Finland, 1990b.

——— Upper modelling: current states of theory and practise, 1990c. PENMAN Development Note, USC/Information Sciences Institute.

——— Language as constraint and language as resource: a convergence of metaphors in systemic-functional grammar. Technical report, GMD/Institut für Integrierte Publikations- und Informationssysteme, Darmstadt, Germany, 1991. Paper presented at the International Workshop on Constraint-based Formalisms for Natural Language Generation, 27–30 November 1990, Bad Teinach. 1990d.

Bateman, J.A. and Hovy, E.H. Computers and text generation: principles and uses. In C.S. Butler, editor, *Computers and Texts: An Applied Perspective*. Basil Blackwell, Oxford, England, 1991.

Bateman, J.A., Kasper, R.T., Moore, J.D. and Whitney, R.A. A general organization of knowledge for natural language processing: the PENMAN upper model. Technical report, USC/Information Sciences Institute, Marina del Rey, CA, 1990.

Bateman, J.A., Kasper, R.T., Schütz, J.F.L. and Steiner, E.H. A new view on the translation process. In *Proceedings of the European Chapter of the Association for Computational Linguistics*, Manchester, England. April 1989. Association for Computational Linguistics.

Bateman, J.A. and Matthiessen, C.M.I.M. Uncovering the text base. In H. Bluhme and H. Keqi, editors, *Selected Papers from the International Conference on Research in Text and Language, Xi'an Jiaotong University, Xi'an, P.R. China, 29–31 March 1989*. To appear.

Bateman, J.A., Matthiessen, C.M.I.M., Nanri, K. and Zeng, L. Multilingual text generation: an architecture based on functional typology. In *International Conference on Current Issues in Computational Linguistics*, Penang, Malaysia, 1991a. Also available as technical report of the Department of Linguistics, University of Sydney.

——— The re-use of linguistic resources across languages in multilingual generation components. In *Proceedings of the 1991 International Joint Conference on Artificial Intelligence*, Sydney, Australia, 1991b. Los Altos, CA: Morgan Kaufman.

Bateman, J.A. and Momma, S. The nondirectional representation of Systemic Functional Grammars and Semantics as Typed Feature Structures. Technical report, GMD/Institut für Integrierte Publikations- und Informationssysteme, Darmstadt and Institut für Maschinelle Sprachverarbeitung, Universität Stuttgart resp., January 1991.

Bateman, J.A. and Oshika, B.T. Computer generation and control of spoken discourse, 1989. (Declined) Proposal prepared for the National Science

Foundation; Information Sciences Institute, PENMAN note, Marina del Rey, CA.

Bateman, J.A. and Paris, C.L. Phrasing a text in terms the user can understand. In *Proceedings of the Eleventh International Joint Conference on Artificial Intelligence*, Detroit, MI, 1989. IJCAI-89.

——— Constraining the deployment of lexicogrammatical resources during text generation: towards a computational instantiation of register theory. In E. Ventola, editor, *Recent Systemic and Other Views on Language*. Benjamins, Amsterdam, 1990.

Bates, M. and Ingria, R. Controlled transformational sentence generation. In *19th Annual Meeting of the Association for Computational Linguistics*, Stanford University, 1981. Association for Computational Linguistics.

de Beaugrande, R. *Text Production: Toward a Science of Composition*. Ablex, Norwood, NJ, 1984.

Becker, J.D. The phrasal lexicon. In R.C. Schank and B.L. Webber, editors, *Theoretical Issues in Natural Language Processing-1 (TINLAP)*, pages 70–3. Cambridge, MA, 1975.

Benson, J.D. and Greaves, W.S., editors. *Systemic Perspectives on Discourse, Volume I: Selected Theoretical Papers from the 9th International Systemic Workshop*. Ablex, Norwood, NJ, 1985.

Bernstein, B. *Class, Codes, and Control 1: Theoretical Studies Towards a Sociology of Language*. Routledge and Kegan Paul, London, 1971.

Berry, M. Systemic linguistics and discourse analysis: a multilayered approach to exchange structure. In M. Coulthard and M. Montgomery, editors, *Studies in Discourse Analysis*. Routledge and Kegan Paul, London, 1981.

———, editor. *Nottingham Linguistic Circular: Special Issue on Systemic Linguistics*. University of Nottingham, England, 1984.

Bloomfield, L. *Language*. Henry Holt and Co. and Allen and Unwin Ltd., New York and London, 1933.

Bohm, D. *Wholeness and the Implicate Order*. Routledge and Kegan Paul, London, 1979.

Brachman, R.J. A structural paradigm for representing knowledge. Technical Report BBN Report 3605, Bolt, Beraneck and Newman, Inc., Cambridge, MA, 1978.

Brachman, R.J., Fikes, R. and Levesque, H.J. KRYPTON: A functional approach to knowledge representation. *IEEE Computer*, 16 (10), 1983.

Brachman, R.J. and Levesque, H.J., editors. *Readings in Knowledge Representation*. Morgan Kaufman, Los Altos, CA, 1985.

Brachman, R.J. and Schmolze, J. An overview of the KL-ONE knowledge representation system. *Cognitive Science*, 9 (2), 1985.

Bresnan, J. Polyadicity: Part I of a theory of lexical rules and representations. In T. Hoekstra, H. van der Hulstra, and M. Moortgat, editors, *Lexical Grammar*. Foris, Dordrecht, 1980. Also appears in J. Bresnan, editor, *The Mental Representation of Grammatical Relations*. The MIT Press, Cambridge, MA, 1982.

———, editor. *The Mental Representation of Grammatical Relations*, The MIT Press, Cambridge, MA, 1982.

Bresnan, J. and Kaplan, R. Lexical-functional grammar: a formal system for grammatical representation. In J. Bresnan, editor, *The Mental Representation of Grammatical Relations*, pages 173–281. The MIT Press, Cambridge, MA, 1982.

Brew, C. Partial descriptions and systemic grammar. In *13th International*

*Conference on Computational Linguistics (COLING-90)*, pages 36–41, Helsinki, Finland, 1990, Volume I.

Brown, P. and Levinson, S.C. *Politeness: Some Universals in Language Usage*. Cambridge University Press, Cambridge, 1987. Revised version of 'Universals in language usage: politeness phenomena', originally published in E. Goody, editor, *Questions and Politeness: Strategies in Social Interaction*. Cambridge University Press, Cambridge, 1978.

Brown, R. and Gilman, A. The pronouns of power and solidarity. In T. Sebeok, editor, *Style in Language*. The MIT Press, Cambridge, MA, 1960.

Bull, W.E. *Time, Tense and the Verb*. University of California Press, Berkeley and Los Angeles, CA, 1963.

Bühler, K. *Sprachtheorie: die Darstellungsfunktion der Sprache*. Fischer, Jena, 1934.

Burton, D. *Dialogue and Discourse*. Routledge and Kegan Paul, London, 1980.

Butler, C.S. *Systemic Linguistics: Theory and Applications*. Batsford, London, 1985.

——— Communicative function and semantics. In M.A.K. Halliday and R.P. Fawcett, editors, *New Developments in Systemic Linguistics, Volume I*. Frances Pinter, London, 1987.

——— Systemic linguistics, semantics and pragmatics. In E. Steiner and R. Veltman, editors, *Pragmatics, Discourse and Text: Some Systemically Inspired Approaches*. Frances Pinter, London. 1988.

Cadwallader, S. *Cooking Adventures for Kids*. Houghton Mifflin, Boston, MA, 1974.

Caffarel, A. Mediating between grammar and context: bi-stratal exploration of the semantics of French tense. Technical report, Department of Linguistics, University of Sydney, Australia, November 1990. Batchelor's Honours thesis.

Chafe, W.L. Creativity and verbalization and its implications for the nature of stored knowledge. In R.O. Freedle, editor, *Discourse Processes: Advances in Research and Theory. Volume I: Discourse Production and Comprehension*. Ablex, Norwood, 1977.

——— The flow of thought and the flow of language. In T. Givòn, editor, *Syntax and Semantics 12: Discourse and Syntax*, pages 159–81. Academic Press, New York, 1979.

Charniak, E. and Wilks, Y., editors. *Semantic Nets as Memory Models*. North-Holland, Amsterdam, 1976.

Chester, D. The translation of formal proofs into English. *Artificial Intelligence*, 7 (3), 1976.

Chomsky, N. *Lectures on Government and Binding*. Foris, Dordrecht, 1981.

Clancy, P.M. and Downing, P. The use of *wa* as a cohesion marker in Japanese oral narratives. In J. Hinds *et al.*, editors, *Perspectives on Topicalization: The Case of Japanese 'wa'*, pages 3–56. John Benjamins, Amsterdam, 1987.

Clippinger, J. *Meaning and Discourse: A Computer Model of Psychoanalytic Speech and Cognition*. Johns Hopkins University Press, Baltimore, MD, 1978.

Close, R. Will in if-clauses. In S. Greenbaum, G. Leech, and J. Svartvik, editors, *Studies in English Linguistics for Randolph Quirk*. Longman, London, 1979.

Comrie, B. *Aspect* Cambridge University Press, Cambridge, 1976.

Cumming, S. The lexicon in text generation. Technical Report ISI/RR-86-168, USC/Information Sciences Institute, 1986.

Cummings, M. SYSPRO: a computerized method for writing system networks and deriving selection expressions. In R. Steele and T. Threadgold, editors, *Language Topics: Essays in Honour of Michael Halliday*. John Benjamins Publishing Co., Amsterdam and Philadelphia, 1987.

Dahl, Ö. *Tense and Aspect Systems*. Basil Blackwell, Oxford, England, 1985.

Dale, R. Cooking up referring expressions. In *Proceedings of the Twenty-Seventh Annual Meeting of the Association for Computational Linguistics*, Vancouver, BC, June 1989. Association for Computational Linguistics.

Dale, R., Mellish, C.S. and Zock, M., editors. *Current Research in Natural Language Generation*. Academic Press, 1990. Selected Papers from the 1989 European Natural Language Generation Workshop, Edinburgh, April.

Daneš, F. Functional sentence perspectives and the organization of the text. In F. Daneš, editor, *Papers on Functional Sentence Perspectives*, pages 106–28. Academia, Prague, 1974.

Danlos, L. Conceptual and linguistic decisions in generation. In *Proceedings of the 10th International Conference on Computational Linguistics*, pages 319–35, Stanford, CA, July 1984.

——— *The Linguistic Basis of Text Generation*. Cambridge University Press, Cambridge, 1987.

Danlos, L., Laporte, E. and Emerard, F. Synthesis of spoken messages from semantic representations (semantic-representation-to-speech system). In *Proceedings of Coling86: 11th International Conference on Computational Linguistics*, pages 599–604, Bonn, 1986.

Davey, A. *Discourse Production: A Computer Model of Some Aspects of a Speaker*. Edinburgh University Press, Edinburgh, 1978. Published version of Ph.D. dissertation, University of Edinburgh, 1974.

Davis, J.R. and Hirschberg, J. Assigning intonational features in synthesized spoken directions. In *The 26th Annual Meeting of the Association for Computational Linguistics*, pages 187–93, 1988.

Davis, J.R. and Schmandt, C.M. The back seat driver: real time spoken driving instructions. In *IEEE Vehicle Navigation and Information Systems Conference*, pages 146–50, Canada, 1989. IEEE.

Dik, S.C. *Functional Grammar*. North-Holland, Amsterdam, 1978.

——— Generating answers from a linguistically coded knowledge base. In G. Kempen, editor, *Natural Language Generation: Recent Advances in Artificial Intelligence, Psychology, and Linguistics*. Kluwer Academic Publishers, Boston/Dordrecht, 1987. Paper presented at the Third International Workshop on Natural Language Generation, August 1986, Nijmegen, The Netherlands.

Diver, W. The chronological system of the English verb. *Word*, 19, 1963.

Dreyfus, H.L. *What Computers Can't Do: A Critique of Artificial Reason*. Harper and Row, New York, 1972.

——— Heidegger's existential phenomenology, 1977. Unpublished course notes to Philosophy 152B, University of California at Berkeley.

——— From micro-worlds to knowledge representation: AI at an impasse. In J. Haugeland, editor, *Mind Design*, pages 161–204.

Emele, M.C. FREGE: Entwicklung und Implementierung eines objektorientierten Front-End-Generator für das Deutsche. Technical report, University of Stuttgart, 1986. Master's thesis.

Emele, M.C., Heid, U., Momma, S. and Zajac, R. Interactions between linguistic constraints: Procedural vs. declarative approaches. *Journal of Machine Translation*, 1991. Also available as: Project Polygloss Paper, Institut für Maschinelle Sprachverarbeitung, University of Stuttgart, Germany. 1990a.

——— Organizing linguistic knowledge for multilingual generation. In *13th International Conference on Computational Linguistics (COLING-90)*, Helsinki,

Finland, 1990. Also available as: Project Polygloss Paper, Institut für Maschinelle Sprachverarbeitung, University of Stuttgart, Germany. 1990b.

Emele, M.C. and Zajac, R. Typed unification grammars. In *13th International Conference on Computational Linguistics (COLING-90)*, Volume III, pages 293–8, Helsinki, Finland, 1990. Also available as: Project Polygloss Paper, Institut für Maschinelle Sprachverarbeitung, University of Stuttgart, Germany.

Erman, L.D., Hayes-Roth, F., Lesser, V.R. and Reddy, D.R. The HEARSAY-II speech understanding system: Integrating knowledge to resolve uncertainty. *Computing Surveys*, 12: 213–53, 1980. Reprinted in: *Readings in Artificial Intelligence*, B.L. Webber and N.J. Nilssen, editors, pages 349–89. Morgan Kaufman Pub. Inc., Los Altos, CA, 1981.

Ervin-Tripp, S. Sociolinguistics. *Advances in Experimental Social Psychology*, 4, 1969.

Fawcett, R.P. Generating a sentence in systemic functional grammar, 1973. Mimeo. Reprinted in M.A.K. Halliday and J.R. Martin, editors, *Readings in Systemic Linguistics*, 1981.

——— *Cognitive Linguistics and Social Interaction: Exeter Linguistic Studies 3*. Exeter University and Julius Groos Verlag, Exeter and Heidelberg, 1980.

——— Language generation as choice in social interaction. In M. Zock and G. Sabah, editors, pages 27–49, 1988.

——— The computer generation of speech with discoursally and semantically motivated intonation. In *5th International Workshop on Natural Language Generation, 3–6 June 1990*, Pittsburgh, PA, 1990: 164–73a. Organized by K.R. McKeown (Columbia University), J.D. Moore (University of Pittsburgh) and S. Nirenburg (Carnegie Mellon University).

Fawcett, R.P. and Tucker, G.H. Demonstration of GENESYS: a very large semantically based systemic functional grammar. In *Proceedings of 13th International Conference on Computational Linguistics*, Volume I, pages 47–9. Helsinki, 1990.

Fawcett, R.P., van der Mije, A. and van Wissen, C. Towards a systemic flowchart model for discourse structure. In R.P. Fawcett and D. Young, editors, *New Developments in Systemic Linguistics*, Volume 2, pages 116–43. Pinter Publishers, London, 1988.

Fillmore, C.J. The case for case. In E. Bach and R.T. Harms, editors, *Universals in Linguistic Theory*. Holt, Rinehart and Wilson, New York, 1968.

Findler, N.V. *Associative Networks: Representation and Use of Knowledge by Computers*. Academic Press, New York, 1979.

Firbas, J. On defining the theme in functional sentence analysis. *Travaux Linquistique de Prague*, 1: 267–80, 1966.

Foley, W. and Van Valin, R. *Functional Syntax and Universal Grammar*. Cambridge University Press, Cambridge, 1984.

Ford, C.C. Overlapping relations in text structure. In S. De Lancey and R.S. Tomlin, editors, *Proceedings of the Second Annual Meeting of the Pacific Linguistics Conference*, Eugene, 1987. Department of Linguistics, University of Oregon.

Fox, B.A. *Discourse Structure and Anaphora in Written and Conversational English*. Cambridge University Press, Cambridge, 1987.

Friedman, J. Directed random generation of sentences. *Communications of the Association for Computing Machinery*, 12 (6), 1969.

Fries, P.H. On the status of theme in English: arguments from discourse. *Forum Linguisticum*, 6 (1): 1–38, 1981. Reprinted in J.S. Petöfi and E. Soezer, editors,

*Micro and Macro Connexity of Discourse*, Hamburg: Buske (Papers in Text Linguistics 45), 1983.

——— On repetition and interpretation. *Forum Linguisticum*, 7 (1): 50–64, 1982.

——— Language features, textual coherence and reading. *Word*, 37 (1/2): 13–29, 1986.

——— Towards a componential approach to text. In M.A.K. Halliday, J. Gibbons, and N. Howard, editors, *Proceedings of the 1987 AILA Meeting*. AILA, Australia, 1987.

——— Toward a discussion of the flow of information in text. In S.A. Thompson and W.C. Mann, editors, *Text Description: Diverse Analyses of a Fund-raising Text*. Benjamins, Amsterdam, forthcoming.

Gazdar, G., Klein, E., Pullum, G. and Sag, I.A. *Generalized Phrase Structure Grammar*. Blackwell Publishing and Harvard University Press, Oxford, England and Cambridge, MA, 1985.

Givòn, T., editor. *Topic Continuity in Language*. Benjamins, Amsterdam, 1983.

Gleason, Jr., H.A. *Linguistics and English grammar*. Holt, Rinehart and Winston, New York, 1986.

Goffman, E. On face work. *Psychiatry*, 18: 213–31, 1955.

Goldman, N. *Computer Generation of Natural-Language from a Deep Conceptual Base*. Ph.D. thesis, Yale University, 1974.

——— Conceptual generation. In R.C. Schank, editor, *Conceptual Information Processing*. North-Holland Publishing Co., Amsterdam, 1975.

Granville, R. Cohesion in computer text generation: Lexical substitution. Technical Report MIT/LCS/TR-310, MIT, Cambridge, MA, 1983.

Gregory, M. Aspects of varieties differentiation. *Journal of Linguistics*, 3: 177–98, 1967.

Gregory, M. and Carrol, S. *Language and Situation: Language Varieties and their Social Contexts*. Routledge and Kegan Paul, London, 1978.

Grimes, J.E. *The Thread of Discourse*. Mouton, The Hague, 1975.

——— Context structure patterns. In S. Allèn, editor, *Text Processing*. Almqvist and Wiksell, Stockholm, 1982.

Gross, M. On the failure of generative grammar. *Language*, 55 (4): 859–86, 1979.

Grosz, B.J. The representation and use of focus in a system for understanding dialogs. In *Proceedings of 5th International Joint Conference on Artificial Intelligence (IJCAI-77)*, pages 67–76, Pittsburgh, PA, 1977. International Joint Conferences on Artificial Intelligence.

——— Discourse knowledge. In D.E. Walker, editor, *Understanding Spoken Language*. North-Holland, New York, 1978.

Grosz, B.J. and Sidner, C.L. Attention, intentions and the structure of discourse. *Computational Linguistics Journal*, 12 (3): 175–204, 1986.

Gunji, T. *Japanese Phrase Structure Grammar*. Reidel Publishing Company, Dordrecht, 1987.

Halliday, M.A.K. The linguistic basis of a mechanical thesaurus, and its application to English preposition classification. *Mechanical Translation*, 3, 1956.

——— Categories of the theory of grammar. *Word*, 17: 241–92, 1961. Reprinted in abbreviated form in Halliday (1976) edited by G.R. Kress, pages 52–72.

——— Linguistics and machine translation. *Zeitschrift für Phonetik, Sprachwissenschaft und Kommunikationsforschung*, 15, 1962.

——— Class in relation to the axes of chain and choice in language. *Linguistics*, 2:

5–15, 1963. Reprinted in abbreviated form in Halliday (1976) edited by G.R. Kress, pages 84–7.
——— The linguistic study of literary texts. In H. Lunt, editor, *Proceedings of the Ninth International Congress of Linguistics*, 1964.
——— Some notes on 'deep' grammar. *Journal of Linguistics*, 2 (1): 57–67, 1966. Abridged version in Halliday (1976) edited by G.R. Kress.
——— Notes on transitivity and theme in English: Parts 1 and 2. *Journal of Linguistics*, 3: 37–81 and 199–244, 1967a.
——— *The Intonation of British Spoken English*. Mouton, The Hague, 1967b.
——— Notes on transitivity and theme in English: Part 3. *Journal of Linguistics*, 4: 179–215, 1968.
——— Options and functions in the English clause. *Brno Studies in English*, 8: 82–8, 1969. Reprinted in Halliday and Martin, editors, *Readings in Systemic Linguistics*. Batsford, London, 1981.
——— Functional diversity in language, as seen from a consideration of modality and mood in English. *Foundations of Language*, 6 (3): 327-51. 1970.
——— *Explorations in the Functions of Language*. Edward Arnold, London, 1973.
——— *Learning How to Mean: Explorations in the Development of Language*. Edward Arnold, London, 1975.
——— The English verbal group. In G.R. Kress, editor, *Halliday: System and Function in Language*. Oxford University Press, London, 1976a.
——— The form of a functional grammar. In G.R. Kress, editor, *Halliday: System and Function in Language*. (Oxford University Press, London, 1976b. Revised version of paper 'On Functional Grammars' originally read to the Seminar on the Construction of Complex Grammars, Cambridge, MA. Also, a further version has appeared in B. Bernstein, editor, *Class Codes and Control, Vol. II*. Routledge and Kegan Paul, London, 1973.)
——— Text as semantic choice in social contexts. In T. van Dijk and J. Petöfi, editors, *Grammars and Descriptions*. Walter de Gruyter, Berlin, 1977. Abridged version in M.A.K. Halliday (1978), *Language as Social Semiotic*.
——— *Language as Social Semiotic*. Edward Arnold, London, 1978.
——— Modes of meaning and modes of saying: types of grammatical structure and their determination by different semantic functions. In D.J. Allerton, E. Carney, and D. Holdcroft, editors, *Function and Context in Linguistic Analysis. Essays Offered to William Haas*. Cambridge University Press, Cambridge, 1979.
——— Modes of meaning and modes of expression. In D. Holdcroft, D. Allerton, and E. Carney, editors, *Function and Context in Linguistic Analysis*. Cambridge University Press, Cambridge, 1980.
——— Types of structure. In M.A.K. Halliday and J.R. Martin, editors, *Readings in Systemic Linguistics*, pages 29–41. Batsford, London, 1981/65. Reprinted version of original paper from 1965.
——— Language as code and language as behaviour: a systemic-functional interpretation of the nature and ontogenesis of dialogue. In R.P. Fawcett, M.A.K. Halliday, S. Lamb, and A. Makkai, editors, *The Semiotics of Culture and Language*, Volume I. Frances Pinter, London, 1984 (Open Linguistics Series).
——— *An Introduction to Functional Grammar*. Edward Arnold, London, 1985a.
——— A grammar for casual conversation? In R. Hasan, editor, *Discourse on Discourse: Workshop Reports from the Macquarie Workshop on Discourse Analysis*. Applied Linguistics Association of Australia, Sydney, Australia, 1985b. Occasional Papers Number 7.

——— Systemic background. In J.D. Benson and W.S. Greaves, editors, *Systemic Perspectives on Discourse, Volume I*. Ablex, Norwood, NJ, 1985c.

——— Language and the order of nature. In N. Fabb, D. Attridge, A. Durant and C. MacCabe, editors, *The Linguistics of Writing*, pages 135–54. Manchester University Press, Manchester, 1987.

——— The history of a sentence: an essay in social semiotics. In R.M.B. Bosinelli, editor, *Language Systems and Cultural Systems: Proceedings of the International Symposium on Bologna, Italian Culture and Modern Literature*. University of Bologna, October 1988.

——— How do you mean? In M. Davies and L. Ravelli, editors, *Selected Papers from the Seventeenth International Systemic Congress*. Forthcoming. University of Stirling, July 1990.

Halliday, M.A.K. and Fawcett, R.P., editors. *New Developments in Systemic Linguistics. Volume I*. Frances Pinter, London, 1987.

Halliday, M.A.K. and Hasan, R. *Cohesion in English*. Longman, London, 1976.

——— *Language, Context and Text: A Social Semiotic Perspective*. Deakin University Press, Geelong, Victoria, 1985 (Language and Learning Series). Also: Oxford University Press, London, 1989.

Halliday, M.A.K., McIntosh, A. and Strevens, P. *The Linguistic Sciences and Language Teaching*. Longman, London, 1964.

Halliday, M.A.K. and Martin, J.R., editors. *Readings in Systemic Linguistics*. Batsford, London, 1981.

Halliday, M.A.K. and Matthiessen, C.M.I.M. Historical survey of systemic linguistics. In F.C.C. Peng and J. Ney, editors, *Current Approaches to Syntax*. Benjamins and Whurr, Amsterdam and London, 1990 (volume in preparation).

——— *The Bloomington Lattice*. de Gruyter, Berlin, in preparation.

Hasan, R. Text in the systemic-functional model. In W. Dressler, editor, *Current Trends in Text Linguistics*. de Gruyter, Berlin, 1978.

——— The grammarian's dream: lexis as most delicate grammar. In M.A.K. Halliday and R.P. Fawcett, editors, *New Developments in Systemic Linguistics, Volume I*. Frances Pinter, London, 1987.

——— Offers in the making: a systemic-functional approach, 1987 MS. Unpublished manuscript, Macquarie University.

Havránek, B. The functional differentiation of the standard language. In B. Havránek and M. Weingart, editors, *Spisnovná cestina a jazyková kultura*. Georgetown University Press, 1932. Reprinted in P. Garvin, editor, *A Prague School Reader on Esthetics, Literary Structure, and Style*, 1964.

Hayes, P. On semantic nets, frames and associations. In *Proceedings of the 5th International Joint Conference on Artificial Intelligence*, pages 99–107, 1977.

Heidorn, G. Augmented phrase structure grammar. In *Theoretical Issues in Natural Language Processing-1 (TINLAP)*, pages 1–5, Cambridge, MA, June 1975.

Henderson, E. J.R. Firth in retrospect: a view from the eighties. In R. Steele and T. Threadgold, editors, *Language Topics: Essays in Honour of Michael Halliday*, Volume I. John Benjamins Publishing Co., Amsterdam and Philadelphia, 1987.

Hendrix, G. Semantic knowledge. In D. Walker, editor, *Understanding Spoken Language*. North-Holland, New York, 1978.

——— Encoding knowledge in partitioned networks. In N.V. Findler, editor, *Associative Networks: Representation and Use of Knowledge by Computers*. Academic Press, New York, 1979.

Henrici, A. Notes on the systemic generation of a paradigm of the English clause.

In M.A.K. Halliday and J.R. Martin, editors, *Readings in Systemic Linguistics*. Batsford, London, 1981. Reprinted from 1965 Working Paper for the O.S.T.I. Programme in the Linguistic Properties of Scientific English.

Highton, N.B. and Highton, R.B. *The Home of Vegetarian Cookery*. Faber and Faber, London.

Hinds, J. Case marking in Japanese. *Linguistics*, 20: 541–57, 1983a.

——— Topic continuity in Japanese. In T. Givòn, editor, *Topic Continuity in Discourse: A Quantitative Cross-Language Study*. John Benjamins Publishing Company, Amsterdam, 1983b.

Hinds, J., Maynard, S.K. and Iwasaki, S., editors. *Perspectives on Topicalization: The Case of Japanese 'wa'*. John Benjamins, Amsterdam, 1987.

Hjelmslev, L. *Omkring sprogteoriens grundlaeggelse*. Akademisk Forlag, København, 1943.

Hobbs, J.R. Overview of the TACITUS project. In *Proceedings of DARPA's 1986 Strategic Computing Natural Language Processing Workshop*. DARPA, 1986.

Hobbs, R.J. and Shieber, S.M. An algorithm for generating quantifier scopings. *Computational Linguistics Journal*, 13 (1/2): 47–63, January–June 1987.

Hornstein, N. Towards a theory of tense. *Linguistic Inquiry*, 8: 521–58, 1977.

——— The study of meaning in natural language: three approaches to tense. In N. Hornstein and D. Lightfoot, editors, *Explanation in Linguistics. The Logical Problem of Language Acquisition*. Longman, London, 1981.

Houghton, G. and Pearson, M. The production of spoken dialogue. In M. Zock and G. Sabah, editors, *Advances in Natural Language Generation: An Interdisciplinary Approach*, Volume I, pages 112–30. Pinter Publishers, London, 1988.

Hovy, E.H. Generating natural language under pragmatic constraints. *Pragmatics*, 11 (6): 689–719, 1987a.

——— Some pragmatic decision criteria in generation. In G. Kempen, editor, *Natural Language Generation: Recent Advances in Artificial Intelligence, Psychology, and Linguistics*. Kluwer Academic Publishers, Boston/Dordrecht, 1987b. Paper presented at the Third International Workshop on Natural Language Generation, August 1986, Nijmegen, The Netherlands.

——— *Generating Natural Language under Pragmatic Constraints*. Ph.D. thesis, Yale University, 1987c. (Technical report: YALEU/CSD/RR 521. Also published by Lawrence Erlbaum Associates, Hillsdale, NJ, 1988.)

——— Planning coherent multisentential texts. In *The Proceedings of the 26th Annual Meeting of the Association for Computational Linguistics*, pages 163–9. Association for Computational Linguistics, June 1988. 1988a.

——— Two types of planning in language generation. In *Proceedings of the 26th Annual Meeting of the Association for Computational Linguistics*, State University of New York, Buffalo, New York, 7–10 June 1988. 1988b.

——— New possibilities in machine translation. Technical report, USC/Information Sciences Institute, Marina del Rey, CA, 1989a. Proposal prepared to encourage new DARPA initiatives in Machine Translation.

——— Pragmatics and natural language generation. *Artificial Intelligence Journal*, Fall 1989b. Also available in the ISI Reprint Series as report number RS-89-233, USC/Information Sciences Institute, Marina del Rey, CA.

——— Approaches to the planning of coherent text. Presented at the Fourth International Workshop on Natural Language Generation. Santa Catalina Island, CA, July 1988. In C.L. Paris, W.R. Swartout, and W.C. Mann, editors, *Natural Language Generation in Artificial Intelligence and Computational Linguistics*. Kluwer Academic Publishers, Dordrecht, July 1990.

Hovy, E.H., Appelt, D. and McDonald, D.D. Workshop on text planning and natural language generation, August 1988. Sponsored by American Association for Artificial Intelligence.

Hovy, E.H. and McCoy, K.F. Focusing your RST: a step towards generating coherent multisentential text. In *Proceedings of the 11th Annual Conference of the Cognitive Science Society*, pages 667–74, University of Michigan, Ann Arbor, MI, 16–19 August 1989. Lawrence Erlbaum Associates, Hillsdale, NJ.

Hu, Z., Zhu, Y. and Zhang, D. *Systemic-Functional Grammar*. Hunan Educational Publishers, Hunan, P.R. China, 1990 (in Chinese).

Hudson, R.A. Constituency in a systemic description of the English clause. *Lingua*, 18: 225–50, 1967. Reprinted in M.A.K. Halliday and J.R. Martin, editors, *Readings in Systemic Linguistics*. Batsford, London, 1981.

——— *English Complex Sentences*. North-Holland, Amsterdam, 1971.

——— An item-and-paradigm approach to Beja syntax and morphology. *Foundations of Language*, 9: 504–48, 1973. Reprinted in M.A.K. Halliday and J.R. Martin, editors, *Readings in Systemic Linguistics*. Batsford, London, 1981.

——— Systemic generative grammar. *Linguistics*, 139: 5–42, 1974.

——— *Arguments for a Non-transformational Grammar*. Chicago University Press, Chicago, 1976.

——— *Word Grammar*. Basil Blackwell, Oxford, 1984.

Inoue, K. 'Empathy and Syntax' re-examined: a case study from the verbs of giving in Japanese. *Annual Meeting of the Chicago Linguistics Society*, 15: 149–59, 1979.

Iordanskaja, L.N., Kittredge, R. and Polguère, A. Implementing a meaning-text model for language generation. In *COLING-88*, 1988.

——— Lexical selection and paraphrase in a meaning-text generation model. Presented at the Fourth International Workshop on Natural Language Generation. Santa Catalina Island, CA, July 1988. In C.L. Paris, W.R. Swartout, and W.C. Mann, editors, *Natural Language Generation in Artificial Intelligence and Computational Linguistics*. Kluwer Academic Publishers, Dordrecht, July 1990.

Isabelle, P. Machine translation at the TAUM group, 1984. Paper presented at the ISSCO *Tutorial on Machine Translation*.

Jackendoff, R. *Semantic Interpretation in Generative Grammar*. The MIT Press, Cambridge, MA, 1972.

——— *Semantics and Cognition*. The MIT Press, Cambridge, MA, 1983.

——— The status of thematic relations in linguistic theory. *Linguistic Inquiry*, 18 (3): 369–411, 1987.

——— *Semantic Structures*, The MIT Press, Cambridge, MA, 1990.

Jacobs, P. PHRED: a generator for natural language interfaces. *Computational Linguistics Journal*, 11, 1985.

——— Why text planning isn't planning, August 1988. Presented at the AAAI-88 Workshop on Text Planning and Realization, organized by E.H. Hovy, D. Appelt, D. McDonald and S. Young.

Johnson, D.E. Jets: a Japanese-English translation system based on relational grammar. Technical report, IBM Research Report, Tokyo Scientific Center, Tokyo, Japan, 1988.

de Joia, A. and Stenton, A. *Terms in Systemic Linguistics. A Guide to Halliday*. Batsford, London, 1980.

Joshi, A.K. The relevance of tree adjoining grammar to generation. In G. Kempen, editor, *Natural Language Generation: Recent Advances in Artificial Intelligence, Psychology, and Linguistics*. Kluwer Academic Publishers, Boston/Dordrecht,

1987. Paper presented at the Third International Workshop on Natural Language Generation, August 1986, Nijmegen, The Netherlands.

Kasper, R.T. *Feature Structures: A Logical Theory with Application to Language Analysis*. Ph.D. thesis, University of Michigan, Computer and Communication Sciences, 1987a.

——— A unification model for disjunctive feature descriptions. In *Proceedings of the 25th Annual Meeting*, Stanford, CA, July 1987. Association for Computational Linguistics. Also available as report ISI/RS-87-187, USC/Information Sciences Institute, Marina del Rey, CA. 1987b.

——— An Experimental Parser for Systemic Grammars. In *Proceedings of the 12th International Conference on Computational Linguistics, August 1988*, Budapest, Hungary, 1988. Association for Computational Linguistics. Also available as Information Sciences Institute Technical Report No. ISI/RS-88-212, Marina del Rey, CA.

——— A flexible interface for linking applications to PENMAN's sentence generator. In *Proceedings of the DARPA Workshop on Speech and Natural Language*, 1989. Available from USC/Information Sciences Institute, Marina del Rey, CA. 1989a.

——— Unification and classification: an experiment in information-based parsing. In *Proceedings of the International Workshop on Parsing Technologies*, pages 1–7, 1989b. 28–31 August 1989, Carnegie-Mellon University, Pittsburgh, Pennsylvania.

Kay, M. Functional grammar. In *Proceedings of the 5th Meeting of the Berkeley Linguistics Society*, pages 142–58. Berkeley Linguistics Society, 1979.

——— Parsing in functional unification grammar. In B.J. Grosz, K. Sparck-Jones, and B.L. Webber, editors, *Readings in Natural Language Processing*, pages 125–38. Morgan Kaufman Publishers, Los Altos, CA. 1986. Reprinted from D.R. Dowty, L. Kartunnen and A. Zwicky, editors, *Natural Language Parsing*, pages 251–78. Cambridge University Press, Cambridge, 1982.

Kehl, W. GEOTEX: ein System zur Verbalisierung geometrischen Konstruktionen, 1986. Diplomarbeit. Stuttgart University, Institut für Informatik.

Kempen, G. Language generation systems. In I. Batori, W. Lenders, and W. Putschke, editors, *Computational Linguistics: An International Handbook on Computer Oriented Language Research and Applications*. Walter de Gruyter, Berlin and New York, 1986.

——— *Natural Language Generation: Recent Advances in Artificial Intelligence, Psychology, and Linguistics*. Kluwer Academic Publishers, Dordrecht, 1987. Selected papers presented at the Third International Workshop on Natural Language Generation, August 1986, Nijmegen, The Netherlands.

Kittredge, R. The significance of sublanguage for automatic translation. In S. Nirenburg, editor, *Machine Translation: Theoretical and Methodological Issues*, pages 59–67. Cambridge University Press, London, 1987.

Kittredge, R. and Lehrberger, L., editors. *Sublanguage: Studies of Language in Restricted Semantic Domains*. de Gruyter, Berlin and New York, 1982.

Klatt, D.H. Review of text-to-speech conversion for English. *Journal of the Acoustical Society of America*, 82 (3): 737–93, 1987.

Kobsa, A. and Wahlster, W. *Computational Linguistics: Special Issue on User Modeling*, 14 (3). The MIT Press, Cambridge, MA, September 1988.

Kukich, K. Knowledge-based report generation: a technique for automatically generating natural language reports from databases. In *Proceedings of the Sixth International ACM SIGIR Conference*, Washington, DC, 1983. ACM SIGIR.

——— Explanation structures in XSEL. In *Proceedings of the 23rd Annual Meeting of the Association for Computational Linguistics*, Chicago, Illinois, 1985. Association for Computational Linguistics.

Kuno, S. *The Structure of the Japanese Language*. The MIT Press, Cambridge, MA, 1973.

——— Subject, theme and the speaker's empathy. In C.N. Li, editor, *Subject and Topic*. Academic Press, New York, 1976.

Kuno, S. and Kaburaki, E. Empathy and syntax. *Linguistic Inquiry*, 8: 627–72, 1977.

Lamb, S.M. *Outline of Stratificational Grammar*. Georgetown University Press, Washington, DC, 1966.

Langacker, R.W. *Foundations in Cognitive Grammar*. Stanford University Press, Stanford, CA, 1987.

Leech, G. *Principles of Pragmatics*. Longman, London, 1983.

Levy, D.M. Communicative goals and strategies: between discourse and semantics. In T. Givòn, editor, *Syntax and Semantics*, Volume 12, pages 183–210. Academic Press, New York, 1979.

Lockwood, D. *Introduction to Stratificational Linguistics*. Harcourt Brace Jovanovich, New York, 1972.

Lowth. *English Grammar*. 1762.

McCord, M.C. On the form of a systemic grammar. *Journal of Linguistics*, 11: 195–212, 1975.

——— Procedural systemic grammars. *International Journal of Man–Machine Studies*, 9: 255–86, 1977.

McCoy, K.F. The ROMPER system: Responding to object-related misconceptions using perspective. In *Proceedings of the 24th Annual Meeting of the ACL*, New York City, NY, June 1986. Association of Computational Linguistics.

McCoy, K.F. and Cheng, J. Focus of attention: constraining what can be said next. In C.L. Paris, W.R. Swartout, and W.C. Mann, editors, *Natural Language Generation in Artificial Intelligence and Computational Linguistics*. Kluwer Academic Publishers, Dordrecht, July 1990. Presented at the Fourth International Workshop on Natural Language Generation. Santa Catalina Island, CA, July 1988.

McCoy, K.F., Vijay-Shanker, K. and Yang, G. Using tree adjoining grammars in the systemic framework. In *5th International Workshop on Natural Language Generation*, 3–6 June 1990, pages 1–8, Pittsburgh, PA, 1990. Organized by K.R. McKeown (Columbia University), J.D. Moore (University of Pittsburgh) and S. Nirenburg (Carnegie Mellon University).

McDonald, D.D. Natural language production as a process of decision making under constraint. Ph.D. thesis, MIT, Cambridge, MA, 1980.

——— Language production: the source of the dictionary. In *The Nineteenth Annual Meeting of the Association for Computational Linguistics*, Stanford University, CA, June 1981.

——— Natural language generation: complexities and techniques. In S. Nirenburg, editor, *Theoretical and Methodological Issues in Machine Translation*. Cambridge University Press, Cambridge, 1986.

McDonald, D.D. and Conklin, J.E. Salience as simplifying metaphor for natural language generation. In *Proceedings of the Third National Conference on Artificial Intelligence*, Washington, DC, 1983. American Association of Artificial Intelligence.

McDonald, D.D., Meteer, M.W. and Pustejovsky, J. Factors contributing to efficiency in natural language generation. In G. Kempen, editor, *Natural Language Generation: Recent Advances in Artificial Intelligence, Psychology, and Linguistics*. Kluwer Academic Publishers, Boston/Dordrecht, 1987. Paper presented at the Third International Workshop on Natural Language Generation, August 1986, Nijmegen, The Netherlands.

MacGregor, R. and Bates, R. The LOOM knowledge representation language. In *Proceedings of the Knowledge-Based Systems Workshop*, 1987. Held in St. Louis Missouri, 21–23 April 1987. Also available as ISI reprint series report, RS-87-188, USC/Information Sciences Institute, Marina del Rey, CA.

MacGregor, R. and Brill, D. The LOOM manual, 1989. USC/Information Sciences Institute, Marina del Rey, CA.

MacGregor, W. The metafunctional hypothesis and syntagmatic relations, 1989. Draft manuscript: Bond University, Gold Coast, Australia.

McKeown, K.R. Generating natural language text in response to questions about database structure. Ph.D. thesis, University of Pennsylvania, May 1982. Also a Technical report, No. MS-CIS-82-05, University of Pennsylvania, 1982.

——— *Text Generation: Using Discourse Strategies and Focus Constraints to Generate Natural Language Text*. Cambridge University Press, Cambridge, 1985.

McKeown, K.R. and Swartout, W.R. Language generation and explanation. In *Annual Reviews in Computer Science*, 1987.

McKeown, K.R., Wish, M. and Matthews, K. Tailoring explanations for the user. In *International Joint Conference on Artificial Intelligence*, Los Angeles, CA, 1985. International Joint Conference on Artificial Intelligence.

Malinowski, B. *Supplement I*. Harcourt, Brace, and Co., Inc., 1923. Supplement to C.K. Ogden and I.A. Richards, *The Meaning of Meaning*.

Mallery, J.C., Hurwitz, R. and Duffy, G. Hermeneutics: from textual explication to computer understanding. In S. Shapiro, editor, *The Encyclopedia of Artificial Intelligence*. John Wiley and Sons, London, 1987.

Mann, W.C. The anatomy of a systemic choice. *Discourse Processes*, 1983a. Also available as USC/Information Sciences Institute, Research Report ISI/RR-82-104, 1982.

——— An overview of the PENMAN text generation system. Technical Report ISI/RR-83-114, USC/Information Sciences Institute, Marina del Rey, CA, 1983b.

——— Discourse structure for text generation. Technical Report ISI/RR-84-127, Information Sciences Institute, February 1984. 4676 Admiralty Way, Marina del Rey, CA.

Mann, W.C., Bates, M., Grosz, B.J., McDonald, D.D., McKeown, K.R. and Swartout, W.R. Text generation: the state of the art and the literature. Technical Report ISI/RR-81-101, Information Sciences Institute, Marina del Rey, CA, 1981. Also available as a Technical Report at the University of Pennsylvania, number MS-CIS-81-9; and in *American Journal of Computational Linguistics* (April–June), 8 (2): 62–9, 1982.

Mann, W.C. and Matthiessen, C.M.I.M. Demonstration of the Nigel text generation computer program. In J.D. Benson and W.S. Greaves, editors, *Systemic Perspectives on Discourse*, Volume I. Ablex, Norwood, NJ, 1985.

Mann, W.C., Matthiessen, C.M.I.M. and Thompson, S.A. Rhetorical structure theory and text analysis. In W.C. Mann and S.A. Thompson, editors, *Text Description: Diverse Analyses of a Fund Raising Text*. John Benjamins, Amsterdam, 1989. Volume in preparation. Also available as Information Sciences

Institute, Report, ISI/RR-89-242, Marina del Rey, CA.

Mann, W.C. and Moore, J.A. Computer as author: results and prospects. Technical Report ISI/RR-79-82, Information Sciences Institute, USC/Information Sciences Institute, Marina del Rey, CA, 1980.

——— Computer generation of multiparagraph text. *American Journal of Computational Linguistics*, 7 (1): 17–29, Jan–Mar. 1981.

Mann, W.C. and Thompson, S.A. Rhetorical structure theory: a theory of text organization. In L. Polanyi, editor, *The Structure of Discourse*. Ablex Publishing Corporation, Norwood, NJ, 1987. Also available as USC/Information Sciences Institute Technical Report Number RS/-87-190.

Marr, D. *Vision*, Chapter 3: From images to surfaces, pages 99–267. W.H. Freeman and Company, San Francisco, 1982.

Martin, J.R. Process and text: two aspects of human semiosis. In J.D. Benson and W.S. Greaves, editors, *Systemic Perspectives on Discourse*, Volume I. Ablex, Norwood, NJ, 1985.

——— The meaning of features in systemic linguistics. In M.A.K. Halliday and R.P. Fawcett, editors, *New Developments in Systemic Linguistics*, Volume I. Frances Pinter, London, 1987.

——— Hypotactic recursive systems in English: toward a functional interpretation. In J.D. Benson and W.S. Greaves, editors, *Systemic Functional Approaches to Discourse: Selected Papers from the Twelfth International Systemic Workshop*. Ablex, Norwood, NJ, 1988.

——— Interpersonal grammaticalization: mood and modality in Tagalog. *Philippine Journal of Linguistics*, 1990 (special monograph issue celebrating the 25th anniversary of the Language Study Centre, Philippine Normal College).

——— *English Text: System and Structure*. John Benjamins, Amsterdam, in press.

——— Macro-proposals: meaning by degree. In S.A. Thompson and W.C. Mann, editors, *Text Description: Diverse Analyses of a Fund Raising Text*. Benjamins, Amsterdam, forthcoming.

Martin, J.R. and Matthiessen, C.M.I.M. Systemic typology and topology. Technical report, Department of Linguistics, University of Sydney, Sydney, Australia, 1990.

Martin, J.R. and Rothery, J. The ontogenesis of written genre. Technical Report Project Report, no. 2, Sydney University: Linguistics Department (Working Papers), 1981.

Matthiessen, C.M.I.M. A grammar and a lexicon for a text production system. In *Proceedings of the 19th Annual Meeting of the Association for Computational Linguistics*, 1981.

——— Choosing primary tense in English. *Studies in Language*, 7 (3), 1983.

——— Choosing tense in English. Technical Report ISI/RR-84-143, USC/Information Sciences Institute, Marina del Rey, CA, 1984.

——— The systemic framework in text generation: Nigel. In J.D. Benson and W.S. Greaves, editors, *Systemic Perspectives on Discourse*, Volume I. Ablex, Norwood, NJ, 1985.

——— Notes on the organization of the environment of a text generation grammar. In G. Kempen, editor, *Natural Language Generation: Recent Advances in Artificial Intelligence, Psychology, and Linguistics*. Kluwer Academic Publishers, Boston/Dordrecht, 1987. Paper presented at the Third International Workshop on Natural Language Generation, August 1986, Nijmegen, The Netherlands.

——— Representational issues in systemic-functional grammar. In J.D. Benson and

W.S. Greaves, editors, *Systemic-functional Approaches to Discourse*. Ablex, Norwood, NJ, 1988a. Also available as USC/Information Sciences Institute Reprint Series Report ISI/RS-87-179.

——— Semantics for a systemic grammar: the chooser and inquiry framework. In J.D. Benson, M. Cummings, and W.S. Greaves, editors, *Linguistics in a Systemic Perspective*. Benjamins, Amsterdam, 1988b. Also available as USC/Information Sciences Institute, Reprint Series Report ISI/RS-87-189, Marina del Rey, CA.

——— Generic structure potential and rhetorical schemas, 1988c. ms. USC/Information Sciences Institute.

——— Systemic theory and text generation: some central design considerations. In *Proceedings of the First Australian–Japanese Joint Symposium on Natural Language Processing*, Department of Computer Science, Melbourne University, Melbourne, 27–29 November 1989.

——— Lexico(grammatical) choice in text generation. Presented at the Fourth International Workshop on Natural Language Generation. Santa Catalina Island, CA, July 1988. In C.L. Paris, W.R. Swartout, and W.C. Mann, editors, *Natural Language Generation in Artificial Intelligence and Computational Linguistics*. Kluwer Academic Publishers, Dordrecht, 1990a.

——— Lexicogrammatical cartography: English systems. Technical report, University of Sydney, Linguistics Department, 1990b. Ongoing expanding draft.

——— Metafunctional complementarity and resonance in syntagmatic organization. Technical report, Linguistics Department, University of Sydney, Sydney, Australia, 1990c.

——— Semantic interfaces in text generation. In *13th International Conference on Computational Linguistics (COLING-90)*, pages 322–9, Helsinki, Finland, 1990. Volume 2. 1990d.

——— Systemic perspectives on tense in English. In M. Berry, C.S. Butler, and R.P. Fawcett, editors, *Meaning and Choice in Language: Studies for Michael Halliday; Volume 2: Grammatical structure, a functional interpretation*. Ablex, Norwood, NJ, to appear.

Matthiessen, C.M.I.M. and Halliday, M.A.K. Systemic functional grammar. In F.C.C. Peng and J. Ney, editors, *Current Approaches to Syntax*. Benjamins and Whurr, Amsterdam and London, 1989, forthcoming.

Maynard, S.K. Discourse functions of the Japanese theme marker *wa*. Ph.D. thesis, Northwestern University, Illinois, 1980.

Meehan, J.R. TALE-SPIN, an interactive program that writes stories. In *Proceedings of IJCAI-77*. International Joint Conference on Artificial Intelligence, 1977.

Mellish, C.S. Implementing systemic classification by unification. *Journal of Computational Linguistics*, 14 (1): 40–51, 1988.

Meteer, M.W. Defining a vocabulary for text planning, August 1988. Presented at the AAAI-88 Workshop on Text Planning and Realization, organized by E.H. Hovy, D. Appelt, D. McDonald and S. Young.

——— The SPOKESMAN natural language generation system. Technical Report BBN Report No. 7090, BBN Systems and Technologies Corporation, Cambridge, MA, 1989.

——— The implications of revisions for natural language generation. Presented at the Fourth International Workshop on Natural Language Generation. Santa Catalina Island, CA, July 1988. In C.L. Paris, W.R. Swartout, and W.C. Mann, editors, *Natural Language Generation in Artificial Intelligence and Computational*

*Linguistics*, pages 155–78. Kluwer Academic Publishers, Dordrecht, July 1990.

Meteer, M.W., McDonald, D.D., Anderson, S.D., Forster, D., Gay, L.S., Huettner, A.K. and Sibun, P. MUMBLE-86: Design and implementation. Technical Report 87-87, COINS, University of Massachusetts, 1987.

Minsky, M. A framework for representing knowledge. In *Theoretical Issues in Natural Language Processing 1*, 1975. See also: paper of the same name in P.H. Winston, editor, *The Psychology of Computer Vision*. McGraw Hill, New York, 1975. Reprinted in R.J. Brachman and H.J. Levesque, editors, *Readings in Knowledge Representation*. Los Altos, Kaufman, 1985.

Mizutani, O. and Mizutani, N. *How to be Polite in Japanese*. The Japan Times, Ltd., Tokyo, Japan, 1987.

Monaghan, J. *The Neo-Firthian Tradition and its Contribution to General Linguistics*. Niemeyer, Tübingen, 1979.

Moore, J.D. A reactive approach to explanation in expert and advice-giving systems. Ph.D. thesis, University of California, Los Angeles, 1989.

Moore, J.D. and Paris, C.L. Constructing coherent texts using rhetorical relations. In *Proceedings of the Tenth Annual Conference of the Cognitive Science Society*. Cognitive Science Society, August 1988.

——— Planning text for advisory dialogues. In *Proceedings of the 27th Annual Meeting of the Association for Computational Linguistics*, pages 203–11. Association for Computational Linguistics, June 1989.

Moser, M.G. An overview of NIKL, the new implementation of KL-ONE. In *Research in Natural Language Understanding*. Bolt, Beraneck, and Newman, Inc., Cambridge, MA, 1983. BBN Technical Report 5421.

Moses, L. *TOPS-20 User's Manual*. USC/Information Sciences Institute, Internal manual, Marina del Rey, CA.

Nebel, B. and Sondheimer, N.K. A logical-form and knowledge-base design for natural language generation. In *Proceedings of the AAAI-86 Conference*, Philadelphia, PA, 11–15 August 1986, pages 612–18, 1986.

Nesbitt, C. and Plum, G. Probabilities in a systemic grammar: the clause complex in English. In R.P. Fawcett and D. Young, editors, *New Developments in Systemic Linguistics; Volume 2: Theory and Application*, pages 6–38. Pinter, London, 1988.

O'Donnell, M. A dynamic model of exchange, 1989a. To appear in: *Word*.

——— Experiments in parsing. Technical report, University of Sydney, Linguistics Department, Sydney, Australia, 1989b.

——— Function potential grammar. Technical report, Department of Linguistics, University of Sydney, Sydney, Australia, January 1990.

O'Toole, M. A systemic-functional semiotics of art. In P.H. Fries and M. Gregory, editors, *Discourse in Society: Functional Perspectives*. Ablex, Norwood, NJ, in press.

Painter, C. *Into the Mother Tongue: A Case Study in Early Language Development*. Frances Pinter, London, 1984 (Open Linguistics Series).

Paris, C.L. Determining the level of expertise of a user of a question answering system. Technical Report 84-3-paris-1, Columbia University, 1984. New York City, NY.

——— The use of explicit user models in text generation: tailoring to a user's level of expertise. Ph.D. thesis, Columbia University Department of Computer Science, 1987. To be published by Pinter Publishers, London.

——— The use of explicit user models in a generation system for tailoring answers to the user's level of expertise. In A. Kobsa and W. Wahlster, editors, *User Models in Dialog Systems*. Springer Verlag, Symbolic Computation Series, Berlin/Heidelberg/New York/Tokyo, 1988.

——— Generation and explanation: building an explanation facility for the explainable expert systems framework. Presented at the Fourth International Workshop on Natural Language Generation. Santa Catalina Island, CA, July 1988. In C.L. Paris, W.R. Swartout, and W.C. Mann, editors, *Natural Language Generation in Artificial Intelligence and Computational Linguistics*. Kluwer Academic Publishers, Dordrecht, July 1990.

——— Text generation: a survey paper. In N.M. Ide, editor, *Methodologies in Humanities Computing*. University of Pennsylvania Press, 1991.

Paris, C.L., Swartout, W.R. and Mann, W.C., editors. *Natural Language Generation in Artificial Intelligence and Computational Linguistics*. Kluwer Academic Publishers, Dordrecht/London/Boston, 1990.

Parker-Rhodes, A.F. *Inferential Semantics*. The Humanities Press, New York, NY, 1978 (Harvester Studies in Cognitive Science).

Patten, T. Interpreting systemic grammar as a computational representation: a problem solving approach to text generation. Ph.D. thesis, Edinburgh University, Scotland, 1986.

——— *Systemic Text Generation as Problem Solving*. Cambridge University Press, Cambridge, 1988a.

——— Compiling the interface between text planning and realization, August 1988. Workshop on text planning and Natural Language Generation, Sponsored by AAAI; Organized by E.H. Hovy, D. Appelt, D. McDonald and S. Young. 1988b.

Patten, T. and Ritchie, G. A formal model of systemic grammar. In G. Kempen, editor, *Natural Language Generation: Recent Advances in Artificial Intelligence, Psychology, and Linguistics*. Kluwer Academic Publishers, Boston/Dordrecht, 1987. Paper presented at the Third International Workshop on Natural Language Generation, August 1986, Nijmegen, The Netherlands.

Patten, T. and Stoops, D.S. Real-time generation from systemic grammars. In *5th International Workshop on Natural Language Generation*, 3–6 June 1990, Pittsburgh, PA, 1990. Organized by K.R. McKeown (Columbia University), J.D. Moore (University of Pittsburgh) and S. Nirenburg (Carnegie Mellon University).

Penman Project. PENMAN documentation: the Primer, the User Guide, the Reference Manual, and the Nigel manual. Technical report, USC/Information Sciences Institute, Marina del Rey, CA, 1989.

Pike, K.L. Language as particle, wave, and field. *The Texas Quarterly*, 2 (2): 37–54, 1959. Reprinted in R. Brend, editor, *Kenneth L. Pike: Selected Writings*. Mouton, The Hague, 1972.

Pike, K.L. and Pike, E. *Text and Tagmeme*. Frances Pinter, London, 1982.

Pollard, C. Lecture notes on head-driven phrase structure grammar. Technical report, Center for the Study of Language and Information, Stanford University, Stanford, CA, 1985.

Pollard, C. and Sag, I.A. *Information-based Syntax and Semantics*, Volume I. Chicago University Press, Chicago, 1987. Center for the Study of Language and Information; Lecture Notes Number 13.

Postal, P. *Constituent Structure: A Study of Contemporary Models of Syntactic Description*. Mouton, The Hague, 1964.

Poynton, C.McK. Names as vocatives: forms and functions. *Nottingham Linguistics Circular*, 13, 1984.

Poynton, C.McK. Amplification as a mode of realisation: attitudinal modification in the nominal group. In M. Berry, C.S. Butler, and R.P. Fawcett, editors, *Meaning and Choice in Language: Studies for Michael Halliday; Volume 2: Grammatical Structure, a Functional Interpretation*. Ablex, Norwood, NJ, forthcoming.

Pratt, R.L. Quantifying the performance of text-to-speech synthesizers. *Speech Technology*, pages 54–64, March/April 1987.

Prince, E.F. Toward a taxonomy of given-new information. In P. Cole, editor, *Radical Pragmatics*. Academic Press, New York, 1981.

Prior, A.N. *Past, Present and Future*. Oxford University Press, London, 1967.

Quillian, R. Word concepts: a theory and simulation of some basic semantic capabilities. *Behavioral Science*, 12: 410–30, 1967. Reprinted in R.J. Brachman and H.J. Levesque, editors, *Readings in Knowledge Representation*. Morgan Kaufman, Los Altos, 1985.

Quirk, R., Greenbaum, S., Leech, G. and Svartvik, J. *A Grammar of Contemporary English*. Longman, London, 1972 (GCE).

Ravelli, L.J. Metaphor, mode and complexity: an exploration of co-varying patterns, 1985. B.A. Honours thesis in Linguistics, University of Sydney.

Reichenbach, H. *Elements of Symbolic Logic*. Macmillan, London and New York, 1947.

Reichman, R. *Making Computers Speak Like You and Me*. The MIT Press, Cambridge, MA, 1985.

Rubinoff, R. Adapting MUMBLE: Experience with natural language generation. In *Proceedings of the fifth Annual Conference on Artificial Intelligence*, American Association of Artificial Intelligence, 1986.

Rösner, D. Ein System zur Generierung von deutschen Texten aus semantischen Repräsentationen. Ph.D. thesis, Institut für Informatik, Stuttgart University, Stuttgart, Germany, 1986.

——— The automated news agency: the SEMTEX generator for German. In G. Kempen, editor, *Natural Language Generation: Recent Advances in Artificial Intelligence, Psychology, and Linguistics*. Kluwer Academic Publishers, Boston/Dordrecht, 1987. Paper presented at the Third International Workshop on Natural Language Generation, August 1986, Nijmegen, The Netherlands.

——— The generation system of the SEMSYN project: towards a task-independent generator for German. In M. Zock and G. Sabah, editors, *Advances in Natural Language Generation: An Interdisciplinary Perspective*, Volume 2, Frances Pinter, London, 1988.

Sacerdoti, E. *A Structure for Plans and Behavior*. Elsevier North-Holland, Amsterdam and New York, 1977.

Samlowski, W. Case grammar. In E. Charniak and Y. Wilks, editors, *Computational Semantics*. North-Holland, Amsterdam, 1976.

Sampson, G. *Schools of Linguistics*. Stanford University Press, Stanford, 1980.

Schank, R.C. *Dynamic Memory: A Theory of Reminding and Learning in Computers and People*. Cambridge University Press, New York, 1982.

Schank, R.C. and Abelson, R.P. *Scripts, Plans, Goals and Understanding*. Lawrence Erlbaum Associates, Hillsdale, NJ, 1977.

Schank, R.C., Goldman, N., Reiger, C. and Riesbeck, C.K. MARGIE: memory, analysis, response generation and inferences in English. In *Proceedings of IJCAI-73*. International Joint Conference of Artificial Intelligence, 1973.

Schank, R.C. and Kass, A. Knowledge representation in people and machines. In

U. Eco, M. Santabrogio, and P. Vidli, editors, *Meaning and Mental Representations*. Indiana University Press, Bloomington, IN, 1988.

Schiffrin, D. *Discourse Markers*. Cambridge University Press, Cambridge, 1987.

Schmolze, J.G. and Israel, D.L. KL-ONE: Semantics and classification. In C.L. Sidner *et al.*, editors, *Research in Knowledge Representation for Natural Language Understanding*, Annual Report, 1 September 1982–31 August 1983, pages 27–39, Bolt, Beraneck and Newman, Cambridge, MA, 1983. BBN Laboratories Report No. 5421.

Scott, D.R. and de Souza, C.S. Getting the message across: a computational grammar of text. Technical report, Philips Research Laboratories and Departamento de Informática, PUC, Redhill, England and Rio de Janeiro, Brazil, 1989.

Scragg, G.W. Semantic nets as memory models. In E. Charniak and Y. Wilks, editors, *Computational Semantics*. North-Holland, Amsterdam, 1976.

Searle, J.R. Minds, brains, and programs. *Behavioral and Brain Sciences*, 3: 417–24, 1980. Reprinted in J. Haugeland, editor, *Mind Design*, pages 282–306, 1981. Cambridge, MA. Bradford Books/MIT Press.

Sefton, P.M. Making plans for Nigel (or defining interfaces between computational representations of linguistic structure and output systems: adding intonation, punctuation and typography systems to the PENMAN system). Technical report, Linguistics Department, University of Sydney, Sydney, Australia, November 1990. Bachelor's Honours thesis.

Shibatani, M. Grammatical relations and surface cases. *Language*, 53 (4): 789–809, 1977.

Shieber, S.M. *An Introduction to Unification-based Approaches to Grammar*. Center for the Study of Language and Information, Stanford University, Stanford, CA, 1986. CLSI Lecture Notes, No. 4.

Sidner, C.L. The use of focus as a tool for disambiguation of definite noun phrases. In D.L. Waltz, editor, *Theoretical Issues in Natural Language Processing 2; TINLAP 2*, pages 86–95. Association for Computing Machinery, 1978 (University of Illinois at Urbana-Champaign, 25–27 July 1978).

——— Towards a computational theory of definite anaphora comprehension in English discourse. Ph.D. thesis, MIT, Cambridge, MA, 1979. Appears as Technical Report No. AI-TR-537.

——— Focusing for interpretation of pronouns. *American Journal of Computational Linguistics*, 7 (4): 217–31, 1981.

Sigurd, B. Computer simulation of spontaneous speech production. In *Tenth International Conference on Computational Linguistics (COLING-84)*, 1984.

Simmons, R. and Slocum, J. Generating English discourse from semantic nets. *Communications of the Association for Computing Machinery*, 15 (10): 891–905, 1972.

Sinclair, J. and Coulthard, R.M. *Towards an Analysis of Discourse*. Oxford University Press, London, 1975.

Sinclair, J.McH. Collocation: a progress report. In R. Steele and T. Threadgold, editors, *Language Topics: Essays in Honour of Michael Halliday*, pages 319–32. John Benjamins, Amsterdam, 1987.

Skuce, D. and Monarch, I. Ontological issues in knowledge base design: some problems and suggestions. In *Proceedings of the Banff Workshop on Knowledge Acquisition*, Banff, Canada, 1990.

de Smedt, K. and Kempen, G. Incremental sentence production, self-correction and co-ordination. In G. Kempen, editor, *Natural Language Generation: Recent*

*Advances in Artificial Intelligence, Psychology, and Linguistics*, pages 365–76. Kluwer Academic Publishers, Boston/Dordrecht, 1987. Paper presented at the Third International Workshop on Natural Language Generation, August 1986, Nijmegen, The Netherlands.

Smith, B.C. Levels, layers, and planes. Master's thesis. MIT, Cambridge, MA, 1978.

Sondheimer, N.K., Weischedel, R.M. and Bobrow, R.J. Semantic interpretation using KL-ONE. In *Proceedings of Coling-84*, pages 101–7, 1984.

Sowa, J. Generating language from conceptual graphs. *Computers and Mathematics with Applications*, 9 (1): 29–43, 1983a.

——— *Conceptual Structures*. Addison-Wesley, Menlo Park, CA, 1983b.

Steiner, E.H. *Die Entwicklung des Britischen Kontextualismus*. Groos, Heidelberg, 1983.

——— Some fragments of a systemic grammar of German for a computational environment. Technical report, GMD/Institut für Integrierte Publikations- und Informationssysteme, Darmstadt, West Germany, 1990. Paper presented at the 17th Annual International Systemic Congress, Stirling University, Scotland, 3–7 July.

——— *Language, Action, and Interpretation*. Mouton and de Gruyter, Berlin and New York, forthcoming.

Steiner, E.H., Bateman, J.A., Maier, E., Teich, E. and Wanner, L. KOMET: Department plan. Technical report, GMD/Institut für Integrierte Informations- und Publikationssysteme, Darmstadt, West Germany, 1990a.

——— Of mountains to climb and ships to sink: generating German within a functional approach to text generation. Technical report, GMD/Institut für Integrierte Informations- und Publikationssysteme, Darmstadt, West Germany, 1990b.

Steiner, E.H., Eckert, U., Weck, B. and Winter, J. The development of the EUROTRA-D system of semantic relations. In E.H. Steiner *et al.*, editors, *From Syntax to Semantics: Insights from Machine Translation*. Frances Pinter, London, 1988.

Steiner, E.H. and Reuther, U. Semantic relations. EUROTRA reference manual, Version 6, 1989 (Commission of the European Community).

Steiner, E.H., Schmidt, P. and Zelinsky-Wibbelt, C., editors. *From Syntax to Semantics: Insights from Machine Translation*. Frances Pinter, London, 1988.

Suchman, L.A. *Plans and Situated Actions: The Problem of Human-Machine Communication*. Cambridge University Press, Cambridge, 1987.

Swartout, W.R. XPLAIN: a system for creating and explaining expert consulting systems. *Artificial Intelligence*, 21 (3): 285–325, September 1983. Also available as ISI/RS-83-4.

Swartout, W.R. and Smoliar, S.W. Explaining the link between causal reasoning and expert behavior. In *Proceedings of the Symposium on Computer Applications in Medical Care*, Washington, DC, November 1987. Also to appear in P.L. Miller, editor, *Topics in Medical Artificial Intelligence*. Springer-Verlag, Berlin/Heidelberg/New York/Tokyo.

Tabuchi, A. Nihon-go bun seisei no tame no systemic bunpou no sakusei (The development of a systemic grammar for the generation of Japanese text), 1986. Bachelor's thesis (in Japanese), Department of Electrical Engineering, Kyoto University, Kyoto, Japan.

Talmy, L. The relation of grammar to cognition. In B. Rudzka-Ostyn, editor,

*Topics in Cognitive Linguistics*. John Benjamins, Amsterdam, 1987.

Tannen, D. What's in a frame? surface evidence for underlying expectations. In R.O. Freedle, editor, *Discourse Processes: Advances in Research and Theory. Volume 2: New Directions in Discourse Processing*. Ablex, Norwood, 1979.

Teich, E. Systemic linguistics in natural language processing. Master's thesis, Universität des Saarlandes, Saarbrücken, West Germany, 1989 (Magisterarbeit).

——— A systemically based treatment of 'raising' and 'control' in the context of machine translation. In E. Ventola, editor, *Recent Systemic and Other Views on Language*. Benjamins, Amsterdam, 1990.

——— A systemic grammar of German for text generation. In M. Davies and L. Ravelli, editors, *Papers from the Seventeenth International Systemic Congress; University of Stirling, July 1990*. 1991.

Tsui, A.B.M. Systemic choice and discourse processes. *Word* 40 (1/2): 163–88, 1989.

Tucker, G.H. Initial specification of lexis for prototype generators 0, 1 and 2. COMMUNAL Report Number 5, Computational Linguistics Unit, University of Wales College of Cardiff, 1988.

Tung, Y-W., Matthiessen, C.M.I.M. and Sondheimer, N.K. On parallelism and the PENMAN language generation system. Technical Report ISI/RR-88-195, USC/Information Sciences Institute, Marina del Rey, CA, 1988.

Turner, G. Social class and children's language of control at age five and age seven. In B. Bernstein, editor, *Class, Codes and Control 2: Applied Studies Towards a Sociology of Language*. Routledge and Kegan Paul, London, 1973.

Ultan, R. The nature of future tenses. In J. Greenberg, E. Moravscik and C. Ferguson, editors, *Universals of Human Language*. Stanford University Press, Stanford, CA, 1978.

Uszkoreit, H. Categorical unification grammars. In *Proceedings of COLING-86*, 1986. Also appears as Center for the Study of Language and Information Report No. CSLI-86-66, Stanford, CA.

van Leeuwen, T. The consumer, the producer and the state: analysis of a television news item. In T. Threadgold, E.A. Grosz, G. Kress and M.A.K. Halliday, editors, *Language, Semiotics, Ideology*, pages 203–24. The Sydney Association for Studies in Society and Culture, Sydney, Australia, 1986.

Ventola, E. Contrasting schematic structures in service encounters. *Applied Linguistics*, 4, 1983.

——— The dynamics of genre. *Nottingham Linguistics Circular*, 14, 1984.

——— *The Structure of Social Interaction: A Systemic Approach to the Semiotics of Service Encounters*. Frances Pinter, London, 1987.

Wanner, L. and Bateman, J.A. A collocational based approach to salience-sensitive lexical selection. In *5th Natural Language Generation Workshop, June 1990*, Pittsburgh, PA, 1990. A shorter version also appeared as *Lexical Cooccurrence Relations in Text Generation* in the Proceedings of the Twelfth Annual Conference of the Cognitive Science Society, Cambridge, MA.

Webber, B.L. *Computational Linguistics: Special Edition on Tense and Aspect*, 14 (2). MIT Press, Association for Computational Linguistics, Cambridge, MA, 1988.

Weischedel, R.M. A hybrid approach to representation in the JANUS natural language processor. In *27th Annual Meeting of the Association for Computational Linguistics*, 26–29 June 1989, pages 193–202, Vancouver, BC, 1989. The Association for Computational Linguistics.

Wekker, H.Chr. *The Expression of Future Time in Contemporary British English*. North-Holland, Amsterdam, 1976.

Wheeler, T. *Sri Lanka, A Travel Survival Kit*. Lonely Planet Publications, South Yarra, Victoria, Australia.

Whorf, B. *Whorf: Language, Thought, and Reality: Selected Writings*. The MIT Press, Cambridge, MA, 1940/1956 (edited by J. Carrol).

Wilkins, J. *An Essay Towards a Real Character and a Philosophical Language*. London, 1668.

Winograd, T. *Understanding Natural Language*. Academic Press, New York, 1972.

——— What does it mean to understand language? *Cognitive Science*, 4: 209–41, 1980.

——— *Language as a Cognitive Process, Volume I: Syntax*. Addison Wesley, New York, 1983.

Winograd, T. and Flores, F. *Understanding Computers and Cognition: A New Foundation for Design*. Ablex, Norwood, NJ, 1986.

Woods, W.A. Transition network grammars for natural language analysis. *Communications of the Association for Computing Machinery*, 13, 1970.

——— What's in a link: foundations for semantic networks. In D.G. Bobrow and A.M. Collins, editors, *Representation and Understanding: Studies in Cognitive Science*. Academic Press, New York, 1975. Also reprinted in R.J. Brachman and H.J. Levesque, editors, *Readings in Knowledge Representation*, pages 217–41. Morgan Kaufman, Los Altos, CA, 1985.

Yngve, V.H.A. Random generation of English sentences. In *The 1961 Conference on Machine Translation of Languages and Applied Language Analysis*, London, 1962. Her Majesty's Stationery Office.

Zock, M. and Sabah, G., editors. *Advances in Natural Language Generation: An Interdisciplinary Perspective*, Volume 2. Pinter Publishers, London, 1988.

# Index